PLANT METAPHORS IN PROPHETIC CONDEMNATIONS OF ISRAEL AND JUDAH

ANCIENT ISRAEL AND ITS LITERATURE

Corrine L. Carvalho, General Editor

Number 49

SBL PRESS

PLANT METAPHORS IN PROPHETIC CONDEMNATIONS OF ISRAEL AND JUDAH

Tina M. Sherman

SBL PRESS

 **PRESS**

Atlanta

Copyright © 2023 by Tina M. Sherman

Library of Congress Control Number: 2023948735

Contents

Acknowledgments

This project owes its genesis to a suggestion by Marc Zvi Brettler that I compile an annotated bibliography of recent studies of biblical metaphor. After reading approximately twenty years of published works, covering both theory and application, I found a gap in the existing research that I thought I could fill: instead of exploring a specific text or metaphorical theme, I would take a comprehensive approach to a range of metaphors to see if I could discern patterns in their selection and use. My goals were both practical and methodological. I wanted to understand better how the biblical authors perceived the world around them, and I also wanted to find new ways to use cognitive metaphor theories to enhance our understanding of biblical metaphor.

I am grateful to Dr. Brettler for his encouragement and thoughtful feedback as this project progressed. I offer my sincere thanks as well to the faculty at Brandeis University, especially David P. Wright and Tzvi Abusch, for their support over the years. Special thanks go to the SBL Metaphor Group—Ryan P. Bonfiglio, Hanne Løland Levinson, Pierre Van Hecke, and Andrea L. Weiss—for the opportunity to share early versions of my research and for their helpful comments on the project. I am also grateful to Bernard M. Levinson for his friendship and wise counsel over the years.

To my parents, who passed away while I was working on this project, I owe a debt of gratitude for their unwavering support and belief in me. Thanks also to my extended family, including my friends, the Reillys, for taking up the drumbeat of encouragement these last few years. Finally, on a lighter note, I would like to express my appreciation for the prophetic authors—for their creativity and empathy as much as for their righteous anger and biting social commentary. Also deserving acknowledgment are fig trees and other woody plants—for inspiring (and frustrating) me with their many mysteries.

Tables and Figures

Tables

Figures

Abbreviations

AB	Anchor (Yale) Bible
ABD	Freedman, David Noel, ed. *Anchor Bible Dictionary*. 6 vols. New York: Doubleday, 1992.
ABIG	Arbeiten zur Bibel und ihrer Geschichte
ACEBTSup	Amsterdamse Cahiers voor Exegese en bijbelse Theologie Supplement Series
AEL	Lichtheim, Miriam. *Ancient Egyptian Literature*. 3 vols. Berkeley: University of California Press, 1971–1980.
AIL	Ancient Israel and Its Literature
Atiqot	ʿAtiqot
b.	Babylonian talmudic tractate
BA	*Biblical Archaeologist*
BASOR	*Bulletin of the American Schools of Oriental Research*
BDB	Brown, Francis, S. R. Driver, and Charles A. Briggs. *A Hebrew and English Lexicon of the Old Testament*. Oxford: Clarendon, 1907.
BHQ	Biblia Hebraica Quinta
Bib	*Biblica*
BibInt	*Biblical Interpretation*
BibInt	Biblical Interpretation Series
BJSUCSD	Biblical and Judaic Studies from the University of California, San Diego
BZAW	Beihefte zur Zeitschrift für die alttestamentliche Wissenschaft
CAD	Gelb, Ignace J., et al., eds. *The Assyrian Dictionary of the Oriental Institute of the University of Chicago*. 21 vols. Chicago: Oriental Institute of the University of Chicago, 1956–2010.
CBQ	*Catholic Biblical Quarterly*
CBQMS	Catholic Biblical Quarterly Monograph Series

CC	Continental Commentaries
CHANE	Culture and History of the Ancient Near East
CLR	Cognitive Linguistics Research
ConBOT	Coniectanea Biblica: Old Testament Series
COS	Hallo, William W., and K. Lawson Younger Jr., eds. *The Context of Scripture*. 4 vols. Leiden: Brill, 1997–2006.
CTL	Cambridge Textbooks in Linguistics
DCH	Clines, David J. A., ed. *Dictionary of Classical Hebrew*. 9 vols. Sheffield: Sheffield Phoenix, 1993–2016.
DULAT	Olmo Lete, Gregorio del, and Joaquín Sanmartín. *A Dictionary of the Ugaritic Language in the Alphabetic Tradition*. Translated and edited by W. G. E. Watson. 3rd ed. 2 vols. HdO 112. Leiden: Brill, 2015.
ECC	Eerdmans Critical Commentary
ET	English translation
ETL	*Ephemerides Theologicae Lovanienses*
FAT	Forschungen zum Alten Testament
HACL	History, Archaeology, and Culture of the Levant
HALOT	Koehler, Ludwig, Walter Baumgartner, and Johann J. Stamm. *The Hebrew and Aramaic Lexicon of the Old Testament*. Translated and edited under the supervision of Mervyn E. J. Richardson. 2 vols. Leiden: Brill, 2001.
HANE/S	History of the Ancient Near East/Studies
HBAI	*Hebrew Bible and Ancient Israel*
HdO	Handbook of Oriental Studies
HSM	Harvard Semitic Monographs
IBHS	Waltke, Bruce K., and Michael O'Connor. *An Introduction to Biblical Hebrew Syntax*. Winona Lake, IN: Eisenbrauns, 1990.
ICC	International Critical Commentary
JAJ	*Journal of Ancient Judaism*
JAOS	*Journal of the American Oriental Society*
Jastrow	Jastrow, Marcus. *Dictionary of the Targumim, the Talmud Babli and Yerushalmi, and the Midrashic Literature*. Peabody, MA: Hendrickson, 2005.
JBL	*Journal of Biblical Literature*
JESHO	*Journal of the Economic and Social History of the Orient*
JNSL	*Journal of Northwest Semitic Languages*

Joüon	Joüon, Paul, and T. Muraoka. *A Grammar of Biblical Hebrew*. SubBi 27. Rome: Pontifical Biblical Institute, 2006.
JSem	*Journal for Semitics*
JSOT	*Journal for the Study of the Old Testament*
JSOTSup	Journal for the Study of the Old Testament Supplement Series
JSS	*Journal of Semitic Studies*
JTS	*Journal of Theological Studies*
KAI	Donner, Herbert, and Wolfgang Röllig. *Kanaanäische und aramäische Inschriften*. 2nd ed. Wiesbaden: Harrassowitz, 1966–1969.
LAI	Library of Ancient Israel
LHBOTS	Library of Hebrew Bible/Old Testament Studies
LSAWS	Linguistic Studies in Ancient West Semitic
LXX	Septuagint
mpl	masculine plural
ms	masculine singular
MT	Masoretic Text
NEA	*Near Eastern Archaeology*
NETS	Pietersma, Albert, and Benjamin G. Wright, eds. *A New English Translation of the Septuagint*. New York: Oxford University Press, 2007.
NICOT	New International Commentary on the Old Testament
NovT	*Novum Testamentum*
OBO	Orbis Biblicus et Orientalis
OTE	*Old Testament Essays*
OTL	Old Testament Library
OTM	Oxford Theological Monographs
OTS	Old Testament Studies
PEQ	*Palestine Exploration Quarterly*
PJ	*Palästina-Jahrbuch*
RBS	Resources for Biblical Study
RevExp	*Review and Expositor*
RINAP	Royal Inscriptions of the Neo-Assyrian Period
Siphrut	Siphrut: Literature and Theology of the Hebrew Scriptures
SJ	Studia Judaica
StBibLit	Studies in Biblical Literature (Lang)

SubBi	Subsidia Biblica
Taʿan.	Taʿanit
TDOT	Botterweck, G. Johannes, Helmer Ringgren, and Heinz-Josef Fabry, eds. *Theological Dictionary of the Old Testament*. Translated by John T. Willis et al. 17 vols. Grand Rapids: Eerdmans, 1974–2021.
TZ	*Theologische Zeitschrift*
VT	*Vetus Testamentum*
WO	*Die Welt des Orients*
ZA	*Zeitschrift für Assyriologie und Vorderasiatische Archäologie*
ZAW	*Zeitschrift für die alttestamentliche Wissenschaft*
ZDPV	*Zeitschrift des Deutschen Palästina-Vereins*

Introduction

The agrarian economies of the ancient Near East needed peace to foster prosperity. Warfare within the homeland disrupted the lives and livelihoods of commoners in numerous ways. People living on farms or in unwalled settlements generally fled from approaching armies, seeking refuge in walled towns or leaving the region altogether. Those who dwelled in, or escaped to, a town risked famine, thirst, and pestilence if the enemy besieged that town, and anyone captured by the invading army faced the possibility of death, deportation, or enslavement.[1] Moreover, besieging armies often consumed or destroyed the crops and vegetation in the region surrounding the town, either to support their own siege activities or to punish the besieged. If victorious, they might also destroy the towns and settlements that they conquered, leaving behind displaced, impoverished, and starving people. In extreme cases, an invading army could take steps to make the land uninhabitable by reducing its capacity to produce food in the future. Texts from the ancient Near East describe, for example, sowing weeds into crop land and destroying fruit trees, which take years to cultivate before they produce fruit.[2]

---

1. See Israel Eph'al, *The City Besieged: Siege and Its Manifestations in the Ancient Near East*, CHANE 36 (Leiden: Brill, 2009), 57–68; and Charlie Trimm, *Fighting for the King and the Gods: A Survey of Warfare in the Ancient Near East*, RBS 88 (Atlanta: SBL Press, 2017), 311–92. The success of Assyrian siege tactics in the eighth century may have led to a change in behaviors. In a situation where walled towns were less able to withstand a siege, people may have chosen to leave an invaded region altogether, returning only after the attacking army had departed. See Ernst Axel Knauf, "Was There a Refugee Crisis in the Eighth/Seventh Centuries BCE?," in *Rethinking Israel: Studies in the History and Archaeology of Ancient Israel in Honor of Israel Finkelstein*, ed. Oded Lipschits, Yuval Gadot, and Matthew J. Adams (Winona Lake, IN: Eisenbrauns, 2017), 159–72.

2. See Trimm, *Fighting for the King and the Gods*, 367–79; Aren M. Maeir, Oren Ackermann, and Hendrik J. Bruins, "The Ecological Consequences of a Siege: A

Even those who escaped the most devastating effects of warfare could experience significant hardship. The simple inability to properly cultivate fields and care for fruit trees during years when armies stalked the land carried both short- and long-term consequences. The first year, uncultivated fields and untended trees meant crop shortages and the potential for famine in the region. In addition, the unplowed land provided a haven for locusts to lay their eggs, which could then develop into crop-destroying swarms in the second year and beyond. The cumulative effect of such disasters could lead people to permanently abandon their homes rather than face years of struggle and famine.[3]

For those in the modern era who have never experienced warfare in their own homelands, it may be easy to overlook the extent to which the prophetic corpus presents an image of life in a war-torn region—not only in its combat imagery, but also in its descriptions of denuded lands, famine, pests, and pestilence.[4] In the decades surrounding the demise of Israel in the eighth century BCE and of Judah in the sixth, an international struggle over control of the southern Levant frequently brought battles into the homelands of the two kingdoms. At various points, Assyria, Aram-Damascus, Egypt, and Babylonia each waged campaigns to acquire hegemonic control over the kingdoms in the region. In addition, from

---

Marginal Note on Deuteronomy 20:19–20," in *Confronting the Past: Archaeological and Historical Essays on Ancient Israel in Honor of William G. Dever*, ed. Seymour Gitin, J. Edward Wright, and J. P. Dessel (Winona Lake, IN: Eisenbrauns, 2006), 239–43; and Avraham Faust, "Settlement, Economy, and Demography under Assyrian Rule in the West: The Territories of the Former Kingdom of Israel as a Test Case," *JAOS* 135 (2015): 765–89.

3. In a seventeenth-century BCE letter from Mari, following the war between Zimri-lim and Eshnunna, the governor of Qaṭṭunān describes his challenges in preventing the people from leaving the city during the first year of the locust swarms. Without military assistance in killing the locusts in the third year, "the plague could have easily led to a total abandonment of the settlement of the region due to the flight of the populace and the cessation of farming." See Karen Radner, "Fressen und gefressen werden: Heuschrecken als Katastrophe und Delikatesse im Alten Vorderen Orient," *WO* 34 (2004): 13 (my translation).

4. Some of the images of damaged landscapes and reduced populations may reflect the effects of a natural disaster, such as the devastating earthquake that struck the Levant in the mid-eighth century BCE, damaging settlements throughout the region. See Steven A. Austin, Gordon W. Franz, and Eric G. Frost, "Amos's Earthquake: An Extraordinary Middle East Seismic Event of 750 B.C.," *International Geology Review* 42 (2000): 657–71.

time to time, the kings of Israel or Judah would attempt, sometimes as part of an alliance with other Levantine rulers, to gain independence from their current hegemon, leading that kingdom to eventually return to the region to reestablish its authority by force.[5]

The burden of these periods of warfare would often have fallen most heavily upon the common people of Israel and Judah—those outside the royal administration and the elites of society—who had little formal power or influence within the kingdoms. Yet the spare retelling of the fall of Israel and Judah that appears in the historiographical texts of the Bible focuses primarily on the actions and fates of the rulers and their officials. The responses to events within the two kingdoms that reside within the prophetic corpus, however, do provide a window into the experience of the common people.

The images of warfare and its aftereffects appear in both literal and metaphorical forms, in some cases placed side by side. Isaiah 1:7–8, for example, declares of Judah:

ארצכם שממה עריכם שרפות אש אדמתכם לנגדכם זרים אכלים אתה
ושממה כמהפכת זרים: ונותרה בת־ציון כסכה בכרם כמלונה במקשה
כעיר נצרה:

[7] Your land is a desolation, your cities burned with fire. Strangers devour the land in front of you, and it is desolate, as overthrown by strangers. [8] And Daughter Zion is left like a booth in a vine-yard, like a hut in a cucumber field, like a city "guarded."[6]

The passage follows a literal description of a kingdom devastated by war-fare (1:7) with a metaphorical version that depicts Judah as a postharvest vineyard and field, with Jerusalem presented as the only structure left standing after the produce has been gathered (1:8).[7]

---

5. See J. Maxwell Miller and John H. Hayes, *A History of Ancient Israel and Judah*, 2nd ed. (Louisville: Westminster John Knox, 2006).

6. Unless otherwise indicated, all translations are my own. To facilitate discussion and comparison of the features of the metaphors analyzed here and in the chapters that follow, translations of the biblical text will generally attempt to preserve the basic literal sense, even the syntax, of the Hebrew passages. As such, the phrasing may at times seem awkward by the standards of modern written English. For passages that are more difficult to render into clear English, translations may include an explanatory gloss or alternate translation in brackets.

7. See also the more detailed discussion of this passage in ch. 4.

Similarly, Jer 8:13 and 14a present a harvesting metaphor of gathered grapes and figs alongside an exclamation in which the speaker orders the people, in literal terms, to flee an approaching army and gather in fortified cities:

אסף אסיפם נאם־יהוה אין ענבים בגפן ואין תאנים בתאנה והעלה נבל ואתן
להם יעברום:
על־מה אנחנו ישבים האספו ונבוא אל־ערי המבצר ונדמה־שם

[13] "Gathered, I will end them," says YHWH. "There are no grapes on the vine, and there are no figs on the fig tree, and the leaf withers. (What) I have given them will pass away from them."
[14a] "Why are we sitting (here)? Gather together so that we may go to the fortified cities and stand still there!"[8]

That the verb אסף appears in both verses to express the action of gathering—of fruit in 8:13 and people in 8:14—creates a connection between the two images and leaves the impression that the gathered fruit represents the people gathering in the fortified cities. The image is not a hopeful one, however; just as farmers gather fruit to consume it, so the people gather for their own destruction (8:14b–17).[9]

The prophetic authors were more than simply keen observers of the misfortunes of their homelands.[10] They also claimed that YHWH had

---

8. Translations of נדמה in 8:14 range from "let us be silent" (KJV, ASV) to "let us … meet our doom" (JPS) and "let us … perish" (RSV). Grammatical analyses of the form have yielded several potential interpretations. The simplest explanation takes נדמה as a *qal* plural cohortative of דמם-I, "to be silent, still; to cease," but *DCH* also suggests that the verb, with emendation, could be a *qal* form of דמם-II, "to weep," or a *niphal* form of דמם-IV, "to maltreat, destroy" (*DCH* 2:450–51, s.vv. "דמם-I–IV"). The prophetic author probably intended to convey the sense that death or suffering awaits the people in the city, but rendering נדמה as either "let us be silent" or "let us perish" fails to adequately convey the wordplay present in the juxtaposition of two verbs that represent different modes of inaction: ישב, "to sit," and דמם-I, "to be silent, still." The translation offered here highlights the contrast in the verse as the speaker, with some irony, rejects sitting motionless in the countryside as the enemy advances in favor of seeking the equally dubious fate of standing still in a fortified city.

9. See further the discussion of this passage in ch. 7.

10. For purposes of this study, which focuses on the development and expression of ideas about Israel and Judah in specific prophetic passages, the authenticity of the prophecies matters less than their content. To avoid confusing claims about the authorship of specific texts with questions about the named prophets as historical figures, I

given them special insight into the causes and courses of these events.[11] The prophets frequently lay the blame for the troubles of Israel and Judah not on any foreign enemies, but on their own people. On this point, a pattern emerges from the data. The history of Israel and Judah suggests that a direct connection can often be drawn between a ruler's foreign policy—especially his decision whether to seek allies or rebel against the kingdom's current hegemon—and the threats facing the kingdom or the harm inflicted upon it. Thus, we expect to find prophetic passages that condemn the kings' foreign policy decisions (e.g., Isa 30:1–5; Jer 2:17–19).

More often, however, the prophetic authors look elsewhere for their explanations of their own kingdom's situation. They argue that YHWH has afflicted, or will afflict, the kingdom, either personally or through a human agent, because the kingdom has failed to properly serve its god. It has not adhered to YHWH's requirements for social justice (e.g., Isa 1:21–23; Ezek 22:12–13; Amos 2:6–8; Mic 3:9–11), or it has not worshiped YHWH exclusively or properly (e.g., Jer 16:10–12; Hos 2:4–15; Amos 2:4–5; Mic 1:5–7). In fact, to the extent that foreign policy plays a role in the prophetic accusations, it appears in complaints that the kingdom's leaders have disobeyed YHWH in their handling of foreign alliances. In other words, properly serving YHWH includes adopting a YHWH-approved foreign policy.[12] The prophets' explanations of the events of their day demonstrate an important aspect of their worldview: that divine favor or wrath consis-

---

use the names of the prophetic texts only to refer to the text, never to the prophet as an individual. When I wish to speak of those responsible for the composition of a specific passage in the prophetic corpus, I use the general terms "prophet," "author," or "prophetic author." That said, the discussion of specific passages will address questions about the dates of the texts as needed to support the analysis of the development of the metaphors in the texts.

11. On the role of the prophet in mediating communications between the divine and human realms, see Martti Nissinen, "Prophetic Intermediation in the Ancient Near East," in *The Oxford Handbook of the Prophets*, ed. Carolyn J. Sharp, Oxford Handbooks (Oxford: Oxford University Press, 2016), 5–22. For a discussion more specifically of biblical prophecy and the relationship of the prophet to the state, see the essays in Christopher A. Rollston, ed., *Enemies and Friends of the State: Ancient Prophecy in Context* (University Park, PA: Eisenbrauns, 2018).

12. Hans M. Barstad discusses this aspect of Hosea's complaints about Ephraimite and Israelite foreign policy. See Barstad, "Hosea and the Assyrians," in *"Thus Speaks Ishtar of Arbela": Prophecy in Israel, Assyria, and Egypt in the Neo-Assyrian Period*, ed. Robert P. Gordon and Hans M. Barstad (Winona Lake, IN: Eisenbrauns, 2013), 91–110.

tently operates as a determining factor in whether a kingdom thrives or falters, and therefore examining the cause and effect of historical events requires consideration of everything that may have incurred divine favor or wrath.[13]

1.1. Patterns in Prophetic Metaphorical Imagery

The prophetic authors employed a wide variety of metaphors to communicate their ideas about the sources of YHWH's anger with his people and about the consequences of that anger. A detailed examination of the evidence, however, suggests that three images in particular held greater appeal than others as vehicles for depicting the kingdoms of Israel and Judah: (1) a flock of small cattle (e.g., Jer 23:1–4; Ezek 34); (2) a woman (e.g., Hos 2:4–15; Jer 3:6–10; Ezek 16; 23); and (3) a plant or plants (e.g., Isa 5:1–7; Ezek 19:10–14; Mic 7:1–7). Scholars often refer to these three categories as *pastoral*, *marital*, and *agricultural* metaphors, though the terms *woman* and *plant* constitute more accurate category names for the last two sets of metaphors, primarily because not all woman metaphors employ marital imagery and not all agricultural metaphors employ plant imagery.[14] All three metaphor types are attested in biblical and extrabiblical texts, and the prophetic authors exploit particular features of each image to convey their messages.

Pastoral metaphors often provide a way to highlight how a kingdom's leaders have contributed to the fate of the people. Occasionally, YHWH plays the role of shepherd to his people, who are a disobedient flock (Hos

---

13. For a discussion of success or failure in warfare as a proxy for divine favor or wrath, see Nili Wazana, "'War Crimes' in Amos's Oracles against the Nations (Amos 1:3–2:3)," in *Literature as Politics, Politics as Literature: Essays on the Ancient Near East in Honor of Peter Machinist*, ed. David S. Vanderhooft and Abraham Winitzer (Winona Lake, IN: Eisenbrauns, 2013), 479–501.

14. The category *agricultural metaphors* is both too broad and too narrow for purposes of defining the boundaries of plant metaphors in the prophetic corpus. Agriculture may refer to both plant and animal farming, thus overlapping with pastoral metaphors. In addition, the category name creates a distinction between cultivated and wild plants that may exclude wild plant metaphors that otherwise have meaningful similarities to cultivated plant metaphors. On marital metaphors as a problematic category name for metaphors depicting Israel or Judah as a woman, see Sharon Moughtin-Mumby, *Sexual and Marital Metaphors in Hosea, Jeremiah, Isaiah, and Ezekiel*, OTM (Oxford: Oxford University Press, 2008), 6–30.

4:16; 13:5–8).[15] More common, however, are passages in which the behavior of bad leaders causes the people to stray into disobedience or exile. For example, Jer 50:6–7 describes the leaders of Judah as shepherds who have led the flock of Judah astray from the pasture of YHWH's protection. The author extends the metaphor to describe the consequences of straying for the people, depicting flight from enemies or exile as a scattering of the flock and military defeat as the consumption of the flock by predators. That pastoral imagery lends itself well to condemning leaders flows naturally from the fundamentally hierarchical nature of the relationship between a shepherd and the flock that he leads. Indeed, the metaphor of a king or leader as a shepherd of his people was common in the ancient Near East.[16]

In contrast to pastoral metaphors, woman metaphors usually do not explicitly differentiate between leaders and commoners. Instead, they conceptualize a kingdom or city, as a collective whole, as a human female. Passages of this type hold the entire kingdom or city accountable for its sins. Consequences, including military conquest, may take the form of physical punishment of the woman's body, or it may be expressed in terms of seizure or destruction of her family or property. For example, Hos 2:4–15 accuses Israel of apostasy by describing the kingdom as YHWH's wife, who has been unfaithful to him by consorting with other deities. As a result, YHWH intends to punish her by stripping her of both clothing and wealth, leaving her poor and unprotected, vulnerable to attacks by her lovers, meaning other kingdoms and their deities.[17]

---

15. Pierre van Hecke, "Pastoral Metaphors in the Hebrew Bible and in Its Ancient Near Eastern Context," in *The Old Testament in Its World: Papers Read at the Winter Meeting, January 2003, The Society for Old Testament Study and at the Joint Meeting, July 2003, The Society for Old Testament Study and Het Oudtestamentisch Werkgezelschap in Nederland en België*, ed. Robert P. Gordon and Johannes C. de Moor, OTS 52 (Leiden: Brill, 2005), 200–217.

16. See G. Ernest Wright, "The Good Shepherd," *BA* 2.4 (1939): 44–48; Joan Goodnick Westenholz, "The Good Shepherd," in *Schools of Oriental Studies and the Development of Modern Historiography: Proceedings of the Fourth Annual Symposium of the Assyrian and Babylonian Intellectual Heritage Project, Held in Ravenna, Italy, October 13–17, 2001*, ed. A. Panaino and A. Piras, Melammu Symposia 4 (Milan: Mimesis, 2004), 281–310; and van Hecke, "Pastoral Metaphors." That small cattle such as sheep and goats also tend to follow a lead animal from the flock similarly aligns well with the leader-commoner dynamic in many of these metaphors. This flock behavior may have contributed to the term for "ram" also developing the sense of "leader" in biblical and extrabiblical texts (*DCH* 1:210–11, s.v. "אַיִל").

17. The passage depicts the kingdom of Israel—comprising people and land—as a woman for purposes of the overall accusation and punishment, but the author also

Like the metaphor of a leader as a shepherd, the metaphor of a city as a woman is also attested in extrabiblical texts from the ancient Near East. The feminine gender of the Hebrew nouns עיר and קריה, meaning "city" or "town," may have contributed to the biblical authors' adoption and development of this metaphor.[18] In addition, since the kingdoms of the ancient Near East often originated with a single city and its immediate environs, references to a kingdom's main city frequently serve as a metonym for the kingdom as a whole. Consequently, the prophetic audience would have readily comprehended the metaphor of a city as a woman as potentially referring more broadly to the kingdom.

Finally, like woman metaphors, plant metaphors for Israel and Judah usually represent the kingdom as a collective whole. For example, Jer 2:21 describes apostate Judah as a vine, planted by YHWH, that has turned away from him as it has grown. At the same time, by drawing on various parts of a single plant, or by using more than one type of plant, these metaphors can also differentiate between different groups or types of people within the collective. Thus, the vine metaphor in Ezek 19:10–14 distinguishes the rulers of Judah from the people by depicting the rulers as twigs on a vine branch and the people as grapes. As a result of the multiple ways to elaborate on the basic metaphor of a kingdom as a plant, plant metaphors allow differentiation of responsibility for the kingdom's fate, much as pastoral metaphors distinguish between the leader-shepherd and people-flock. In the case of Ezek 19:10–14, the overgrowth of the royal branch that leads to the downfall of the entire vine (with its fruit) conveys the message that the people are suffering for the actions of their leaders.[19]

Metaphors depicting people as plants were both highly conventional and highly productive in the ancient Near East. They provide the foundation for numerous common Hebrew terms found in the Bible, as when offspring are referred to as פרי, "fruit," or זרע, "seed."[20] The ubiquity of such

---

extends the metaphor by incorporating her children into the image, who represent the current generation of people within the kingdom, whom YHWH will now disown (2:6–7). Another type of extension of the woman metaphor presents different cities as sisters (Jer 3:6–10; Ezek 16; 23).

18. Christl M. Maier, *Daughter Zion, Mother Zion: Gender, Space, and the Sacred in Ancient Israel* (Minneapolis: Fortress, 2008), 61–74.

19. See ch. 5 for additional discussion and analysis of Jer 2:21 and Ezek 19:10–14.

20. For a discussion of these and other common terms and expressions, see Tikva Frymer-Kensky, "The Planting of Man: A Study in Biblical Imagery," in *Love and Death in the Ancient Near East: Essays in Honor of Marvin H. Pope*, ed. John H. Marks

metaphors means that comprehension of expressions in which a whole city or a kingdom is a plant or plants would likely have posed no problem for the prophetic audience. Metaphors that present kingdoms or cities as plants are not well attested outside the Bible, but at least two texts from Mesopotamia describe the city of Babylon as a date or date palm tree.[21] The date palm grew well in Mesopotamia, and in addition to the uses of its fruit as both a food source and a sweetener, its wood provided building material to a region that otherwise does not produce many trees.[22] That combination of prolific growth and economic significance probably contributed to the sense that the tree or its fruit could serve as a symbol for an important city like Babylon. A similar dynamic may have contributed to the relative popularity of viticulture metaphors for depicting Israel and Judah among the biblical authors.[23]

1.2. Patterns in the Prophetic Condemnations

In addition to the employment of a common set of metaphors to depict Israel and Judah, a second pattern also appears in the prophecies that condemn the kingdoms. The material contains two types of messages. The first, and by far more numerous, type simply expresses an accusation of collective wrongdoing and a pronouncement of doom. For example, Isa

---

and Robert M. Good, (Guilford, CT: Four Quarters, 1987), 129–36. For biblical and extrabiblical examples of metaphors of people as plants in the context of warfare, see Nili Samet, "On Agricultural Imagery in Biblical Descriptions of Catastrophes," *JAJ* 3 (2012): 2–14.

21. Selena Wisnom, *Weapons of Words: Intertextual Competition in Babylonian Poetry; A Study of Anzû, Enūma Eliš, and Erra and Išum*, CHANE 106 (Leiden: Brill, 2019), 233. In addition, a late Babylonian hymn may compare the city of Borsippa and its main shrine, Ezida, to "groves of date trees whose crowns reach the clouds." See Steven W. Cole, "The Destruction of Orchards in Assyrian Warfare," in *Assyria 1995: Proceedings of the Tenth Anniversary Symposium of the Neo-Assyrian Text Corpus Project, Helsinki, September 7–11, 1995*, ed. Simo Parpola and Robert M. Whiting (Helsinki: Neo-Assyrian Text Corpus Project, 1997), 29. The imagery in the poem is suggestive of trees, though the text does not specifically mention date palms. For the text of the hymn, see F. Köcher, "Ein spätbabylonischer Hymnus auf den Tempel Ezida in Borsippa," *ZA* 53 (1959): 236–40.

22. Cole, "Destruction of Orchards," 29–30.

23. Victor H. Matthews, "Treading the Winepress: Actual and Metaphorical Viticulture in the Ancient Near East," *Semeia* 86 (1999): 19–32. See further the discussion of the appeal of viticulture metaphors in ch. 3.

1:4–9 first accuses Judah of rejecting YHWH. The passage then details the consequences of that rejection, describing the conquered kingdom metaphorically: as a beaten body, covered in wounds and sores (1:5–6); as a harvested vineyard and field (1:8); and as barely escaping the fate of the destroyed cities of Sodom and Gomorrah (1:9). In 1:7, the author ensures that the audience will understand the metaphors by presenting more literal images of Judah's towns burned down and its crops consumed by the invading army. Thus, the message in Isa 1:4–9 has two components: an accusation of wrongdoing; and a pronouncement of doom. Variations of this type of condemnation might be simpler still, depicting only the accusation or only the announced doom.

The second type of condemnation is more complex. These metaphors still usually include accusation and punishment elements like those of the simpler metaphors, but they add to the image a more detailed depiction of the kingdom that they are condemning. They construct a national identity for Israel or Judah that emphasizes a collective history, character, and fate for the people and their land. The basic condemnation in Isa 5:1–7, for example, describes Israel and Judah as a vineyard that will be trampled and consumed by cattle (5:5), just as a conquering army destroys the land, captures its people, and consumes its resources. The author does not simply call Israel and Judah a vineyard, however. Rather, he begins in 5:1–2 with a creation myth for the two kingdoms. It describes the people as a grapevine variety that YHWH chose, planted, and cultivated on his land. Yet despite all of YHWH's effort on their behalf, the people have produced nothing but the rotten grapes of injustice and unrighteousness (5:7).[24] A comparison of Isa 1:4–9 and 5:1–7 demonstrates how both the simple and the complex condemnations may include within their structure the language and imagery of conflict and warfare—burning, trampling, capturing, consuming—but only the complex condemnations craft a national identity for the kingdom, which their authors use to show their audience how YHWH views them.

The chapters that follow explore both types of metaphors—the simple collective condemnations and the national identity condemnations—in passages that employ plant metaphors. The relative popularity of plant metaphors and the wide variety of plant options available to the biblical authors for depicting Israel and Judah make these metaphors an optimal choice for examining the ways that the prophetic authors conceived of

---

24. See the detailed analysis of Isa 5:1–7 in ch. 4.

Israel and Judah in their condemnations of the two kingdoms. Studying how different authors used the same basic image—kingdom as plant—but molded that image to suit their message helps to identify the factors or considerations that may have constrained the authors' conceptualizations of their subjects. Among the questions it raises is why some plants seem to have proven more compelling than others for depicting Israel and Judah. In addition, the analysis of metaphors that employ a common basic image highlights the aspects of that image with which the authors felt free to innovate. In other words, identifying the norms of conceptualizing the Israelite and Judahite experience in terms of plant imagery also helps to identify and explore that which appears to be abnormal.

Finally, the discussion addresses the rhetorical strategy and effect of those metaphors that construct an Israelite or Judahite national identity. The analysis will demonstrate that among the plants of the southern Levant, viticulture metaphors and metaphors combining grapevines and fig trees proved particularly useful as vehicles for criticizing the kingdoms of Israel and Judah. While the origins and structures of these metaphors differ, grapevines and fig trees carried positive connotations as symbols of Israel and Judah for the people of the two kingdoms—or at least for the people with whom the prophetic authors interacted. They used their audience's preexisting, positive conceptions of Israel or Judah as a land of grapevines and fig trees as the foundation for constructing a national identity for the people. They then transformed or deconstructed that identity to condemn one or both kingdoms. In so doing, they encouraged their audience to adopt a new perspective on the kingdoms. Examining the dynamics of the creation of national identity in the complex condemnations will thus facilitate an exploration of not just how the prophetic authors *thought* about the people of the two kingdoms, but also how they used their metaphorical prophecies to *reason* about their homeland's past, present, and future.[25]

1.3. Nations, Nationalism, and National Identities

The preceding discussion has employed the term *national identity* to describe the way that some prophetic authors portrayed the kingdoms of

---

25. On reasoning through metaphor, see Barbara Dancygier and Eve Sweetser, *Figurative Language*, CTL (New York: Cambridge University Press, 2014), 38–41.

Israel and Judah. The application of national identity theory to an ancient polity requires justification, however, because nations and nationalism, from which national identities derive, are modern phenomena. Most scholars of nationalism argue that the features that characterize nations—such as fixed territorial boundaries, a legal system that establishes a common set of rights and responsibilities for all members, and members who view themselves as active participants in the life of the nation—only emerged in the modern era.[26] Empires, kingdoms, and other types of states existed prior to that time, as did communities with a shared culture, but none of those premodern collectives exhibited the features above that define modern nations.[27]

At the same time, theories of nationalism and national identity formation may still be instructive for understanding currents of thought that arose in ancient communities. Benedict Anderson's definition of a modern nation provides a useful basis for examining the development of national identities in the prophetic corpus. According to Anderson, a nation is "an imagined political community—and imagined as both inherently limited and sovereign."[28] That a nation is imagined reflects the reality that the members of a nation will not all know each other personally, but they may nevertheless perceive themselves to be part of the nation. The limitations of a nation are the criteria by which it distinguishes itself from other nations, and its sovereignty refers to the state and its control of a bounded territory.[29] Subsequent scholarship on the concept of nations has offered a more nuanced view of the aspect of sovereignty. A claimed territory is a feature common to all modern nations, but not all nations have independent control of the state in which they reside. As such, control of the state is a possible, but not necessary, feature of nations.[30]

---

26. For a more detailed discussion of these and other features of nations, see Anthony D. Smith, "When Is a Nation?" *Geopolitics* 7.2 (2002): 5–32.

27. Not all scholars of nationalism align with the modernist position discussed here. Other influential schools of thought, the most prominent being perennialism, argue that nations may have their origins in ancient ethnic or cultural communities. For an overview of the debate from each perspective, see Smith, "When Is a Nation?"; and Alexander Maxwell, "Primordialism for Scholars Who Ought to Know Better: Anthony D. Smith's Critique of Modernization Theory," *Nationalities Papers* 48 (2020): 826–42.

28. Benedict Anderson, *Imagined Communities: Reflections on the Origin and Spread of Nationalism*, rev. ed. (London: Verso, 2006), 6.

29. Anderson, *Imagined Communities*, 6.

30. Montserrat Guibernau, "Nations without States: Political Communities in the Global Age," *Michigan Journal of International Law* 25 (2004): 1251–82. Among

If nations are communities whose existence depends, in part, on members seeing themselves as part of the nation, then nationalism and national identities provide a way to foster that sense of membership and to unite the nation's members in support of national goals or ideals. In general, research has shown that in modern "prenationalist societies," people may turn to nationalism when they begin to perceive injustice in their experience within the social hierarchy. Thus, for example, Liah Greenfeld and Jonathan Eastwood argue that nationalism in sixteenth-century England arose when people outside the aristocracy began to experience upward mobility in society for the first time, which led them to question the norms of their day regarding inherited social positions.[31]

Most modernist scholars of nationalism date the origins of nations and nationalism later than this—often attributing these developments to the late eighteenth or early nineteenth centuries and associating them with the rise of capitalism or the industrial revolution.[32] Anderson adds that nations and nationalism were made possible by the development of mass printing capabilities that facilitated the widespread distribution and exchange of new ideas throughout a community.[33] While Greenfeld and Eastwood do not dismiss these developments as contributing to the spread of nationalism within individual countries, they argue that the origins of nationalism should be sought by asking a different question: "What sorts of cognitive problems did these individuals [who turned to nationalism and national identity] have that were solved by constructing a new image

---

the examples Guibernau cites as nations without independent states are Catalonia, Quebec, and Scotland (1254). The elements of Guibernau's definition of *nation* align with those of Anderson's model, but Guibernau expresses them differently. He describes the imagined community as "a human group conscious of forming a community," speaks of its limits in terms of the members "sharing a common culture" and "having a common past and a common project for the future," and defines its sovereignty as being "attached to a clearly demarcated territory" and "claiming the right to decide upon its political destiny" (Guibernau, "Nationalism without States," in *The Oxford Handbook of the History of Nationalism*, ed. John Breuilly [Oxford: Oxford University Press, 2013], 592).

31. Liah Greenfeld and Jonathan Eastwood, "National Identity," in *The Oxford Handbook of Comparative Politics*, ed. Charles Boix and Susan C. Stokes (Oxford: Oxford University Press, 2009), 256–73.

32. Maxwell, "Primordialism," 827.

33. Anderson, *Imagined Communities*, 36.

of the social world?"[34] They suggest that the egalitarian principles that underlie nationalism appeal to budding nationalists because they address a perceived injustice in the existing social structure.[35]

Studies of nationalism in nations that do not control the state in which they reside also find a pattern of perceived injustice as providing the inspiration for a nationalistic response. People in nations of this type may look back to a time when the nation did govern itself, and they may associate the loss of that power with experienced or perceived conflict and oppression. They may also resent the state that governs them as restricting their freedom and sapping their resources without providing benefits that offset these costs. Finally, they may fear that their own culture is being "replaced by an increasingly pervasive global culture."[36]

The precise conditions that have fostered modern nationalism did not exist in ancient Israel and Judah, but an analogous set of pressures could have given rise to similar ideas in the minds of the prophetic authors. In the last decades of Israel and of Judah, the experience of the trauma of warfare and conquest, the ongoing threats from neighboring kingdoms, and the periods of subjugation by one kingdom or another suggest conditions akin to those of modern nations that must submit to a state that they do not control. The prophetic authors could remember or imagine an earlier time when their kingdom was free of hegemonic control, and many would have lived through at least one cycle of attempted rebellion and renewed conquest within their kingdom, giving them living memories of violent conflict and oppression.

In addition, both Israel and Judah profited well from their position atop major trade routes linking Arabia and Africa to Anatolia and Mesopotamia.[37] Tribute demands by hegemonic powers essentially functioned as a tax on these profits. In exchange, Israel and Judah gained protection against attacks from other kingdoms, including from the hegemon itself. In fact, John S. Holladay Jr. refers to Assyrian hegemony as a "protection racket," whereby the vassals paid Assyria not to destroy them:

---

34. Greenfeld and Eastwood, "National Identity," 265.

35. Greenfeld and Eastwood, "National Identity," 265–66.

36. Guibernau, "Nationalism without States," 594. See also Guibernau, *Nations without States: Political Communities in a Global Age* (Cambridge: Polity, 1999).

37. David A. Dorsey, *The Roads and Highways of Ancient Israel* (Baltimore: Johns Hopkins University Press, 1991).

In the complex reciprocal relationship between Assyria and its smaller neighbors, the tributary system was mostly about money and the things that money could buy—ideally, at no cost to the Assyrian Empire, except for the trouble of making the rounds of the neighborhood to collect the rent and protection money and to beat up and rob the "deadbeats."[38]

The prophetic authors generally did not advocate rebellion against their kingdom's hegemon, but they may nevertheless have recognized and resented the coercive nature of the hegemon's actions. Finally, beyond the issues of conflict and oppression, prophetic complaints about Israel or Judah adopting the practices of other kingdoms or people groups, especially with regard to worshiping deities other than YHWH, assert that such behaviors constitute an unwelcome change in the Israelite and Judahite cultures (e.g., Isa 2:5–8; Ezek 8).

The social problems of modern prenationalist societies also have rough parallels in the late Iron Age conditions in Israel and Judah. The displacement and poverty that would have arisen as a consequence of warfare within the homeland probably contributed to the social injustices decried by the prophets—such as taking bribes, fraud, and usury (e.g., Isa 1:21–23; Ezek 22:12–13; Amos 2:6–8)—by enlarging the population that was vulnerable to exploitation. These issues highlighted the distance between the elites of the kingdom and the poorest commoners, and the prophetic denunciations of those in power indicate that the prophets, at least, perceived the experiences of the poor as unjust. Moreover, just as modern nationalist movements may respond to perceived injustice between social strata by advocating political change, so the prophetic authors sometimes offer solutions appropriate to their circumstances and worldview. They do not call for wholesale restructuring of society. Several passages do, however, declare that in the future, YHWH will replace the kingdom's current leaders with new leaders who will uphold justice for all the people (e.g., Isa 1:26; Jer 3:15; Ezek 34:23–24).

Since the prophetic corpus represents the work of multiple authors and editors from different locations and time periods, we should not expect to find a uniform perspective on the sources of the problems facing Israel and Judah. That said, we do find some similarity in the prophetic

---

38. John S. Holladay Jr., "Hezekiah's Tribute, Long-Distance Trade, and the Wealth of Nations ca. 1000–600 BC: A New Perspective," in Gitin, Wright, and Dessel, *Confronting the Past*, 312–13.

responses to these problems. The social and cultural pressures present in Israel and Judah at the end of the eighth and seventh centuries appear to have inspired quasi-nationalist ideas or sentiments in some of the prophets. We can see in select passages descriptions of the people of Israel or Judah as joined in a unified community in which the members, by means of their ability to affect the favor or wrath of the national deity, are active participants in determining the fate of the nation. These texts may set limits on the nation by distinguishing it from neighboring kingdoms in terms of features such as genealogy, shared history, and culture. In addition, they frequently emphasize the sovereignty of their nation by claiming that the community is, or should be, governed by a common set of divine laws and by including territorial claims for Israel or Judah. Further, these assertions about Israel and Judah hold regardless of the state of the state— as independent kingdom, vassal, or imperial province.

The specific set of features that the prophets claim for their imagined, limited, and sovereign communities constitute constructed national identities for Israel and Judah. In this context, *national identity* refers to a set of claims, perceptions, and beliefs about the aspects of one nation that unify it and that distinguish it from other nations. The aspects most often highlighted in constructions of national identity include attributing to the nation and its members: a collective past, present and future; a common culture; a national territory; and a national character (i.e., a common conception of what constitutes a typical member of the nation).[39]

Since national identity is based on human claims, perceptions, and beliefs, the aspects that define the nation may not always comport with history or objective reality. For example, the biblical authors frequently assert that there was a time in Israel's past when the Israelites practiced exclusive worship of YHWH, and that this practice set them apart from other peoples. This claim is probably exaggerated. More likely is that the Israelites' cultic practices were quite similar to those of their neighbors, with a national god and a variable set of local deities or venerated ancestors that people in their communities and families also served.[40] In the

---

39. Ruth Wodak et al., *The Discursive Construction of National Identity*, trans. Angelika Hirsch, Richard Mitten, and J. W. Unger, 2nd ed. (Edinburgh: Edinburgh University Press, 2009), 27–29. A more detailed discussion of the construction of national identity follows in ch. 2.

40. See Ziony Zevit, *The Religions of Ancient Israel: A Synthesis of Parallactic Approaches* (London: Continuum, 2001); John Bodel and Saul M. Olyan, *Household*

postexilic period and beyond, however, claims about this historical connection to YHWH as their sole deity served to differentiate Jews from other peoples. Belief in the history of their originally exclusive relationship with YHWH became part of their identity.

The process of constructing a national identity primarily happens through discourse, as people speak or write about a nation. Individuals who identify with the same nation will generally share similar ideas about the nation's defining features, but the details of how they understand, describe, and prioritize those features often differ. As a result, when we examine how the prophetic authors constructed national identities for Israel and Judah, we should expect to find broad similarities in their conceptualizations, but also variation in the details of those conceptualizations. For example, several of the metaphorical condemnations contain an account of Israel's origins that presents Israel as having a long history as YHWH's people, but no two of these accounts are exactly alike. In addition, constructed national identities may serve different strategies, including reinforcing, changing, or breaking down existing conceptions of the nation. In the case of the prophetic condemnations, because they wish to change something about their society, we should expect to find more focus on changing or breaking down existing perspectives on the kingdoms of Israel and Judah. Finally, these strategies may or may not be consciously pursued; in some cases, they may simply arise as a product of the speaker's goals for speaking and attitudes toward the nation.[41]

Any study that seeks to apply a modern political or sociological theory to an ancient community risks introducing anachronisms into its analysis and conclusions. It is therefore important to carefully define how and to what extent the theory in question may reasonably apply to the community under study. To be clear, this study does not constitute a sociological exploration of nationalism among the Israelites and Judahites. Though the prophetic authors often call for social or cultural reforms, no evidence exists to suggest that they were trying to engender a political movement to

---

and Family Religion in Antiquity, The Ancient World: Comparative Histories (Malden, MA: Wiley-Blackwell, 2008); Rainer Albertz and Rüdiger Schmitt, *Family and Household Religion in Ancient Israel and the Levant* (Winona Lake, IN: Eisenbrauns, 2012); and Albertz et al., eds., *Family and Household Religion: Toward a Synthesis of Old Testament Studies, Archaeology, Epigraphy, and Cultural Studies* (Winona Lake, IN: Eisenbrauns, 2014).

41. Wodak, *Discursive Construction*, 7–48.

impose these changes upon the kingdoms by force of popular will.[42] The prophetic authors do use rhetoric that shares some features common to modern conceptions of national identity, but they do so in support of their own goals and messages. Indeed, many of the passages that construct a national identity for Israel or Judah preclude the possibility of forming a nationalist movement by immediately destroying the nation that they have just created. In effect, the prophets create straw man national identities for the purpose of knocking them down. Therefore, this study is limited to examining the *rhetorical use* of national identity by the prophets in their condemnations of Israel and Judah. National identity theory facilitates the analysis by providing a framework and language for discussing the features of this rhetoric.

Applying the concept of national identity to an ancient community also raises questions about terminology that must be addressed. Though biblical scholarship has often used the terms *nation* or *city-state* to refer to Israel and Judah, in the discussion that follows, I consistently describe the historical entities of Israel and Judah as kingdoms. As Megan Bishop Moore and Brad Kelle argue, the term "more accurately reflects their patron-client character, bureaucratic organization, and sociological similarity to other ancient civilizations."[43] In addition, while I do follow the well-established convention of describing YHWH as a national deity, I otherwise reserve nation and related terms for use in discussing the communities and identities conceptualized (often in metaphor) by the prophetic authors.

Finally, it is important not to confuse kingdom propaganda with the national identities studied here. Kingdom propaganda focuses on celebrating the power of the deity or the king. It may mention the people of the kingdom, but it shows little interest in depicting them as a *nation*, as a distinctive political community whose members participate in the life

---

42. Moreover, the reach of the prophetic messages would likely have been insufficient to foster such a movement. The audiences for the prophetic ideas were probably limited to the cities in which the authors lived and the circles in which they moved—constrained during the preexilic period by the lack of widespread literacy among the populace, and perhaps also by the absence of either motive or means to broadly distribute the prophetic communications within the kingdom.

43. Megan Bishop Moore and Brad Kelle, *Biblical History and Israel's Past: The Changing Study of the Bible and History* (Grand Rapids: Eerdmans, 2011), 324. See also Raz Kletter, "Chronology and United Monarchy: A Methodological Review," *ZDPV* 120 (2004): 15–34, esp. 19–29.

of the nation and are perceived as equal in some meaningful way.[44] What makes the prophetic metaphors studied here analogous to modern constructions of national identity is precisely that explicit conceptualization of, and focus on, the people of Israel or Judah as an empowered community whose defining characteristics apply to king and commoner alike. Passages lacking that community element are better described as kingdom metaphors, not national metaphors.

1.4. Plant Metaphors in the Prophetic Condemnations

As discussed above, this study focuses on just one of the three main metaphorical themes that the prophets used to craft messages about Israel and Judah: plants. While the dynamics of the depictions of Israel and Judah in the pastoral and woman metaphors in the prophetic corpus deserve further study, within the prophetic condemnations, those two categories are more constrained than plant metaphors. Pastoral metaphors tend to have weakly drawn identity elements. Only rarely do the prophetic authors employ such metaphors to create a vision of their kingdom's origins or distant collective past. Instead, these passages tend to focus on the recent experience or future state of the people. In addition, they show little interest in differentiating among different types of flock animals, and they often focus primarily on the leaders-shepherds, rather than on the kingdom-flock as a whole. If the flock becomes the main subject, that change generally occurs only at the point when the author speaks of a future restoration for the people or kingdom. Therefore, these metaphors lend themselves best to understanding how the prophetic authors perceived their leaders or conceptualized an idyllic future for their kingdom.

By contrast, several of the woman metaphors have very well-defined identity elements, so they give a clear impression of how the prophets viewed the kingdoms. They do not, however, employ a very diverse set of depictions of women. In most cases, they focus on the image of a promiscuous woman, either presenting her as a prostitute or as an unfaithful wife. The lack of variety makes woman metaphors in the condemnations less useful for examining a range of metaphor options available to the

---

44. Greenfeld and Eastwood, "National Identity," 258. Greenfeld and Eastwood are quick to point out that equality comes in various forms: "For some, equality may be conceptualized in terms of equal civil rights, in others an equal share in the dignity of a 'glorious' but authoritarian society" (265 n. 13).

prophetic authors or for evaluating the factors that might have governed their choice of images.

Conversely, the wide variety of plant metaphors in the prophetic corpus offers ample opportunity to explore the choices that the prophetic authors made in conceptualizing the two kingdoms. Within that broader set of images, only a narrow subset of the various crops produced and plants grown in the region appear in complex metaphors that construct a national identity. That ancient agricultural practices are reasonably well understood facilitates a close examination of the messages of these metaphors. Finally, plant metaphors also appear in reference to kingdoms other than Israel and Judah, making it possible to compare how the prophets perceived Israel or Judah versus their perceptions of other kingdoms.[45]

To facilitate the examination of both plant metaphors and their use in the construction of national identity in the prophetic corpus, chapter 2 provides an overview of the methodological approach to metaphor and to national identity employed in the remaining chapters. The chapter establishes the common set of terms and concepts for speaking about metaphor and national identity that will govern the study. It also identifies several of the metaphors commonly used by the biblical authors to depict conflict and discusses how the prophetic authors incorporated these metaphors into their plant imagery, converting activities associated with peacetime into portraits of warfare and conquest.

The remaining chapters explore the range of plant metaphors employed in prophetic condemnations of Israel and Judah. Chapters 3–7 progressively examine those plants that the prophetic authors used most often to depict their homelands: grapevines and fig trees. Since the number and variety of viticulture metaphors greatly exceeds that of fig metaphors, the analysis of this material is not evenly distributed. After chapter 3 provides an overview of viticulture and viticulture metaphors in the Bible and the ancient Near East, chapters 4, 5, and 6 address vineyard, vine, and wine and intoxication metaphors, respectively.[46] Chapter 7 then covers meta-

---

45. The prophets also occasionally apply the image of a kingdom or city as a woman to other states (e.g., Isa 47; Nah 3:4–7), so woman metaphors share that advantage with plant metaphors, though to a lesser extent.

46. Most detailed examinations of biblical viticulture imagery focus more on using the texts to reconstruct the practice of viticulture in ancient Israel than on comparing different passages' use of this imagery to create meaning for their audience. See, e.g., Jack M. Sasson, "The Blood of Grapes: Viticulture and Intoxication in the Hebrew

phors based on figs and fig trees, giving special attention to the frequent pairing of fig trees and grapevines. Since fig imagery has not received significant attention in biblical scholarship, chapter 7 also offers overviews of the features of figs and fig trees and of fig imagery in the Bible before turning to the use of the tree and its fruit in metaphors about Israel and Judah.

Chapter 8 completes the examination of the various plants employed in prophetic condemnations of people and communities. The chapter organizes the evidence into two broad categories—metaphors about grasses, and metaphors about woody plants—and it analyzes patterns in the structure and expression of the metaphors in each category.[47] The latter category name, "woody plants," aligns with biblical uses of the Hebrew word עֵץ, which can apply to a range of plants that have hard stems, including trees, bushes, and vines. For purposes of analyzing the conceptual structure of metaphors based on these varied plants, referring to them using one of the standard translation values for עֵץ, such as "tree" and "wood," would be misleading, and it could obscure patterns that exist across the range of these metaphors.[48]

Chapters 4–8 also include detailed discussions of the metaphorical construction of national identity. Each of these chapters presents the full set of prophetic national identity condemnations of Israel or Judah based

---

Bible," in *Drinking in Ancient Societies: History and Culture of Drinks in the Ancient Near East*, ed. Lucio Milano, HANE/S 6 (Padua: Sargon, 1994), 399–419; and Carey Ellen Walsh, *The Fruit of the Vine: Viticulture in Ancient Israel*, HSM 60 (Winona Lake, IN: Eisenbrauns, 2000). These studies are enormously helpful for understanding the technical details underlying the viticulture metaphors, but they add less to our understanding of the structure or rhetorical strategies underlying these metaphors.

47. Prior studies that have looked broadly at plant metaphors in the prophetic corpus or in specific prophetic texts tend to offer an overview of the topic rather than a detailed analysis and comparison of the metaphorical images employed in different passages or by different authors. See, e.g., Patricia K. Tull, "Persistent Vegetative States: People as Plants and Plants as People in Isaiah," in *The Desert Will Bloom: Poetic Visions in Isaiah*, ed. A. Joseph Everson and Hyun Chul Paul Kim, AIL 4 (Atlanta: Society of Biblical Literature, 2009), 17–34; and Samet, "On Agricultural Imagery." Kirsten Nielsen (*There Is Hope for a Tree: The Tree as Metaphor in Isaiah*, JSOTSup 65 [Sheffield: JSOT Press, 1989]) does offer an in-depth exegesis of the tree metaphors in Isaiah, however. In addition, Job Y. Jindo (*Biblical Metaphor Reconsidered: A Cognitive Approach to Poetic Prophecy in Jeremiah 1–24*, HSM 64 [Winona Lake, IN: Eisenbrauns, 2010]) examines the plant metaphors in Jer 1–24 as expressions of a larger biblical concept of Israel as YHWH's "royal garden" (152).

48. See *DCH* 6:519–25, s.v. "עֵץ."

on the image or images that are the subject of the chapter. In addition, chapters 4, 5, and 7 each offer a case study of the most complete identity metaphor of its type. Chapter 4 studies the Song of the Vineyard in Isa 5:1–7, chapter 5 examines the vine metaphor in Ezek 19:10–14a, and chapter 7 analyzes the grapes and figs metaphor in Hos 9:10–17. These case studies provide a more in-depth assessment of the message of each passage and of how the prophetic author has used plant imagery to construct a national identity for Israel and/or Judah in service of that message. Since the prophets never employ wine or intoxication as the central image in the construction of a national identity for Israel or Judah, chapter 6 does not include a case study. It does, however, discuss the identity metaphor of Moab as wine in Jer 48:11–12. In addition, chapter 8 includes analyses of two unusual examples of identity metaphors: (1) the depiction of Assyria as a cedar tree in Ezek 31; and (2) the image of Judah as an olive tree in Jer 11:14–17.

Finally, chapter 9 addresses the broader implications of the findings from this study. After presenting a synthesis of the results from the preceding chapters, it considers the national identity metaphors as a group, highlighting several broad patterns in the data that offer insight into the genesis and development of ideas about Israel and Judah as kingdoms and nations. The chapter also includes a discussion of directions for further research to fill in remaining gaps in the systematic mapping of constructed national identities in the prophetic corpus. It closes with an assessment of several benefits of the methodological approach taken in this study for identifying and analyzing patterns in biblical metaphor.

While the study overall spends significantly more time on viticulture metaphors than on metaphors of other plants, ultimately, the project is less about exploring a specific image than it is about systematically analyzing the ways that the prophetic authors conceptualized kingdoms, especially Israel and Judah, including tracing the development of the sources and structures of those conceptualizations.[49] In this way, this study contrib-

---

49. By contrast, other recent studies of viticulture metaphors have focused on particular images or on theological aspects of the expressions. See, e.g., Kon Hwon Yang, "Theological Significance of the Motif of Vineyard in the Old Testament" (PhD diss., Golden Gate Baptist Theological Seminary, 1996); and Jeremy Daniel Smoak, "Building Houses and Planting Vineyards: The Inner-Biblical Discourse of an Ancient Israelite Wartime Curse" (PhD diss., University of California, Los Angeles, 2007). One exception is Jennifer Metten Pantoja, who examines the metaphor of YHWH as a vint-

utes to the body of evidence demonstrating that the utility of metaphor analysis within biblical scholarship includes, but is not limited to, exegesis of particular passages. Rather, a careful examination of the metaphorical material in the Bible can also yield insights into how the Israelites thought and reasoned about their world.

---

ner within a broader frame of YHWH as a planter. See her *The Metaphor of the Divine as Planter of the People*, BibInt 155 (Leiden: Brill, 2017).

2

Frameworks for Studying Metaphor and National Identity

Over forty years ago, George Lakoff and Mark Johnson published *Metaphors We Live By*, in which they argued for a new understanding of the role of metaphor in human cognition. They rejected the idea that metaphor simply represents decorative language and instead claimed that metaphor is fundamental to human thought.[1] From everyday interactions to artistic expression to technical discourse, humans regularly use metaphor to organize and express our thoughts, to explain abstract concepts, to introduce new ideas, and to extend our lexica. While interest in the study of metaphor had been growing prior to the publication of *Metaphors We Live By*, the work helped to generate a tidal wave of new research, not only in metaphor theory and literary analysis, but also in the cognitive and linguistic sciences and in a diverse array of other fields.[2] Though *Metaphors We Live By* focuses on the use of metaphor in everyday discourse, incorporation of Lakoff and Johnson's model, known as conceptual metaphor

---

1. George Lakoff and Mark Johnson, *Metaphors We Live By, with a New Afterword* (Chicago: University of Chicago Press, 2003), 3–6; the volume was originally published in 1980.

2. Twenty-five years before the release of *Metaphors We Live By* in 1980, Max Black published his influential "Metaphor," *Proceedings of the Aristotelian Society* 55 (1955): 273–94. The year 1979 saw the publication of the first edition of *Metaphor and Thought*, a well-known collection of essays on metaphor and metaphor theory edited by Andrew Ortony (Cambridge: Cambridge University Press, 1979; 2nd ed., 1993). For subsequent publications, see, e.g., the twenty-eight chapters in *The Cambridge Handbook of Metaphor and Thought*, ed. Raymond W. Gibbs Jr. (Cambridge: Cambridge University Press, 2008), which includes entries discussing metaphor and such topics as artificial intelligence, emotion, psychotherapy, art, and music.

theory (CMT), has also become commonplace in studies of metaphor in literary contexts, including studies of biblical metaphor.[3]

In the decades since its introduction, a number of scholars have challenged aspects of CMT, in some cases proposing adjustments or expansions to the model, and in other cases offering new theories to either supplement or replace it.[4] This chapter provides an overview of the hybrid analytical model that I have adopted to examine plant metaphors in the prophetic corpus. Key concepts and vocabulary from the CMT framework provide the foundation for the analysis and discussion, with modifications and supplements to incorporate additional theoretical concepts and tools that can yield further insights into the metaphorical material or its underlying conceptual structure.[5]

2.1. Studying Biblical Metaphor: A Hybrid Approach

According to CMT, a metaphor represents a systematic mapping of elements from one conceptual domain to another. The theory views simile

---

3. George Lakoff and Mark Turner expanded the theory for application to literary metaphor in Lakoff and Turner, *More Than Cool Reason: A Field Guide to Poetic Metaphor* (Chicago: University of Chicago Press, 1989). Lakoff subsequently further developed CMT under the name contemporary theory of metaphor (CTM). See Lakoff, "The Contemporary Theory of Metaphor," in Ortony, *Metaphor and Thought*, 202–51. For a more recent treatment of conceptual metaphor theory, see Zoltán Kövecses, *Metaphor: A Practical Introduction*, 2nd ed. (Oxford: Oxford University Press, 2010). The study of metaphor in ancient Near Eastern texts outside the Bible has caught on more slowly, but see the recent collection of essays, Marta Pallavidini and Ludovico Portuese, eds., *Researching Metaphor in the Ancient Near East*, Philippika 141 (Wiesbaden: Harrassowitz, 2020).

4. E.g., Alice Deignan discusses a number of empirical studies that test elements of CMT in *Metaphor and Corpus Linguistics*, Converging Evidence in Language and Communication Research 6 (Amsterdam: Benjamins, 2005). See also Raymond W. Gibbs Jr., "Evaluating Conceptual Metaphor Theory," *Discourse Processes* 48 (2011): 529–62; Francisco José Ruiz de Mendoza Ibáñez and Lorena Pérez Hernández, "The Contemporary Theory of Metaphor: Myths, Developments and Challenges," *Metaphor and Symbol* 26 (2011): 161–85; and Zoltán Kövecses, "Recent Developments in Metaphor Theory: Are the New Views Rival Ones?," *Review of Cognitive Linguistics* 9 (2011): 11–25.

5. The model employed here owes much to the cognitive linguistic approaches to figurative language presented in Dancygier and Sweetser, *Figurative Language*.

in the same way, as a mapping of elements between two domains.[6] In the examples "a king is a shepherd" (metaphor) and "a king is *like* a shepherd" (simile), both expressions map elements from a domain containing information about shepherds to elements in a domain containing information about kings. This similarity in basic structure means that we can analyze metaphor and simile in similar ways. Thus, the discussion of the features of metaphor in this chapter will also apply to simile.

Conversely, metonymy involves only a single domain. Instead of mapping elements from one domain to another, a metonymy maps elements within a single domain.[7] For example, YHWH promises Solomon in 1 Kgs 9:4–5 that if he and his heirs live righteous lives, YHWH will ensure that they continue to rule over Israel: והקמתי את־כסא ממלכתך על־ישראל לעלם, "I will establish your royal throne [lit. the throne of your kingdom] over Israel forever" (9:5). The author of this passage uses one element from the KINGDOM domain, THRONE, to refer to another element of the KINGDOM domain, DYNASTY. *Throne* in this expression is therefore a metonymy for dynasty. Metonymy differs from simile and metaphor, but since its conceptual structure also employs a domain and mappings, much of the discussion of domain features and behaviors below also applies to metonymy.

The two domains engaged in a metaphor are called the source and the target. The target is the literal subject of the metaphor, and the source is the concept with which the target is metaphorically identified. A conceptual metaphor expresses the relationship between the two domains, and it is written in the form TARGET IS SOURCE.[8] In the conceptual metaphor ARGUMENT IS WAR, the main subject of the metaphor, ARGUMENT, is the

---

6. This discussion of simile is primarily concerned with its domain-level structure. It does not address the details of how specific expressions of similes and metaphors may create meaning in different ways. Such issues will be discussed as needed in the analysis that follows. For an overview of the history of scholarship on simile and a discussion of simile's properties, see Dancygier and Sweetser, *Figurative Language*, 137–48. See also William Croft and D. Alan Cruse, *Cognitive Linguistics*, CTL (Cambridge: Cambridge University Press, 2004), 211–16; and Carol Lynn Moder, "*It's Like Making a Soup*: Metaphors and Similes in Spoken News Discourse," in *Language in the Context of Use: Discourse and Cognitive Approaches to Language*, ed. Andrea Tyler, Yiyoung Kim, and Mari Takada, CLR 37 (Berlin: Mouton de Gruyter, 2008), 301–20.

7. On metonymy and its relationship to metaphor, see Kövecses, *Metaphor*, 171–93; and Croft and Cruse, *Cognitive Linguistics*, 216–19.

8. Conceptual metaphors are conventionally written in SMALL CAPS to distinguish them from specific linguistic expressions of metaphor.

target. The concept employed to express something about the nature of arguments, WAR, is the source. Conceptual metaphor theory distinguishes between linguistic expressions of a metaphor and the underlying conceptual metaphor that structures such linguistic expressions.[9] The following phrases represent linguistic expressions of the conceptual metaphor ARGUMENT IS WAR:

> I *demolished* his argument.
> Your claims are *indefensible.*
> He *attacked every weak point* in my argument.
> His criticisms were *right on target.*[10]

In each expression, the speaker employs one or more terms (shown in italics) that are literally associated with the source domain of WAR to say something about the target domain of ARGUMENT that is the subject of the sentence. The links from elements in the source domain to elements in the target domain are called mappings.[11] For example, expressions of ARGUMENT IS WAR might map the element of SOLDIERS to that of DEBATERS and the element of COMBAT to that of DEBATE.

2.1.1. Conceptual Domains and Semantic Frames

Conceptual metaphor theory defines the relationship between source and target as a mapping from one domain to another. A different construct, however, that of semantic frames, often proves more useful than domains for the analysis of figurative language.[12] A domain contains the set of concepts, and information about the relationships between those concepts, that are associated with a particular word or topic.[13] Domains need not be

---

9. Lakoff and Turner, *More Than Cool Reason*, 50.

10. ARGUMENT IS WAR—both the conceptual metaphor and the linguistic expressions of it shown here—is the first metaphor example that Lakoff and Johnson present in *Metaphors We Live By* (4, emphasis original).

11. Lakoff and Johnson, *Metaphors We Live By*, 265.

12. Dancygier and Sweetser, *Figurative Language*, 17–21. For a more detailed discussion of the history and nature of domains and frames, see Croft and Cruse, *Cognitive Linguistics*, 7–39; and Alan Cienki, "Frames, Idealized Cognitive Models, and Domains," in *The Oxford Handbook of Cognitive Linguistics*, ed. Dirk Geeraerts and Hubert Cuyckens (Oxford: Oxford University Press, 2007), 170–87.

13. Cienki, "Frames," 181–82.

constrained by the context in which they appear, and therefore a domain evoked by a metaphor may contain large amounts of information that is irrelevant to understanding that metaphor. For example, the domain of BATTLE could include information about all types of battles, both real and fictional, from all periods of history. As such, the expression "she *shot down* each of their claims" could evoke images ranging from hurling stones with a sling to firing a plasma cannon.

In everyday discourse, that breadth of options has little effect on the hearer's ability to comprehend the metaphorical expression, since the metaphor does not depend on a specific type of weapon or shooting context. A later interpreter seeking to examine how a speaker or her contemporary audience would have understood the metaphor, however, would want to exclude from the domain any projectile weapons unknown to the speaker. In practice, biblical scholars often do just that: They narrow the scope of their metaphorical domains by imposing contextual constraints on the domain content. Such approaches can work, but they increase the risk that vaguely or variably defined domain boundaries may lead to flawed analyses of specific metaphors.

By contrast, semantic frames carry constraints by definition that narrow their content and make them context-dependent.[14] According to Karen Sullivan, "*semantic frames* consist of sets of elements and relations which are abstracted from real-world situations."[15] Domains consist of interrelated concepts associated with a *word* or *subject*, while frames contain interrelated elements associated with a *situation*. The two concepts therefore share the aspects of both content and relations. The situational basis of frames, however, narrows and gives specific structure to their content in ways that words or subjects may not necessarily do for a domain. In other words, frames have more formal structure than domains, and therefore analysis based on frames more clearly requires analysis of frame structures.

A frame's content is formally limited by the speaker's knowledge of the real-world situation evoked by the frame. For the sake of clarity, I employ a modified version Sullivan's definition to make this assumption

---

14. Dancygier and Sweetser, *Figurative Language*, 17.

15. Sullivan, *Frames and Constructions in Metaphoric Language*, Constructional Approaches to Language 14 (Amsterdam: Benjamins, 2013), 15, emphasis original. Sullivan treats frames as elements within a metaphorical domain whose contents provide structure to the domain (23–24).

about frame content explicit: "semantic frames consist of sets of elements and relations that are abstracted from real-world situations *that are known to the speaker*." The implication of this definition, of course, is that if the speaker's knowledge of the situation that evokes the frame is incorrect or incomplete, then the frame content evoked by the frame in a metaphor will also be incorrect or incomplete. Of course, this aspect of a speaker's knowledge holds true for metaphor interpretation regardless of the theoretical approach. Max Black made a similar observation about his interaction theory of metaphor in 1955: "From the expert's standpoint, the system of commonplaces [evoked by a given word] may include half-truths or downright mistakes (as when a whale is classified as a fish); but the important thing for the metaphor's effectiveness is not that the commonplaces shall be true, but that they should be readily and freely evoked."[16]

In the example of the BATTLE frame, when examining a biblical author's battle metaphors, the analyst must study ancient wars and warfare to better understand what the author would have known, or believed, about battle. The elements included in the BATTLE frame for a biblical author could include opposing armies, siege practices for both the besieger and the besieged, various types of hand-held weapons, and perhaps horses and chariots. It could also include elements related to the aftermath of battles, including roles and actions for both the winner and the loser. An important additional consequence of the definition of frame content in terms of the speaker's knowledge is that frame content can change over time.[17] For example, if Ernst Axel Knauf is correct that the effectiveness of Assyrian siege warfare tactics changed behaviors by the end of the eighth century BCE, such that people would leave a region in the face of an approaching army rather than seeking the dubious security of a walled town,[18] then that suggests that the frame of WARFARE also changed in the late eighth century. Waiting out a siege—hoping that reinforcements would arrive or that the enemy would give up and depart before the town's food ran out—once represented a valid defense strategy for towns that could not defeat their enemies in open battle.[19] Now either flight or surrender would have seemed the only options for avoiding destruction. In addition, for the

---

16. Black, "Metaphor," 287.
17. Croft and Cruse, *Cognitive Linguistics*, 12.
18. Knauf, "Was There a Refugee Crisis," 159–72.
19. Ephʿal, *City Besieged*, 106–13.

people, walled towns may no longer have represented places of refuge, but rather places where certain defeat could be followed by death, deportation, or enslavement.

Critical to the interpretation of metaphorical expressions is the issue of the viewpoint of the speaker. As Barbara Dancygier and Eve Sweetser argue:

> Metaphor is not just thinking but *reasoning* about one domain in terms of another.… Metaphoric mappings crucially involve mapping not just objects and qualities and relations, but also inferences about causes, results, and other aspects of the structure of the two domains. *Viewpoint* on a situation does affect inferential structure, so viewpoint on a source domain should affect which inferences are mappable to the target.[20]

With the prophetic speakers, the question of viewpoint presents an unusual challenge, since the prophet often claims to speak for YHWH. The analysis in the chapters that follow generally treats the prophetic speaker as an honest communicator, which means that speech that the prophet attributes to YHWH will be treated as the prophet's sincere perception of what YHWH has communicated to him. As a result, in passages in which both the prophet and YHWH speak, it assumes each holds their own perspective.

The summary of the BATTLE frame above highlights three features of frames that distinguish them from domains and that assist interpreters in highlighting and assessing the speaker's viewpoint and the inferences mapped in a metaphorical expression. First, frames explicitly structure their content in terms of the relations between their elements as the frame's situation plays out from beginning to end.[21] The BATTLE frame does not simply contain armies; it contains opposing armies, an attacker and a defender, and a victor and a vanquished. Second, the situational aspect of frames also facilitates consideration of the speaker's viewpoint and context.[22] For example, does the speaker address the situation from the perspective of the attacker or the defender? Is she examining a scene of approaching or ongoing battle, or does she stand in its aftermath? Is the speaker expressing a lament or a condemnation?

Finally, a third helpful feature of frames derives from their origins as abstractions from real-world situations:

---

20. Dancygier and Sweetser, *Figurative Language*, 39, emphasis original.
21. Sullivan, *Frames*, 18, 25.
22. Cienki, "Frames," 172–73.

> The definition of a *frame* also involves gestalt structure: that is, an expression referring to some aspect of a frame structure gives conceptual access to the entire structure, so that evoking one aspect of a frame provides access to the entire frame, and individual frame components are understood in the context of the entire frame.[23]

Since the speaker has knowledge of the situation evoked by the frame, mentioning one element of it will evoke the entire situation in the speaker's mind, thereby making the entire frame available to the speaker as the discourse continues. To the extent that the audience also has knowledge about the situation, the entire frame will also be available to the audience. Thus, in our BATTLE example, the expression "she *shot down* each of their claims" evokes not only the image of the confrontation between the shooter and her opponents, but also the entire situation of battle.

Evoking the entire situation does not necessarily mean that either speaker or audience consciously runs through the entire battle scenario in their mind. Rather, it means that the whole situation becomes available to speaker and audience for additional mappings and inferences as the discourse continues. Therefore, in the battle example, the speaker could continue the description of the argument by saying that "the opponents attacked on another front," that "they hacked at the foundation of her argument," and that "in response, she gathered her defenses." Attacking on another front suggests a broader battlefield than just the initial scene in which shots are fired, hacking at an argument brings a new weapon into the metaphor, and gathering defenses extends the female subject's role from combatant to battle leader.

The speaker could even draw on elements of battle external to combat, such as claiming that "they adjusted their plan of attack," referring to a planning period prior to the beginning of combat, or "she not only defeated their current argument; she burned their whole theory to the ground," referring to burning down the city of a defeated opponent. Having access to the entire frame of BATTLE means that the speaker can use these phrases from various points and aspects of battle together coherently and that the audience can understand them. For biblical scholars as interpreters of ancient metaphors, the frame evoked by a metaphorical expression is not what the scholar knows about the subject but what the speaker knew. Therefore, to

---

23. Dancygier and Sweetser, *Figurative Language*, 17. See also Croft and Cruse, *Cognitive Linguistics*, 12; and Sullivan, *Frames*, 19.

take full advantage of the power of frames for analyzing biblical metaphor, the scholar must understand, to the extent possible, the frame that would have been evoked in the speaker's mind when expressing the metaphor.

As noted above, frames often prove more useful than domains for analyzing metaphorical expressions. Both domains and frames contain the information necessary to understand such expressions, but domains tend to be more broadly defined as containing all interrelated concepts relevant to a given subject, while frames by definition constrain their content to the limits of the speaker's knowledge, viewpoint, and context. Thus, frames facilitate a close examination of the speaker's circumstances in order to understand the frame evoked by the speech. At the same time, for metaphor analysis, the frame concept works better with some types of frames than others, because some frames more effectively evoke situations than others.

The concept of semantic frames was first introduced by Charles Fillmore in the 1970s, but it owes its origins to Fillmore's earlier work on the "semantic 'valence' of verbs," meaning the combinatory properties of verbs that are based on the verb's meaning rather than its form.[24] That original connection to verbs may explain why definitions of frames tend to refer to scenarios and situations. For example, Fillmore describes frames as follows:

> Frame semantics is first of all an approach to describing the meanings of independent linguistic entities by appealing to the kinds of conceptual structures that underlie their meanings and that motivate their use. These conceptual structures, called frames, can be schematizations of particular situation types and their components such as the events or states expressed by simple verbs or adjectives, e.g., *lift* or *similar*; large-scale institutional scenarios such as commercial translations or judicial process; patterns of contrast such as that between winning and losing; networks of relationships such as what is found in kinship terminology, and a great many others. The words or other linguistic entities in a text or discourse **evoke** or **project** their frames in the minds of the language user and figure in the cognitive process of language interpretation.[25]

Because they were originally conceived and developed as a way to describe the meanings of words that express events and states, frames lose their

---

24. Charles Fillmore, "Frame Semantics," in *Encyclopedia of Language and Linguistics*, ed. Keith Brown, 2nd ed. (New York: Elsevier, 2006), 615–16.

25. Fillmore, "Frame Semantics," 613, emphasis original.

advantage over domains for metaphor analysis when the word in question does not express an event or a state. In such cases, frames begin to look much like domains; both contain all of the information that the speaker knows about the domain's subject, and neither necessarily evokes a specific scenario or situation when elements from the domain or frame are expressed. The BATTLE example above demonstrated the difference between a BATTLE domain and a BATTLE frame, but what if the domain/frame was an object, such as ROCK? Saying the word *rock* might bring to mind the properties of rock (and rocks), where rock is located, and what people do with rock, but the word does not evoke a specific situation. Nor does it provide guidance for determining the elements and their relations that the speaker intends to evoke by mentioning rock.

This limitation does not negate the usefulness of frames for metaphor analysis, but it does have implications for the study of national identity construction in plant metaphors, because like rock, the names of nations and plants do not evoke scenarios or situations. As such, the primary frames of metaphors that identify nations with plants have less inherent structure than frames that do evoke situations or scenarios. That said, each linguistic expression of an identity metaphor contains additional content that fleshes out the details of the identity by placing the nation-object into one or more specific scenarios that would evoke frames reflecting the speaker's knowledge, viewpoint, and context.

For example, Isa 5:1–7 presents Israel and Judah as a vineyard. The underlying conceptual metaphor, expressed as TARGET IS SOURCE, describes a relationship between two nonscenario-based frames: ISRAEL/JUDAH IS A VINEYARD.[26] The extended description of the vineyard within this identity metaphor, however, adds to the image the speaker's scenario-based message that YHWH planted and cultivated the nation-vineyard, but that the people-vines have angered YHWH by producing only the bad fruit of injustice, and therefore YHWH intends to abandon the nation-vineyard. Thus, the passage as a whole will evoke not only the ISRAEL/JUDAH and VINEYARD frames, but also specific scenario-based

---

26. The metaphor makes no meaningful distinction between Israel and Judah, so I treat them here as representing a single frame. In reality, Israel and Judah were separate kingdoms. As such, the metaphor creates a perceived reality in which the two kingdoms constitute a single "nation." See the discussion later in this chapter about "imagined communities" for the theoretical basis of this conception of nations. See also the discussion of Isa 5:1–7 in ch. 4.

frames such as PLANTING, CULTIVATING, and HARVESTING. Most of the metaphor analysis in this study will focus on simple expressions with mappings between source and target frames. For discussions of concepts that are particularly broad and unstructured, however—viticulture, for example—I will generally use the term domain instead.

2.1.2. Defining Key Terms and Features of Semantic Frames

A second example of a conceptual metaphor, this time drawn from the prophetic corpus, will demonstrate the principles discussed to this point and provide an opportunity to elaborate on the features of frames that are relevant to the analysis in this book. Jeremiah 15:7a reads:

ואזרם במזרה בשערי הארץ

I will scatter them with a winnowing fork among the gates of the land.

This passage appears in a prophecy in which YHWH accuses Jerusalem of abandoning him (i.e., not worshiping him properly) and describes the punishment that he has planned for the city (15:5–9). As shown in figure 2.1, this expression of the conceptual metaphor EXILING IS WINNOWING uses information from the source frame, WINNOWING, to say something about the target frame, EXILING.

Conceptual Metaphor: EXILING IS WINNOWING

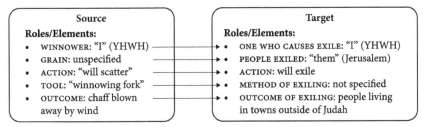

Fig. 2.1. The winnowing metaphor in Jeremiah 15:7a

Each frame in the metaphor evokes a situation as understood by the speaker. Thus, the two frames in the example contain what the speaker knows about winnowing and about exiling.

The various pieces of information within a frame are called elements or roles. The roles and their relationships often provide a basic script for the situation evoked in the frame.[27] In the WINNOWING frame, we have roles for a WINNOWER, a GRAIN that he winnows, the ACTION of scattering (by winnowing), a winnowing TOOL that the winnower uses, and the OUTCOME of the winnowing. Specific terms from the metaphorical expression are said to fill the frame roles or elements. In the EXILING frame, "I" (YHWH) fills the role of the ONE WHO CAUSES EXILE, and "them" (Jerusalem) fills the PEOPLE EXILED role. In the WINNOWING frame, "will scatter" fills the action role, and "winnowing fork" fills the TOOL role, and so on. The points of correspondence between roles in the WINNOWING frame and those in the EXILING frame are the mappings. Thus, the WINNOWER role maps to the ONE WHO CAUSES EXILE role, the GRAIN role maps to the PEOPLE EXILED role, and so on. Regarding formatting, frame names and frame elements or roles appear in small caps; conceptual metaphors, which represent relationships between frames, also appear in small caps (e.g., EXILING IS WINNOWING).[28]

Finally, this example demonstrates the importance of frame selection and the consideration of the goals of the metaphor analysis when defining conceptual metaphors. Since this study focuses on metaphors about kingdoms and nations, I could have defined the conceptual metaphor in Jer 15:7a in terms of its depiction of Jerusalem (as a metonymic reference to Judah): JERUSALEM IS GRAIN. The resulting analysis of the roles and mappings in the expression "I will scatter them with a winnowing fork among the gates of the land" would look similar to the discussion above, which suggests, incorrectly, that precision in defining conceptual metaphors does not matter.

Defining the metaphor from the perspective of the kingdom foregrounds the range of source frames that the biblical authors employ to depict Judah, but it obscures whether the same source frames also appear in metaphors of other kingdoms. It also obscures details about the action taken with respect to the grain (and with the kingdom that is the metaphor's target). Winnowing constitutes one option among several actions, including harvesting and threshing, that appear in biblical grain meta-

---

27. Sullivan, *Frames*, 18.

28. The use of small caps for frame and element names is not conventional for CMT but rather is adapted from the formatting approach employed by Sullivan, *Frames*, 20.

phors. Defining them all as grain metaphors makes it easier to overlook details such as whether some actions appear more often than others in metaphors about Judah or whether the winnowing and harvesting source frames tend to map to different target frame actions. Thus, the way that the conceptual metaphors are defined in an analysis may not be misleading in interpreting specific expressions, but it may make a difference in the ability to organize and analyze nuances in the data about a set of similar metaphorical expressions.

Not all metaphorical expressions allow such flexibility in defining the underlying conceptual metaphor. Notice that both versions of the conceptual metaphor for Jer 15:7a, EXILING IS WINNOWING and JERUSALEM IS GRAIN, also appear as mappings between the target and source frames in figure 2.1. Simple, one-situation metaphors permit this type of transposition, defining the underlying conceptual metaphor in terms of more than one of the metaphor's mappings. More complex metaphorical structures generally lack the same flexibility. Again referring to the example of Isa 5:1–7, the complete scenario depicted in the metaphor includes descriptions of the vintner (YHWH) planting and cultivating the vineyard (Israel/Judah), discovering that the grapes are bad, and declaring his intention to abandon the vineyard. The only elements common to all of these actions are the vineyard and the vintner. Thus, only the conceptual metaphors ISRAEL/JUDAH IS A VINEYARD or YHWH IS A VINTNER provide an overarching structure that can incorporate all of the details in verses 1–7.

2.1.3. Other Useful Features of Conceptual Metaphor Theory

Beyond identifying the structural aspects of metaphor—the elements and relations within frames or domains and the mappings between source and target—CMT also addresses several ways in which metaphorical expressions guide the listener's interpretation of the metaphor. While metaphors evoke the entirety of both the source and target frames, they only explicitly map a subset of elements in those frames. The choice of elements that are mapped from the source frame in a metaphorical expression serves to highlight the corresponding aspects of the target frame. Highlighting some elements of a frame may also cause other elements to be hidden or downplayed. In the example from Jer 15:7a, "I will scatter them with a winnowing fork among the gates of the land," the term "winnowing fork" highlights the part of the winnowing process that involves throwing the grain into the air and allowing the wind to carry the chaff, the inedible portion of the grain, away. The word "scatter" further highlights the chaff and what happens to it when the wind catches it. The image thus gives the impression that all of the people of Jerusalem will be scattered across the world.

At the same time, the purpose of winnowing is to remove the chaff from the grain. While the wind takes the chaff away, the good, edible grain, which significantly outweighs the chaff, falls back to the ground. This metaphor's focus on the fate of the chaff hides the fate of the grain. Absent that hiding effect, the metaphor would be less effective as a threat of national destruction, since it could imply that either the city of Jerusalem or some of the people in it will go unpunished, and only the worthless will suffer.[29] An author may also prime the audience to interpret the metaphor as intended by placing the expression in a context that reinforces the metaphor's message.[30] Jeremiah 15, for example, surrounds the winnowing metaphor in verse 7a with threats of destruction in 15:6 and 15:7b–9. This helps to ensure that the audience focuses on the mapping of blown chaff to exiled people and ignores the unspoken potential mapping of good wheat to a saved city or people.[31]

The expression in Jer 15:7a represents a fairly simple metaphor and message. More complex messages require more complex metaphorical structures, which can be achieved by elaborating on, extending, or combining metaphors.[32] Elaboration refers to adding detail to an existing mapping in a metaphor. For example, an author who wanted to strengthen the message of displacement in Jer 15:7a might elaborate more fully on distances that the chaff will travel or the locations where it will land. Extension, which adds new mappings to the expression, offers another way to complicate a metaphor's message. Jeremiah 15:7a describes the scattering of the chaff, but had the author wanted to explicitly claim within the metaphor that the people will suffer or die in exile, he could have extended the image to describe the chaff landing in a fire at the end of its travels. Finally, combination involves using more than one metaphor (or simile) in a single passage. Isaiah 17:13, for example, crafts an

---

29. For a discussion of highlighting and hiding, see Kövecses, *Metaphor*, 91–93.

30. On priming, see Dancygier and Sweetser, *Figurative Language*, 35–38.

31. See further the discussion of Jer 15:7 in ch. 4.

32. For a discussion of elaborating, extending, and combining (which they call composing), see Lakoff and Turner, *More Than Cool Reason*, 67–72; and Kövecses, *Metaphor*, 53–55.

image of YHWH dispersing Judah's enemies by combining an extended simile of fleeing armies as a receding wave with two similes of those same armies as blown chaff and tumbleweed:

לְאֻמִּים כִּשְׁאוֹן מַיִם רַבִּים יִשָּׁאוּן וְגָעַר בּוֹ וְנָס מִמֶּרְחָק וְרֻדַּף כְּמֹץ הָרִים לִפְנֵי־רוּחַ וּכְגַלְגַּל לִפְנֵי סוּפָה׃

Peoples—like the sound of masses of water they roar, but he rebukes it, and it flees far away, driven off like chaff to the hills before a wind, or like tumbleweed before a gale.[33]

2.1.4. Blending Theory

The CMT framework provides the basic model and language for the metaphor analysis in this study, but it has some limitations. The theory originally focused on unidirectional source-to-target mappings, and as a result, it lacked tools and terms for assessing interaction effects in combinations of metaphors like that in Isa 17:13. In such cases, combining CMT with (conceptual) blending theory (BT) may facilitate a more complete analysis of the passage.[34] Blending theory attempts to explain the mental processes involved in human cognition.[35] For example, when a person encounters a metaphor such as ARGUMENT IS WAR, their mind evokes the two frames—ARGUMENT and WAR—and it develops a coherent understanding of what it means to relate those frames to each other. Blending theory offers an explanation of how the mind achieves that understanding of the metaphor.

The BT model for processing a simple metaphor begins with four mental spaces (as opposed to the two-domain model of CMT). A mental

---

33. The combination of similes in Isa 17:13 is obvious. A more subtle example appears in Dylan Thomas's "Do Not Go Gentle into That Good Night." The title itself, which is also the first line of the poem, already combines three conceptual metaphors: DEATH IS A DEPARTURE (*do not go*); DEATH IS AN ADVERSARY (*gentle*); and A LIFETIME IS A DAY (*night*) (Lakoff and Turner, *More Than Cool Reason*, 34).

34. For a discussion CMT and BT as complementary approaches, see Joseph E. Grady, Todd Oakley, and Seana Coulson, "Blending and Metaphor," in *Metaphor in Cognitive Linguistics: Selected Papers from the Fifth International Cognitive Linguistics Conference, Amsterdam, July 1997*, ed. Raymond W. Gibbs Jr. and Gerard J. Steen (Amsterdam: Benjamins, 1999), 101–24.

35. Gilles Fauconnier and Mark Turner, *The Way We Think: Conceptual Blending and the Mind's Hidden Complexities* (New York: Basic Books, 2002).

space is a container for conceptual material. Two of the four BT spaces are input spaces. In an analysis of a simple metaphor, the input spaces correspond to CMT's source and target domains. A third space, called the generic space, contains features, often at a schematic level, that the input spaces have in common. The fourth space is called the blend or blended space. The generic space maps its content to each of the input spaces, which in turn map their more detailed content to the blend. The creation of the blended space via activation of the generic and input spaces is called "running the blend."[36]

Blending theory is more scalable and flexible than CMT. By design, blends can have multiple input spaces; they are not limited to just a source and a target. In fact, input spaces can themselves be blends or source-to-target metaphorical mappings that contribute to a larger blend. Input spaces may also contain nonfigurative language that can be blended with figurative language. In addition, where CMT focuses on source-to-target mappings, BT conceptualizes both source and target mapping to the blend. As a result, BT can accommodate more complex interactions between source and target or among several metaphors that have been combined in a passage. Blending theory therefore facilitates the analysis of constructions that combine multiple metaphors or that mix metaphor with other types of figurative or nonfigurative language.

In the example of Isa 17:13, the first simile presents an image of YHWH rebuking a wave, representing the armies of Judah's enemies, and causing it to recede. In the rest of the passage, the two wind-related similes convey the idea of YHWH blowing on the enemy armies, depicted as chaff and tumbleweed, to scatter them or drive them away. On its own, the wave simile might suggest that YHWH gives a verbal command that encourages the wave to depart. When the wave simile is blended with the two wind-related similes, however, the interaction of the three images adds meaning to each of them. The wave simile now creates an image not of YHWH speaking to the waves, but of YHWH shouting at them, blasting them with the force of his rebuke and pushing them into retreat. The two wind similes, on the other hand, no longer simply represent force applied to push the enemies away. Instead, the wind now also takes on the sense of a rebuke.

Blending theory goes much more deeply into cognitive processes than this study of metaphor requires, but three aspects of the theory can add

---

36. Fauconnier and Turner, *Way We Think*, 39–50.

depth and insight to an analysis of complex metaphors. The first is the concept of the blend, which, as discussed above, guides the interpreter to consider how multiple inputs may interact in the creation of meaning. The second is the concept of compression, which is common to most blends. Compression refers to the process of mentally reducing the distance that exists between elements in the real world so that the elements can be considered in relation to each other in the blend.[37]

For example, Jer 15:7a blends an image of YHWH scattering his people across the known world with an image of a human scattering chaff as far as the wind can carry it. The two images operate on vastly different scales in terms of the size of the main actors in each scenario and the physical distance over which their respective victims are scattered. The mental process of compression works to reduce the global-sized image of YHWH scattering the people down to the size of the image of the human scattering chaff. This allows the mind to consider the two images side-by-side to see how they interact. Compression operates frequently in national metaphors in the prophetic corpus, as the mind reduces the literal image of the nation down to the size of a plant or flock or woman. Compression also works in reference to time, as when a centuries-long national history must be reduced to a metaphorical representation of that time span in terms of the length of an agricultural season or the lifespan of a human.

The third useful aspect of BT derives from the generic space in the model. As noted above, the generic space contains features and elements that are common to all of the input spaces in a blend. For example, in a metaphor that relates individual combat to harvesting wheat, the generic space would contain elements that are common to both, such as entities representing the actor and the one acted upon. It would also include physical motions that the two frames share, including an abstracted image that represents both swinging a sword and wielding a sickle. Essentially the concept of the generic space encourages the interpreter to consider content and structural similarities between the input spaces at an abstract level to understand whether and how the scenarios in the two frames that have been evoked by the metaphor overlap as each scenario runs its script from beginning to end. In the generic space, we can imagine the abstracted scenarios as something like stick figures in a hand-drawn animated car-

---

37. Fauconnier and Turner, *Way We Think*, 92–93. See also Dancygier and Sweetser, *Figurative Language*, 86.

toon. As in the grain harvesting metaphor, visualizing the scenarios in this way adds insight to how the two frames and the mappings between them conceptually align, and it may facilitate identifying the submetaphors underlying complex metaphorical expressions.

2.1.5. Conventional Metaphors

Returning now to CMT, recall that the model originated as a way to analyze how metaphor structures everyday language. Conceptual metaphor theory calls these everyday metaphors *basic* or *conventional* metaphors:

> Basic conceptual metaphors are part of the common conceptual apparatus shared by members of a culture. They are systematic in that there is a fixed correspondence between the structure of the domain to be understood and the structure of the domain in terms of which we are understanding it. We usually understand them in terms of common experiences. They are largely unconscious, though attention may be drawn to them. Their operation in cognition is mostly automatic. And they are widely conventionalized in language, that is, there are a great number of words and idiomatic expressions in our language whose interpretations depend upon those conceptual metaphors.[38]

While this definition assumes that all conventional metaphors are common and automatic, the degree to which any particular metaphor exhibits these features varies. Conceptual metaphors and the expressions derived from them may be more or less conventional—more or less common and automatic—for a particular culture. They may also be conventional for one community within a culture, but not conventional for the culture as a whole.[39]

Among the conceptual metaphors often cited as examples of conventional metaphor are LIFE IS A JOURNEY, DEATH IS REST, and PEOPLE ARE PLANTS.[40] Based on their prevalence in the biblical corpus, these metaphors also appear to have been conventional for the ancient Israelites. For example, regarding living a righteous life, the biblical authors exhort the people to come learn YHWH's ways ונלכה בארחתיו, "so that we may walk in his paths" (Isa 2:3; Mic 4:2), they say of a buried king that he … וישכב

---

38. Lakoff and Turner, *More Than Cool Reason*, 51.
39. Lakoff and Turner, *More Than Cool Reason*, 55.
40. Lakoff and Turner, *More Than Cool Reason*, 52.

עַם־אֲבֹתָיו, "laid down with his fathers" (1 Kgs 2:10), and they describe a wise man who knows YHWH's teachings as כְּעֵץ שָׁתוּל עַל־פַּלְגֵי מַיִם, "like a tree planted by streams of water" (Ps 1:3).[41] In everyday language, speakers generally employ more common idioms and expressions based on these conventional metaphors. Poetic texts also routinely employ conventional metaphors, but the creativity of poetry often leads to uncommon elaborations, extensions, and combinations of metaphors. In other words, even the most common conventional conceptual metaphors may give rise to unique specific linguistic expressions.[42] Poetic texts may also question common or conventional metaphors by challenging their underlying assumptions and inferences.[43]

The analysis of plant metaphors that follows will examine both the structure and the expression of prophetic metaphors that condemn kingdoms and nations. Achieving that end requires identifying conventional conceptual metaphors within the structures of these prophetic metaphors. The discussion will not address every conventional metaphor in these expressions. Rather, it will focus on two types of conventional metaphors that help to shape the conceptualizations and condemnations of the kingdoms. First, by definition, plant metaphors about communities employ the metaphor PEOPLE ARE PLANTS. The conventionality of PEOPLE ARE PLANTS across multiple cultures in the ancient Near East has been amply demonstrated, so additional discussion of that metaphor is not needed here.[44]

Second, many of the prophetic condemnations employ one of the following metaphors for conflict within their metaphorical structures: WARFARE IS INDIVIDUAL COMBAT, CONFLICT IS BURNING, and CONQUEST IS EATING. For each of these metaphors, the attacker in the conflict may be either human or divine. Thus, *warfare*, for example, includes both human battles and divine attacks (in the sense of an individual deity attacking a

---

41. Numerous additional biblical examples exist for each of these metaphors. See, e.g., LIFE IS A JOURNEY (Deut 31:29; 1 Kgs 8:25; Isa 53:6; Jer 6:16; Ps 56:14); DEATH IS REST or DEATH IS SLEEP (Gen 47:30; Deut 31:16; Isa 14:8, 11; Ps 13:4; Job 3:11–19); and PEOPLE ARE PLANTS (2 Sam 23:6; Jer 17:8; Ps 128:3; Job 24:20; Song 2:3).

42. Lakoff and Turner, *More Than Cool Reason*, 50.

43. Lakoff and Turner, *More Than Cool Reason*, 51–52. For an example of questioning, see the discussion of Ezek 15 in ch. 8. The passage takes a preexisting positive metaphor of Judah as a vine and explains, at length, that vines have no value because their wood is useless for anything but burning.

44. Frymer-Kensky, "Planting of Man," 129–36.

human population). Establishing the conventionality of these three metaphors requires a set of criteria by which to evaluate them, preferably one that aligns with Lakoff and Turner's definition of conventional metaphor, quoted above. By that standard, a conventional metaphor would have the following properties:

- It is common to members of the same culture.
- It generates a large number of expressions within that culture.
- The structure of the mappings between source and target is fixed, or systematic, such that elements A, B, and C from the source frame consistently map to elements A′, B′, and C′, respectively, in the target frame (and therefore A never maps to B′ or C′).
- The source frame probably derives from a common human experience.

In addition, according to CMT, conventional metaphors represent commonplace ways of thinking and speaking: "A metaphor is conventional to the extent that it is automatic, effortless, and generally established as a mode of thought among members of a linguistic community."[45]

The criteria below for identifying a conventional metaphor in the biblical corpus focus on assessing the extent to which the metaphor demonstrates these properties:

1. The biblical texts contain numerous examples of expressions based on the conceptual metaphor.[46]

---

45. Lakoff and Turner, *More Than Cool Reason*, 55. Determining whether a metaphorical expression was effortless to produce would seem to require direct access to the biblical authors, which we do not have, but the criteria provided here can help to assess whether a metaphor was "automatic" and "generally established as a mode of thought" in ancient Israel and Judah.

46. "Numerous," in this case, cannot be defined in terms of a minimum number of expressions. Rather, the number of expressions of a conventional metaphor can only be considered numerous if a relatively large number of the biblical passages that discuss the metaphor's target employ the metaphor. Thus, five similar expressions about a target that otherwise appears dozens of times in the Bible would constitute weak evidence of conventionality, while the evidence of conventionality would seem stronger if the five expressions refer to a target that only appears ten times in the biblical corpus.

2. These expressions appear in passages from at least two different biblical genres, and (preferably) in both poetry and prose.[47]

3. If the biblical authors spoke about the metaphor's target in more than one way—using either more than one conceptual metaphor or both metaphorical and nonmetaphorical terms—then they used the metaphor under study at rates comparable (or better) to the alternate ways of speaking about the target.

4. The expressions map several elements and terms from the source domain.

5. The structure of the metaphorical mappings remains consistent across all expressions of the metaphor, meaning the elements from the source domain consistently map to the same corresponding elements in the target frame.

6. The source frame probably derives from a common human experience.

Metaphors that meet the first two criteria establish their widespread use among the biblical authors, and therefore offer evidence that the metaphors were probably common in ancient Israelite culture. They also help to demonstrate that the metaphors represent established modes of thought, as does the third criteria, because it assesses the frequency with which the metaphor is used relative to other ways of speaking of the metaphor's target. In other words, if the biblical authors use metaphorical and literal terms to speak about a single target at roughly equivalent rates, then that suggests that the metaphorical mode is a relatively common way to think about that target.

Metaphors that meet the fourth and fifth criteria would be considered "systematic," in that they consistently map a variety of elements and terms from source to target in a way that preserves "a fixed cor-

---

47. The presence of the same conceptual metaphors in texts from other ancient Near Eastern linguistic communities would further support their conventionality, since it would suggest either that these modes of thought had been operative long enough to become broadly distributed or that the conceptual connection between the source and target was so natural that the metaphor spontaneously arose in several languages. The converse principle does not hold, however, because, as Lakoff and Turner note, metaphors can be conventional for one community, or even for a subgroup within a larger community, but unconventional for another (Lakoff and Turner, *More Than Cool Reason*, 55).

respondence" between the source frame and target frame structures.[48] Finally, the sixth criterion should be assessed from the perspective of the biblical author: Does the situation in the frame derive from a common experience in ancient Israel or Judah? A metaphor may be conventional without reflecting a common experience, however, so the sixth criterion is more descriptive than determinative for conventionality.

While these criteria help to determine which metaphors to include as conventional, they are less effective for excluding other metaphors as not conventional. Some metaphors that appear in the Bible that do not display these properties may, in fact, have been conventional for the Israelites, but they simply did not warrant frequent use by the biblical authors.[49] The converse situation, however—that biblical metaphors that display the above properties were not conventional—seems quite unlikely. If the essence of conventional metaphor is that it reflects routine and varied use of terms from one frame to describe another frame, then the above criteria establish such patterns of use. Certainly, they establish a degree of conventionality for the metaphors among the biblical authors. In addition, while the possibility exists that one or more of these metaphors could have been conventional only to the biblical authors, and not to their audiences, this also seems doubtful, in part because some of the verbal expressions of these metaphors have fossilized into idioms, which suggests long-term, regular use of the expression.[50] Moreover, the texts involved developed over centuries and arose out of different schools of thought and different locations. This diversity in authorship makes it unlikely that the texts represent a way of communicating that was unique to those who wrote them.

An evaluation of the three conflict metaphors—WARFARE IS INDIVIDUAL COMBAT, CONFLICT IS BURNING, and CONQUEST IS EATING— demonstrates that they all satisfy the first two criteria for conventionality: the biblical corpus contains numerous examples of each metaphor, and in each case, the metaphor appears in at least two different biblical genres

---

48. Lakoff and Turner, *More Than Cool Reason*, 51.

49. An analogous situation exists with biblical *hapax legomena*, some of which may have been fairly common in ancient Hebrew. See Edward Ullendorff, "Is Biblical Hebrew a Language?," in *Is Biblical Hebrew a Language? Studies in Semitic Languages and Civilizations* (Wiesbaden: Harrassowitz, 1977), 3–17.

50. Deignan, *Metaphor and Corpus Linguistics*, 150.

and in both poetry and prose. The following is a partial list of passages containing examples of each metaphor:

- WARFARE IS INDIVIDUAL COMBAT: Exod 9:15; Lev 26:17; Num 14:45; Josh 10:4; Judg 1:5; 2 Sam 5:24; 2 Kgs 14:10; 2 Chr 14:11; Isa 5:25; Mic 6:13; Ps 135:10
- CONFLICT IS BURNING: Gen 19:24; Num 21:28; Deut 32:22; 1 Kgs 14:10; Isa 9:17–19; Jer 5:14; Ezek 28:18; Amos 1:4; Pss 97:3; 118:12; Prov 26:21; Lam 2:3
- CONQUEST IS EATING: Gen 49:27; Deut 7:16; 2 Sam 18:8; Isa 9:11; Jer 2:3; Ezek 34:10; Hos 13:8; Mic 3:3; Pss 14:4; 21:10; 124:3; Prov 30:14; Job 16:9; Lam 2:5

The third criterion works well for establishing the conventionality of WARFARE IS INDIVIDUAL COMBAT, because it happens that a large number of terms for warfare in the biblical corpus derive from the INDIVIDUAL COMBAT frame. Thus, any descriptions of warfare that use these terms are expressions of WARFARE IS INDIVIDUAL COMBAT.

The third criterion cannot so easily be employed to determine whether either CONFLICT IS BURNING or CONQUEST IS EATING were conventional, though. Each metaphor represents an alternative way of speaking about conflict, so the third criterion would require comparing their popularity relative to each other. It makes little sense to identify the most common metaphors for conflict in the biblical corpus and then to define one of them as unconventional simply because it appears less often than the others. The third criterion does prove useful, however, for assessing relative degrees of conventionality of these metaphors. By that measure, WARFARE IS INDI-VIDUAL COMBAT is the most conventional of the three by a significant margin, while CONFLICT IS BURNING and CONQUEST IS EATING appear to be comparable to each other in conventionality.

The sets of examples of WARFARE IS INDIVIDUAL COMBAT, CONFLICT IS BURNING, and CONQUEST IS EATING above were chosen both because they show the variety of texts and text types in which the metaphors appear and because the expressions of the metaphors in those passages employ a variety of terms within a consistent set of source-to-target mappings. The examples therefore help to establish that all three metaphors also meet the fourth and fifth criteria, which relate to systematicity. To put the concept of systematicity in more concrete terms, table 2.1 lists examples of some of the more common terms for individual combat, including verbal roots, nouns, and idioms, that appear in biblical warfare accounts in expressions of WARFARE IS INDIVIDUAL COMBAT:[51]

Table 2.1. Examples of mappings in
expressions of WARFARE IS INDIVIDUAL COMBAT

Term	Individual Combat	Warfare
נכי	to strike, kill	to attack, defeat
מכה	a blow, wound	an attack, defeat
נגף	to injure by striking (*qal*); to be injured by striking (*niphal*)	to successfully attack, defeat (*qal*); to be defeated (*niphal*)
מגפה	a damaging blow, wound	a successful attack, defeat
תפש	to take hold of	to take control over
ביד	in the hand of [a person]	subject to the control, power of [a leader or kingdom]

In each case, an element from the INDIVIDUAL COMBAT frame maps to a corresponding element in the WARFARE frame. The metaphor maps not just individual elements but also the whole structure of the source frame onto the target frame, such that words for striking in INDIVIDUAL COMBAT consistently map to words for attacking in WARFARE, words for wounding in INDIVIDUAL COMBAT consistently map to words for defeating in WARFARE, and so on. The consistency in the structure even works at the level of nuances of usage for a single word, as in Hebrew נפל, "to fall," whose meaning varies depending on which combatant serves as the subject of the verb. When the attacker falls upon the attacked, נפל carries an attacking sense in individual combat that can also metaphorically map to a similar sense in warfare of one army attacking another. However, an attacked person falling in combat, signifying that the person has been struck or killed, would map to an attacked army or city experiencing a defeat in war.

---

51. The table focuses on the system of terms with senses that represent mappings between the frames of INDIVIDUAL COMBAT and WARFARE. It omits any senses that the cited terms may carry that are not related to the metaphor WARFARE IS INDIVIDUAL COMBAT.

A similar table of mappings could be prepared for CONFLICT IS BURN-ING and CONQUEST IS EATING. Expressions of CONFLICT IS BURNING, for example, consistently map the one who starts the fire to the attacker, and they map a variety of terms for burning or causing a fire—such as אש יצא, בער, and להט—to attacking. Likewise, expressions of CONQUEST IS EATING consistently map various terms for the eater—whether person, animal, or thing—to the attacker, and terms for the item eaten—such as bread, prey, or person—to the attacked. Finally, all three metaphors meet the sixth criteria: they rely on source frames derived from common human experi-ences: fighting; burning; and eating.[52]

2.1.6. Conflict Metaphors within Prophetic Plant Metaphors

To understand how the conventional conflict metaphors help to struc-ture the plant metaphors in the prophetic condemnations, it is helpful to keep in mind the basic structure of a CONFLICT frame, including the pri-mary roles and relations within that frame. Figure 2.2 (p. 50) presents the roles most likely to be mapped in biblical expressions of conflict, though not every expression will map all of these elements. The elements also represent the basic script for a conflict: that one entity attacks another (ATTACKER and ATTACKED) in some way (MEANS OF ATTACK), for some reason (MOTIVATION FOR ATTACK), and with a particular result (OUT-COME OF ATTACK). Attack, here, refers to any aggressive move, whether physical, social, or verbal.

For any given expression, the message of the author will drive the por-trayal of the elements. In other words, while the frame itself represents a neutral view of conflict, fillers for a particular expression may present the ATTACKER as hero or villain, just as they may present the ATTACKED

---

52. BURNING IS EATING, a submetaphor frequently incorporated into expressions of CONFLICT IS BURNING, also meets all six criteria. Indeed, the metaphor appears to have been highly conventional in ancient Israel and Judah. Not only does it occur in a wide variety of contexts and forms, but the most common verb for eating, אכל, is used to express the action of a fire burning (i.e., consuming by fire) at rates comparable to those of common literal roots that mean "to burn," such as שרף and בער. This brief overview of WARFARE IS INDIVIDUAL COMBAT, CONFLICT IS BURNING, and CONQUEST IS EATING attempts to provide sufficient information about each metaphor to set up the discussion in the chapters that follow of how the conflict metaphors help structure plant metaphors. A more detailed examination of the use of these three meta-phors within the broader biblical corpus will be forthcoming.

(DIVINE) CONFLICT Frame
Roles/Elements:
- ATTACKER
- ATTACKED
- MEANS OF ATTACK
- MOTIVATION FOR ATTACK
- OUTCOME OF ATTACK

Fig. 2.2. The basic structure of a CONFLICT frame

as victim or foe. In addition, the MEANS and the MOTIVATION FOR THE ATTACK may be presented as righteous or not and the OUTCOME as positive or not. Of course, more nuanced expressions may represent positions in between any of these poles. Finally, the viewpoint of the expression may vary—in most cases running the script with a focus on either the ATTACKER (*A attacked B*) or the ATTACKED (*B was attacked by A*).

In many of the plant metaphors in the prophetic condemnations, the conventional metaphors for conflict provide a link between the plant-based source frame and the target frame of military conquest or a divine attack. Because both eating and burning are actions that can be directly taken against plants, when the metaphors CONQUEST IS EATING or CONFLICT IS BURNING are incorporated into a plant metaphor, the conflict metaphor itself fills one of the source-to-target mappings. For example, figure 2.3 shows the standard mapping for a metaphor that depicts a military conquest of a city as a forest fire.

Conceptual Metaphor: MILITARY CONQUEST IS A FOREST FIRE

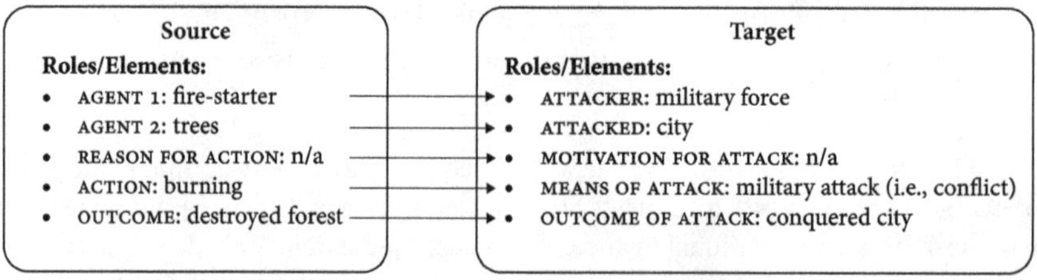

Source	Target
Roles/Elements:	**Roles/Elements:**
• AGENT 1: fire-starter	• ATTACKER: military force
• AGENT 2: trees	• ATTACKED: city
• REASON FOR ACTION: n/a	• MOTIVATION FOR ATTACK: n/a
• ACTION: burning	• MEANS OF ATTACK: military attack (i.e., conflict)
• OUTCOME: destroyed forest	• OUTCOME OF ATTACK: conquered city

Fig. 2.3. The incorporation OF CONFLICT IS BURNING within a plant metaphor

As the diagram demonstrates, CONFLICT IS BURNING would fill the mapping between the ACTION taken against the plants in the FOREST source frame (burning) and the MEANS OF ATTACK element in the CONQUEST target frame (conflict). In a similar way, CONQUEST IS EATING may fill the source-to-target mappings between the OUTCOME in the PLANT-BASED source frame (eating) and the OUTCOME OF ATTACK in the CONQUEST target frame (conquest).

The relationship between the conflict and plant metaphors is more complex with WARFARE IS INDIVIDUAL COMBAT. Since a person cannot engage in individual combat with a plant, WARFARE IS INDIVIDUAL COMBAT cannot simply fill either the ACTION → MEANS OF ATTACK or OUTCOME → OUTCOME OF ATTACK mappings between the PLANT-BASED frame and the CONQUEST frame. Instead, these metaphors draw on a shared set of physical motions or actions that occur in both plant and individual combat contexts. For example, harvesting may require cutting down or beating plants, and these physical motions have parallels in the act of striking an opponent in individual combat.

Structurally, in depictions of warfare in terms of some plant-based activity, WARFARE IS INDIVIDUAL COMBAT serves as an intermediary between the plant-based source frame and the warfare target frame. In these cases, the INDIVIDUAL COMBAT frame becomes the source frame for warfare imagery and the target frame for plant imagery. The relationship between the source and target frames in this structure looks something like the transitive property in mathematics:

If $a = b$, and $b = c$, then $a = c$.

For example, in the metaphor WARFARE IS HARVESTING, the transitive property allows us to conceptualize the connections among the source and target frames as follows:

	Target Frame	Source Frame
If	WARFARE (a)	IS INDIVIDUAL COMBAT (b),
and	INDIVIDUAL COMBAT (b)	IS HARVESTING (c),
then	WARFARE (a)	IS HARVESTING (c).

The INDIVIDUAL COMBAT frame thus connects the WARFARE and HARVESTING frames.[53] Not all plant metaphors engage one or more of the

_____

53. The transitive property provides a useful way of explaining the relationships between these metaphors, but the analogy is limited in its applicability by the

conventional conflict metaphors, but for those that do, analyzing this aspect of their metaphorical structure will enrich our overall understanding how plant metaphors create meaning for the audience.

In the chapters that follow, the modified CMT framework discussed here will guide the analysis of both specific metaphorical expressions and the underlying conceptual metaphors that structure these expressions. For exploration of the national identity components in many of these passages, however, metaphor theory alone does not suffice to explain the content and rhetorical strategies of the prophetic authors. Therefore, the analysis incorporates an additional theoretical model derived from studies of national identity and national identity formation.

2.2. Analyzing the Construction of National Identity

As discussed in chapter 1, the national identity metaphors present in the prophetic corpus derive from a sort of quasi-nationalistic impulse. Nations, nationalism, and national identity are modern phenomena.[54] Nevertheless, some of the factors that led to the rise of modern nations and nationalist movements also appear to have been present in Israel and Judah at the end of the eighth and seventh centuries, creating conditions in which ideas similar to modern nationalism may have arisen in the minds of some of the prophets. The question then becomes how to understand and evaluate these ideas. On this point, theories about collective identity, and specifically national identity, offer a solution; they provide a vocabulary and structure for analyzing national identities that proves useful also for analyzing ancient quasi-national identities.

The approach used here adopts a modified version of Anderson's definition of a modern nation as "an imagined political community—and imagined as both inherently limited and sovereign."[55] Anderson argues

---

unidirectional nature of metaphor. The fact that the mappings from one frame to the next work in one direction, and in the specific order given, does not mean that the same mappings will work if the order of the frames is reversed or otherwise disarranged. In other words, with metaphor, if the arrangement "if a = b and b = c, then a = c" works, that does not imply that the arrangement "if c = b and b = a, then c = a" will yield identical mappings and meanings.

54. For a summary of many of the different criteria by which modern scholarship defines the concept of a nation, see Ruth Wodak et al., *Discursive Construction*, 18–30.

55. Anderson, *Imagined Communities*, 6. See also the discussion of Anderson's

that the nation is imagined because the people of a nation do not know each other personally, and therefore their connection as a collective exists primarily because they think of themselves as a nation. The limits of a nation refer to the criteria by which the people distinguish their own nation from other nations, and its sovereignty refers to the nation's state and the clearly defined territory that the state controls.[56]

The one necessary modification to this model relates to the issue of sovereignty: while every nation associates itself with a specific territory, not every modern nation includes a state. This adjustment represents an important decoupling of the concepts of nation and state, so that each may be considered separately in the study of modern nations.[57] The imagined nature of nations is fundamental to understanding the construction of national identity in the prophetic metaphors. Regardless of how other Israelites and Judahites viewed themselves in relation to their communities and kingdoms, when the prophetic authors created their national identity metaphors, they did so from the perspective of imagining themselves as members of a (quasi-)nation. They then fleshed out the identity of that nation by placing limits on it in terms of its territory, its defining features, and how it differs from other nations.

While the discussion thus far may seem to suggest that each prophetic author constructed a single national identity, the reality is that national identities have no fixed form; they are subject to change over time as new circumstances affect how the speaker interprets the nation's past, present, and anticipated future.[58] Therefore, even identities constructed by the same prophetic author need not include the same details or lead to the same conclusions about how the prophet viewed the nation. Nor should we expect that two authors speaking of the same nation create identical images of that nation. Indeed, the differences in the various conceptualizations of Israel and Judah as nations are at least as important

---

theory and how it has sometimes been misunderstood or misapplied in subsequent scholarship in Maxwell, "Primordialism," 826–42.

56. Anderson, *Imagined Communities*, 6–7.

57. Guibernau, "Nations without States," 1251–82. Guibernau cites Catalonia, Scotland, Quebec, and the Kurds as examples of nations without states (1261–64, 1268–71, 1274–76). See also Guibernau, *Nations without States*.

58. Ohad David and Daniel Bar-Tal, "A Sociopsychological Conception of Collective Identity: The Case of National Identity as an Example," *Personality and Social Psychology Review* 13 (2009): 365–66.

as the similarities, because they invite further inquiry about how they differ and why.

Exploring such differences requires examining the specific situation and context within which each particular identity developed.[59] For purposes of this study, a national identity includes a prophet's claims, perceptions, and beliefs about the features that unify his own nation and that differentiate it from other nations. The prophet's situation comprises the immediate historical circumstances within which the prophetic text was composed, including aspects of the prophetic author's circumstances (location, role in society, etc.). Context is the broader historical, political, social, and religious reality of the world around the prophetic author. Modern identity studies may collect direct evidence from individuals for both perceived national identity features and situational and contextual information. In addition, the availability of direct evidence from multiple sources and perspectives allows researchers to examine identity formation dynamics, at both the individual and group levels, from multiple perspectives. Application of identity theory to the study of ancient individuals and societies requires a different approach. In the case of biblical prophecy, the available evidence includes the prophetic texts and what is known about the history and societies of ancient Israel, Judah, and their neighbors in the ancient Near East.

Presumably, the prophetic authors communicated what they believed to be true or what they wanted others to believe to be true. As such, the prophetic texts may serve as direct evidence of individual claims, perceptions, and beliefs. Moreover, multiple authors, to the extent that they can be differentiated, constitute multiple sources. A greater challenge lies in gleaning situational information from the available evidence. After all, determining with any confidence the date and author of a specific text may not be possible. In addition, while some prophetic passages feature verbal exchanges between a prophet and his subject or audience,[60] none of the

---

59. Richard D. Ashmore, Kay Deaux, and Tracy McLaughlin-Volpe, "An Organizing Framework for Collective Identity: Articulation and Significance of Multidimensionality," *Psychological Bulletin* 130 (2004): 103–4. The definitions of the prophets' situation and context employed here derive from those developed by Ashmore, Deaux, and McLaughlin-Volpe for use in examining collective identity. See also the discussion of context and collective identity in David and Bar-Tal, "Sociopsychological Conception of Collective Identity," 371–72.

60. John T. Willis, "Dialogue between Prophet and Audience as a Rhetorical Device in the Book of Jeremiah," *JSOT* 33 (1985): 63–82.

national identity metaphors include such explicit interactions. Therefore, we lack situational evidence for how these passages were received by the Israelites and Judahites. The one exception would be if we could determine that one text is directly responding to another; such texts may provide evidence for how a later prophet reacted to the ideas of an earlier one. In that case, the later prophet's situation would include knowledge of the earlier text. In addition, the ways that the prophetic authors present their identity metaphors sometimes suggest that the text constitutes an interaction with a preexisting conception of Israel or Judah held by their audience. As such, we may glean from them a sense of one aspect of the prophet's situation—how the audience viewed their kingdom at the time that the prophet created the identity metaphor.

Finally, in most cases, we have at least a general sense of the contexts for the prophetic metaphors. Even absent a precise date and author for each text, archaeological and textual evidence offer some information about the history and society of Israel and Judah at the close of the Iron Age. These differences in the amounts of available situational versus contextual evidence mean that context will provide most of the background against which individual texts will be evaluated, occasionally supplemented by limited situational information.

With these assumptions and limitations in mind, this study treats the prophetic metaphors about Israel and Judah as evidence related to the authors' own conceptualizations of their kingdoms and of their people as nations. Moreover, since the prophetic authors directed their work toward an audience, the national identities they present also constitute attempts to foster and shape a particular perspective on Israelite or Judahite national identity. The national identity model offered by Ruth Wodak and her colleagues provides a helpful framework for examining and discussing the details of the prophetic conceptions of national identity.[61] Its focus on how people construct national identities as they speak or write about nations aligns well with idea that the prophets created their national identity metaphors as they composed prophecies about their people.

Wodak and her colleagues developed their model specifically to study the dynamics of Austrian national identity during the mid-1990s, though they also took pains to ensure that their approach could be employed to study other nations. They present a set of five

---

61. Wodak et al., *Discursive Construction*.

core components that routinely appear in Austrian constructions of national identity:

1. A narrative about the nation's past;
2. A shared culture;
3. A "common political present and fate";
4. A "national body";
5. A "national character."[62]

A nation's narrative tells the story of its origins, history, or development.[63] Shared culture would include elements such as language and religion, as well as other common aspects of the people's lifestyles, behaviors, and habits. The concept of a shared political present and fate means that the speaker perceives that the people of the nation currently share a common experience because of their association with the nation and that the speaker anticipates that, in the future, what happens to one member of the nation will happen to all. The national body includes territorial claims for the nation or landmarks or other distinctive geographic or architectural features that characterize the speaker's nation and that distinguish it from other nations.[64]

Finally, national character refers to the set of features that answer the question "What does being a member of the nation mean?" The concept may include stereotypes about how the typical member of the nation behaves or claims that the people share a common ancestry or place of birth. It may also include the individual's sense of connection to

---

62. Wodak et al., *Discursive Construction*, 29–31.

63. Narrative identity theories posit that identity is formed through the development, over time, of a personal or group narrative. See Phillip L. Hammack Jr., "Theoretical Foundations of Identity," in *The Oxford Handbook of Identity Development*, ed. Kate C. McLean and Moin Syed, Oxford Library of Psychology (Oxford: Oxford University Press, 2015), 21–23. While these theories developed on a separate, though related, path from other theories of social and collective identity, the concept of an identity narrative has subsequently been incorporated into some comprehensive approaches to identity and identity formation. Three of the frameworks that contribute to this study do include the concept of a collective or national narrative. See Ashmore, Deaux, and McLaughlin-Volpe, "Organizing Framework," 96–97; David and Bar-Tal, "Sociopsychological Conception of Collective Identity," 365–66, 368–69; and Wodak et al., *Discursive Construction*, 18–31.

64. Wodak et al., *Discursive Construction*, 31.

or pride in the nation.[65] Some overlap may occur between the first four elements of the model and the fifth element of national character. This duplication occurs because the first four elements in the model speak to the features of the nation as a collective whole, while national character focuses on the individual as a member of the nation. As such, national character may include the "typical" individual's role in or relationship to the nation's past, present, future, culture, and body.

Generally speaking, the model as defined by Wodak and colleagues fits well with the content of the prophetic national identity metaphors. The five identity elements in the Austrian model offer a simple way to categorize the various mappings in these metaphors, and to understand whether and how the prophetic authors use concepts that are common to modern national identities. The elements also provide a baseline against which to judge whether or not a particular metaphor constructs a national identity. Not all metaphors use all five identity elements, so I established some general criteria that a metaphor must meet in order to qualify as an identity metaphor. By definition, all condemnation metaphors accuse the people of some misdeed or condemn them to some form of suffering, and many of them do both. They therefore include the element of a shared present or fate. Generally, a passage must also have at least two of the other four elements to qualify as containing a constructed national identity. The presence of a national narrative and a national body carry the most weight in my assessments of whether a particular metaphor constitutes an identity metaphor, because these features, more so than culture or character, create a tangible link that connects the people to each other and to a specific geographic area.

One additional advantage to this model lies in the discussion of how constructed national identities serve different strategies. These strategies may or may not be consciously pursued; in some cases, they may simply arise as a product of the speaker's goals for speaking and their attitude toward the nation. Wodak and colleagues identify three main categories of strategy in constructing national identities. First, "constructive" strat-

---

65. Wodak et al., *Discursive Construction*, 29–30. In their interviews and focus groups, Wodak and her team framed the question as "What does being Austrian mean?" Answers ranged from biographical details, such as ancestry, citizenship, or where a person was born or raised, to behavioral features, including being "easygoing" and "humorous," to having a positive sense of belonging to Austria (115–17, 150–57, 193–94).

egies work to support the nation as it currently stands by emphasizing both what unites the nation and what differentiates it from other nations. They create or propagate a new identity designed to unify the people, or they defend a threatened existing identity by reproducing or justifying it. Second, "transformative" strategies aim to change the nation's current identity. Third, "destructive" strategies seek to destroy aspects of the nation's current identity, and they generally fail to offer an alternative in its place.[66] In combination with the identity elements, these discursive strategies provide the primary tools employed in the following chapters for identifying, analyzing, and discussing the elements of national identity when they appear in the prophetic condemnation metaphors.

---

66. Wodak et al., *Discursive Construction*, 32–33.

3
Viticulture Metaphors: An Introduction

Grapevines—and, more broadly, viticulture—figure prominently in biblical depictions of the landscape, culture, and prosperity of ancient Israel and Judah. In the stories of the foundations of humanity, one of the first acts of Noah after the flood is to plant a vineyard (Gen 9:20). Oded Borowski argues that "the biblical tradition that Noah planted a vineyard after the flood suggests that the biblical writers were aware of the antiquity of viticulture and the location of domestication of the vine."[1] A more likely explanation of the narrative is that the Noah tradition reflects not only the importance of viticulture to the Israelite culture and economy, but also the biblical author's conception of his people as a nation of vintners. The narratives of the wilderness period offer another example of viticulture's significance. According to Num 13:23, when the Israelite spies bring back to their camps the produce found in Canaan, their haul includes a giant grape cluster so big that it requires two people to carry it:

ויבאו עד־נחל אשכל ויכרתו משם זמורה ואשכול ענבים אחד וישאהו
במוט בשנים ומן־הרמנים ומן־התאנים:

They came to the river valley of Eshcol, and they cut from there
a branch with one cluster of grapes (and they carried it on a pole
between two [of them]) and some pomegranates and some figs.

The pomegranates and figs gathered at the end of this verse appear almost as an afterthought in comparison to the image of the massive grape cluster, which indicates how much the presence of grapes contributed to the perception of Canaan as a good land.

---

1. Oded Borowski, *Agriculture in Iron Age Israel* (Winona Lake, IN: Eisenbrauns, 1987), 102.

The importance of viticulture to the Israelites also appears in metonymic expressions in which vineyard ownership (sometimes presented
in combination with the ownership of houses or fields) represents prosperity.[2] Proverbs declares that wise men and women prosper because they
put in the effort needed to ensure the success of their vineyards (Prov
24:30–34; 31:16).[3] First Samuel indicates that kings had the power to steal
or bestow wealth by taking or granting vineyards and fields (1 Sam 8:14;
22:7). Ezekiel 28:26a describes postexilic prosperity in terms of building
houses and planting vineyards:

וישבו עליה לבטח ובנו בתים ונטעו כרמים וישבו לבטח

And they will live on it [their land] securely. And they will build
houses and plant vineyards and live securely.

The author emphasizes in this verse that YHWH will provide the security
necessary for the people to live in their homeland. The building of houses
and planting of vineyards thus primarily represents the concept of prosperity, perhaps with the added entailment of a settled life.[4]

Finally, several passages express the idea of being blessed or cursed
by differentiating between planting vineyards and consuming their fruit.
In blessings, the people will both plant their vineyards and consume the
produce (e.g., Isa 65:21; Jer 31:5; Amos 9:14), while in curses, they plant
the vineyards, but others consume the fruit or wine (e.g., Deut 28:30;

---

2. See also the discussion in ch. 7 of the association between prosperity and the
combination of grapevines and fig trees.

3. Proverbs 24:30–34 places כרם as a parallel for שדה, "field," which might imply
that the actions of the lazy, foolish man in the proverb include neglect of his vineyard.
In Prov 31:16, however, the woman acquires a שדה presumably to plant a כרם in it. The
relationship between שדה and כרם in Prov 31:16 raises the question of whether the
two terms in Prov 24:30–34 also refer to a single plot of land, meaning both passages
focus on the care of a vineyard as a sign of wisdom. The reference to the stone wall
in 24:31 also suggests that a vineyard, not a field, dominates the image in the passage,
since the biblical evidence elsewhere suggests that vineyards could be enclosed by a
wall or hedge to keep out people or animals (Num 22:24; Isa 5:5; Ps 80:13).

4. Jeremiah 35 also associates vineyard ownership with a settled life, as the Rech-
abites describe their commitment to their nomadic lifestyle by reaffirming their ancestral vow never to own houses, fields, or vineyards nor consume the produce of the
vine (35:6–10). See also the discussion in ch. 7 of sitting under vine and fig tree as a
metonym for prosperity.

Amos 5:11; Zeph 1:13). This formula appears only in reference to Israel or Judah, and thus usually directs the blessing or curse toward the Israelites or Judahites. Joshua 24:13, however, represents a variation on the curse, as YHWH declares that the Israelites are consuming the fruit of vineyards planted by the people of Canaan, whom YHWH drove from the land:

ואתן לכם ארץ אשר לא־יגעת בה וערים אשר לא־בניתם ותשבו בהם
כרמים וזיתים אשר לא־נטעתם אתם אכלים:

I have given to you land in which you have not toiled, and cities that you did not build, and you have dwelled in them. Vineyards and olive trees that you did not plant, you have consumed.

In this passage, and a similar version in Deut 6:11, the Israelites benefit from the misfortune of the Canaanites.[5]

Ultimately, vines and vineyards came to represent Israel and Judah themselves. The following four chapters explore how the prophetic authors used frames from the VITICULTURE domain to express their conceptions, and condemnations, of Israel and Judah. The prophetic authors did not restrict their use of viticulture metaphors to Israel and Judah, however. To the extent that metaphors condemning other kingdoms may help shed light on the authors' use of the VITICULTURE domain, these other metaphors will also be included in the discussion. The analysis will begin in this chapter with an overview of the nature of prophetic viticulture metaphors and the challenges of presenting a comprehensive analysis of the material. Attention will then turn to the use of viticulture metaphors to express collective condemnation.

3.1. Overview of Prophetic Viticulture Metaphors

Some thirty-seven passages in the prophetic corpus contain metaphors that employ terms from a viticulture source frame to say something about a human target frame.[6] The targets of these metaphors are almost always cities, kingdoms, or nations; only four passages use viticulture metaphors

---

5. For additional discussion of this theme, see Smoak, "Building Houses."

6. Some passages that describe Israel or Judah as a woody plant may also have originated as viticulture metaphors (e.g., Isa 37:31; Nah 2:3). Because these metaphors lack terms that unambiguously place them within the VITICULTURE domain, however, it is difficult to know whether their authors conceptualized the nation specifically as a

in reference to individuals or groups (Isa 34:4; Jer 23:9; Ezek 17:5–10; Zeph 1:12). The challenge of analyzing these metaphors below the general domain level of VITICULTURE lies in determining how to define their frames. Expressions of these metaphors fall fairly naturally into two groups. The first group, containing twenty-six metaphors, employs mainly plant-related imagery—vineyards, vines, or grapes. The second group contains eleven metaphors that ignore the plant and instead focus on wine and its intoxicating effect. Since the imagery in these two groups generally does not overlap, their metaphors will be discussed separately. This chapter and the two that follow it examine the plant-based metaphors, which provide the greatest variety and complexity among the viticulture metaphors. Chapter 6 then addresses the wine- and intoxication-based metaphors.

Organizing the twenty-six plant-based viticulture metaphors into categories that will help facilitate their analysis poses a challenge. Studies of viticulture metaphors often refer to them, rather imprecisely, as either vine metaphors or vineyard metaphors: ISRAEL IS A VINE or ISRAEL IS A VINEYARD. The problem with this approach is that the biblical authors are often less interested in defining their plant-based target than they are in describing what happens to that target. They may describe destroying vine branches or their fruit, but they often fail to specify whether the underlying object of the metaphor is a vine or a vineyard.[7] For example, Isa 18:5 depicts defeating an opponent in terms of pruning:[8]

כי־לפני קציר כתם־פרח ובסר גמל יהיה נצה וכרת הזלזלים במזמרות ואת־
הנטישות הסיר התז:

For before the harvest, when the bud is finished and the blossom becomes a developing unripe grape, he will cut off the shoots with a pruning knife, and the running canes he will remove, he will pull away.

This is a typical conquest metaphor that incorporates WARFARE IS INDIVIDUAL COMBAT within its structure. The action of lopping off the shoots and

---

vine or more generally as a fruit-bearing woody plant. Therefore, such passages have been excluded from this analysis.

7. Even passages that reference a vine may do so as an element of the VINEYARD frame, thus obscuring whether the expression in question constitutes a vine metaphor or a vineyard metaphor.

8. See below for a discussion of the pruning details in this passage.

canes maps to the image of a soldier attacking a series of opponents. The larger context indicates that it describes the defeat of an enemy kingdom, but does the passage depict pruning a single vine or a whole vineyard?

Collective condemnation metaphors like this one tend to focus on the source elements that map to people, such as branches or fruit, while elements that map to the more abstract concepts of city, kingdom, or nation, such as a vine or vineyard, remain a blurry background to the image. Unfortunately, educated guessing rarely helps to resolve the ambiguity. For example, we can assume that the Israelites and Judahites generally cultivated their vines in groups—that is, in vineyards—rather than as single vines, because one vine would not produce a sufficient quantity of grapes to support even the minimal needs of a single individual. We might then conclude that because pruning in ancient Judah occurred in vineyards, the image in Isa 18:5 is probably that of a vineyard. Such a conclusion, however, overlooks the fact that figurative language is not as bound by the dictates of logic as is literal description. While a reference to pruning in literal terms would almost certainly suggest the presence of multiple vines, in figurative language, the action taken could apply to either a vineyard or a vine. In other words, the element of PRUNING belongs to both source frames—VINEYARD and VINE—and therefore the underlying image in Isa 18:5 could be either one. As a result, if the goal is to count how many vineyard and vine metaphors appear in the prophetic corpus, Isa 18:5 would have to go in a third, undefined category.

An additional concern in the categorization of viticulture metaphors, as discussed in chapter 2, is that the approach of choosing a single object by which to categorize these expressions of collective condemnation may obscure similarities and differences in the frame element mappings across multiple metaphors. Separating vine and vineyard imagery, for example, may hide the way that both categories include some expressions that map people to grapes and some that map people to branches or to whole vines. Adopting a different approach—framing these metaphors by the action taken within the expression—avoids the issues associated with using plant-based targets and allows us to take advantage of a common frame structure that applies to any plant-based viticulture metaphor that depicts that action. As a result, we can compare the use of branch imagery in pruning metaphors or the use of grapes in harvesting expressions. The analysis that follows in this chapter examines how the actions of pruning, harvesting, and wine-making structure the majority of the expressions of collective condemnation in prophetic viticulture metaphors.

3.2. Collective Condemnation Viticulture Metaphors

Of the twenty-six metaphors in the prophetic corpus that contain plant-based terms from the VITICULTURE domain, twenty-two appear in condemnation prophecies about a nation, kingdom, or city.[9] This total includes both collective condemnation and national identity metaphors. In describing a shared fate for the target—a nation, kingdom, or city— these metaphors rely on the conceptual relationship A GROUP OF PEOPLE IS A WOODY PLANT.[10] They may also include in their structure one or more of the conventional conquest metaphors discussed in chapter 2.

Table 3.1. Viticulture metaphors in the prophetic condemnations

Plant Outcome	Relevant Biblical Passages
Pruning	Isa 16:8; **18:5–6; Jer 5:10**
Harvesting	*Isa 1:4–9;* 24:13; 65:8; **Jer 6:9;** *8:13; 49:9;* Obad 5; Mic 7:1–7
Grape-Treading	*Isa 3:13–15;* **63:1–6;** *Joel 4:13–14*
Cattle Grazing/ Trampling	*Isa 3:13–15; 5:1–7; Jer 12:7–13* (at v. *10*)
Uprooting	*Ezek 19:10–14*
Neglect/ Abandonment	*Isa 5:1–7*
Fruitlessness	*Hos 9:10–17*
Burning	*Ezek 15; 19:10–14*
Stripping Vine	*Hos 10:1–2*
None Specified	*Jer 2:21; 48:32–33*

As shown in table 3.1, the condemnation or common fate action for eight passages derives from the HARVESTING frame, while a smaller number of pas-

---

9. Of the remaining four metaphors, two appear in restoration prophecies (Isa 27:2–6; Hos 14:6–8), one maps vine and fig leaves to a group of celestial deities (Isa 34:4), and one maps an individual to a vine (Ezek 17:5–10).

10. See ch. 8 for an overview of the conceptual structure of woody-plant metaphors.

sages employ frames for the viticultural processes that precede and follow the harvest: PRUNING (three passages) and GRAPE-TREADING (three passages).[11] Most of the collective condemnation metaphors and some of the national identity metaphors draw from one of these three frames. The national identity metaphors also draw their common fate imagery from other aspects of viticulture, including the perceived threat of cattle grazing on or trampling a vineyard (three passages), the uprooting of a vine (one passage), the neglect or abandonment of a vineyard (one passage), and fruitlessness (one passage). Finally, three passages include actions not necessarily belonging to the VITI-CULTURE frame—burning (two passages) and stripping a vine of its shoots and fruit (one passage)—and two contain national vine metaphors that do not construct a common fate within the metaphor.

Since these passages describe condemnation and punishment, we might expect them to depict the total destruction of the vine or vineyard. This is not the case, however. Instead, the condemnation actions generally align with normal activities associated with viticulture, activities that usually would not pose a serious threat to the survival of the vine(s). The portrayal may contain an element of hyperbole in its imagery, especially in cases that depict warfare as viticulture, but the actions taken, even at their most extreme, would not normally kill a grapevine. This pattern is easier to explain in the context of collective condemnation metaphors than in national identity metaphors. Most collective condemnation metaphors fail to specify whether the underlying image is a vine or a vineyard, which means that they essentially lack mappings for the abstract concept of the kingdom or nation. They therefore express widespread death and destruction among the people without addressing the survival of the kingdom or nation as a whole. As such, it might be fairer to say that these passages do not contemplate the fate of the vine or vineyard, rather than that they preserve that life.

On the other hand, most of the national identity metaphors both contemplate the fate of the national plant(s) that they condemn and pre-

---

11. Table 3.1 contains twenty-five entries because three passages are counted twice. Isaiah 3:13–15 appears in the count for both grape-treading and grazing/trampling by cattle, because the action in the metaphor changes between 3:14 and 3:15. In addition, Ezek 19:10–14 includes both uprooting and burning in its description of the fate of Judah; and Isa 5:1–7 includes both cattle grazing/trampling and neglect/abandonment. Passages shown in bold text are discussed in some detail in this chapter. Passages shown in italics are discussed further in chs. 4, 5, 7, or 8.

serve the life of the plant(s). The inability to produce fruit in Hos 9:10–17 does not destroy the vine itself. The burning metaphors in Ezekiel seem threatening, but Ezek 15 speaks only of the branches of vine wood, and thus avoids addressing the fate of the vine as a whole, and Ezek 19:10–14 describes burning the vine's branches and fruit, in addition to uprooting the whole plant, but the vine survives, transplanted into the desert. The few passages that do significantly threaten the national plant(s) do so in terms of natural events—the grazing or trampling of a vineyard by cattle (Isa 3:13–15; Jer 12:7–13) or the lack of care by its owner (Isa 5:1–7)—rather than wanton destruction by humans.

This near universal absence of metaphors that destroy either vine or vineyard requires explanation. One possibility is that the imagery reflects an ideological aversion to destroying fruit trees in warfare. Certainly, the practice was known in the ancient Near East. Records from Assyria, the Hittite Empire, and Egypt describe extensive destruction of fruit trees in military campaigns against external enemies or in response to internal rebellions.[12] In biblical narrative, Samson sets fire to the Philistine grain fields, vineyards, and olive trees in Timnah as revenge for a broken marriage contract (Judg 15:1–8), and in a campaign against Moab, the prophet Elisha instructs the kings of Israel, Judah, and Edom to destroy the Moabites' fruit trees and the fields where they grow crops (2 Kgs 3:15–27).

Both biblical and extrabiblical evidence suggests, however, that the wanton destruction of fruit trees, even in the context of waging warfare, may have been more the exception than the rule. For example, Assyrian texts contain numerous reports of destroying the fruit trees of their opponents in war, but these actions appear primarily in the context of punishment inflicted on those who had rebelled against the empire. Even that practice does not seem to have been consistently applied. Sennacherib's campaign in the west in 701 BCE was a response to the rebellion of several Levantine states, including Judah.[13] Yet none of the Assyrian records or reliefs indicate that they destroyed fruit trees in the southern Levant, and the relief depicting the defeat of Lachish shows the fruit trees still standing in the background.[14]

---

12. Jacob L. Wright, "Warfare and Wanton Destruction: A Reexamination of Deuteronomy 20:19–20 in Relation to Ancient Siegecraft," *JBL* 127 (2008): 423–58.

13. Miller and Hayes, *History of Ancient Israel and Judah*, 416–21.

14. Wright, "Warfare," 443.

The accounts of fruit tree destruction may also have served as propaganda. In cases where a rebelling party had escaped defeat, total destruction of that rebel's fruit trees was claimed as proof that the Assyrian king had nevertheless achieved his goals in waging the war.[15] Finally, the Assyrians may have used the progressive destruction of fruit trees as a pressure tactic to coerce the people of a besieged town to surrender.[16] Such measures, however, would likely have been more useful to smaller kingdoms or tribal groups—those that did not have the resources to maintain a professional army with expertise in breaking through city walls. Since the Assyrians had both a professional army and siege expertise, they probably would not have needed to employ coercive techniques very often.[17]

Several biblical narratives also allude to the idea that fruit trees often survived during wartime. The idealized image of the Israelites' conquest of Canaan describes them conquering the land and benefiting from its fruit trees, which they did not plant (Deut 6:11; Josh 24:13). In the narrative of Sennacherib's campaign against Jerusalem, the Rabshakeh tells the people of the city that if they surrender, they will be allowed to return, at least temporarily, to their own homes to eat from their own vines and fig trees (2 Kgs 18:31–32; Isa 36:16–17). While this speech might suggest an Assyrian attempt to use coercion to draw out the Jerusalemites, the narrative contains no indication that the Assyrians are threatening the Judahite vines and fruit trees.[18] Finally, the accounts of the days after the destruction of Jerusalem include descriptions of the Babylonians either assigning the poor who were not exiled to work in fields and vineyards (2 Kgs 25:12) or giving them fields and vineyards (Jer 39:10). Jeremiah also describes

---

15. Wright, "Warfare," 430–45. For an overview of warfare and the military in the ancient Near East that addresses the strategic and tactical considerations faced both by the great empires and those who rebelled against them, see Israel Eph'al, "On Warfare and Military Control in the Ancient Near Eastern Empires: A Research Outline," in *History, Historiography, and Interpretation: Studies in Biblical and Cuneiform Literatures*, ed. Hayim Tadmor and Moshe Weinfeld (Jerusalem: Magnes, 1983), 88–106. See also Eph'al, *City Besieged*.

16. Cole, "Destruction of Orchards," 36.

17. Wright, "Warfare," 430–45.

18. Wright, "Warfare," 444 n. 86. Contra Nili Wazana, who sees a threat in these words. Wazana, "Are the Trees of the Field Human? A Biblical War Law (Deuteronomy 20:19–20) and Neo-Assyrian Propaganda," in *Treasures on Camels' Humps: Historical and Literary Studies from the Ancient Near East Presented to Israel Eph'al*, ed. Mordechai Cogan and Dan'el Kahn (Jerusalem: Magnes, 2008), 274–95.

how those who remained in Judah after the fall of Jerusalem harvested wine and figs and oil in abundance, presumably from the vineyards and orchards of those who had been taken to Babylonia (Jer 40:9–12).

Self-interest may explain this apparent tendency to preserve fruit trees. Destroying fruit trees hurts both the invaded territory and the invaders, because it robs all parties of both a food source and an income source (via trade). Newly planted fruit trees need anywhere from two to twenty years to develop before they produce their first crop, so destroying them means crippling fruit production not just in the current season, but for years to come.[19] An invading kingdom may not have wanted to destroy the fruit-production capabilities of a territory it intended to control, since that action would impoverish the new territory, making it difficult for the residents to either support themselves or pay tribute.[20] Granted, a besieging army very likely would have done significant ecological damage to the immediate area around a town, but that destruction was probably more attributable to consuming local resources to supply the needs of the attacking army and to support siege operations than to punitive efforts to denude the land.[21] Indeed, a concern for preserving sources of food and income probably motivated the biblical law prohibiting destruction of fruit trees as part of extended siege operations against a city (Deut 20:19–20).[22]

---

19. The impact would be even more severe if fruit-growers adhered to the principle contained in Lev 19:23–25, which prohibits consumption of a new tree's fruit until its fifth year.

20. Wright ("Warfare," 453) makes a similar observation. Conquered land could also be granted to the king's officials or allies (Cole, "Destruction of Orchards," 34). Such grants would presumably be more valuable if the land included productive orchards or vineyards. On the other hand, if the invader simply wanted to weaken the conquered territory without assuming control of it, then destroying the land might have been an appealing tactic (Trimm, *Fighting for the King and the Gods*, 316–92).

21. Maeir, Ackermann, and Bruins, "Ecological Consequences of a Siege," 239–43.

22. Wright ("Warfare," 434) suggests that vineyards are not mentioned in the law against cutting down fruit trees because they were not valuable enough for an invading army to target for destruction, either to coerce an enemy to surrender or to punish them for rebellion. Setting aside his judgment about the low economic value of wine, which is probably incorrect, his argument overlooks the way that the Israelites conceptualized grapevines. While modern botany distinguishes between trees and vines, evidence from the biblical corpus indicates that the word עץ can refer to any woody plant, whether tree or vine or shrub. (See also the discussion of woody plants in ch. 8.) Deuteronomy 20:19–20 does not mention specific fruit trees by name. Rather, it

Of course, even if there was a cultural preference for preserving fruit trees, nothing prevented the biblical authors from presenting *images* of the nation as vines chopped down or burned.[23] The absence of such imagery suggests that the aversion operated more on the level of the subconscious than conscious; in most cases, it simply may not have occurred to the prophetic authors to include the total destruction of vines or vineyards in their metaphoric mappings. The prophetic viticulture metaphors are deeply grounded in the Israelite experience of viticulture. From planting to pruning to harvesting, the mappings in these metaphors appear to reflect ancient practices, rather than imaginative figures drawn from the VITICULTURE domain. For example, the prophetic authors rarely personify the vine or vineyard in any significant way. The image represents the nation, and some natural plant behaviors do map to human behaviors, but there exists no prophetic equivalent to Jotham's fable, in which the trees choose a king for themselves (Judg 9:8–15).[24] That tendency toward realism may have kept the prophetic authors largely within the bounds of their chosen viticulture source frames in their constructions of a common fate for a kingdom or nation. About the furthest that they push the image is to express the viticulture-related actions in hyperbolic terms or in terms that are reminiscent either of warfare or individual combat.[25]

3.2.1. Pruning Metaphors

Pruning metaphors derive from the practice of trimming excess branches from domesticated grapevines (*Vitis vinifera L.*) to maximize the potential for a good crop of grapes. Vine branches grow and produce fruit in predictable stages. Each year, a vine will produce new branches, called shoots, from buds that developed on the previous year's shoots. A new shoot grows in length from its tip. At regular intervals as it grows, the shoot will

---

prohibits the felling of any עץ that produces food. There is no reason to believe that they would exclude grapevines from that category.

23. See the discussion in ch. 8 of destructive imagery used with plants that are not fruit trees.

24. Even Ezek 17, which Daniel Block describes as a fable, limits the vine to actions a plant could take—primarily growing in a particular direction—rather than depicting the vine as exhibiting human behaviors. Daniel Block, *The Book of Ezekiel: Chapters 1–24*, NICOT (Grand Rapids: Eerdmans, 1997), 523–53.

25. Most plant metaphors in the prophetic condemnations display a similar tendency toward realism. See further the discussion in ch. 8.

sprout leaves, flower clusters, or tendrils. The flower clusters will develop into fruit. The tendrils are short, leafless structures that wrap themselves around anything that stands in proximity to the shoot. Their purpose is to help support the weight of the shoot. A typical shoot will produce at least ten to twelve leaves and one or two flower clusters in a single season.

A shoot produces fruit only once, during its first season of growth. In its second season, the shoot itself will become a woody branch, called a cane or cordon, from which new shoots will grow.[26] Growing shoots, producing leaves and tendrils, and developing fruit all draw on the vine's energy and nutrients. Pruning practices developed in part to manage a vine's resources, balancing the need to allow shoots and leaves to grow to produce energy for the vine (via photosynthesis) with the desire to remove canes and shoots in order to redirect the vine's resources toward producing fruit.[27]

While pruning always serves the overall goal of managing fruit production, the type of pruning needed varies at different points in the process of cultivating a vine. In modern practice, for a vine's first few years, new shoots are routinely pruned from it to prevent fruiting and to direct all of the vine's energy toward producing a strong stock and a small number of canes that will provide the foundation for all future fruiting. Thereafter, the now mature vine is pruned in two different ways. First, in the winter, when the vine is dormant, older shoots and canes are removed to concentrate the vine's energy and nutrients on producing new shoots and fruit. This type of pruning also helps to shape the vine as it grows, so that it does not extend outside of the vineyard or encroach on other vines or crops.[28]

The second type of pruning for mature vines serves a different purpose. Israel's dry summer season is ideal for grape-growing. The vines and grapes primarily receive irrigation via dew, rather than rain, so the grapes remain relatively dry.[29] In an adverse year, however, excess moisture on

---

26. Edward W. Hellman, "Grapevine Structure and Function," in *Oregon Viticulture*, ed. Edward W. Hellman, (Corvallis: Oregon State University Press, 2003), 5–19; and G. L. Creasy and L. L. Creasy, *Grapes*, Crop Production Science in Horticulture 16 (Wallingford: CABI, 2009), 18–20, 25, 29–35.

27. For additional discussion of pruning practices as described in biblical and other ancient texts, see Walsh, *Fruit of the Vine*, 119–22. See also the brief summaries in Borowski, *Agriculture*, 109–10; and Matthews, "Treading the Winepress," 26.

28. Creasy and Creasy, *Grapes*, 105; Walsh, *Fruit of the Vine*, 119–20.

29. Walsh, *Fruit of the Vine*, 33.

the grapes would make the fruit more susceptible to fungal infestation. In addition, the fruit requires sunlight for ripening and to develop sugars in the juice.[30] To manage these issues, in the spring, once grapes have begun to form on the vine, the vine is pruned to clear excess foliage, allowing air to circulate around the grape clusters to evaporate any excess moisture and letting some sunlight reach the fruit. New shoots that did not produce fruit are a prime target for the spring pruning, because they can be removed without reducing the vine's overall grape yield.[31]

The spring pruning may also be better characterized as more of a process than a one-time event. New, fruitless shoots may continue to sprout along the vine canes throughout the growing season. In addition, since vine shoots do not develop terminal buds on the tips of the branches that would limit their growth, they could theoretically continue to increase in length indefinitely. Under the right conditions, a single shoot can grow to a length of several yards or more over the course of a season. As a result, new or growing shoots may need to be cut back more than once to prevent them from blocking the sun away from the grapes.[32]

Evidence for maturation and winter pruning appears in Roman writings from the first century CE, in the works of Pliny, Columella, and Virgil, but the biblical corpus makes no mention of either of these types of pruning.[33] Leviticus 19:23–25 commands the Israelites not to *consume* the fruit of their vines for the first four years after planting, a statement that suggests that these young vines were allowed to *produce* fruit rather than being pruned to prevent fruiting.[34] In the New Testament, John 15:2 refers to the benefits of pruning unproductive shoots and canes in a metaphor in which Jesus compares himself to a vine pruned by his divine father: πᾶν κλῆμα ἐν ἐμοὶ μὴ φέρον καρπόν, αἴρει αὐτό, καὶ πᾶν τὸ καρπὸν φέρον καθαίρει αὐτὸ ἵνα καρπὸν πλείοναφέρῃ, "He removes every branch in me that bears no fruit. Every branch that bears fruit he prunes to make it bear more fruit" (NRSV). The text makes no mention of the timing of such pruning during the agricultural year, but the practice described in this

---

30. Walsh, *Fruit of the Vine*, 33, 38.
31. Creasy and Creasy, *Grapes*, 140–45.
32. Creasy and Creasy, *Grapes*, 143.
33. For the Roman evidence, see Walsh, *Fruit of the Vine*, 119.
34. The law further commands that the fourth year's produce be dedicated to YHWH, meaning that only in the fifth season would the people begin to enjoy the fruits of their labor.

metaphor could easily fit within the goals of spring pruning.[35] Absent evidence to the contrary, the most reasonable supposition may be that the practices of pruning newly planted vines and of pruning mature vines in the winter had not yet developed in Israel or Judah during the biblical era.[36]

By contrast, we do have biblical and extrabiblical evidence that the Israelites pruned their mature vines in the spring. In Isa 18:5 we see that the text depicts defeating an opponent in terms of a pruning cycle that begins when the grape berries are starting to form on the vine:

כי־לפני קציר כתם־פרח ובסר גמל יהיה נצה וכרת הזלזלים במזמרות ואת־
הנטישות הסיר התז:

For before the harvest, when the bud is finished and the blossom becomes a developing unripe grape, he will cut off the shoots with a pruning knife, and the running canes[37] he will remove, he will pull away.

The description of the actions taken in this verse comports well with the modern practice of pruning fruitless and overgrown shoots or canes as a method of managing the vine's foliage. As noted earlier, grape shoots produce fruit only in their first year of growth. In the spring, as the weather turns warmer and the vine begins to grow, the new shoots need time to develop before they can sprout flowers and produce grapes. The harvest mentioned in this passage must therefore refer to the wheat harvest, which occurred in late spring. The vines would not have had sufficient time to bloom before the early spring barley harvest.

The Gezer Calendar, which dates to tenth-century BCE Israel, also describes a period for pruning (ירחו זמר) that occurs in the spring or early

---

35. Pruning also receives mention twice in the Deuterocanonical Books, in texts that date to the first few centuries CE. As with John 15:2, however, the relevant passages provide no information about the timing of the practice (4 Macc 1:29; 2 Esdr 16:43).

36. Winter pruning is not essential either to the vine's survival or to its production of fruit. Each year, a vine will naturally produce far more dormant buds for the next year's growth than its existing foliage can sustain through photosynthesis. On an unpruned vine, a certain percentage of the new buds will therefore not develop sufficiently to survive the winter or to achieve bud break the next spring. In effect, the vine prunes itself (Creasy and Creasy, *Grapes*, 115).

37. For the translation of נטישות, see the discussion of Jer 5:10 below.

summer.[38] It situates this two-month pruning cycle after the winter grains have been harvested, slightly later than the description in Isa 18:5. This discrepancy may reflect different choices about how to sequence two events in the calendar whose timing overlapped in the late spring, or it may indicate that the pruning cycle started later for the community that produced the Gezer Calendar. A third possibility is that זמר in the calendar refers to both pruning and harvesting grapes.[39] The important point is that each of these solutions would reflect a practice of pruning vines during the growing season, not during the winter.

Understanding the timing and nature of vine pruning cycles in ancient Israel and Judah allows additional insight into the three pruning metaphors in the prophetic corpus, because it provides a sense of what the vines would have looked like before and after the pruning. Before, the vine would be lush with foliage and larger in size than the previous year, with new growth sprouting randomly from the one-year-old canes that had been the previous season's shoots. Afterward, the vine would have a more orderly appearance; the foliage would be thinner but still present, giving the grapes and leaves more access to the sun, and any shoots that

---

38. Walsh, *Fruit of the Vine*, 34–41, 172 n. 28. Several scholars have argued that ירחו זמר refers to a grape harvest in June–July (see, e.g., Borowski, *Agriculture*, 33, table 1; and 37, table 3). That timing appears to be a little too early, given the way that grapes develop over the course of a season. New vine shoots require two to three months to grow before they blossom and develop fruit. If spring in Israel begins in March, then the spring pruning, described in Isa 18:5 as occurring after the grapes have formed, would likely have begun no earlier than May. The grape berries then need an additional two to three months (or more) to develop and ripen, which would place the grape harvest in July or August (Hellman, "Grapevine Structure," 18). Support for this estimate appears in the Temple Scroll (11Q19), which refers to a festival for the first wine of the season on the third day of Av (i.e., July–August). The text specifies that this is when the people will begin to eat grapes, suggesting that this is also the time that the earliest grapes had ripened enough to become edible (21:4–10).

39. Aaron J. Koller, *The Semantic Field of Cutting Tools in Biblical Hebrew: The Interface of Philological, Semantic, and Archaeological Evidence*, CBQMS 49 (Washington, DC: Catholic Biblical Association of America, 2012), 106–8. Koller argues that זמר in the Hebrew Bible always refers to pruning, but that the Gezer Calendar may represent a dialect in which זמר refers to harvesting grapes. He follows Borowski and others in assigning the grape harvest in the Gezer Calendar to the months of June and July (see previous note), but he also acknowledges that זמר in the Gezer Calendar could refer to "any activity that involves cutting something off a grape vine," which would include both pruning and harvesting (106).

had grown too long or had not produced fruit would be cut back. Piles of cut branches and shoots would also lie either at the base of the vines or off to the side waiting to be used or discarded.[40]

Pruning metaphors map the PEOPLE element to BRANCHES of the vine, the removal of which conveys the sense of death or exile.[41] Since pruning serves to manage the vine, these metaphors may map the idea of correction or redirection of the vine's growth to the concept of a rebuke. Thus, they leave room for a less destructive outcome than total conquest. None of the pruning metaphors in the prophetic corpus exploit the longer-term implications of this idea of pruning as correction, however, meaning we do not see claims of an improved nation, postpruning, in these metaphors.

In addition, pruning metaphors may draw on a conventional concept that associates height with pride or with power and prestige.[42] In tree metaphors, the plant's height may represent its target's power or prestige (e.g., Amos 2:9). Excessive height may also convey the idea that the tree's target is too proud (e.g., Ezek 31:10). Since free-standing vines do not achieve significant height, that mapping is reimagined for the VINE frame as associating cane or shoot length with power and prestige (Isa 16:8; Jer 48:32; Ps 80:12).[43] It is less clear whether any of the passages that employ this mapping connect it to excessive pride. In each case, the expression seems more admiring of the vine's reach than critical of it. The metaphor maps

---

40. Ezekiel 15 and John 15:6 provide some evidence that such branches were used for firewood (Matthews, "Treading the Winepress," 26).

41. Absent explicit mappings, it is difficult to determine whether the prophetic authors make any meaningful distinction between death and exile in some of these plant metaphors. For one thing, if the point of the prophecy is to alarm the audience with a dire warning, then the metaphor may contain an element of hyperbole: "You are all going to die!" For another, the metaphor DEATH IS A DEPARTURE appears to have been conventional in ancient Israel and Judah, just as it is in English today. The biblical authors frequently describe death as ירד שאול, "descending to Sheol" (e.g., Gen 37:35; 1 Kgs 2:6; Isa 14:11; Ezek 31:15–17; Ps 30:4; Job 7:9; Prov 5:5). In addition, Prov 14:12 (= 16:25) speaks of the דרכי־מות, "paths of [i.e., toward] death"; and Ps 49:18 reminds us that a rich man לא במותו יקח הכל, "cannot take anything [with him] when he dies." Therefore, conquest imagery that includes the idea of a departure could be referring either to death or to exile.

42. The basic metaphors POWER IS UP, PRESTIGE IS UP, and PRIDE IS UP provide the foundations for more complex metaphors that associate these concepts with the height of an object. See the discussion of this mapping in woody-plant metaphors in ch. 8.

43. Psalm 80 is unique in mapping both the vine's height (v. 11) and its cane length (v. 12) to power and prestige.

the image of the vine's shoots approaching or crossing the sea or some other location to the nation extending its influence—probably via trade in grape products—outside its own national borders.[44] The metaphor of a pruned national vine in these cases thus carries with it a sense of diminished power and prestige.

The Israelites used a מזמרה (< זמר, "to prune"), a short, possibly curved, blade with a handle, to prune their vines.[45] The use of the tool lends itself well to incorporating the conventional metaphor WARFARE IS INDIVIDUAL COMBAT into the CONQUEST IS PRUNING structure. The physical actions of individual combat—striking an opponent with a weapon, the opponent falling to the ground, the survivor moving on to the next opponent—map to the actions of pruning the vine. Evidence for an additional element of resonance between the two frames resides in prophetic passages that reference repurposing metal implements—turning weapons into tools (Isa 2:4; Mic 4:3) or tools into weapons (Joel 4:10). In each case, the transformation occurs between a sword (חרב) and the cutting blade for a plow (את; i.e., a ploughshare), and between a spear (חנית) and a pruning knife (מזמרה).[46] If the ancient Israelites repurposed metals to forge either weapons or tools, depending on the needs of the community, that would have created a persistent conceptual connection between farming and fighting.[47]

---

44. The mapping probably draws on the practical reality of transporting wine from one country to another. Wine skins, and especially wine jars, were heavy and relatively fragile, making overland transport both costly and risky. As a result, the economic viability of wine trade often relied on the availability of water transport, either by river or by sea. Marvin A. Powell, "Wine and the Vine in Ancient Mesopotamia: The Cuneiform Evidence," in *The Origins and Ancient History of Wine*, ed. Patrick E. McGovern, Stuart J. Fleming, and Solomon H. Katz, Food and Nutrition in History and Anthropology 11 (Luxembourg: Gordon & Breach, 1995), 107–8.

45. Walsh, *Fruit of the Vine*, 121; and Koller, *Semantic Field of Cutting Tools*, 109–11.

46. The precise meaning of את is disputed. The standard Hebrew dictionaries render the term as "ploughshare" or as the head or blade of an ax (see BDB, s.v. "[אֵת] III," 88; *HALOT*, s.v. "אֵת III"; and *DCH* 1:453, s.v. "[אֵת] III"). While he does not offer a conclusion about the nature of an את, Koller (*Semantic Field of Cutting Tools*, 91–93) does point out how easy the conversion between sword and ploughshare would be: "In order to beat a straight blade into a ploughshare, a blacksmith would fold over the sides of the tip; in time of war, a ploughshare can easily be converted to a weapon by banging the sides flat again" (91).

47. Walsh (*Fruit of the Vine*, 122) notes: "Since metals were still not inexpensive in the Iron II period, tools would likely have been forged into weapons and then back again after the battle ended."

Of the three pruning metaphors in the prophetic corpus, only Isa
18:5 maps a single vinedresser in its image. In that case, the vinedresser
is YHWH. The remaining two pruning metaphors in Isa 16:8 and Jer 5:10
create an image of battle, a composite of multiple instances of individual
combat, by describing a scene in which multiple vinedressers prune the
vine(s).[48] Presumably, an attacking army would be larger than the typical
number of vinedressers needed to prune a vineyard, which means these
metaphors compress the number of soldiers in an invading army so that
they can be mapped to a team of vinedressers. For example, Jer 5:10 presents Jerusalem as an overgrown vineyard. To remedy the problem, YHWH
commands the pruning of the city's rows of vines:

עלו בשרותיה ושחתו וכלה אל־תעשו הסירו נטישותיה כי לוא ליהוה המה:
Go up among her rows and destroy, but do not make an end.
Remove her running canes, for they are not YHWH's.

The use of plural imperative forms in the orders indicates that YHWH's
speech addresses more than one person.

This verse contains two rare terms whose interpretation is key to understanding the mappings in its CONQUEST IS PRUNING metaphor: נטישותיה
(< נטישה, "a running cane" [as in a branch that grows away from the main
plant]); and שרותיה (< שרה, "a row or terrace").[49] The word נטישה appears
three times in the biblical corpus, in this verse and in two other prophetic
viticulture metaphors (Isa 18:5; Jer 48:32). The verbal root from which
this noun derives, נטש, carries the sense of leaving something untended
or relinquishing control over it, an action that either allows the subject to
go wild on its own or allows another to take it over.[50] The nominal form,

---

48. The discussion here classifies Isa 16:8 as a pruning metaphor, but an alternate
interpretation argues that it may instead represent an intoxication metaphor. The difference depends on whether שרק refers to vine shoots or tendrils, as per Otto Kaiser,
or to wine, as per J. J. M. Roberts and Hans Wildberger. See Kaiser, *Isaiah 13–39:
A Commentary*, trans. R. A. Wilson, OTL (Philadelphia: Westminster, 1974), 59, 73;
Roberts, *First Isaiah: A Commentary*, Hermeneia (Minneapolis: Fortress, 2015), 230;
and Wildberger, *Isaiah 13–27: A Commentary*, trans. Thomas H. Trapp, CC (Minneapolis: Fortress, 1997), 112.

49. *HALOT*, s.v. "שָׂרָה"; and *DCH* 8:560, s.v. "שָׂרָה I or II." Both *HALOT*, s.v.
"נְטִישָׁה," and *DCH* 5:676, s.v. "נְטִישָׁה" offer "tendril" as a translation value.

50. In this sense, נטש applies to leaving a field untended (Exod 23:11) or allowing a group of people to scatter (1 Sam 30:16), but it also refers to turning control of a

נטישה, therefore probably refers not to shoots or canes in general, but to untended or unrestricted growth from a vine.

Such an understanding of the term is consistent with its appearance in the metaphor about Moab in Jer 48:32, where it refers to vine branches that have "crossed over the sea," indicating that they have grown beyond Moab's boundaries.[51] It is also consistent with Isa 18:5, which uses the image of pruning vine branches to describe YHWH's rejection of a proposed alliance between Cush and Judah against Assyria. The נטישות in Isa 18:5 thus represent a kingdom transgressing a perceived boundary.[52] In the case of Jer 5:10, the author describes the נטישות as לוא ליהוה, "not YHWH's," suggesting that the boundaries transgressed by the vines represent YHWH's requirements of his people.[53] In addition, by describing the people as "not YHWH's" the prophet essentially defines them as outsiders deserving to be cut from the vine of Judah.

The second obscure term, שרותיה (< שרה), is a *hapax legomenon* that is generally taken to be related to שור, "wall," or שורה, "row or terrace."[54] Ancient Israelites usually planted their vineyards and fruit trees on terraced hills, with retaining walls built below each terrace level to shore up the hillside and prevent soil erosion.[55] Absent the rest of the verse, a scholar might reasonably conclude that the term derives from שור and

---

flock over to another shepherd (1 Sam 17:20) or to YHWH allowing his people to be conquered (2 Kgs 21:14).

51. Jeremiah 48:32 uses the image of the vine runners to describe the Moabite wine trade.

52. The pruned vine could map to: (1) The kingdom of Cush driven back to their homeland in order to prevent the alliance with Judah (Roberts, *First Isaiah*, 250). (2) The Judahites, punished for transgressing the boundaries that YHWH has set for them by seeking an alliance with Cush rather than trusting in YHWH's protection. Brevard S. Childs, *Isaiah*, OTL (Louisville: Westminster John Knox, 2001), 138–39. Or (3) the Assyrians, prevented by YHWH from attacking Judah, thereby rendering the alliance with Cush unnecessary. George Buchanan Gray, *A Critical and Exegetical Commentary on the Book of Isaiah: I–XXXIX*, ICC (New York: Scribners, 1912), 315; and Joseph Blenkinsopp, *Isaiah 1–39: A New Translation with Introduction and Commentary*, AB 19 (New York: Doubleday, 2000), 311.

53. Jack R. Lundbom comments that "the trailing branches are symbols of influence and national pride," but he does not connect that observation to his analysis of the passage. Lundbom, *Jeremiah 1–20: A New Translation with Introduction and Commentary*, AB 21A (New York: Doubleday, 1999), 389.

54. *HALOT*, s.v. "שָׂרָה"; and *DCH* 8:560, s.v. "שָׂרָה I," or "שָׂרָה II."

55. Walsh, *Fruit of the Vine*, 94–96.

constitutes a literal reference to the city walls of Jerusalem. The presence of נטישה, however, which belongs to the VITICULTURE domain, supports instead the common viewpoint that שרה derives from the same domain and refers to a row or terrace, or perhaps to the retaining wall of a terrace.[56]

In one short verse, the author has blended two vineyard metaphors: one theological and one military. The first metaphor depicts the vineyard terraces as representing the boundaries of proper cultic observance. The people map to vine branches, and those described as running canes, who have grown beyond the vineyard terraces, map to people who are not serving YHWH properly (5:11). Jeremiah 5:1–9, which precedes this verse, suggests that the entire population, both poor and rich alike, would map to the running canes of 5:10. The vineyard has significantly overgrown its boundaries. The second metaphor presents Jerusalem as the vineyard and an invading army as vine trimmers. The people of Jerusalem still map to vine branches, while the dead in battle map to the trimmed canes. The blend allows the author to suggest that those killed by the invading army have been cut down for their sins, a message consistent with the content of the surrounding text in Jer 5.[57]

A number of commentators erroneously reject the notion of a pruning image in this verse and instead assert that the metaphor describes the total destruction of the vine. Jack Lundbom argues that the idea of a surviving remnant does not fit the context or date of the passage—that in Jeremiah, the concept of a remnant appears only in later passages and editorial additions. He therefore reinterprets וכלה אל־תעשו, arguing that אל carries an asseverative force: "and won't you make an end?"[58] Leslie Allen,

---

56. Lundbom, *Jeremiah 1–20*, 388.

57. A possible, but perhaps unintended, implication of the blend is that just as the vineyard prospers from the pruning, so Jerusalem will prosper for having been invaded and cleared of apostates. Nothing in the surrounding text, however, suggests that the prophet wishes to convey such a hopeful message to his audience. That said, while the analysis here relates to the passage in its current position in the MT, the material in Jer 5 does not appear to represent a unified composition. See John Bright, *Jeremiah: Introduction, Translation, and Notes*, AB 21 (Garden City, NY: Doubleday, 1965), 42. The metaphor fairly clearly presents invasion as punishment for transgression, but the elements drawn from elsewhere in the chapter regarding the nature of the people's error and the extent of the punishment may not reflect the original intent of the prophecy.

58. Lundbom, *Jeremiah 1–20*, 386, 388. While Lundbom reinterprets אל as asseverative, he also hedges by arguing that the passage allows for partial survival. He claims

William Holladay, and William McKane emend the line to remove the negative particle.[59] While such adjustments have the benefit of making the message of Jer 5 more internally consistent, they lack support in the texts and versions.[60]

More importantly for purposes of this discussion, however, is that the interpretation of 5:10 as presenting a pruning metaphor need not be rejected on the basis of the level of destruction conveyed through the metaphor. Rather, the passage may simply present conquest through an exaggerated image of pruning. A freshly pruned vine, especially if that vine started out in an overgrown state, would be significantly reduced from its former size. In addition, the process of trimming long canes or shoots would leave a scene of vegetative carnage in its wake, with leafy branches scattered on the ground at the vine-trimmers' feet. As such, an image of pruning would sufficiently convey the message of the conquest of its target without resorting to arguments that cutting off the branches—an act that would not kill real vines—serves here to express the killing of the metaphorical vineyard.

Rejecting Jer 5:10 as a pruning metaphor also fails on methodological grounds. Lundbom argues that "we are not talking here about a pruning, but a thorough stripping of the vine-rows."[61] The level of destruction,

---

that כלה means "'to end (fully),' but not necessarily in an absolute sense" (388). Given this analysis, it is not clear why he so emphatically declares that this passage does not represent a pruning metaphor (389).

59. Allen, *Jeremiah: A Commentary*, OTL (Louisville: Westminster John Knox, 2008), 75; Holladay, *Jeremiah 1: A Commentary on the Book of the Prophet Jeremiah, Chapters 1–25*, Hermeneia (Philadelphia: Fortress, 1986), 183, 186; McKane, *Introduction and Commentary on Jeremiah I–XXV*, vol. 1 of *A Critical and Exegetical Commentary on Jeremiah*, ICC (Edinburgh: T&T Clark, 1986), 120.

60. This is especially true for the removal of אל, as McKane (*Jeremiah*, 120) acknowledges. For example, the corresponding verse in the LXX suggests that its *Vorlage* included the word: ἀνάβητε ἐπὶ τοὺς προμαχῶνας αὐτῆς καὶ κατασκάψατε, συντέλειαν δὲ μὴ ποιήσητε· ὑπολίπεσθε τὰ ὑποστηρίγματα αὐτῆς, ὅτι τοῦ κυρίου εἰσίν, "Go up upon her battlements, and raze, but do not make a full end; leave behind her under-props, because they are the Lord's" (NETS). While the verse as a whole presents an image of battle rather than the pruning of a vineyard, the syntax of the Greek translation precisely mirrors that of the MT, with the one exception that it lacks an equivalent term for לוא in the MT's phrase כי לוא ליהוה המה, "for they are not YHWH's."

61. Lundbom, *Jeremiah 1–20*, 389. He further argues that the imagery in the verse could represent a literal army chopping off the branches of the vines in a literal vineyard, or it could represent the metaphorical equivalent of that army and vineyard

however, does not determine whether an expression constitutes a pruning metaphor. Rather, the determining factor is whether the expression evokes the PRUNING frame by using terms from that frame. The example of Isa 18:5–6 presents an image of significant destruction of a vine or vineyard, as the branches cut from it will feed the local animals for a year (18:6). Yet 18:5 describes a spring pruning in some detail. The timing of the action, expressed in terms of the formation of unripe grapes on the shoots, coincides with viticultural practice. In addition, the author describes using מזמרות, pruning knives, to trim two types of branches: the vine-trimmers will כרת הזלזלים, "cut off the shoots" and הנטישות הסיר, "remove the running canes." Given the number of explicit pruning references in this passage, it would not make sense to interpret it as anything other than a pruning metaphor, even if the level of destruction is beyond what would occur in real life.

Applying this logic to Jer 5:10, the evidence suggests that this passage also contains a pruning metaphor. First, it shares language with the pruning metaphor in Isa 18:5–6. Both passages use the same phrase to describe the removal of the running canes from the vines: הנטישות הסיר in Isa 18:5 and הסירו נטישותיה in Jer 5:10. Using terms from the PRUNING frame would evoke that frame and guide the audience to see the image as one of vine pruning. Second, the level of destruction in the detailed pruning metaphor in Isa 18:5 demonstrates the weakness of using that criterion to argue that Jer 5:10 cannot be a pruning metaphor.[62]

3.2.2. Harvesting Metaphors

While pruning metaphors map the element of PEOPLE to BRANCHES, harvesting metaphors map PEOPLE to FRUIT. The idea of death or exile takes the form of the image of grapes picked from a vine or vineyard. A potential distinction in the pruning and harvesting depictions of the national target lies in the sense that vine prunings are relatively useless, while grapes are

---

(391). In theory, damaging fruit trees would be a way to punish an opponent without causing long-term harm to the ability of a conquered territory to grow fruit. It is not clear, however, that such a practice has a basis in reality. To the best of my knowledge, none of the available sources regarding the destruction of fruit trees as a warfare tactic depict cutting off only the branches of the trees.

62. Based on this analysis, that Holladay (*Jeremiah 1*, 183, 186) both rejects Jer 5:10 as a pruning metaphor and argues that it is directly dependent on Isa 18:5 makes little sense.

not. For the most part, however, harvesting metaphors hide the goodness of grapes by not focusing on the qualities of the fruit.[63] Instead, the metaphors typically enter the harvesting scene at the point when the grapes have already been gathered. The imagery therefore lacks descriptions of harvesting actions suggestive of individual combat. Instead, the metaphors focus on the total or near total absence of the grapes from the vine or vineyard. In other words, where pruning metaphors for conquest tend to depict the violence of combat, harvesting metaphors instead present an image of the emptiness of the land in the aftermath of a war.

This focus holds even in passages that look ahead to a future conquest. See, for example, the anticipatory descriptions of a depopulated land as bare vines (and fig trees) in Jer 8:13 and of survivors as gleanings left behind after the harvest in Isa 24:13. The grape harvest was a time for celebration in ancient Israel, a time for singing and dancing, as a family or community worked together to bring in the harvest and make wine from it (Isa 16:10; Jer 48:33).[64] Depicting a nation as a postharvest vineyard creates a stark contrast to the normal harvesting scene and emphasizes the silence after the celebration. The images generally express no anger toward the conquering enemy, no condemnation of the enemy's actions; rather, they focus on judgment of or mourning for the postharvest nation (see, e.g., Isa 1:7–9; Mic 7:1–7).[65]

Among the harvesting metaphors, Jer 6:9 provides a rare description of a scene that occurs during the harvesting process, though it includes no mappings reflecting the revelry of the occasion.[66] The passage presents an

---

63. An exception lies in Mic 7:1–7, which declares that the picked fruit represents the good people of Judah, who have departed, leaving only degenerates behind. In this case, the passage does not appear to present a postconquest scene. Instead, the author may have had in mind a mapping of the fruit to an idealized ancestral generation.

64. Borowski, *Agriculture*, 110; Walsh, *Fruit of the Vine*, 179–86. Grapes begin to deteriorate quickly after they reach peak ripeness, so the harvest must be accomplished within just a few days' time. To meet that need, families or towns would have needed to work together to bring the grapes in before they overripened (Walsh, *Fruit of the Vine*, 170–71, 179).

65. An exception to the general pattern for harvesting metaphors occurs in Isa 3:13–15, whose primary purpose is to depict the leaders of Judah as the enemy and to condemn them for harvesting the vineyard. See further the discussion of this passage in ch. 4.

66. The only other metaphor that references part of the harvesting process appears in Isa 65:8, which describes Israel as a cluster of apparently bad grapes. The

image of depopulation as an act of gathering every last grape remaining on the vine:

כה אמר יהוה צבאות עולל יעוללו כגפן שארית ישראל השב ידך כבוצר
על־סלסלות:

Thus says YHWH of Hosts, "They shall surely glean, like the vine, the remnant of Israel." "Bring your hand back, like a grape-picker, over the branches."

The change from third person to second in YHWH's speech has led some scholars to propose emending the verse, but the passage can be understood without emendation.[67] YHWH first describes what will be done to Judah and then speaks to one of the attackers to instruct him in the process of gleaning the nation.[68]

Gleaning refers to a second pass over the vines to gather any grapes that may have been missed during the primary harvest of the fruit.[69] In this context, and because the text refers to gleaning the remnant of Israel, many scholars argue that the passage maps the conquest of Israel and Judah to the stages of the harvest. While the primary harvest in such interpretations invariably includes the fall of Samaria, arguments differ about

---

metaphor calls on YHWH not to destroy the entire cluster, because some of the grapes contain good juice. The image may indicate that grape clusters were examined after picking to identify and remove any rotten fruit. It also reflects the reality that many grape diseases begin in one grape and then spread to the whole cluster (Creasy and Creasy, *Grapes*, 185–205).

67. Holladay, McKane, and Carroll prefer emending the 3mpl imperfect יעוללו to a 2ms imperative עולל. The solution serves more to smooth out an awkward text than to correct a real interpretive problem in the passage. See Robert P. Carroll, *Jeremiah: A Commentary*, OTL (London: SCM, 1986), 194; Holladay, *Jeremiah 1*, 210; McKane, *Jeremiah*, 143, 145.

68. Lundbom (*Jeremiah 1–20*, 424) also sees the two phrases as having different addressees. The first is a general statement, and the second directs encouragement at a particular gleaner.

69. Leviticus 19:10 and Deut 24:21 prohibit vineyard owners from collecting these gleanings. Instead, they should be left for those who sit at the margins of society, and who therefore face a greater threat of food insecurity. This includes the poor, the resident alien, the orphan, and the widow. If these laws reflect customary practice in ancient Israel and Judah, then the metaphor in Jer 6:9 apparently presents YHWH as violating custom. The alternative that it depicts the powerful invading enemy as akin to society's most vulnerable seems less likely.

the mapping of the gleaning, whether it refers to the Assyrian campaign in Judah in 701 BCE or to the Babylonian conquest in the early sixth century BCE.[70] In either case, for most scholars, the harvesting image maps to a military conquest, with the plural command mapping an army of soldiers to a group of harvesters, while the singular command governs a single soldier-harvester.[71]

At first glance, the imagery seems less suggestive of combat than some harvesting metaphors. Yet the verb עלל I, which, especially in the *poel*, carries the sense of "to glean, to deal severely with," demonstrates a conceptual link between the HARVESTING and CONQUEST frames. The root עלל I appears to have achieved conventional status in usage with either frame.[72] In addition, the knife used for pruning vines (מזמרה) may also have been used for cutting grape clusters from the vine during the harvest.[73] If vine clusters were cut from the vine in this way during gleaning, then this harvesting metaphor would incorporate the conceptual metaphor WARFARE IS INDIVIDUAL COMBAT in the same ways as the pruning metaphors discussed in the previous section.[74] On the other hand, if

---

70. E.g., Holladay (*Jeremiah 1*, 212–13) identifies the first harvest as the fall of Samaria in 721 BCE, and he understands the second harvest as a reference to events in Judah in the late seventh and early sixth centuries BCE. Lundbom (*Jeremiah 1–20*, 424) makes a similar argument for this passage as describing a harsh punishment in two stages, first by Assyria (which includes both the conquest of Samaria and the campaign in Judah) and second by the Babylonians in Judah.

71. By contrast, McKane (*Jeremiah*, 143–45) interprets this verse as a command to Jeremiah, mapping the gleaning to saving a remnant of the nation.

72. *DCH* 6:425–26, s.v. "עלל I," concludes that the base meaning of the *qal* is "to do, do repeatedly." Several biblical passages use עלל I without any apparent reference to harvesting a crop (e.g., the *hitpael* forms in Exod 10:2; Judg 19:25; 1 Sam 31:4). Two others apply it exclusively to harvesting, without apparent reference to warfare (e.g., the *poel* forms in Lev 19:10; Deut 24:21). In addition, the noun עללות always refers to "gleanings" from a harvest (though it is worth noting that in the biblical corpus, the word only appears in expressions of WARFARE IS HARVESTING): Judg 8:2; Isa 17:6; 24:13; Jer 49:9; Obad 5; and Mic 7:1.

73. Borowski, *Agriculture*, 109; Walsh, *Fruit of the Vine*, 172–73.

74. Walsh (*Fruit of the Vine*, 171–72) proposes that grape harvesting involved two main actions. The grape harvest received the name בציר (< בצר, "to cut off"), because harvesters used a pruning knife to cut the clusters from the vine; אסף, on the other hand, refers to the second action of taking the grape clusters and placing them in containers. Hebrew אסף carries the same meaning in reference to other types of produce as well.

gleaning constituted a process of picking the remaining grapes by hand, then the gleaning image would be more reminiscent of capturing an enemy than combatting one.

3.2.3. Grape-Treading Metaphors

The second stage of the harvest occurs when the grapes are crushed to extract their juice. Metaphors based on this action map the crushed grapes to defeated humans. Two of the three grape-treading metaphors in the prophetic corpus present simple images. Isaiah 3:13–15 describes Judah as a vineyard and maps the poor to crushed and ground grapes, while Joel 4:13–14 maps people to grapes in its description of the day of judgment as harvesttime, when the wine press and wine vat are full of grapes and newly pressed juice, respectively.[75] The third metaphor, in Isa 63:1–6, is more elaborate, describing in detail the image of YHWH treading out the vintage that is the kingdom of Edom (63:1).[76] The main mappings relevant to the analysis here appear in 63:2–3:

מדוע אדם ללבושך ובגדיך כדרך בגת׃ פורה דרכתי לבדי ומעמים אין־
איש אתי ואדרכם בפי וארמסם בחמתי ויז נצחם על־בגדי וכל־מלבושי
אגאלתי׃

² "Why is there red on your clothes, and your garments like one who treads in a wine press?" ³ "The wine press I have trodden alone. From the peoples no man was with me. I trod them in my

---

75. Outside the prophetic corpus, Lam 1:15 also includes a grape-treading metaphor of this type, in which YHWH treading over Judah in a winepress maps to his punishment of the kingdom. For a discussion of biblical winepress imagery and its reception history, see Joshua Schwartz, "Treading the Grapes of Wrath: The Wine Press in Ancient Jewish and Christian Tradition," *TZ* 49 (1993): 215–28, 311–24.

76. The biblical authors frequently portray Edom as an enemy. Eventually, Edom came to represent an "arch-symbol of evil and depravity." Shalom M. Paul, *Isaiah 40–66: Translation and Commentary*, ECC (Grand Rapids: Eerdmans, 2012), 560. In this passage, Edom has been interpreted in various ways: Paul views it as the sole victim; Westermann as representative of all the kingdoms of the world being destroyed; and Blenkinsopp as simply providing the location at which YHWH has destroyed all of the kingdoms of the world. See Paul, *Isaiah 40–66*, 560; Claus Westermann, *Isaiah 40–66: A Commentary*, trans. David M. G. Stalker, OTL (Philadelphia: Westminster, 1969), 384; and Joseph Blenkinsopp, *Isaiah 55–66: A New Translation with Introduction and Commentary*, AB 19B (New York: Doubleday, 2003), 249.

anger and trampled them in my rage. Their 'juice' spattered my garments, and all my clothes I stained."

In this passage, the first speaker in 63:2 sees YHWH approaching and calls out his question about YHWH's appearance. YHWH then explains his condition in 63:3.

Prior to the creation of mechanized wine presses, extracting juice from grapes involved placing the grapes in a wine press and then having humans walk over the grapes to break the skins and press the juice out of the flesh.[77] Most wine presses had a large, flat surface upon which the grapes would be crushed. This treading floor was connected to a vat or container into which the juice would flow. The metaphor in this passage reflects the reality that as the grape-treaders stomped, and as the grape skins burst, some of the juice would splatter on the workers' clothing. Grape juice derives its color from the grape skins. While it may be that both green and red grapes were grown in ancient Israel, the descriptions of grape juice or wine that appear in the biblical texts, including in this passage, liken the liquid to blood and are therefore based on the crushing of red grapes.[78] In the case of Isa 63:1–2, the mapping of red grapes in the metaphor allows the author to create two wordplays: (1) between the אדם, "red," of YHWH's garments (63:2) and the name of the victim: אדום, Edom;[79] and (2) between בציר, "grape harvest," and the name of a major city in Edom, בצרה, Bozrah.[80] The choice of the VITICULTURE domain as source for this metaphor may not simply be in service of the play on the word "red," however. Jeremiah

---

77. The excavation of the large wine press installation at Beit Ṣafafa included a small, plastered structure that archeologists speculate held water for washing or purification. It was probably used by the grape-treaders before they worked on the treading floor. See Nurit Feig, "Excavations at Beit Ṣafafa: Iron Age II and Byzantine Agricultural Installations South of Jerusalem," *Atiqot* 44 (2003): 201.

78. Sasson, "Blood of Grapes," 401. Genesis 49:11 also compares grape juice from Judahite grapes to blood.

79. For variations on the use of wordplay with the name Edom (אדום) and the color red (אדם), see Gen 25:25, in which Esau, the founding father of Edom, is born covered in red hair (שער), which itself is a play on שעיר Seir, a region of Edom. See also Gen 25:29–34 (esp. v. 30), which contains a folk etymology for Edom based on a story about Esau selling his birthright for a serving of "red" food prepared by his brother, Jacob.

80. Bozrah has been identified with Buseirah in Edom (Paul, *Isaiah 40–66*, 561–62). Paul also comments in some detail on the element of wordplay in this passage.

49:9 (and the similar passage in Obad 5) also applies the image of a har-vested vineyard to Edom, suggesting that like its neighbors, Israel, Judah, and Moab, Edom may also have cultivated grapes.[81]

As noted above, the metaphor in Isa 63:1–6 maps people to trodden grapes. The metaphor incorporates combat imagery into its structure through the figure of the grape-treader (and because grapes can "bleed" red juice). Thus, 63:1–6 focuses on mapping the blood-spattered garments of a soldier who has killed one or more opponents to the juice-spattered clothing of YHWH as the grape-treader. In this way, the author juxtaposes pleasing sights and smells of freshly pressed grapes—as well as the shouts of the grape-treaders as they tread out the vintage—with the gruesome reality of battle. In addition, the passage transforms the image of music and celebration that typically accompanied the treading of the grapes to one of celebration over a defeated foe.[82] The author emphasizes this impression as YHWH claims to have achieved both victory and vengeance in his punishment of Edom (63:1, 4–5). YHWH's description of treading the grapes in anger lends a sense of battle intensity to the scene.[83]

3.3. The Appeal of Viticulture Metaphors

The following chapters will address how the prophetic authors employed various viticulture frames in their depictions of Israel and Judah. Also important, however, is why viticulture would have generated such a large number of national metaphors relative to other plant-based source frames. On this point, three factors seem relevant: financial, cultural, and environmental. The financial benefits to viticulture operated on two levels. First, though much of the wine produced in Israel and Judah prob-ably served domestic needs, their kings could also profit from the export

---

81. Evidence for the practice of viticulture in Edom is only available from the Roman period, but Paul (*Isaiah 40–66*, 562) argues that Edom took control of territory in southern Judah after the Babylonian conquest, so the Edomites may have engaged in viticulture at that time.

82. For the treading of grapes as a time of celebration, see Borowski, *Agriculture*, 110; and Walsh, *Fruit of the Vine*, 179–86.

83. Jeremiah 25:30 compares the image of YHWH shouting a challenge to his foes to the shouts of a grape-treader. The author does not develop the image, however, so the simile serves mainly to highlight the sound, and perhaps also the visual, of the grape-treader at work, rather than to evoke the entire GRAPE-TREADING frame.

of wine, especially to Egypt and the cities of the Mediterranean.[84] Second, vineyard ownership also represented personal wealth for common Judahites, perhaps even more so than for kings. J. David Schloen argues that in Israel and Judah, especially prior to the end of the eighth century, fields for growing grains may have been allocated by a clan's elders annually, according to each household's needs and capabilities. He suggests, however, that land for crops that required a significant investment in time and effort, such as vineyards and olive groves, may have been more permanently ceded to particular family lines.[85] As such, the acquisition of land for the cultivation of a vineyard would represent a more stable, long-term source of prosperity for a family. The idea of aspiring to plant a vineyard because it represents long-term financial security appears to be reflected in biblical passages, discussed in the introduction to this chapter, that describe the future restoration of Israel or Judah in terms of the people planting vineyards and enjoying their produce (e.g., Isa 65:21; Jer 31:5; Amos 9:14).

On a cultural level, the biblical accounts of the grape harvest describe a festive atmosphere, with shouting or singing to accompany the grape-treaders as they worked (Judg 9:27; Isa 16:10; Jer 48:33). As noted earlier, once grapes start to ripen, they must be harvested quickly to avoid over-ripening. As a result, the grape harvest and the making of wine would have been a community-wide effort.[86] The positive associations of wine-making with celebration would have made viticulture an appealing source for images of the nation.

Finally, vines and vineyards were part of the natural scenery for the people living in the region. Archaeologists have unearthed wine-making installations dating to the Iron Age that indicate the production of

---

84. Since wine is expensive to transport over land, these exports would probably have been carried by sea from Philistine ports. See Avraham Faust and Ehud Weiss, "Judah, Philistia, and the Mediterranean World: Reconstructing the Economic System of the Seventh Century B.C.E.," *BASOR* 338 (2005): 71–92.

85. Schloen, "Economy and Society in Iron Age Israel and Judah: An Archaeological Perspective," in *The Wiley Blackwell Companion to Ancient Israel*, ed. Susan Niditch, Wiley-Blackwell Companions to Religion (Chichester: Wiley & Sons, 2016), 433–53. The greater emphasis in the biblical corpus on vineyards as symbols of prosperity suggests that vineyard ownership may have been either more common or more valued than ownership of olive groves. On olives and olive trees in the prophetic corpus, see ch. 8.

86. Borowski, *Agriculture*, 110; Walsh, *Fruit of the Vine*, 170–71, 179–86.

wine in the highlands of Samaria and Jerusalem. In Israel, the Samaria ostraca detail shipments of wine and oil to Samaria from locations in the surrounding region. In Judah, the Iron Age II evidence for winemaking— primarily wine vats—extends from north of Jerusalem south to Hebron and its environs.[87] A decline in pollen produced by olive trees in the Judean Highlands in the second half of the eighth century BCE may indicate an "intensification of settlement activity"—that is, removing trees, including olive trees, and cultivating vineyards on the cleared land—during this period.[88] Archaeological studies of eighth- and seventh-century sites in the region have also suggested that wine production may have been one of the primary functions of these new sites.[89] Particularly for the prophets and their audiences, what could have been more natural than to imagine their people or land as a vine or vineyard when their cities literally sat nestled among the vines?

3.4. Conclusions: Framing Viticulture Metaphors

This chapter began with a discussion of the challenge of classifying and analyzing viticulture metaphors based on whether the underlying object in the metaphor is a vineyard, or a vine, or grapes, because the prophetic authors are often less interested in defining what type of plant-based object their target kingdom is than in describing what happens to that object. In many cases, therefore, examining the imagery based on the actions taken in the metaphorical scenario offers greater opportunities for comparison and analysis of patterns in the use of viticulture imagery.

As the examples discussed here have demonstrated, expressions of collective condemnation in viticulture metaphors may blend imagery from individual combat with scenes typical of farm life. In addition, many of these expressions take advantage of communal aspects of vineyard

---

87. Wolfgang Zwickel, "Weinanbaugebiete in alttestamentlicher Zeit," in *Ein pralles Leben: Alttestamentliche Studien; Für Jutta Hausmann zum 65. Geburtstag und zur Emeritierung*, ed. Petra Verebics, Nikolett Móricz, and Miklós Köszeghy, ABIG 56 (Leipzig: Evangelische Verlagsanstalt, 2017), 311–23.

88. Israel Finkelstein and Dafna Langgut, "Climate, Settlement History, and Olive Cultivation in the Iron Age Southern Levant," *BASOR* 379 (2018): 153–69. On Iron Age II settlement patterns around Jerusalem, see also Yigal Moyal and Avraham Faust, "Jerusalem's Hinterland in the Eighth–Seventh Centuries BCE: Towns, Villages, Farmsteads, and Royal Estates," *PEQ* 147 (2015): 283–98.

89. Smoak, "Building Houses," 119–22.

management. They use the images of teams of vinedressers or harvesters to incorporate armies, rather than individual soldiers, into the viticulture scene. Moreover, several passages, especially the more fully elaborated ones, make effective use of mood by contrasting the grim reality of battle and conquest with the celebratory atmosphere of the grape harvest.

The approach of framing viticulture metaphors by action does not work in all cases, however. In national identity metaphors, the underlying object plays a central role in the conceptualization of the nation. None of the national identity metaphors depict the nation as grapes, but several of them use the image of a vine or a vineyard. Depictions of a nation as a single vine may differ in fundamental ways from those of a nation as a vineyard, because the two frames may contain different elements or may emphasize common elements in different ways. Land, for example, may play a different role in vineyard metaphors than in vine metaphors, because vineyards by definition occupy a specific plot of land, while vines have a much smaller footprint and may be moveable. The importance of the central object to national identity metaphors means these metaphors should be examined using object-based frames, even when they employ actions similar to those that structure the collective condemnation metaphors discussed in this chapter—pruning, harvesting, or grape-treading. Chapters 4 and 5 will therefore shift to analyzing national identity metaphors framed in terms of two physical objects in the VITICULTURE domain: VINEYARD and VINE.

4
Vineyard Metaphors

Metaphorical uses of the word כרם, "vineyard," are relatively rare in the Hebrew Bible. Of the sixty-two biblical passages in which כרם appears, only nine (15 percent) can be considered vineyard metaphors.[1] Of the five vineyard metaphors in the prophetic corpus, four occur in prophetic condemnations: Isa 1:4–9; 3:13–15; 5:1–7; and Jer 12:7–13. The fifth, in Isa 27:2–6, occurs in a restoration prophecy and thus is excluded from this study.[2] While the four condemnations imagine Judah or Jerusalem as a vineyard, only Isa 5:1–7 constitutes a national identity metaphor. The other three metaphors express messages of collective judgment, either of Jerusalem or Judah as a whole or of their leaders. The discussion that fol-

---

1. Two other passages also require comment, because they present, in parallel lines, the words גפן, "vine," and שדמה, "field" (as a general term for a terraced plot of land that could support a vineyard; *HALOT*, s.v. "שְׁדֵמָה"): Deut 32:32–33 and Isa 16:8–10. Both passages use שדמות, "fields," as the setting for a metaphor that compares a group of people to a vine. Thus, they invoke a VINE source frame that includes the element of a VINEYARD/שדמה. Finally, Jer 5:10, which was discussed in ch. 3, appears to conceptualize its target as a vineyard, but the primary focus of the metaphor and its mappings is what happens to the vines. Since the vineyard serves as a background to the growth and pruning activity, the passage is closer to a vine metaphor than a vineyard metaphor.

2. Isaiah 27:2–6 was most likely composed to reverse the punishment described in the vineyard metaphor in Isa 5:1–7. See Marvin A. Sweeney, "New Gleanings from an Old Vineyard: Isaiah 27 Reconsidered," in *Early Jewish and Christian Exegesis: Studies in Memory of William Hugh Brownlee*, ed. Craig A. Evans and William F. Stinespring (Atlanta: Scholars Press, 1987), 51–66; Benjamin J. M. Johnson, "'Whoever Gives Me Thorns and Thistles': Rhetorical Ambiguity and the Use of מי יתן in Isaiah 27.2–6," *JSOT* 36 (2011): 105–26; and John T. Willis, "Yahweh Regenerates His Vineyard: Isaiah 27," in *Formation and Intertextuality in Isaiah 24–27*, ed. J. Todd Hibbard and Hyun Chul Paul Kim, AIL 17 (Atlanta: Society of Biblical Literature, 2013), 201–7. The four remaining biblical vineyard metaphors appear in the Song of Songs as expressions of the metaphor A WOMAN IS A VINEYARD: Song 1:6; 2:15; 7:13; and 8:11–12.

lows will begin with these collective condemnation metaphors, presenting them chronologically according to their estimated date of composition. It will then offer an in-depth case study of the national identity metaphor in Isa 5:1–7.

4.1. Collective Condemnation Vineyard Metaphors

The prophecy in Isa 3:13–15 likely contains one of the oldest of the vineyard metaphors.[3] The author wraps the image of a ravaged vineyard in the frame of a judicial proceeding to accuse Judah's leaders of exploiting the poor. The metaphor begins in 3:14 and probably continues into 3:15:

יהוה במשפט יבוא עם־זקני עמו ושריו ואתם בערתם הכרם גזלת העני
בבתיכם: מלכם תדכאו עמי ופני עניים תטחנו נאם־אדני יהוה צבאות:
[14] YHWH enters into judgment with the elders of his people and its leaders: "It is you who have grazed bare the vineyard; the plunder of the poor is in your houses! [15] What is with you? You crush my people, and the face of the poor you grind," says my Lord, YHWH of Hosts.

The phrasing in 3:14 suggests that the metaphor is drawing on a preexisting conceptualization of Judah as a vineyard.[4] The author calls Judah

---

3. The superscription to the book of Isaiah sets the prophet's career in the second half of the eighth century BCE, during the reigns of the Judahite kings from Uzziah to Hezekiah (1:1), but most scholars now attribute significant portions of the book to later authors and editors. The standard approach divides the book into three periods: First Isaiah (chs. 1–39); Second Isaiah (chs. 40–55); and Third Isaiah (chs. 56–66). (Some scholars reject the theory of a Third Isaiah and assign all of chapters 40–66 to Second Isaiah.) Second and Third Isaiah appear to derive from the exilic and postexilic periods, respectively. First Isaiah contains the material generally attributed to the eighth century (esp. chs. 1–12), though it also includes later insertions (including chs. 24–27 and 33–35) and editorial adjustments. For an overview of recent debate over the composition, redaction, and dating of Isaiah, including arguments against the early dating of material in First Isaiah, see Ulrich Berges, "Isaiah: Structure, Themes, and Contested Issues," in *The Oxford Handbook of the Prophets*, ed. Carolyn J. Sharp, Oxford Handbooks (New York: Oxford University Press, 2016), 153–70.

4. So also Hans Wildberger, *Isaiah 1–12: A Commentary*, trans. Thomas H. Trapp, CC (Minneapolis: Fortress, 1991), 142. The problem for understanding the passage as referring to a literal vineyard is that it contains no indication of what "the vineyard" is.

הכרם, "the vineyard," rather than כרם, "a vineyard," and offers no introduction to set up that metaphor. An audience that lacked prior knowledge of the identity of the vineyard would struggle to relate the image of consuming it to the accusation of exploiting the poor, particularly since the passage otherwise seems to employ terms not typical of the VINEYARD frame. On what basis would that audience understand the association between a vineyard and poor people, who belong to the segment of society least likely to own vineyards? The connection of these two elements makes more sense if it represents the author playing with an already known conception of Judah.

The conventional metaphor CONQUEST IS EATING structures the metaphor in 3:14, as it depicts the theft of wealth from Judahites who are poor as the consumption (בער II) of the vineyard.[5] Some commentators interpret the accusation against the leaders as mapping them to bad shepherds who have allowed animals to graze in the vineyard.[6] If that were the intent, however, the author could have used the *hiphil* form of בער, "to allow to be grazed," rather than the *piel*, "to graze."[7] Instead, the author directly accuses the leaders themselves of doing the grazing. Implicit in the use of בער for consuming, rather than a more typical verb for human eating, such as אכל, "to eat," is the notion that Judah's elders and leaders are animals. The image may derive from conventional metaphors that associate a human leader with a dominant male sheep or goat: A LEADER IS AN איל,

---

5. Gray (*Isaiah*, xxi–xxii, 69) argues that the grazing sense of בער either developed from the destroying sense of the root (Num 24:22; Deut 17:7; 2 Sam 4:11; 1 Kgs 14:10), or that it developed as an independent root. The close conceptual connections in Biblical Hebrew between burning and consuming and between burning and conquest, however, make it more likely that both the grazing and destroying senses of בער arose as metaphorical extensions of בער's burning sense. That the eating sense of בער conveys an image of total consumption, akin to what happens when fuel is burned, also suggests that the original literal sense of בער was likely that of burning.

6. Gray, *Isaiah*, 69; Wildberger, *Isaiah 1–12*, 142. In other words, Gray and Wildberger incorrectly interpret Isa 3:14 as describing a scene similar to the legal case presented in Exod 22:4 (22:5 ET). That law requires restitution when a man causes or allows his cattle to graze someone else's vineyard or field. Isaiah 3:14 does raise the issue of unlawful grazing of a vineyard, but where the law holds the owner of the cattle accountable for the act, Isa 3:14 directly accuses the cattle, which represent Judah's leaders.

7. E.g., the *hiphil* form appears in the grazing law in Exod 22:4 (22:5 ET), discussed in the previous footnote.

"RAM" (e.g., Exod 15:15; Ezek 17:13) or A LEADER IS AN עתוד, "MALE GOAT OR SHEEP" (e.g., Isa 14:9; Ezek 34:17, which employs both עתוד and איל).[8]

While the grazing image in 3:14 is relatively clear, the precise referent for the vineyard remains an open question, one that depends on the intended mappings in 3:15. The two verbs in the verse do not appear in viticulture-related contexts elsewhere in the Bible. The root דכא typically refers either to something that is physically crushed (Isa 19:10; Job 4:19) or to someone who is metaphorically crushed, as an expression of conquest or oppression (Isa 57:15; Pss 72:4; 89:11; 94:5). The root טחן, on the other hand, usually refers to grinding grains, but it also appears in two references to crushing or grinding the idol in the golden calf narrative (Exod 32:20; Deut 9:21).[9] The evidence from these terms would seem to suggest that the vineyard metaphor does not extend past 3:14. In that case, then, the vineyard could map to the land of Judah. The poor who live in the land would remain human within the metaphor, and the consumed vines and fruit would map to what has been stolen from the poor. In other words, the passage would essentially constitute a metaphoric expression of the metonymic relationship, discussed at the beginning of chapter 3, in which vineyard ownership represents prosperity. By consuming the vineyard, Judah's leaders are consuming the income of the poor.

On the other hand, the act of treading on grapes in order to press the juice from them could conceivably also be described as crushing or grinding. In addition, Lam 3:34 declares that YHWH punishes humans by לדכא תחת רגליו, "crushing [them] under his feet," thereby identifying the action of דכא as something that can be done by pressing an object under foot. A closer look at the evidence thus leaves open two possibilities: (1) that one or both of these terms were associated with viticulture, and they are simply not attested as such in the Bible; or (2) that the author has creatively employed two nonviticulture terms in Isa 3:15 after priming the audience in 3:14 to reinterpret those terms from the perspective of the VINEYARD frame. In either case, the effect would be to extend the viticulture metaphor into 3:15, mapping the poor to grapes, and the grape juice to what has been stolen from the poor. Since the poor now are no longer human

---

8. Ezekiel 34:17–22 also presents an image of exploitative leader-cattle. In that case, the leaders consume the best of the land and its water and leave nothing good for the weakest of the flock.

9. For grinding grains, see Gray, *Isaiah*, 69.

and separate from the vineyard, but instead map to the fruit, the mapping for the vineyard as a whole would also shift from referring to the land of Judah to more broadly referring to the nation of Judah.

The passage itself contains insufficient detail to definitively settle the question, but it seems more likely than not that the author intended to continue the vineyard metaphor into 3:15. The verb דכא appears in only eighteen verses in the biblical corpus, and טחן only in seven. Had the author simply wanted to describe the unjust treatment of the poor, he could have done so using more common verbs meaning "to oppress," such as ענה II (esp. *piel*; seventy-five verses) or עשק (thirty-four verses), which appear frequently in laws and narratives about mistreating the Israelites or about exploiting those in need.[10] Instead, he chose terms whose frame structure could align with that of grape-treading.

The two verses together thus represent a progression of thought, with the vineyard initially referring mainly to the land of Judah in 3:14, but with 3:15 extending the mapping to also include the vineyard's produce. The filler of the ATTACKER element shifts from animals in 3:14a to grape-tread-ers, those who crush the grapes to release their juice, in 3:14b–15. That change of mapping is made clear by the description of the actions in the two verses. While cattle are as capable as grape-treaders of crushing grapes under foot, cattle have no houses and would not preserve the juice for later consumption. The vineyard ultimately fills the role of sympathetic victim in this metaphor, though the image is not one of military conquest, but of exploitation of the weak by the powerful. After accusing the leaders of consuming the vineyard, the author narrows the focus so that this destruc-tion maps only to the oppression of the poor. Along the way, the author reframes his own reference to the vineyard, shifting it from an image of the land of Judah to one that identifies the poor with the nation of Judah. The resulting blend takes individuals who normally occupy the fringes of soci-ety and instead places them at its center: as the poor go, so goes the nation.

The second collective condemnation vineyard metaphor, in Isa 1:4–9, presents an image of the vineyard that focuses more on the land of Judah than did Isa 3:13–15. The passage probably reflects conditions in Judah

---

10. *DCH* 6:497–99 and 619–20, s.vv. "ענה II" and "עשק I." The root רצץ (eighteen verses) can also carry the sense of oppressing the poor, and it appears five times paired with עשק, but since its more literal sense relates to smashing or breaking something, it does not constitute a clear conceptual alternative to דכא or טחן (*HALOT*, s.v. "רצץ").

following Sennacherib's successful campaign in the region in 701 BCE.[11] Isaiah 1:4–7 first describes Judah as a beaten body and declares that the nation has been devastated by war, its cities burned, and its land consumed by foreigners. Isaiah 1:8–9 then summarizes Judah's current state in a series of similes:

ונותרה בת־ציון כסכה בכרם כמלונה במקשה כעיר נצורה: לולי יהוה
צבאות הותיר לנו שריד כמעט כסדם היינו לעמרה דמינו:

[8] And Daughter Zion is left like a booth in a vineyard, like a hut in a cucumber field, like a city "guarded." [9] Had YHWH of Hosts not left us a mere remnant, like Sodom we would have become, Gomorrah we would resemble.

The booth in 1:8 refers to a temporary structure in which the grape-pickers would have lodged during the harvest. They may also have used it to store the picked grapes until they were ready to be pressed into juice. The reference to the hut in the cucumber field provides a visual parallel to the vineyard line, since in ancient Israel, both grapes and cucumbers would have grown on low, spreading vines.[12] Mapped to Jerusalem, the images of the two unstable structures emphasize the claim in 1:9 that the city has only survived due to YHWH's decision to spare it.[13] In addition, the association of the booth and hut with harvesttime activities places the similes of the vineyard and field in that specific context.

The third simile in 1:8 differs from the first two. The key term, נצורה, has been variously interpreted as describing either a guarded (< נצר, "to

---

11. Blenkinsopp, *Isaiah 1–39*, 183; Brevard S. Childs, *Isaiah*, OTL (Louisville: Westminster John Knox, 2001), 17; Roberts, *First Isaiah*, 22; and Wildberger, *Isaiah 1–39*, 183. Otto Kaiser, however, argues that the passage was composed after the destruction of Jerusalem by the Babylonians in 587 BCE. See Kaiser, *Isaiah 1–12: A Commentary*, trans. John Bowden, 2nd ed., OTL (Philadelphia: Westminster, 1983), 20–21.

12. The Israelites probably cultivated free-standing vines that spread out on the ground. (See the discussion in ch. 5.) It is not clear whether the Judahites would have grown cucumbers on a scale large enough to require a hut for lodging workers or for storage of the picked vegetables. Thus, the image in the second simile may not precisely reflect reality.

13. Most treatments of this passage comment on the nature of these temporary structures. E.g., Borowski (*Agriculture*, 106) calls them "flimsy," and Blenkinsopp (*Isaiah 1–39*, 184) describes them as "impermanent and precarious."

keep watch [over]") or besieged (< צור, "to tie up, encircle") city.[14] The difference between this third simile and the first two is jarring enough that many scholars have argued that it requires reinterpretation or emendation. Some suggest that the image reflects a pastoral scene (e.g., "refuge in the sheepfold"; or "ass's foal in a pen").[15] Gray adjusts the translation so that it describes a scene of a structure in a field—"like a tower for the watch"—an image that more closely aligns with the previous two similes in the verse.[16] These approaches overlook the way the author plays with the imagery by using a word that could be associated with either defense or attack. A similar ironic blend of the images of a location guarded and a location attacked appears in Jer 4:17, which describes a besieged Jerusalem as a field surrounded by guards.

The quotation marks surrounding "guarded" in the translation of Isa 1:8, here, highlight this use of ambiguous language to evoke the double meaning that the city has survived, and thus was guarded, but that the surrounding territory has been destroyed by a besieging army. Visually, it presents yet another image of a structure surrounded by an empty field. By comparing Jerusalem to a besieged city, however, the author blends the combat scene with those of the vineyard and the cucumber field at harvesttime, thereby clarifying the message of the verse. The third simile is thus neither indicative of a corrupted text nor discordant within the series of similes in 1:8. Rather, it contextualizes the previous two images. It also creates a bridge to 1:9, whose reference to Sodom and Gomorrah draws on traditions of once prosperous cities that were destroyed for their sins, never to be repopulated or rebuilt.[17]

In the context of 1:7's graphic description of the devastated land, as well as the comparison to Sodom and Gomorrah in 1:9, the vineyard simile offered in 1:8 suggests a postharvest scene, the vines nearly picked clean of grapes, the branches perhaps disheveled from being manhandled

---

14. *HALOT*, s.vv. "נצר"; "צור I."

15. Respectively, Kaiser, *Isaiah 1–12*, 17; Wildberger, *Isaiah 1–12*, 18–20.

16. Gray, *Isaiah*, 14.

17. The details of the Sodom and Gomorrah traditions vary. One version of the narrative appears in Gen 18:16–19:29. Ezekiel 16:46–50 also references the two cities, though the accounting of their sins differs from that described in Gen 18–19. Elsewhere in the prophetic corpus, comparisons to Sodom and Gomorrah sometimes focus on their sins (Isa 1:10; Jer 23:14), but more frequently refer to their destruction (Isa 13:19; Jer 49:18; Amos 4:11; Zeph 2:9).

as the grape clusters were removed from them, and the ground trampled by the grape-pickers. The blend of the harvest and warfare imagery casts a sinister air over the celebratory atmosphere of the harvest by reworking it into an image of conquest by an enemy army. The author here focuses on the state of the conquered land, however, rather than on the actions of the nation's conquerors. The audience enters the scene during the aftermath of both harvest and conquest, when the land stands mangled, empty, and still. The prophetic author offers an image both sad and sympathetic, expressing relief that Jerusalem still stands but mourning the loss of the vitality and fruitfulness of the preharvest, preconquest land.[18]

The third collective condemnation vineyard metaphor, in Jer 12:7–13, was composed perhaps a century after the events depicted in Isa 1:4–9. The passage offers a different image of postconquest desolation based on the conceptualization of Judah as YHWH's vineyard.[19] In 12:10, the author grounds the metaphor not in the concept of harvest, but rather in the image of the vineyard as overrun by cattle:

רעים רבים שחתו כרמי בססו את־חלקתי נתנו את־חלקת חמדתי למדבר
שממה:

Many shepherds have destroyed my vineyard. They have trampled my allotted field.[20] They have turned my delightful field into a desolate wilderness.

---

18. While it does not specifically reference a vineyard, Mic 7:1–7 presents a similar image to that of Isa 1:8. In Mic 7:1, Jerusalem compares itself to the remnants of a fig and grape harvest. Again, the author enters the scene after the harvest, and therefore does not focus on the joyful image of harvesting fruit. Instead, the author keeps the audience's gaze on the present, degenerate state of the nation. The exclamation of woe by the mourning land in 7:1 encourages the audience to sympathize with the land. Both passages also denounce the present generation of Judahites. Isaiah 1:4–9 opens by suggesting that the Judahites have invited their fate (1:4–6), and Mic 7:1–7 argues that all of the good people of Jerusalem have disappeared, leaving only the bad behind (7:2–6). See ch. 7 for additional discussion of Mic 7:1–7.

19. Scholars differ on whether the passage dates to the final years of the seventh century BCE, prior to the Babylonian conquest, and therefore anticipates a future fate (Holladay, *Jeremiah 1*, 386), or whether it reflects backward, either on the destruction of Judah in 598–597 BCE (Lundbom, *Jeremiah 1–20*, 656) or of Jerusalem in 587 BCE. Robert P. Carroll, *Jeremiah: A Commentary*, OTL (London: SCM, 1986), 290.

20. The noun חלקה refers to an assigned plot of land within a community (*HALOT*, s.v. "חֶלְקָה"). The description sets the land of Judah apart from all other kingdoms by claiming it is the portion of the world that was allotted to YHWH (cf. Deut 32:8–9). In

As in Isa 3:14, the passage offers no explanation for the description of Judah as YHWH's vineyard. Rather, the author assumes that the audience already understands why YHWH's "allotted field" takes the form of a vineyard. At the same time, Jer 12:10 differs from Isa 3:14 in connecting the vineyard explicitly to YHWH. Isaiah 3:14 simply calls Judah "the vineyard," whereas Jer 12:10 more closely identifies the land with YHWH by granting YHWH possession of the vineyard.

The image presents a scene of shepherds driving their cattle across a vineyard, trampling the vines in the process.[21] Vineyards in Israel and Judah were most likely enclosed within walls or hedges to prevent such incidents.[22] In this national metaphor, the wall maps to the borders of the land, and the cattle have breached it. The surrounding passages contain several references to the conquest of Judah. In 12:7, YHWH declares that he has given Judah בכף איביה, "into the palm of her enemies." In 12:9 he calls for wild animals to consume the Judahites, and 12:12 speaks of destroyers who have come to attack the people of Judah. Collectively, these verses paint a picture of foreign invasion and make it likely that the shepherds of 12:10 map to foreign kings.[23] The cattle, in turn, map to invading armies, whose rampage across the land damages it just as a herd of cattle overrunning a vineyard or field would do.[24]

---

a similar vein, Jer 12:7–9 describes the people of Judah as YHWH's נחלה, a term that primarily refers to inherited property, but that also appears in metaphorical expressions about the relationship between YHWH and his people (e.g., Deut 4:20; 2 Sam 21:3; Isa 47:6; Ps 78:71). See the brief discussion in Harold O. Forshey, "The Construct Chain *naḥalat YHWH/ᵉlōhîm*," *BASOR* 220 (1975): 51–53.

21. Since the accused take the role of shepherds in the metaphor, the passage more directly evokes the legal situation addressed in Exod 22:4 (22:5 ET), in which a man must make restitution if his cattle destroy another man's field or vineyard, than does Isa 3:14 (see n. 6). The parallel is still limited, however. Jeremiah 12:10 does not map the cattle's consumption of the vineyard's fruit, nor do the surrounding verses in the unit (12:7–13) demand restitution from the shepherds over the destruction of YHWH's vineyard.

22. Walsh, *Fruit of the Vine*, 123.

23. So also Allen, *Jeremiah*, 153; and Holladay, *Jeremiah 1*, 388. As discussed in ch. 1, the image of a deity or king as a shepherd is common in biblical and other ancient Near Eastern texts. The metaphor also appears in Jeremiah, where the prophet several times refers to Judah's leaders as shepherds (e.g., 2:8; 3:15; 10:21; 23:1–4) and also uses the metaphor to refer to invading foreign kings (here and in 6:3).

24. McKane (*Jeremiah*, 274) also discusses how the cattle imagery maps to the destruction caused by invading armies.

The passage overall works both as accusation against the *people* of Judah and as expression of sympathy for the *land* of Judah by mapping the two targets to different types of frames. The accusations against the Judahites in the preceding verses, 12:8–9a, present the people as predatory animals who have treated YHWH as their prey. Thus, the people fill the role of the ATTACKER and YHWH the role of the ATTACKED. Jeremiah 12:9b then invokes the metaphor CONQUEST IS EATING by calling other wild animals to consume the people. This reverses the Judahites' position, using them now to fill the ATTACKED role.[25] In 12:10, on the other hand, the land of Judah, mapped to the vineyard and field, fills only the role of the ATTACKED, never the ATTACKER.[26] In the resulting blend of the two metaphors, the Judahites as wild animals are responsible for their own destruction, but the land of Judah as a vineyard or field is an innocent victim that bears the consequences of the Judahites' actions.[27]

A perhaps unexpected aspect of the three collective condemnation vineyard metaphors is that they all present a generally sympathetic image of Judah as the vineyard. This is most true of Isa 3:13–15, of course, which depicts the vineyard as the victim of the animals that graze on it. Yet even Isa 1:4–9 and Jer 12:7–13, both of which argue that the vineyard deserves its fate, make their case in a tone that suggests that the author feels no satisfaction over the vineyard's destruction. Isaiah 1:4–9 imagines Judah

---

25. McKane (*Jeremiah*, 272–73) comments on the reversal of Judah's fortunes, from predator to prey, in the animal imagery.

26. Allen (*Jeremiah*, 153) argues that 12:10 focuses on the destruction of the land, but he seems to overlook the combined effect of the imagery in the passage, and therefore goes too far in arguing of the passage as a whole that "the disaster is not the destruction of the people but that of the land." Notice the experiential grounding of the images in 12:8–10. In an ironic reversal, the people who were predators attacking YHWH in 12:8–9a are themselves attacked by predators in 12:9b. In 12:10, however, since predators would not normally trample a vineyard or field, the land instead falls prey to cattle.

27. Holladay (*Jeremiah 1*, 389) argues that "emotionally and theologically the passage [Jer 12:7–13] has much in common with Isa 5:1–7; there, too, the destructive work of Yahweh is laid alongside his devoted constructive work of earlier years." While that description works well enough for Isa 5:1–7 (see the discussion in the case study below), it bears little resemblance to the content of Jer 12:7–13, which addresses not YHWH's work for Judah, but Judah's identity as YHWH's inherited possession. Holladay appears to have imported details from Isa 5:1–7 into the interpretation of Jer 12:7–13. (See further the discussion of this phenomenon in the example of Jer 2:21 in ch. 5.)

in terms of the mournful image of a postharvest vineyard (1:8), and Jer 12:7–13 both shows YHWH speaking words of mourning over the vineyard (12:10) and depicts the vineyard mourning its own state (12:11).

4.2. Case Study: Isaiah 5:1–7

In contrast to the sympathetic perspectives on the vineyard in the collective condemnations, Isa 5:1–7, also known as the Song of the Vineyard, offers a more critical image that ascribes bad behavior to the vineyard itself. The text contains a complex and detailed construction of national identity that warrants further study, especially because the identity aspect of the text has generally been overlooked in biblical scholarship. Modern treatments of the passage often take prior scholarship as a starting point, to which they then offer modifications or extensions. Such approaches fail to appreciate the extent to which discomfort with the theological implications of a plain text reading of 5:1a—in which the prophet speaks of his deity, YHWH, using an intimate epithet, ידידי, "my beloved"—has spawned decades of exegetical attempts to prove that the text cannot be read so simply. That Isa 5:1–7 often serves as a lens through which other viticulture imagery in the Bible is interpreted makes misinterpretations of the passage particularly problematic, and makes a fresh look at the text all the more necessary.

In the passage, shown below, the speaker announces his intention to sing a song about his beloved (friend) and his friend's vineyard (5:1a). Accordingly, he begins by describing how his friend had prepared a new plot of land for his vineyard, planted a choice variety of grapes on the land, and outfitted the vineyard with everything necessary for its cultivation and protection (5:1b–2a). Yet despite his friend's best efforts and expectations, the vineyard produces stinking grapes (5:2b). Following this recital of the vineyard's history and present state, the singer assumes the role of his friend and asks the audience, rhetorically, "What more could I have done?" (5:3–4) Without waiting for an answer, the friend declares his intention to allow nature to reclaim the land. He will destroy the vineyard's defenses, cease tending the land and the vines, and cut off the vineyard's water supply (5:5–6). In the final verse of the passage, the singer steps out of the song to offer an interpretation of it. He tells his audience that Israel and Judah are YHWH's vineyard, and that the people are the vines that have produced the rotten grapes of injustice (5:7).

אשירה נא לידידי ¹ Let me sing about my beloved,

שירת דודי לכרמו My love song about his vineyard:[28]

כרם היה לידידי My beloved had a vineyard

בקרן בן־שמן: On a fruitful hilltop.

ויעזקהו ויסקלהו ² He broke up its soil, and cleared it of stones,

ויטעהו שרק And planted it with śoreq-grapes.

ויבן מגדל בתוכו He built a tower in the midst of it,

וגם־יקב חצב בו And also a wine press he hewed out in it.

ויקו לעשות ענבים He expected it to produce good grapes,

ויעש באשים: But it produced stinking grapes.

ועתה יושב ירושלם ³ "And now, residents of Jerusalem,

ואיש יהודה And men of Judah,

שפטו־נא ביני Judge between me

ובין כרמי: And my vineyard.

מה־לעשות עוד לכרמי ⁴ What more was there to do for my vineyard

ולא עשיתי בו That I did not do in it?

מדוע קויתי לעשות ענבים Why, when I expected [it] to produce good grapes,

ויעש באשים: Did it produce stinking grapes?

ועתה אודיעה־נא אתכם ⁵ Now let me tell you

את אשר־אני עשה לכרמי What I am doing to my vineyard:

הסר משוכתו Removing its hedge,

והיה לבער So that it may be grazed bare,

---

28. Most scholars rightly reject translating שירת דודי as a possessive expression—"my דוד's song about his vineyard"—because if the דוד wrote the song, he probably would not refer to himself in the first line of the song (i.e., line 3 of 5:1) as ידידי, "my beloved" (Blenkinsopp, *Isaiah 1–39*, 207). Proposals to emend the phrase to שירת דודי, "my love song" or שירת דודים, "a love song" (e.g., Roberts, *First Isaiah*, 70–71) are neither supported by the texts and versions of this passage nor necessary to make sense of the phrase. Rather, שירת דודי should be understood as a construct chain in which the genitive form attributes a quality to the bound form. In such cases, both the genitive and any pronoun attached to it modify the noun in the construct state, and the genitive should be translated adjectivally. See *IBHS*, §9.5.3b, 150–51; and esp. J. A. Weingreen, "The Construct-Genitive Relation in Hebrew Syntax," *VT* 4 (1954): 50. Thus, e.g., Weingreen argues that Ps 42:9b, תפלה לאל חיי, should be translated not as "a prayer to the God of my life," but as "a prayer to my living God" (55). Applying the logic of this principle to שירת דודי, the phrase would therefore be best translated as "my love song" instead of "the song of my beloved." The same rule also governs the translation in 5:7 of נטע שעשועיו as "his delightful planting," instead of "the planting of his delight."

פרץ גדרו Breaking down its wall,

והיה למרמס: So that it may be trampled.

ואשיתהו בתה ⁶ I will make it a waste:

לא יזמר ולא יעדר It shall be neither pruned nor hoed,

ועלה שמיר ושית So that thorns and thistles shall overgrow it.

ועל העבים אצוה And the clouds I will prohibit

מהמטיר עליו מטר: From dropping rain upon it."

כי כרם יהוה צבאות בית ישראל ⁷ For the vineyard of YHWH of Hosts is the house of Israel,

ואיש יהודה נטע שעשועיו And the men of Judah his delightful planting.

ויקו למשפט והנה משפח He expected justice, but instead there was bloodshed,

לצדקה והנה צעקה: Righteousness, but instead there was an outcry.[29]

In 1977, John Willis published a summary of the major theories regarding the genre of Isa 5:1–7, including an uncle's song of wisdom for a prospective bridegroom, a love song sung by either a bride or a groom, or a song sung by a friend of a bridegroom. He then offered his own proposal that the song represents a parable about a disappointed vineyard owner.[30] Gale Yee followed up in 1981, agreeing with Willis that the song constitutes a parable, but arguing that his definition of the form required more precision. Yee ultimately views the passage as a combination of a song and a juridical parable.[31] Most subsequent interpretations of this passage have followed Yee's line of thought in describing the song as containing features of both the lawsuit and parable forms. In this juridical parable, the speaker

---

29. In 5:7, the author employs a wordplay between משפט "law" and משפח "bloodshed" in the third line and צדקה "justice" and צעקה "an outcry" in the fourth line (Roberts, *First Isaiah*, 72). משפח is a *hapax legomenon* that most scholars interpret as related to Arabic *safaḥa* "to pour, spill (blood)" (Wildberger, *Isaiah 1–12*, 185). For an in-depth analysis of the author's use of sound, rhythm, and repetition in the song, see F. W. Dobbs-Allsopp, "Isaiah's Love Song: A Reading of Isaiah 5:1–7," in *Biblical Poetry and the Art of Close Reading*, ed. J. Blake Couey and Elaine T. James (Cambridge: Cambridge University Press, 2018), 149–66.

30. Willis, "The Genre of Isaiah 5:1–7," *JBL* 96 (1977): 337–62. Willis's analysis also addresses the theories that the song represents a polemic against fertility cults, a song by the prophet either about his own vineyard or about YHWH, a drinking song, a lawsuit, a fable, and an allegory.

31. Gale Yee, "A Form-Critical Study of Isaiah 5:1–7 as a Song and a Juridical Parable," *CBQ* 43 (1981): 30–40.

tells the audience a story that leads the audience to pronounce judgment on a misbehaving character, after which the speaker reveals that the misbehaving character represents the audience. In this way, the speaker tricks the audience into condemning themselves.[32]

Those who identify the parable form in Isa 5:1–7 argue that the song hides from the audience the identities of the vintner and vineyard and then asks the audience, in 5:3, to judge the vineyard for producing bad grapes. Since the vineyard represents the people, the song thus induces the people to judge themselves. The most common version of this theory sees the parable also couched in a metaphor: the vintner-vineyard relationship is a metaphor for a broken male-female romantic relationship, which in turn is a parable about the relationship between YHWH and his people. Accordingly, the parable induces the audience to judge not the vineyard, but the unfaithful woman whom the vineyard represents.[33] For each of these theories, the explanation of the parable in 5:7 reveals to the audience that in condemning the vineyard or woman, they have condemned themselves. They must acknowledge the justice in the song's message—that despite the lavish care that YHWH has expended on Judah, the nation has turned away from YHWH's requirement of social justice and will therefore be punished.[34]

While such interpretations correctly identify the social justice message of the song, they overlook a more straightforward explanation of its content. These seven verses contain one of the most complete metaphoric constructions of national identity in the biblical corpus, including all of the major elements: a narrative about the nation's past; a shared culture for members of the nation; a common political present and fate for those members; a national body (i.e., land) on which the nation resides; and a

---

32. Yee, "Form-Critical Study," 33.

33. The summary offered here provides the basic outline of the parable-based theories, though the details of each scholar's analysis of the song vary on a number of points. While some scholars have attempted to map the entire song to the metaphor of a woman as a vineyard, most modern treatments agree that the author does not carry the feminine imagery beyond the first verse (see e.g., Blenkinsopp, *Isaiah 1–39*, 207; and Wildberger, *Isaiah 1–12*, 186). As such, they argue that the feminine imagery serves mainly to help hide the true identity of the vineyard from the audience.

34. The interpretation offered here argues that the song has no feminine imagery. Therefore, the discussion does not address the problems with theories that the passage uses such imagery as a misdirect. For a discussion of these issues, see Willis, "Genre of Isaiah 5:1–7," 361–62.

national character that defines what it means to be a member of the nation. Through this ironic tale, the author of Isa 5:1–7 exploits a preexisting conception of the land of Judah as a vineyard. In the opening lines, the positive account of the nation's origins under YHWH's care creates a shared past and national character that binds the people together and differentiates Judah from other nations. By the end of the song, however, the author has transformed the very national identity that he earlier praised, rejecting the nation's proud self-image as a producer of fine wine and replacing it with an image of a nation that produces only injustice and unrighteousness. The members of the nation, like the vines in the vineyard, will share the common fate of abandonment and destruction.

The song does hide its intent from the audience, but the evidence from this passage, and from First Isaiah's sympathetic portrayals of the vineyard in the two passages discussed above, suggests that the author's purpose was less to misdirect the audience into judging the vineyard than to misdirect them into approving of the vineyard. To that end, the author provides clues to the identities of the vineyard and vintner in 5:1–2 but hides the identity of the vines until the last verse. Ultimately, the surprise for the audience lies not in the fact that the vineyard is *Judah*, but rather in the fact that vineyard is *bad*.[35]

The song builds on a known conception of the land of Judah as a vineyard, but it does not assume that mere mention of the word כרם would automatically bring the kingdom to a listener's mind. Rather, the author provides clues in the opening verses that help the audience to recognize that the song is about YHWH as the vintner and Judah as the vineyard. The author's description of the vintner as ידיד, "my beloved," in 5:1a already associates the vintner with YHWH. The word ידיד and the related terms ידידות, "beloved," and ידדות, "loved one," appear in nine verses in the Bible. The term usually refers to those whom YHWH loves (e.g., Pss 60:7; 108:7), but in one passage it relates to a human's love of YHWH's temple as the place where YHWH resides (Ps 84:2).[36] At first glance, the evidence

---

35. Though he argues that the song hides the identities of the vineyard and vintner, Wildberger's observation (in *Isaiah 1–12*, 180) that the author initially presents the composition as a "harmless song," when in fact it contains a "harsh accusation," also applies to the interpretation offered here. Thanks to J. Blake Couey for the phrasing here regarding the source of the surprise.

36. On the senses and forms of ידי, see Moshe Bar-Asher, "יְדִידְיָה—וה' אֲהֵבוֹ: The Morphology and Meaning of the Word ידיד," in *Studies in Classical Hebrew*, SJ

does not appear to support arguments that ידיד in Isa 5:1 would refer to YHWH. An older tradition, however, offers a different perspective on the range of uses for ידיד.

Ugaritic texts employ the epithet *ydd* in the context of divine kingship and royal ideology.[37] The most frequently used variants in this corpus are *ydd 'l* and, from the same root as *ydd*, *mdd 'l*, both phrases meaning "the beloved of El." The epithet *ydd 'l* typically refers to Mot, the god of death, but *mdd 'l* appears in reference both to Mot and to Yam, the god of the sea.[38] Ugaritic mythology also depicts each of these deities as divine kings. Mot rules the city of the netherworld, and a poorly preserved text about Yam appears to describe a coronation ceremony for him.[39] Moreover, one Ugaritic text refers to Mot three times simply as *ydd*, "beloved."[40] A Uga-

---

71 (Berlin: de Gruyter, 2014), 23–46. The term also appears in the superscription to Ps 45, which describes the psalm as שיר ידידת (45:1). The text extols the virtues and actions of the king in the context of a royal wedding. Christoph Schroeder, "'A Love Song': Psalm 45 in the Light of Ancient Near Eastern Marriage Texts," *CBQ* 58 (1996): 417–32. The phrase שיר ידידת is generally translated as "a love song," but the associations of ידיד with royalty (see discussion in the next footnote) suggest that "love song" may not fully capture the sense of שיר ידידת as a description for this psalm about a king.

37. Nicolas Wyatt, "'Jedidiah' and Cognate Forms as a Title of Royal Legitimation," *Bib* 66 (1985): 112–25. Wyatt discusses evidence that in Egyptian texts, the epithet "beloved-of-DN" designates a royal heir. He then addresses similar epithets in Ugaritic and biblical texts, arguing that in each case, the term refers to a divine or human king. While his approach perhaps too quickly glosses over differences between texts whose composition is separated by centuries, he makes a strong case for the general association of ידיד with royalty and with both human and divine royal ideology.

38. Aicha Rahmouni, *Divine Epithets in the Ugaritic Alphabetic Texts*, trans. J. N. Ford, HdO 93 (Leiden: Brill, 2008), 193–97. Rahmouni indicates that a third entity also appears in Ugaritic texts with the epithet *mdd 'l*. The "sea monster," Arš, who represents "the personified sea" is also described as "beloved of El" (212–18). However, the context in which Arš appears with this epithet suggests that it may represent an alternate identity for, or extension of, Yam.

39. Wyatt, "Jedidiah," 120–21. According to Wyatt, the deity employing the epithet, El, is "intimately concerned with the general principles embodied in the monarchy, that is, the maintenance of social stability, territorial integrity, and so forth, commonly symbolised by cosmic management, lordship of the pantheon, and creativity" (122). In other words, in the contexts in which this epithet appears, both the loving deity and the beloved hold the responsibilities of a monarch—they just do so at different levels of responsibility.

40. Rahmouni, *Divine Epithets*, 193–94.

ritic audience would probably have recognized *ydd* as a shortened form of the known epithet *ydd 'l*, but the text nevertheless indicates that a variant of the epithet existed that did not include the reference to El. In the centuries between the fall of Ugarit and the composition of the biblical texts, a tradition of referring to other divine kings as *ydd 'l*, or simply as *ydd*, may have developed.

The question then becomes, would the epithet ידיד, or ידיד אל, have been employed with YHWH? The two Ugaritic deities referred to as *ydd* shared two characteristics: (1) they were divine kings; and (2) they were sons of El, the head of the pantheon. The biblical corpus contains evidence that YHWH may have met both of these criteria. It includes numerous examples of the conception of YHWH as a divine king (e.g., Exod 15:18; Isa 6:5; 33:22; Mic 4:7; Pss 24:7–10; 93:1–2).[41] In addition, Deut 32:8–9 suggests the existence of a tradition of YHWH as a subordinate, and probably son, of El:

בהנחל עליון גוים בהפרידו בני אדם יצב גבלת עמים למספר בני ישראל:
כי חלק יהוה עמו יעקב חבל נחלתו:

[8] When Most High apportioned the peoples, when he separated the sons of man, he established the boundaries of the peoples according to the number of the sons of Israel. [9] For YHWH's share is his people, Jacob his inherited portion.

In the MT, 32:8 describes עליון, "Most High"—a title used elsewhere of YHWH—dividing up the world into different people groups. Since 32:9 then indicates that Israel (referred to as Jacob) became YHWH's portion (חלק and חבל נחלתו), presumably the purpose of the division in 32:8 was to allocate the peoples to specific deities.[42] A combination of logical inconsistencies within

---

41. See Marc Zvi Brettler, *God is King: Understanding an Israelite Metaphor*, JSOTSup 76 (Sheffield: JSOT Press, 1989); and Anne Moore, *Moving beyond Symbol and Myth: Understanding the Kingship of God of the Hebrew Bible through Metaphor*, StBibLit 99 (New York: Lang, 2009).

42. In this context, the term חלק refers to the share of an estate inherited by an heir. The idea of Israel or the land of Israel as YHWH's portion or inheritance appears several times in the biblical texts, though the passages make no reference to the notion of YHWH as just one deity in a pantheon. While חלק most often refers to YHWH as the Israelites' inherited portion (e.g., Num 18:20; Ps 16:5; Lam 3:24), Israel or Judah become YHWH's inheritance in expressions using חלקה, "allotted land" (only in Jer 12:10), and נחלה, "inherited property." In some expressions, נחלה refers to the people

the text of 32:8 and evidence from other versions of the passage, however, suggests that the original text has been edited or reinterpreted to align with a monotheistic ideology by obscuring YHWH's role within the pantheon.

The MT states that the division of the peoples in 32:8 occurred למספר בני ישראל, "according to the number of the sons of Israel." This division of the world into as many peoples as Jacob had sons makes little sense. First, the biblical authors make no claim that each of these sons founded a people. Second, what purpose would be served by dividing the world up according to the number of Jacob's sons if YHWH was to be the god of all of those sons, but not of all of the other peoples? A scroll from Qumran preserves a version of the text that is probably closer to its original sense. The division of the world in that text occurs למספר בני אלהים, "according to the number of the sons of God [or divine sons]" (4Q37 [4QDeut^j]).[43] In this context, עליון would have originally referred to the title held by El, the head of the Canaanite pantheon: El (עליון) divided up the world according to the number either of his sons or of the divine sons (32:8), and he assigned the portion named Jacob to YHWH (32:9). YHWH, therefore, would have been either El's son or his subordinate.

Parallels between the Ugaritic uses of *ydd* and the examples of ידיד in the biblical corpus also suggest that the epithet could have been used of YHWH. First, in most biblical instances of the term, ידיד and related forms refer to individuals, groups, or the nation as a whole as needing or receiving divine protection or blessing. In several cases, the beloved is also royalty. Thus, the superior-to-subordinate dynamic between YHWH and the beloved is often similar to that between El and Mot or El and Yam in the Ugaritic texts. The biblical examples place YHWH in the role of El, rather than the beloved, so they do not prove that YHWH could be the ידיד, but they do suggest a degree of stability in the basic sense of the

---

(Deut 4:20; Isa 19:25; 63:17; Joel 2:17; Ps 33:12) or to the combination of the people and the land (Jer 12:7–9). In others, נחלה seems to refer mainly to the land of Israel (Exod 15:17; Jer 2:7).

43. The LXX translation, κατὰ ἀριθμὸν ἀγγέλων θεοῦ, "according to the number of divine sons" (NETS), reflects a *Vorlage* similar to the text at Qumran. BHS proposes emending the final phrase of 32:8 to בני אל, "the sons of El," or בני אלים, "divine sons." Joosten, on the other hand, has offered a solution based on the MT. He suggests that dittography of the *yod* in בני and misinterpretation of the word division may account for a shift from an original text that used an attested epithet for the god El, בני שר אל, "the sons of Bull El," to the MT's בני ישראל, "the sons of Israel." Jan Joosten, "A Note on the Text of Deuteronomy xxxii 8," *VT* 57 (2007): 548–55.

epithet in the period between when *ydd* was used at Ugarit and when the biblical authors employed יְדִיד.

An additional example does connect יְדִיד to YHWH, however. The one passage in which יְדִיד (or יְדִידוֹת, in this case) refers to the divine occurs in Ps 84, which praises YHWH's temple as the residence of the divine king. Psalm 84:2 declares: מַה־יְּדִידוֹת מִשְׁכְּנוֹתֶיךָ יְהוָה צְבָאוֹת, "How beloved is your dwelling place, O YHWH of Hosts!" The role of the מִשְׁכָּן "tabernacle" as the resting place for the ark in the wilderness and settlement narratives associates the tabernacle with the ideology of divine kingship, because the ark represented YHWH's throne and footstool.[44] The epithet used of YHWH in the psalm, יְהוָה צְבָאוֹת, is also associated with the kingship of YHWH, as it describes YHWH as leader of a divine host.[45] Finally, in verse 4 of the psalm, the author directly addresses YHWH as מַלְכִּי, "my king." The participation of Ps 84 in the ideology of divine kingship raises the question of whether the reference to the temple as יְדִידוֹת may represent trace evidence that the epithet יְדִיד was once used of YHWH in his role as divine king. At a later point in time, uncomfortable with the prospect of employing the familiar term יְדִיד to directly reference YHWH, use of the epithet may have shifted from YHWH to YHWH's temple.[46]

That the biblical corpus does not preserve additional examples of YHWH as יְדִיד may be more attributable to editorial activity than to authorship. While not definitive, the cumulative weight of the evidence regarding the use of יְדִיד in reference to deities and in the context of divine royal ideology suggests that יְדִיד may have been an epithet used of YHWH. If so, then the description of the vintner as יְדִיד would have helped the audience to identify the vintner as YHWH. Isaiah 5:1a as a whole would then inform the audience that the song is about YHWH and his vineyard.[47]

---

44. Benjamin D. Sommer, "Conflicting Constructions of Divine Presence in the Priestly Tabernacle," *BibInt* 9 (2001): 41–63; and C. Mark McCormick, "From Box to Throne: The Development of the Ark in DtrH and P," in *Saul in Story and Tradition*, ed. Carl Ehrlich and Marsha C. White, FAT 47 (Tübingen: Mohr Siebeck, 2006), 175–86.

45. Martin Rose, "Names of God in the OT," *ABD* 4:1008–9.

46. Though Wyatt's association of יְדִיד with royalty provided the inspiration for the theory offered here, Wyatt himself ("Jedidiah," 115) argues against identifying YHWH as the יְדִיד in Isa 5:1. He instead interprets the beloved in that verse as the Judahite king. He does not explain how his argument relates to 5:7, which explicitly declares that the vineyard is YHWH's and thereby identifies the beloved vintner as YHWH.

47. Other scholars have suggested that יְדִיד was a divine epithet, but they generally do not address the implications of that claim for their interpretation of Isa 5:1–7.

Descriptions of the vineyard in 5:1 and 5:2 also provide clues to the audience that the author intends to invoke a familiar conceptualization of Judah as a vineyard. The vineyard's location as בקרן בן־שמן, literally "on a horn, a son of oil," is obscure (5:1b). Most scholars interpret the "horn" as a reference to a hill or spur of land, with "son of oil" indicating that the hill is fertile or blessed.[48] While such interpretations probably capture some of the intended meaning of the phrase, they may overlook an element of wordplay in the description of the land. For example, the choice of a hilltop may reflect the reality that grains in ancient Israel were grown in the flatlands, leaving the hills for horticulture.[49] Since Jerusalem itself was located in the Judean Highlands, the reference to the vintner planting the vineyard on a hill places the vineyard on terrain similar to that surrounding the city. In addition, the descriptor בן־שמן may have more significance than simply praising the fertility of the land. While the basic meaning of בן is "son," the bound form בן־x or בני־x can also idiomatically indicate a quality or characteristic.[50] Thus, בן־שמן may indicate the characteristic of having or producing oil, and the reference may represent a way of conceptualizing a hill covered in olive trees, as in הר הזתים, "the Mount of the Olives," located to the east of Jerusalem.[51]

E.g., Wildberger (*Isaiah 1–12*, 180) argues that YHWH's identity remains hidden in the song until 5:6, but he concedes that the evidence for ידיד and דוד as divine epithets provides "some support to the notion that Isaiah's audience, insofar as they were paying close attention, could have gotten the idea that the 'friend' or 'beloved' of Isaiah had to be Yahweh." Blenkinsopp (*Isaiah 1–39*, 207) argues more affirmatively that 5:1 hints at the identity of the vintner, but he still views 5:1a as also incorporating the image of a woman as a vineyard in order to focus the text on the vineyard and to "endow the composition with a gnomic, riddle-like quality." It is not clear, however, what the author would gain by puzzling the audience if he is also providing clues to the vintner's identity.

48. Walsh, *Fruit of the Vine*, 93–94. She also mentions the use of שֶׁמֶן specifically to refer to olive oil, while the related terms שָׁמָן "something that is fat" (Gen 27:28) or שָׁמֵן "fat" (Num 13:20) may refer to "the fertility of land" (94).

49. Matthews, "Treading the Winepress," 23.

50. See, e.g., בן־ארבעים שנה, "son of forty years" = "forty-year-old man" in Gen 25:20; or בני־חיל, "sons of valor" = "warriors" in Deut 3:18 (*DCH* 2:205–7, s.v. "בֵּן").

51. This proposal is neither new nor recent. Already in the second century CE, Symmachus translated בקרן בן־שמן as *in cornu in medio olivarum* "in a horn, in the midst of olive trees" (Kaiser, *Isaiah 1–12*, 90 n. 5; my translation). Walsh (*Fruit of the Vine*, 93) also comments that "the value of hill slopes for the Israelites because of their agricultural yield in olives is at least hinted at with Isaiah's unique phrase."

The fact that archaeologists have unearthed wine and oil presses in close proximity to each other in Israel also suggests that the two types of woody plants were grown near each other and on the same type of soil.[52] Moreover, archaeological evidence indicates a drop in olive pollen counts in the Judean Highlands during the late Iron Age. Scholars attribute the change primarily to deforestation as a result of increasing numbers of settlements and to "expansion of viticulture rather than olive orchards."[53] If a decline in olive trees resulted from an increased cultivation of vineyards in their place, then the passage in Isaiah may also allude to that change. In other words, a hill of olive trees as the site of the vineyard may reflect the actual practice of viticulture and the cultivation of new vineyards in Judah in the late eighth century BCE.

If the description of the land connects the vineyard to Judah, the choice of grapes planted in the vineyard further reinforces that message. Ancient vintners understood that the only way to be certain of the grape variety and production capability of a vine is to grow it from an older vine that has produced well in the past.[54] When the speaker declares in 5:2 that the vintner planted שרק, he means that the vintner planted slips, twigs, or cuttings from *śoreq*-vines to ensure that the resulting grapes would breed true.[55]

What, then, is the significance of שרק? The noun שֹׂרֵק appears only three times in the Bible: twice in prophetic metaphors, in Isa 5:2 and Jer 2:21, and once in a place name in the Samson cycle (in Judg 16:4). Two similar terms, שֹׂרֵקָה (Gen 49:11) and שֹׂרֵק (> שֹׂרֵקִים; Isa 16:8), also appear in the context of viticulture. All three terms likely derive from the same root, שרק II, "to shine brightly."[56] The association of the root with the color red is usually taken as an indication that viticultural terms derived from it relate to a variety or varieties of red grapes. The clearest evidence to sup-

---

52. Walsh, *Fruit of the Vine*, 94.

53. Finkelstein and Langgut, "Climate, Settlement History, and Olive Cultivation," 165.

54. Matthews, "Treading the Winepress," 20.

55. Walsh (*Fruit of the Vine*, 13 n. 10) notes that the fact that grapevines are not native to Syria-Palestine "makes the vine an apt metaphor for transplanted, cultivated people." Since viticulture had been widely practiced throughout the Levant for millennia, however, it is not clear that the biblical authors would have known that grapes are not native to the region.

56. *DCH* 8:198, s.v. "שרק II."

port this claim appears in Gen 49:11, which compares the wine from שרקה to blood:

אסרי לגפן עירה ולשרקה בני אתנו כבס ביין לבשו ובדם־ענבים סותה:

Tethering to the vine his young donkey, to the śoreqah-vine[57] his donkey's foal, he washes in wine his garment, in [the] blood of grapes his robe.

The use of שָׂרֹק to describe the color of a horse in Zech 1:8, however, seems inconsistent with the dark red color of grapes.[58] This disconnect warrants a reevaluation of the origin and uses of the root שרק in the context of viticulture.

The place name נחל שרק, Nahal Soreq, may originally have derived from the "shining brightly" sense of שרק II—as in "the Shining Valley." Textual and archeological evidence suggests that the grape variety, שֹׂרֵק, takes its name from its place of origin in נחל שרק, which lies to the west of Jerusalem.[59] The association of a type of wine with the region in which it was produced is attested in both biblical and extrabiblical texts. An inscription from the Babylonian king Nebuchadnezzar II (604–562 BCE) boasts of importing fine wines from several named locations to offer to the Babylonian gods:

Sweet *kurunnu* wine, 'mountain beer,' the purest wine, (and) wine of the lands Izalla, Tu'immu, of Ṣimiri, of Ḫilbūnu, Arnabānu, Sūḫu, of Bīt-Kubāti, and Bītāti—countless (amounts), like water of a river—I

---

57. Scholars usually treat שרק and שרקה as referring to a "choice vine stock" without addressing why the name exists in two different forms. The contexts in which שרק and שרקה appear suggest a solution to this question. In Gen 49:11, שרקה serves as a semantic parallel to גפן, "vine." Isaiah 5:2 and Jer 2:21, on the other hand, refer to planting שרק, which then produces a grapevine. This could indicate that שרק and שרקה relate to different aspects of the same variety of grapes. In each case, the term may reflect an abbreviation of a full name. In the biblical corpus, both ענב, "grape," and נטע, "shoot," are masculine, and גפן is usually feminine; שרק may represent a short form of ענב שרק, used as a general name for the grape variety, or נטע שרק, referring to a slip from a śoreq-vine; שרקה, on the other hand, could be abbreviated from גפן שרקה, referring specifically to the vine that produces śoreq-grapes. Ernst Axel Knauf ("Masrekah," *ABD* 4:600) makes a similar distinction, arguing that שרק refers to the grape and שרקה to the vine, but he does not explain his reasoning.

58. Walsh, *Fruit of the Vine*, 109–10.

59. Walsh, *Fruit of the Vine*, 109–10.

copiously provided (all of this) for the table of the god Marduk and the goddess Zarpanītu, my lords.[60]

Two of the locations in this inscription, Ḥilbūnu and Izalla, may also appear in Ezek 27. Ezekiel 27:18 mentions Tyre profiting from trade in יין חלבון, "the wine of Helbon."[61] In addition, the MT of 27:19 begins with an untranslatable phrase: ודן ויון מאוזל, "and Dan and Yavan from Uzal." This line may represent a corruption from an original text that read: ודני יין מאיזל, "and casks of wine from Izalla."[62] The name שרק may be yet another example of this phenomenon of associating a type of wine with the specific region that produced it.[63]

In support of this theory, textual evidence places vineyards just south of Nahal Soreq, in Timnah (Tel Batash).[64] In the Samson cycle, when Samson marries the woman from Timnah, the narrative describes Samson arriving at כרמי תמנתה, "the vineyards of Timnah" (Judg 14:5). The hilly terrain, soil type, and access to water at Timnah would at least have provided good growing conditions for grapevines.[65] The archaeological evidence is less clear, but it leaves open the possibility that Timnah was a wine producing region in the eighth century BCE. Like many cities in the Shephelah, Timnah may have specialized in olive oil production during the seventh century BCE, but no evidence of oil presses was found in the eighth-century city at that site, which was destroyed by the Assyrians in 701 BCE.

---

60. Nebuchadnezzar II 019, i 21–28, trans. Frauke Weiershäuser and Jamie Novotny, The Open Richly Annotated Cuneiform Corpus (ORACC), http://oracc. museum.upenn.edu/ribo/Q005490/.

61. Powell, "Wine and the Vine in Ancient Mesopotamia," 107–8. Powell identifies Babylonian Hilbunu and biblical Helbon with Arabic Hilbun, "the name for a valley and village in the Anti-Lebanon Mountains northwest of Damascus."

62. Alan R. Millard, "Ezekiel xxvii. 19: The Wine Trade of Damascus," JSS 7 (1962): 201–3. See also Moshe Greenberg, Ezekiel 21–37, AB 22A (New York: Doubleday, 1997), 557.

63. Such an understanding of the origin of a vine as indicative of the grape variety (and quality) is also present in the vine metaphor in Deut 32:32, in which the peoples are condemned because מגפן סדם גפנם, "from the vine of Sodom is their vine." Note, however, that all of the evidence presented dates to the late seventh century BCE or later, so it does not provide clear proof that the connection between location and grape variety or quality was widespread in First Isaiah's time. Still, it establishes the possibility that such an association existed in the late eighth century.

64. Zwickel, "Weinanbaugebiete in alttestamentlicher Zeit," 311–23.

65. Walsh, Fruit of the Vine, 110.

In addition, after Timnah was again destroyed in the late seventh or early sixth century, the small sixth-century settlement at the site appears to have included a winepress.[66]

One explanation for the range of biblical uses of שרק II is that the root developed additional senses over time. First, the location lent its name to the grape variety. Then, the root developed a tertiary sense related to the properties of the grapevine. In some grape varieties, as the vine's green shoots and tendrils age and turn to wood, they also take on a reddish tone.[67] Such a development in the meaning of the root שרק from the color of the grapevine, instead of from the color of its grapes or their juice, would also explain the use of שרק in Isa 16:8. In the context of a metaphor that presents Moab as a pruned vine, the term שרקים probably refers to the vine's tendrils or shoots. Deriving the color sense of שרק from the color of the vine wood also provides a more logical explanation for application of the color term to a horse in Zech 1:8.

Returning to Isa 5:1–7, the significance of the planting of שרק in Isa 5:2 is the grape variety's association with Judah. Genesis 49:11 explicitly connects שרקה to Judah, as Jacob's blessing to his son, Judah, paints a picture of him prospering from the wine produced from śoreqah-vines. The reference to tethering the donkey to the vine in this verse carries a dual meaning. First, mules and donkeys were the mounts of choice for kings in Israel and the ancient Near East, so the donkeys in 49:11 indicate the kingship of Judah.[68] Second, the reference suggests that the śoreq-wine will produce wealth via trade, because the donkey was also commonly used as a pack animal for transporting trade goods.[69] The fact that Nahal Soreq lies to the west of Jerusalem further strengthens the association of śoreq with Judah.[70]

---

66. See George L. Kelm and Amihai Mazar, "Three Seasons of Excavations at Tel Batash: Biblical Timnah," *BASOR* 248 (1982) 1–36; and Kelm and Mazar, "Seventh Century B.C. Oil Presses at Tel Batash, Biblical Timnah," in *Olive Oil in Antiquity: Israel and Neighboring Countries from the Neolithic to the Early Arab Period*, ed. David Eitam and Michael Heltzer, HANE/S 7 (Padova: Sargon, 1996), 243–47.

67. Creasy and Creasy, *Grapes*, 35.

68. Philip J. King and Lawrence E. Stager, *Life in Biblical Israel*, LAI (Louisville: Westminster John Knox, 2001), 115–17, 186.

69. On donkeys and mules in the ancient Near East, see King and Stager, *Life*, 186–87; and Kenneth C. Way, *Donkeys in the Biblical World: Ceremony and Symbol*, HACL 2 (Winona Lake, IN: Eisenbrauns, 2011). See also Dorsey, *Roads and Highways of Ancient Israel*, 13–14; and Holladay, "Hezekiah's Tribute," 309–31.

70. Walsh, *Fruit of the Vine*, 109–10.

Taken together, the biblical evidence suggests: (1) that שֹׂרֵק refers to a particular grape variety common to the region either in or near Judah; (2) that its vine stock was known to produce a desirable and valuable variety of grapes; and (3) that Judah had profited from its cultivation. As such, *śoreq* would probably have been a source of pride for anyone who cultivated it, as well as for Judahites as a whole in their self-conception as a grape- and wine-producing people. Exporting the wine would also likely have provided a source of wealth for Judah's kings. That is the sense that שרקה carries in Gen 49:11, and it would explain why both Isa 5:2 and Jer 2:21 use שרק for their metaphorical representations of Judah. The planting of *śoreq* connects the vine or vineyard to Judah and also affirms for the audience that these vines would produce a high-quality crop.

Having hinted to the audience that the true subjects of the song are YHWH and Judah, the author further praises Judah in 5:2 by describing the vineyard in terms that convey a sense of wealth and prestige, but also in terms that attribute Judah's prosperity to YHWH. The first two lines of 5:2 describe the process of planting the vineyard. That the soil had to be broken and cleared of stones indicates that the vintner selected a new plot of land for his vineyard.[71] He did not assume control over an already cultivated vineyard; rather, he cleared old vegetation so that he could plant a new vineyard.[72] In addition, typically only the wealthy would have had the resources to build a מגדל, "tower," in a vine-

---

71. Eran Viezel ("A Note to ויעזקהו [Isaiah 5,2]," *ZAW* 123 [2011]: 604–7) investigated current cultivation practices among Israeli farmers to better understand the root עזק, a *hapax legomenon*. The root is attested in rabbinic texts with the sense of "to dig in the ground," and most modern translations of 5:2 rely on this sense of the root. Viezel found that since the soil in Israel is naturally dry and rocky, the process of preparing a plot of land for cultivation involves using a special tool to break up the ground and pull the rocks in the soil up to the surface, at which point the rocks can be removed from the field. The actions described in this line of the poem probably reflect a similar process.

72. Matthews ("Treading the Winepress," 25) misses the aspect of time compression in his claim that YHWH in the prophecy is performing the "reconstruction of previously built terraces since they had been used for centuries in the Judean hill country." A similar issue exists with his claim that the "fertile hill" (5:1) is the result of the work of previous farmers in preparing the land. The song looks backward to a distant past and claims that YHWH engaged in the initial cultivation of the land, preparing it for the Israelites.

yard. The tower would have served as lodging for the vineyard workers and guards and would have provided a cool place for storing fermenting wine.[73] The inclusion of a גת, "wine vat," is also noteworthy. Most Judahite villages shared the use of a common wine vat, rather than each family having their own.[74] Cumulatively, the image of the vineyard in the song is one of wealth and prestige, and it reinforces the claimed expectation by the vintner that the vineyard would produce large quantities of juice-filled grapes, because he built the structures needed to process that yield.

After flattering the audience with the description of the rich vineyard, the author then turns the tables and declares that while the vineyard began its life with all of the advantages that the vintner could provide, what it has produced is less than worthless. To the vintner's dismay, despite all his care in selecting the vines and cultivating the vineyard, the vines produce not עִנָבִים, "good grapes," but בְּאֻשִׁים, "stinking grapes" (5:2, 4).[75] Traditionally, the word בְּאֻשִׁים, a *hapax legomenon*, has been translated as wild grapes or unripe grapes.[76] Such translations, however, make little sense in terms of viticulture or semantics. Since vines are propagated via cuttings from proven vine stock, the grapes produced from such vines cannot be genetically flawed unless the vintner has mistakenly planted the wrong type of grapevine. Further, only an inexperienced or incompetent vintner would harvest grapes before

---

73. Matthews, "Treading the Winepress," 27. While early interpretations of the passage focused on the defensive aspect of towers, Marvin L. Chaney notes the archaeological findings suggesting that some of the towers were built in locations that would not make sense if they were for defense. Thus, they must have been for other purposes, such as providing a storage space for newly pressed wine, which needs relatively cool, stable temperatures during fermentation. That said, at harvest time, storing the processed wine in a tower in which the field hands also lived would itself have provided protection for the produce from the vineyard. See Chaney, "Whose Sour Grapes? The Addressees of Isaiah 5:1–7 in Light of the Political Economy," *Semeia* 87 (1999): 108–9.

74. Matthews, "Treading the Winepress," 27.

75. *DCH* interprets בְּאֻשִׁים as a plural *qal* passive participle of בָּאַשׁ, meaning "stinking (ones)" (*DCH* 2:88–89, s.v. "בָּאַשׁ").

76. Wild grapes are usually smaller and more sour than their domesticated cousins. Daniel Zohary and Maria Hopf, *Domestication of Plants in the Old World: The Origin and Spread of Cultivated Plants in West Asia, Europe, and the Nile Valley*, 3rd ed. (Oxford: Oxford University Press, 2000), 152–53; H. P. Olmo, "The Origin and Domestication of the *Vinifera* Grape," in McGovern, Fleming, and Katz, *Origins and Ancient History of Wine*, 33.

they are ripe. It is unlikely that the author would have portrayed YHWH as incompetent.[77]

Moreover, explanations of באשים as wild or unripe grapes fail to account for the meaning of its root, באש, "to stink."[78] Hebrew באשים probably refers to grapes that have been corrupted in a way that befouls their smell. The song tells us that YHWH planted שרק on good land in a well-tended vineyard, so the problem is neither inherent to the vine nor attributable to the vintner. Rather, the problem must have arisen from some outside influence.[79] The most likely culprit is some form of sour rot, a general term for a malady, caused by a variety of microorganisms, in which affected grapes begin to rot on the vine.[80] Sour rot may be hard to identify in its early stages, but it becomes much more noticeable near harvesttime.[81] As the disease progresses, the affected berries split or fall from the vine and produce the scent of vinegar.[82] Anyone who has participated in the harvesting of grapes knows what a feast for the eyes and the nose

---

77. Rejecting the "wild grapes" translation value on similar grounds, see John S. Kloppenborg Verbin, "Egyptian Viticultural Practices and the Citation of Isa 5:1–7 in Mark 12:1–9," *NovT* 44 (2002): 141–42.

78. Yael Avrahami explores the olfactory aspect of באשים, noting the human tendency to view negatively something that smells bad. She also highlights an interesting difference in scholarly approaches to interpreting באשים: "In sharp contrast with the commentators, all lexicographers, from Mandelkern through Clines, point to the obvious etymology of *be'ushim*, the Hebrew root באש, literally 'to carry bad smell,' and thus explain *be'ushim* as rotten grapes." Avrahami, "Foul Grapes: Figurative Smells and the Message of the Song of the Vineyard (Isa 5:1–7)," *VT* 67 (2017): 346–47. Wildberger (*Isaiah 1–12*, 182) also draws on the basic sense of the root to describe the grapes as "stinking, spoiled berries."

79. Contra Matthews ("Treading the Winepress," 28), who blames the vine for producing "unfit" produce.

80. Borowski (*Agriculture*, 160–161) argues instead that the grapes are afflicted with black rot, which affects grapes late in the growing season. The problem with this theory is that black rot is native to North America, not the Near East (Creasy and Creasy, *Grapes*, 200). Driver, on the other hand, proposed anthracnose, a fungal disease thought to be of European origin, as the affliction (see Wildberger, *Isaiah 1–12*, 182). Anthracnose, however, primarily affects grapevines in warm, rainy climates (Creasy and Creasy, *Grapes*, 200).

81. Megan Edina Pond Hall, "Sour Rot on Grapes: Understanding Etiology and Developing Management Strategies" (PhD diss., Cornell University, 2018).

82. André Barata et al., "Influence of Sour Rotten Grapes on the Chemical Composition and Quality of Grape Must and Wine," *European Food Research and Technology* 233 (2011): 183–94. The exact conditions under which sour rot will appear vary,

the grape clusters and juice are. To have that experience replaced with the sight of rotten grapes and the scent of vinegar helps explain the extreme disappointment and disgust expressed by the vintner in the poem. It would likely have produced a visceral reaction in the prophet's audience as well.[83]

At this point, the audience should understand that the vineyard is Judah, but they may not yet realize that they are the vines. In addition, an audience with some knowledge of באשים would probably know not to blame the vintner for the poor yield of his vineyard. If the kingdom has not experienced a recent outbreak of sour rot, they may be wondering where the song is going, since the prosperous vineyards of Judah have produced good grapes and fine wine for them. While the audience ponders how to respond to the vintner's call that they judge whether the vintner or the vineyard is in the wrong, the song proceeds in 5:5–6 with an announcement of doom for the vineyard. In effect, the punishment indicates that the produce of the land is so bad that it cannot be remedied. The vintner declares his intention of not just abandoning his vineyard, but of helping nature reclaim the land.[84]

Mapped to the target of Judah, the vintner's actions against the vineyard—removing its hedge and wall, ceasing efforts to tend the vines and keep the land on which they sit from growing weeds, and refusing to water it (5:5–6)—not only leave the nation unprotected from military invasion or internal unrest; they also indicate YHWH's intention to stop providing for his people. Removing the protective barriers around the vineyard would allow animals (and humans) to pass through the land and trample and consume the vines and fruit.[85] The terms בער, "to graze bare," and

---

though scholars have connected it to the depredations of insects, fungi, and excess moisture on the grapes.

83. The problem goes beyond appearance and smell, however. Juice yields from sour rotten grapes are significantly lower than normal due to the loss of juice from burst or fallen grapes. Moreover, significant quantities of rotten grapes in a wine (> 50 percent) would have negative effects on the wine's color and taste (Barata et al., "Influence of Sour Rotten Grapes," 183–94).

84. The content of the song, with its reference to the grapes and the vintner's expectations of good produce, indicates a harvesttime setting. Since grapevines do not produce edible fruit in their first few years of growth, this suggests that the vineyard has been in production for several years. Years-long anticipation of a good harvest is thus built into the emotion of the song (Matthews, "Treading the Winepress," 24).

85. Kaiser (Isaiah 1–12, 92) comments on the image of removing the hedge and wall as a metaphor for leaving the nation defenseless.

מרמס, "trampled," emphasize dangers to which destroying the vineyard's enclosure exposes the vineyard. The choice of בער expresses the total consumption of the vineyard via the CONQUEST IS EATING metaphor; מרמס similarly evokes the sense of animals trampling over the vines as they feed.[86] The imagery here is similar to that of Isa 3:13–15, which, as discussed above, presents the elders and leaders of Judah as animals grazing on the poor. Isaiah 5:5, however, implies that an invading army fills the ATTACKER role.[87]

Refusing to prune the vines and hoe the land (5:6) represent additional ways of leaving the vineyard undefended. As discussed in chapter 3, pruning removes unproductive branches to help focus the plant's energy on the productive branches. Hoeing serves a similar purpose, clearing away weeds that would take water (and nutrients) away from the vines.[88] In other words, not just animals, but also other plants will be allowed to attack the vineyard. One scene that is rarely mentioned in analyses of this poem is the significance of allowing שמיר ושית, "thorns and thistles," to grow in the vineyard.[89] This word pair is often identified as characteristic of First Isaiah, but considered more broadly, thorns and related plants also appear several times in the prophetic corpus, including in First Isaiah, as metaphors for troublesome people (Isa 9:17; 27:4; Ezek 28:24; Mic 7:4).[90] Thus, the growing of thorny plants in the abandoned vineyard may represent YHWH allowing troublesome people and groups to prosper in the land.[91]

---

86. Wildberger (*Isaiah 1–12*, 183) also highlights the intensity of the destruction implied by the use of בער instead of the more neutral term for grazing, רעה. He further notes that מרמס in the biblical text refers to ground or people trampled by cattle or enemies.

87. The two passages differ more significantly in mapping the victims of the attackers. The exploited poor map to grapes in Isa 3:13–15, but in Isa 5:1–7, the Judahites map to the vines, while their unjust actions are the grapes filled with sour juice.

88. Matthews, "Treading the Winepress," 25; Creasy and Creasy, *Grapes*, 131.

89. Michael Zohary suggests that the word pair שמיר ושית should be understood as expressing the general concept of "thorniness," rather than as a reference to two specific species of thorny plants. See Zohary, *Plants of the Bible* (Cambridge: Cambridge University Press, 1982), 153.

90. Blenkinsopp (*Isaiah 1–39*, 208) sees the references to שמיר ושית in First Isaiah as a "recurrent motif" that refers back to the song. On thorns and related plants as metaphors for troublesome people, see also ch. 8.

91. The biblical corpus also contains numerous examples of the image of a conquered territory as a place overgrown by weeds and other wild plants (Kaiser, *Isaiah 1–12*, 92).

Finally, withholding water means withholding a substance necessary to sustain the life of the plant.[92] It expresses YHWH's intention to cease all efforts to prosper the nation of Judah.[93] Notice, however, that with all the damage to his vineyard that the vintner makes possible, he does not himself pull out the vines that he has planted; his actions are limited to leaving the vineyard undefended and without provision. This concept of divine abandonment, including withholding provision and protection, is similar to that of other ancient Near Eastern cultures, in which misfortune is interpreted as abandonment by an angry deity.[94]

The content of 5:7 offers further support for the claim that the song does not hide the identities of the vintner and vineyard. Notice what the author does not say in this verse. He clearly describes the mappings for the vineyard's vines. He also indicates the identity of the באשים. He does *not* explain the vintner's identity but rather assumes that the audience already knows that the song's topic is כרם יהוה צבאות, "the vineyard of YHWH of Hosts," meaning that they will have already recognized YHWH as the vintner, and that they already conceptualize YHWH as having Judah as his vineyard. Yet the author does not simply redeploy a known metaphor about Judah. Rather, he broadens the identity of the vineyard by describing the vineyard as בית ישראל, "the house of Israel." Then, in the parallel line, he declares what YHWH has planted to be the איש יהודה, "men of Judah." The combination presents a conception of the vineyard as encompassing both Israel and Judah.[95]

---

92. Some scholars struggle with how to interpret the vintner's command that the clouds not rain on the vineyard, because a human vintner would not have the ability to make such a demand, and the juridical parable form requires that the author conceal the identity of the vintner. They therefore suggest that the author gives away the vintner's identity in this verse (e.g., Childs, *Isaiah*, 45; Wildberger, *Isaiah 1–12*, 171). Roberts (*First Isaiah*, 72), on the other hand, views the phrase as hyperbole.

93. Matthews ("Treading the Winepress," 23–24) likens the description of YHWH's withholding rain to a curse commonly invoked against oath breakers in ancient Near Eastern vassal treaties.

94. See Daniel I. Block, "Divine Abandonment: Ezekiel's Adaptation of an Ancient Near Eastern Motif," in *By the River Chebar: Historical, Literary, and Theological Studies in the Book of Ezekiel* (Cambridge: Clarke, 2014), 73–99.

95. Contra Chaney ("Whose Sour Grapes?," 115–16), who argues that the prophecy addresses and condemns only the elites of Judah and Israel, rather than the two nations as a whole. He claims that three key phrases carry specific technical senses in this passage: יושב ירושלם refers to the sitting ruler in Jerusalem, איש יהודה to Judah's

The identification of the vines and their grapes also requires explanation in the text, which may mean that the existing conceptualization of the land of Judah as a vineyard did not consistently or conventionally include mappings for the vines and fruit. The author therefore clarifies that the people represent the vines and that their actions have become like stinking, rotten fruit to YHWH. While they were producing their good grapes and fine wines in literal terms, in metaphorical terms, they were also producing the foul grapes of injustice and unrighteousness.[96] The song thus provides a different conceptualization of injustice than that of Isa 3:13–15. There, the prophet uses a metaphor of crushing grapes and taking the good wine as part of an accusation that Judah's leaders have oppressed the poor by stealing their wealth. Here, the prophet couches the accusation that the people have acted unjustly in terms of a metaphor in which the people are vines who have produced bad grapes.

Ultimately, the Song of the Vineyard constructs an identity for the nation of Judah complete with: (1) a national character defined as deriving from the same vine stock; (2) a shared history as a people chosen, established, and protected by YHWH; (3) a shared culture, defined by the requirement to obey YHWH and the present reality that the prosperity that Judah currently enjoys does not reflect the nation's standing with YHWH, whom they have disobeyed and disappointed; (4) a common fate as a nation in decline—abandoned by its angry god, who will no longer defend or provide for his people; and (5) a defined body of land that includes both historical Israel and present Judah.

Scholarly opinions about the date of the text range from the late eighth century BCE, early in Isaiah's career, to the period after the Assyrian campaign against Judah in 701 BCE.[97] While it is possible that the passage was composed *ex eventu*, the content and message of the song best fits the

---

military elite, and בית ישראל to the royal family in the Northern Kingdom of Israel. In his view, the poem predicts the destruction of elites, but does not address the fate of the rest of the populations of the two nations.

96. On the pairing and significance of משפט and צדקה in the biblical corpus, see Weinberger, *Isaiah 1–12*, 63.

97. Most scholars attribute the poem to First Isaiah. Those who argue for an early date in his career suggest that the misdirect regarding the identity of the vineyard would only have worked during a period before Isaiah's prophecies became well-known (e.g., Wildberger, *Isaiah 1–12*, 179). While Gray (*Isaiah*, 83–84, 87) implies that the poem was likely written after the fall of Samaria, he argues that the content of the text fits any period of Isaiah's career, making specific dating impossible. Kaiser

period between the fall of Samaria and the Assyrian destruction of Judah. The prophecies of First Isaiah, which are set in Jerusalem, frequently hold the threat of Assyrian conquest over the heads of their audience.[98] Isaiah 5:1–7 participates in this theme, though the text never explicitly mentions Assyria. The content of the song suggests that it was probably written after the destruction of the Northern Kingdom, at a point when Judah could conceptually lay claim to the name and territory of Israel, because the Northern Kingdom of Israel no longer existed, and because some portion of Israel's population had taken refuge in Judah. Isaiah 5:3 emphasizes this point by the audience that it addresses: יושב ירושלם and איש יהודה, "the residents of Jerusalem" and "the men of Judah." The separate identification of יושב ירושלם and איש יהודה may serve a greater purpose than simple parallelism.[99] It may also represent a merism intended to capture everyone living in Jerusalem who might logically be part of the nation conceptualized in the song, including both those born in Judah and those who have fled from Israel to Judah as refugees.

The description of the punishment also suggests that the Assyrian campaign of 701 BCE has not yet occurred. From the perspective of constructing a common fate for the nation, incorporating Israel into the nation's identity has the benefit of implying that the punishment has already begun, thereby emphasizing the immediacy of the threat. The fall of Israel proves that YHWH has already abandoned his people. The use of the participle in verse 5—ועתה אודיעה־נא אתכם את אשר־אני עשה לכרמי, "now let me tell you what I **am doing** to my vineyard"—serves to indicate that YHWH's action is both present and ongoing.[100] The verse then continues the present action with infinitive absolute forms to indicate the first two actions already under way: הסר משוכתו, "removing its hedge," and פרץ גדרו, "breaking down its wall." The hedge and wall map to divine protection, which YHWH withheld from Israel. The statement contains

---

(*Isaiah 1–12*, 93), on the other hand, views the passage as explaining the Assyrian invasion after the fact.

98. Peter Machinist, "Assyria and Its Image in the First Isaiah," *JAOS* 103 (1983): 719–37.

99. For a discussion of the word order of Jerusalem and Judah, see Wildberger, *Isaiah 1–12*, 3.

100. Most translations render את אשר־אני עשה as a simple statement of future action "what I will do" (e.g., JPS, KJV, RSV, WEB). Such an interpretation is both possible and plausible, but the solution offered here may fit better with the content of the song and its blending of the fates of Israel and Judah.

an implicit threat that YHWH has already decided to also withhold his protection from Judah.

By contrast, the verbs in 5:6 take the imperfect form, because they address not current actions, but denied or prohibited future actions. The first line of the verse describes the goal of YHWH's present and future inaction. YHWH says of the land, ואשיתהו בתה, "I will make it a waste." The remaining lines describe routine vineyard maintenance and support activities that YHWH intends to end. It will no longer be יזמר, "pruned," or יעדר, "hoed," and YHWH will אצוה מן, "prohibit," the clouds from raining upon it. These lines emphasize that YHWH's denial of protection is not a temporary or half measure, but a long-term and total abandonment of his people. As new threats arise, YHWH will allow them to take their course with no intervention on his people's behalf. In addition, he will withhold the blessings he has previously provided.

Finally, the threats that the song specifies as a result of YHWH's abandonment allow Judah's coming punishment to take a number of forms, from military invasion (mapped to grazing and trampling of animals; 5:5) to internal unrest (mapped to appearance of thorns and thistles; 5:6) to drought (mapped to the absence of rain; 5:6). In other words, according to the song, the punishment of Judah is inevitable, but the form of that punishment remains in doubt. Such a message would be more consistent with a prosperous Judah, rather than one that had already been devastated by the Assyrians. As such, the song probably was composed in the last ten to fifteen years of the eighth century BCE, long enough after the fall of Samaria for the reality of that nation's destruction to have become accepted, but before the Assyrian campaign in Judah in 701 BCE.

The song's depiction of total (or near total) destruction seems at odds with First Isaiah's notion elsewhere that Jerusalem will always be saved.[101] Such a reading, however, may misunderstand the purpose of 5:5–6. The author describes in detail YHWH's abandonment of his people and the threats to which this abandonment has exposed Israel and Judah, but aside from the general claim that the nation will be devastated, the song provides

---

101. Matthews ("Treading the Winepress," 28–29) suggests that the prophecy also carries the intent of future rebirth—that total destruction in ancient Near Eastern stories often foreshadows eventual recreation (without the problems that led to the destruction in the first place). In this case, that would mean a recreated Israel without a monarchy.

no information about the fate of specific towns or individuals.[102] One goal of the passage may have been to persuade the audience to question their self-assurance in their own current prosperity. The choice of metaphorical source frame and the content of the song seems designed to bring Judah's own vineyards to the forefront of the audience members' minds, giving emotional resonance to the threat of destruction contained in the song. The song builds on the awareness in the audience of the crucial role that vineyards and winemaking play in the kingdom's economy, thereby engaging with the audience's self-interest, as loss of their vineyards would mean loss of wealth and food security for them.

In addition, the author seeks to activate his audience's sense of participating in a national identity. By making the audience identify with YHWH's vineyard, the author seeks to deputize them as caretakers of that vineyard, of which only Judah remains. Attending to YHWH's requirements for social justice for the poor becomes an act of self-preservation, a way to avert, or at least limit, YHWH's wrath. In this context, a message of protection for Jerusalem would be counterproductive to the goals of the song, since it would diminish its threatening tone. Indeed, the author may have consciously omitted the theological issue of the inviolability of Jerusalem from the song by making no mention of destroying the structures that the vintner had built inside the vineyard (5:2). Including the tower and wine vat in 5:5–6 would probably have activated a mapping of these structures to Jerusalem. Ignoring the tower and wine vat, however, effectively hides the fate of Jerusalem as an issue in the message of the song. The concern is not the threat to Jerusalem; it is the threat to the nation, comprising the people of Judah and those Israelites who sought refuge in Judah after Assyria conquered Israel.

4.3. Conclusions: The Land of Judah as a Vineyard

The prophetic condemnations include only four clear national vineyard metaphors. A sample size that small makes it difficult to draw firm conclusions about the conceptualization of a nation as a vineyard. A few patterns do emerge from the data, however. First, these expressions seem to treat the vineyard as an indivisible unit: what happens to one, happens to all.

---

102. Matthews ("Treading the Winepress," 28) notes that the state of the vineyard, postdestruction, recalls that of cities abandoned by their deities in Mesopotamian city laments.

Second, three of the four vineyard metaphors specifically highlight the land on which the vineyard is planted (Isa 1:8; 5:1–7; Jer 12:10), an element not usually included in viticulture metaphors.[103] Indeed, two of them omit explicit mappings for people altogether and focus entirely on the land (Isa 1:8; Jer 12:10). Moreover, the land in question in these metaphors is not Israel, but Judah.[104] Vineyard metaphors appear only in texts attributed to Judahite prophets, and their primary concern is Jerusalem or Judah and their inhabitants.

Considering specifically the passages in First Isaiah, these patterns—the vineyard as a unit and the focus on the land and Judah—suggest that the metaphor of the land of Judah as a vineyard may have been relatively common in the late eighth century BCE, but the personification of that vineyard may not have been common. If personification of the vineyard followed its metaphorization, that would also explain how the riddle in Isa 5:1–7 manages to indicate the identities of the vintner and vineyard while hiding the identity of the vines: the audience would not have expected the vines to represent people. If the concept of a personified vineyard was a secondary development, that also means that the origin of the vineyard metaphors was not the conventional conceptual metaphor PEOPLE ARE PLANTS. Instead, the prevalence of vineyards in Judah likely inspired an initial experience-based, essentially visual, metaphor of the land of Judah as a vineyard. That a vineyard consists of a set of plants, however, made it easy to later incorporate mappings from PEOPLE ARE PLANTS (and more

---

103. The vine metaphor in Ezek 19:10 may also allude to an original conception of the land of Judah as a vineyard. The overall passage in 19:10–14 focuses on the fate of the national vine, but a vineyard, which essentially maps to the land of Judah, provides the setting for the beginning of the vine's story, prior to its transplantation to the desert. (See the case study and excursus in ch. 5 for a discussion of this passage.)

104. Howard N. Wallace has suggested that vineyard metaphors in the Bible represent a southern tradition, while vine metaphors derive from a northern tradition. Wallace does not explore his proposal in detail, however, nor does he address the connection of the vineyard metaphors specifically to the land of Judah. In addition, the evidence for the vine metaphor as a northern tradition is unclear, because vine metaphors appear in texts attributed both to Israelite and to Judahite prophets and in passages about both Israel and Judah. See Wallace, "Harvesting the Vineyard: The Development of Vineyard Imagery in the Hebrew Bible," in *Seeing Signals, Reading Signs: The Art of Exegesis; Studies in Honour of Antony F. Campbell, SJ, for His Seventieth Birthday*, ed. Mark A. O'Brien and Howard N. Wallace, JSOTSup 415 (London: T&T Clark, 2004), 127–28.

specifically, A GROUP OF PEOPLE IS A GROUP OF WOODY PLANTS) into the structure of the originally land-based metaphor.

The vineyard metaphors also share a similar approach to and perspective on the vineyard. The authors do not use the vineyard image to directly compare Judah to other kingdoms as vineyards in terms of their relative size or fruitfulness. Instead, the expressions tend to focus inward on events within the land of Judah, though conquest by other kingdoms is envisioned. In addition, all four express the basic viewpoint that the vineyard is good, or at least that it was good at one time, but that bad things have happened within it. The passages hold the Judahites or their leaders responsible for the evil that occurs within the vineyard, but a sympathetic image of the vineyard exists alongside this judgment in three of the four passages (Isa 1:8; 3:13–15; Jer 12:10), and the fourth passage presents the vineyard as having idyllic origins (Isa 5:1–7).

Finally, that three of the four vineyard metaphors reside in First Isaiah has implications for understanding the origins and development of the conceptualization of Judah, specifically, as a vineyard. As noted in the discussion of Isa 3:13–15 above, the description of Judah as הכרם in 3:14 suggests that the author drew on a preexisting conception of Judah as a vineyard. This finding presents a challenge for arguments that Isa 5:1–7 represents an early vineyard metaphor that attempts to deceive the audience about the identity of the vineyard by using an image unknown to the audience. It is not clear how the largely sympathetic perspectives on the vineyard of Judah in Isa 1:8 and 3:14 could have developed as extensions of a passage that thoroughly condemns that vineyard. More likely is that Isa 5:1–7 does not represent the origin of the very conceptualization of Judah as a vineyard, but rather that all three vineyard metaphors in First Isaiah adapt an already existing positive conception of Judah as a vineyard to suit their particular messages.[105] If so, then scholars should be especially care-

---

105. Jeremiah 12:7–13 plays with some of the same themes as Isa 5:1–7, leading some scholars to conclude that the Isaiah passage influenced Jeremiah (Blenkinsopp, *Isaiah 1–39*, 208). The themes in question, however—divine abandonment, the trampling of a vineyard or field by cattle, and Judah as YHWH's vineyard—all appear elsewhere in biblical or extrabiblical texts. In addition, Jeremiah expresses these themes differently than Isa 5:1–7. In Jer 12:7, YHWH abandons his house, not his vineyard. The cattle in Jer 12:10 trample the vineyard, but do not consume it; and the vineyard represents only the land, not the people. Jeremiah 12:7–13 also contains themes not present in Isa 5:1–7, such as the metaphor of people as wild animals. Thus, while Jer

ful to interpret these metaphors individually, rather than treating Isa 1:8 and 3:14 as potentially dependent on Isa 5:1–7.

Extrabiblical evidence may also support the idea that the metaphor of Judah as a vineyard existed as a positive image. In the 1950s, archaeologists working at Tel Ramat Raḥel, located south of Jerusalem, midway between that city and Bethlehem, uncovered evidence that a large royal administrative center or estate had existed at the site from the late eighth or early seventh century through the fourth century BCE.[106] Approximately two kilometers from the estate, at Beit Ṣafafa, archaeologists discovered a large wine press installation capable of processing far more wine than would be typical of a farm or village. Like the earliest construction at Ramat Raḥel, the winepress dates to the late eighth or early seventh century BCE.[107] The "relative rarity of farmsteads in the vicinity" during this period suggests that the territory surrounding Ramat Raḥel was devoted to vineyards owned by the king, the produce of which was processed in wine presses in the region, including the press found at Beit Ṣafafa.[108]

Most scholars now identify Ramat Raḥel with the biblical site of בית הכרם, "the House of the Vineyard."[109] The name appears only twice in the MT, with one additional potential reference in the LXX. A prophecy against Jerusalem in Jer 6:1 calls for a warning signal to be raised at בית הכרם. In order for such a signal to work, בית הכרם would have to be located on an elevated site so that people in the surrounding territory could see it. The

---

12:7–13 may have known Isa 5:1–7, the author's message does not appear to have been constrained by that knowledge.

106. While the eighth-century site was already impressive in its size and architectural details, in the second half of the seventh century, the original buildings were supplemented and transformed to create a lavish royal palace complex. Oded Lipschits et al., "Palace and Village, Paradise and Oblivion: Unraveling the Riddles of Ramat Raḥel," *NEA* 71.1 (2011): 2–49.

107. Feig, "Excavations at Beit Ṣafafa," 191–238.

108. Moyal and Faust, "Jerusalem's Hinterland," 293. The presence of the vineyards and the architectural features of the buildings lead Moyal and Faust to reject the description of the earliest occupation layer at Ramat Raḥel as an administrative center (293; and Lipschits et al., "Palace and Village," 19–20).

109. Lipschits et al., "Palace and Village," 4. The identification of Ramat Raḥel with בית הכרם was originally proposed by Aharoni, who conducted the first significant excavations at the site. For a summary of his assessment of the site, see Yohanan Aharoni, "Beth-haccherem," in *Archaeology and Old Testament Study: Jubilee Volume of the Society for Old Testament Study, 1917–1967*, ed. D. Winton Thomas (Oxford: Clarendon, 1967), 171–84.

installation at Ramat Raḥel sits on one of the highest peaks in southern Judah.[110] Nehemiah 3:14 indicates that בית הכרם became an administrative district in Judea in the postexilic era, which aligns with a period in which the center at Ramat Raḥel was still occupied. Finally, the LXX text of Josh 15:59, which is longer than the MT, includes the name Καρεμ (Karem) in reference to a location near Bethlehem.[111] The location of Ramat Raḥel on a high hill between Jerusalem and Bethlehem and the evidence that the site included an administrative center and a sizeable vineyard thus all comport with the biblical references to בית הכרם.

Two possibilities suggest themselves for the origin of the name בית הכרם. On the one hand, the site could have been named for its location and purpose as a royal vineyard.[112] Since the wine press at Beit Ṣafafa dates to the late eighth or early seventh centuries BCE, the name would probably also date to that time period. From that beginning, the Judahites could have extended the conception metaphorically to represent the land of Judah as a whole, based on the analogy that if the king represents the people, then his estate represents the land. A more likely explanation, however, is that a preexisting metaphor of Judah as a vineyard inspired the name of the palace.[113] Unfortunately, insufficient evidence exists to prove

---

110. Lipschits et al., "Palace and Village," 2–4.

111. Lipschits et al., "Palace and Village," 3–4. Alt's 1925 proposal that the list of towns in Josh 15:20–63 represents a set of Judahite administrative districts started a long debate over the nature and date of this district system. If the basic theory is sound, however, then Karem in the LXX may refer to the administrative center at Ramat Raḥel. Albrecht Alt, "Judas Gaue unter Josia," *PJ* 21 (1925): 100–116.

112. Oded Lipschits and Nadav Na'aman, "From 'Baal-Perazim' to 'Beth-Haccerem': Further Thoughts on the Ancient Name of Ramat Raḥel," *Beit Mikra* 51 (2011): 65–86 [Hebrew]. Both biblical and extrabiblical texts attest to the practice of referring to palaces using names that reflect the buildings' features or uses, rather than their locations. In a prophecy against the kingdom of Israel in Amos, YHWH declares his intention of striking בית־החרף, "the House of the Winter," and בית הקיץ, "the House of the Summer" (Amos 3:15), perhaps referring to the Israelite kings' palaces at Samaria and in Jezreel. See Francis I. Andersen and David Noel Freedman, *Amos: A New Translation with Introduction and Commentary*, AB 24A (New York: Doubleday, 1989), 411. In addition, Jer 36:22 describes the Judahite king, Jehoiakim, in residence in his בית־החרף during the winter season. The idea of the king or other elites having both summer and winter homes also appears in texts from Phoenicia, Babylonia, and Persia. See Shalom M. Paul, "Amos 3:15—Winter and Summer Mansions," *VT* 28 (1978): 358–60.

113. The biblical corpus also contains evidence of giving fanciful names to significant buildings. The palace in Jerusalem provides the clearest example. Descriptions

either of these options. Material in First Isaiah suggests that the conceptualization of Judah as a vineyard already existed at the time that passages such as Isa 3:13–15 and 5:1–7 were composed, but the uncertainty in the dating of both of those passages and the construction of the site at Ramat Raḥel makes it impossible to know which came first.

Even if a preexisting metaphor of Judah as a vineyard did inspire the name בית הכרם, that does not preclude the possibility that the construction of בית הכרם also helped inspire the creation of the specific vineyard metaphors in First Isaiah. After all, Isa 5:8–10 does express antipathy toward the owners of large vineyards, and Isa 3:13–15 takes Judah's leaders to task for consuming the vineyard by oppressing the poor. The decadence of a celebrated royal estate named בית הכרם may have generated prophetic ire about social injustice perpetrated by Judahite elites, and it would have given new resonance to the image of Judah as a vineyard. Righteous anger about Ramat Raḥel would also explain why First Isaiah includes three vineyard metaphors but otherwise shows little interest in using viticultural imagery to represent Judah.[114] The number of vineyard metaphors in First Isaiah compared to the other prophetic texts attests to the salience and vitality of that metaphor for First Isaiah's audience. At the same time, the only other viticulture metaphors in First Isaiah relate to foreign kingdoms (Moab in Isa 16:8–10 and Egypt in Isa 18:5–6). This pattern suggests that viticulture metaphors had not yet become commonplace in the late eighth century BCE. A century and more later, however, Jeremiah and Ezekiel both make extensive use of viticultural imagery, but they do so from the perspective of an already conventionalized association of Judah with vines and vineyards that more closely resembles other plant metaphors in the prophetic corpus.

---

of its construction and contents include the moniker בית יער הלבנון, "the House of the Forest of Lebanon" (1 Kgs 7:2; 10:17, 21; 2 Chr 9:16, 20), and a prophecy against Judah in First Isaiah mentions בית היער, "the House of the Forest" (Isa 22:8). The name likely derives from the cedar columns and beams that supported the structure (1 Kgs 7:1–12). See Mordechai Cogan, *1 Kings: A New Translation with Introduction and Commentary*, AB 10 (New York: Doubleday, 2001), 254.

114. More speculative still is the possibility that, if First Isaiah's vineyard metaphors do constitute a critique of the estate at Ramat Raḥel, then Isa 5:1–7, and in particular verses 1b–2, may have been inspired by a secular song about the king and his new vineyard. Wyatt ("Jedidiah," 115–16) goes so far as to suggest that the vintner in the song is the Judahite king, but he bases his claim on the association of the term ידיד with royal ideology.

5

Grapevine Metaphors

Compared to כרם, for which only 15 percent of the uses of the term are metaphorical, the metaphorical use of גפן, "vine," is both more widespread and more diverse.[1] Of the forty-three passages employing the word גפן, fifteen (35 percent) are metaphorical.[2] In general, vineyards appear to have been used more symbolically—as representing or exemplifying prosperity or a settled life—than metaphorically, while vines more often appear in metaphor, perhaps because they are easier to personify. The prophetic corpus contains nine clear vine metaphors, of which two are excluded from this study. The simile in Hos 14:6–8 appears in a restoration prophecy, and the vine metaphor in Ezek 17:5–10 maps to an individual.[3] The remaining seven vine metaphors are structured using the conceptual metaphors A CITY/KINGDOM IS A VINE or A NATION IS A VINE. Of these, two refer to Moab (Isa 16:8–10; Jer 48:32–33) and five to Israel or Judah (Jer 2:21; 6:9; Ezek 15; 19:10–14; and Hos 10:1–2).[4]

---

1. While גפן may refer to any vine or climbing plant, most biblical instances of this noun are references to grapevines.

2. This count excludes the dream report in Gen 40:1–15 and the fable in Judg 9:8–15. These passages include figurative uses of vine imagery, but the differences in genre and intent make them inappropriate comparators for the prophetic metaphors discussed here.

3. Among the nonprophetic vine metaphors, three describe an individual as a vine (Ps 128:3; Job 15:33; Song 7:9), and two apply the vine image to a city, kingdom, or nation (Deut 32:32–33; Ps 80:9–17).

4. Jeremiah 48:32–33 may represent a reworking of Isa 16:8–10, and as such, these two passages could be considered a single instance of a vine metaphor. The differences between the two texts, however, are significant enough to be attributed to authorship or editing, rather than scribal error or inverted citation. Therefore, each author's decision to use the metaphor is treated as a separate instance.

The prophetic condemnations that employ vine metaphors to represent Israel and Judah show little of the sympathy that appears in the
prophetic vineyard metaphors. Only the kingdom vine in the Moab prophecies (Isa 16:8–10; Jer 48:32–33) receives the prophetic authors' lament. As
with vineyard metaphors, the variety of expressions and mappings indicates that a general conception existed of a national or kingdom vine that
allowed some creativity in the expression of the metaphor. Most vine metaphors focus on a small set of the plant's features and environment. They
address the vine's height, its branches or fruit, or its access to water. One
mapping that is more explicitly expressed in the prophetic vine metaphors
than in other plant metaphors relates to the way that plants appear to grow
toward light and water.[5] Observing this phenomenon may have inspired
the mapping that depicts loyalty as a vine's direction of growth.

In addition, several vine metaphors employ the mapping, discussed
in chapter 3, that associates the length of a vine's branches with power or
prestige. In three passages, an image of a vine's branches growing as far as
the sea maps to a kingdom's participation in international commerce as an
expression of the kingdom's prestige.[6] This mapping appears in both of the
metaphors about Moab (Isa 16:8; Jer 48:32). Outside the prophetic corpus,
Ps 80:9–17 also uses it in verse 12 in its depiction of Israel as a vine: תשלח
קציריה עד־ים ואל־נהר יונקותיה, "She sent out her branches to [the] sea, to
[the] river her shoots."

Not only are there more vine metaphors than vineyard metaphors, in
the prophetic corpus there are also more national identity vine metaphors.
Four of the five prophetic condemnations of Israel and Judah that use the

---

5. Like many plants, grapevines can turn their leaves to catch more or less sunlight, depending on the vine's needs. In addition, vine tendrils tend to grow away from
the light and toward objects around which they can wrap themselves. The vine's roots,
on the other hand, do not technically grow toward water. The roots will grow downward into the earth and outward from the twig or cutting from which it was planted.
As they grow, if the vine's roots find water or nutrients, the vine will produce larger
numbers of roots in that location in order to take advantage of the resources (Creasy
and Creasy, *Grapes*, 18, 23, 34–35). Both the leaf and root activity give the vine the
appearance of growing in a particular direction in response to the stimuli of light or
water. (See Ezek 17:5–10 for imagery that takes advantage of these plant behaviors.)

6. As noted earlier, the image likely derives from the fact that wine was usually
transported by river or sea, because the expense and risk of shipping wine by land
outweighed the potential for profit. See Powell, "Wine and the Vine in Ancient Mesopotamia," 97–122.

image of a national vine construct a national identity for their target kingdom within the metaphor: Hos 10:1–2; Jer 2:21; Ezek 15; and 19:10–14.[7]
The discussion that follows presents these passages in chronological order,
with Ezek 19:10–14 receiving a more detailed analysis as a case study of
the most complex of the vine-based national identity metaphors.

5.1. National Condemnation Vine Metaphors

Probably the earliest of these passages resides in Hos 10:1–8, which relates
to the situation in the Northern Kingdom of Israel in the eighth century
BCE, in the final decade of the kingdom's existence.[8] The presence of
uncommon terms and phrases in 10:1–2 hinders the metaphor's interpretation, but its basic message is still fairly clear. The author maps fruitfulness
to prosperity to argue that the Israelites have incorrectly attributed their
past prosperity to their cultic practices:[9]

גפן בוקק ישראל פרי ישוה־לו כרב לפריו הרבה למזבחות כטוב לארצו
היטיבו מצבות: חלק לבם עתה יאשמו הוא יערף מזבחותם ישדד מצבותם:

[1] A prolific vine is Israel.[10] [His] fruit he makes like him. When his
fruit has had abundance, he has given abundantly to the altars.[11]

---

7. The fifth vine metaphor, in Jer 6:9, is a simple expression of collective condemnation (see discussion in ch. 3).

8. Hans Walter Wolff relates the passage to the events surrounding Hoshea's
assumption of the throne in Israel, ca. 730 BCE. See Wolff, *Hosea: A Commentary on
the Book of the Prophet Hosea*, Hermeneia (Philadelphia: Fortress, 1974), 173. Cornelis
van Leeuwen, on the other hand, places it near the end of Hoshea's reign, ca. 724 BCE.
See his "Meaning and Structure of Hosea X 1–8," *VT* 53 (2003): 367–68.

9. The connection between cultic observance and fruitfulness is a common theme
in Hosea. See James Luther Mays, *Hosea: A Commentary*, OTL (Philadelphia: Westminster, 1969), 139.

10. Following the translation of בוקק offered by Göran Eidevall, *Grapes in the
Desert: Metaphors, Models, and Themes in Hosea 4–14*, ConBOT 43 (Stockholm:
Almqvist & Wiksell, 1996), 156.

11. Lit. "he increased/multiplied for the altars." The translation here treats הרבה
למזבחות as a rough semantic parallel to the following phrase, היטיבו מצבות. In both
cases, the author intends to convey that as Israel prospered, their offerings increased.
This approach contrasts with analyses of this metaphor that view the altars as multi-
plying, e.g., A. A. Macintosh, *A Critical and Exegetical Commentary on Hosea*, ICC
(Edinburgh: T&T Clark, 1997), 385; Eidevall, *Grapes in the Desert*, 156; and Van Leeuwen, "Meaning and Structure," 371.

When his land has had prosperity, they have prospered cult pillars.
[2] Their heart has been false [lit. smooth].[12] Now they will know
their guilt. He will topple[13] their altars, destroy their cult pillars.

The metaphor and its explanation end with 10:2, as the rest of the unit
focuses on events in Israel in more literal terms.

The most significant challenge to interpreting 10:1 lies in determining
the meaning of בוקק. A review of the biblical evidence would suggest that
בוקק carries a negative connotation. Excluding this verse, the root בקק
appears in six verses in the biblical corpus: three *qal*, two *niphal*, and one
poel. In the *qal* and *poel* forms, it carries the sense of "to lay waste," while
the *niphal* carries a passive sense, "to be laid waste."[14] In addition, a potentially related hollow root, בוק, attested in two nominal forms in Nah 2:11,
also refers to "desolation," perhaps deriving from a basic root meaning of
"emptiness."[15] Yet if בוקק in Hos 10:1 represents a *qal* participle, then it
should carry an active, not passive, sense, like the other attested *qal* forms
of בקק: that is, "a ravaging vine is Israel." At first glance, such a translation
does not seem to fit the context of the rest of the verse, which focuses on
what happens to the vine, not what the vine does.[16]

---

12. The phrase חלק לבם probably reflects an idiom that associates smoothness
with falsity. A similar use of חלק with פה occurs in Ps 55:22 in reference to deceptive
speech.

13. Lit. "break the neck of" (*HALOT*, s.v. "ערף II"). Noting Wolff's claim that ערף
appears primarily in nonsacrificial contexts, Eidevall (*Grapes in the Desert*, 156) highlights the ironic reversal of fortune in the use of ערף in this expression, as the altars,
once the site of animal sacrifices, themselves are treated as (nonsacrificial) animals by
having their "necks" broken.

14. *HALOT*, s.v. "בקק I."

15. *HALOT*, s.v. "בוק." Some Hebrew verbs appear to have originated from a two-
letter root combined with more than one weak root letter: "Thus to express the verbal
notion *to lay snares* Hebrew has augmented the stable core קש with an initial weak
element, either י or נ, to give יקש and נקש" (Joüon, §84a, 215). Joüon and Muraoka
note that some cases of ע"ו and ע"ע verbs that are not well attested in the biblical text
present particular challenges to determining whether the forms represent two roots or
a single root with varying weak consonants (§84a, 215).

16. To resolve the issue of בוקק's meaning, Macintosh (*Hosea*, 383–84, 386) posits
that בקק and בוק are by-forms, and that בוק/בקק can carry both transitive "to cause
damage" and intransitive "to show damage" senses. To arrive at this conclusion, however, he appears to have conflated the *qal* and *polel* forms, leading him to support his
claim for the causative sense of the *qal* participle בקקים in Neh 2:3 by citing the caus-

Given the difficulties of translating בוקק according to the attested
senses of בקק in the biblical corpus, most modern treatments of the passage view בוקק as deriving from a second בקק root and carrying a sense
otherwise not attested in the biblical corpus. Following the LXX, Peshitta,
and Vulgate, they translate בוקק as a *qal* participle that describes the vine
as luxuriant or fruitful. Justification for this translation rests on a cognate
verb in Arabic: *baqqa*, meaning "to be (cause to be) plentiful."[17] This study
adopts a similar approach in its translation of 10:1. Reflecting historical
experience of prosperity for Israel, the metaphor describes the nation's
history of cultic practice from some point in the past up to the present
day, and it foreshadows doom in its reference, in 10:2, to Israel coming to
"know their guilt."

That said, given the multivalence of metaphor, it may be that the
author plays with the dual meanings of בקק in 10:1. The biblical evidence
suggests that the root may have carried a specific technical sense when
used in reference to woody plants.[18] Relevant to this question is the use of
בקק in Nah 2:3b, which describes the destruction of Israel via a metaphor of the nation as a woody plant, possibly even a vine: כי בקקום בקקים
וזמריהם שחתו, "for ravagers have ravaged them, and their cut branches
they have destroyed." The term זמורה appears four times in the biblical
corpus, in each case apparently referring to a branch or shoot cut from a
woody plant (Isa 17:10; Ezek 8:17; 15:2; Nah 2:2). That זמורה derives from
זמר, "to prune," leaves open the possibility that the woody plant in the passage is a vine, because vines were routinely pruned.[19]

---

ative sense of *polel* קומם (< קום). He similarly argues for the intransitive sense of *qal*
participle בוקק in Hos 10:1 by citing a similar sense for the *polel* perfect שובב (< שוב).

17. *DCH* 2:250, s.v. "בקק II"; *HALOT*, s.v. "בקק II." Among those who translate
the phrase as referring to a flourishing vine are William Rainey Harper, *A Critical
and Exegetical Commentary on Amos and Hosea*, ICC (New York: Scribner, 1905),
343; Eidevall, *Grapes in the Desert*, 156; Mays, *Hosea*, 137; Van Leeuwen, "Meaning
and Structure," 370; and Wolff, *Hosea*, 170. Andersen and Freedman take the unusual
approach of interpreting בוקק as a *polel* perfect with YHWH as the subject and Israel
the object: "He made Israel, the vine, luxuriant." See Francis I. Andersen and David
Noel Freedman, *Hosea: A New Translation with Introduction and Commentary*, AB 24
(New York: Doubleday, 1980), 547, 549–50.

18. So also Macintosh, *Hosea*, 383.

19. See further the discussion of vine pruning in ch. 3. The content of Nah 2:3b
may therefore contradict the claim by Andersen and Freedman (*Hosea*, 549) that בקק
"can describe a land laid waste, but never a vine."

Yet the term is not restricted to vine cuttings; זמורה apparently also refers to other types of woody-plant cuttings (Ezek 15:2). The connection of זמורה and בקק in Neh 2:3b suggests that בקק may relate to removing branches from a tree, perhaps as one of the steps in converting a tree into lumber for construction or woodworking, though the details offered in the verse provide insufficient information to determine with certainty the precise nature of action taken against the plant. Nevertheless, in the context of Hos 10:1–2, the double meaning of בקק would convey both that the vine is presently proliferating itself through its cultic observance and, in combination with the threat implicit in 10:2, that those same actions will also result in Israel destroying itself: גפן בוקק ישראל פרי ישוה־לו, "Israel is a flourishing/ravaging vine. [His] fruit he makes like him."

In terms of the structure of the vine metaphor in this passage, 10:1 maps elements from the VINE frame outward from the vine: upward to its fruit and downward to its land. The vine itself maps to the nation, while the fruit probably refers to children or descendants, though it may instead provide a semantic parallel to the prosperity of the land and thereby refer to the prosperity of the nation in more general terms.[20] The author here claims that up to now, the Israelites have responded to population growth and to bountiful growing seasons by increasing their offerings at the altars and cult pillars in the land. Some scholars argue that the altars and pillars were dedicated to YHWH worship. The critique in this case would derive from the manner in which the Israelites practiced the cult, rather than the deity served.[21] Others suggest that the issue is worship of deities other than YHWH.[22] In either case, the reference in 10:2 to the people having a "false heart" indicates that the author intends in this passage to condemn the practices of the Israelites. The nation's foreshadowed punishment will

---

20. Wallace ("Harvesting the Vineyard," 118) sees the fruit as "the blessings on the nations which become a snare for them." Van Leeuwen ("Meaning and Structure," 370) takes a similar stance in arguing that the fruit refers to Israel's prosperity. Macintosh (*Hosea*, 383, 388) translates 10:1a as "Israel is a damaged vine whose fruit fails him," and on that basis argues that the fruit represents the altars and pillars that the Israelites created during prosperous times. These proposals are plausible within the context of each scholar's theory of the text, but the reference in 10:1a to the vine making fruit like itself seems to speak more of proliferation of the nation than of general prosperity or the fate of the cult sites.

21. Mays, *Hosea*, 139; Wolff, *Hosea*, 173–74.

22. Andersen and Freedman, *Hosea*, 552; Macintosh, *Hosea*, 388; Van Leeuwen, "Meaning and Structure," 371.

occur in order to teach the people the error of their ways. The destroyer of the altars and cult pillars at the end of 10:2 is not clear, though the most likely referents are Israel or YHWH.[23]

Taken together, these two verses construct a fairly detailed national identity for Israel. While the author has not provided an account of the nation's origins, the passage does offer a sense of national history by distinguishing between past and future, with the present state standing as a turning point in the nation's history. Then, the people prospered and wrongly attributed that prosperity to their cultic observance. Soon, the vine will no longer prosper, and the people will recognize that their destruction is the consequence of their prior cultic practices. In fleshing out the national identity, the author constructs a national body in 10:1 by connecting the people and the land via the description of the land as ארצו, "his land," with the pronoun referring both to Israel and, by association, to its metaphorical representation as a vine. The author also constructs a national culture by attributing to the people a common set of cultic practices. By reinterpreting those practices as responsible for the nation's destruction, rather than its prosperity, the author calls for a transformation of the nation's culture, presumably in the hope of yielding a better long-term common fate than the punishment imminently expected for the nation.

Whereas in Hos 10:1–2 the author directly condemns the cultic practices of the Israelites, the author of the second national identity vine metaphor, in Jer 2:21, instead uses direction of growth to metaphorically express the concept of apostasy:[24]

ואנכי נטעתיך שרק כלה זרע אמת ואיך נהפכת לי סורי הגפן נכריה:

I planted you as *śoreq*, the whole of it true stock [lit. seed]. So how have you been changed into a deviant, an alien vine?

---

23. Andersen and Freedman (*Hosea*, 553) prefer the latter option, as do Mays (*Hosea*, 139), Van Leeuwen ("Meaning and Structure," 371), and Wolff (*Hosea*, 174). Macintosh (*Hosea*, 388–90) argues instead that the pronoun הוא in 10:2 refers to the Israelites' hearts, which will cause them to destroy their own altars and pillars.

24. The content of this verse and the surrounding context do not provide sufficient detail to assign it to a specific historical setting, but there is no reason to think that the verse represents a later insertion into the text. Thus, it most likely dates to the late seventh century BCE (Lundbom, *Jeremiah 1–20*, 278–79).

The first phrase in this verse is relatively straightforward. YHWH is the speaker and the vintner, and as in Isa 5:1–7, שרק refers to a high-quality variety of grapes that were grown in Judah. The second half of the verse makes clear that YHWH is speaking to the vine—as opposed to the land or the grapes—and that the mention of *śoreq* in the first half is not a vocative noun, but rather describes the vine's origins. The first phrase should therefore be translated from that perspective.[25] The phrase ואנכי נטעתיך שרק, "I planted you as *śoreq*," asserts YHWH's specific intent to plant a *śoreq*-vine right from the beginning.

The following phrase reinforces that message by confirming that the twig or cutting that YHWH planted was זרע אמת, "true stock," meaning that it came from a proven *śoreq*-vine.[26] YHWH's action in selecting and planting a particular variety of grape, rather than planting an unspecified type of vine, constructs a national origins account and a national character by mapping that image to the idea that YHWH chose Judah's ancestors from among the peoples of the world and established them in their homeland. The implication in the choice of *śoreq* is that other peoples may map either to *śoreq* or to other types of grapes. As such, being *śoreq* unifies the Judahites as a homogeneous people, but it may not necessarily distinguish

---

25. A translation of "I planted you with *śoreq*" would suggest that YHWH is addressing the land, which conflicts with the address to the vine in the second half of the verse. "I planted you, O *Śoreq*" is also not a viable translation, because then the pronoun on כלה should be in the second person—"all of you"—not third.

26. The phrase זרע אמת, "true seed," seems to conflict with the practical reality that grapevines are not grown from seeds, but from twigs or cuttings taken from proven grapevines of the variety that the vintner wishes to grow (Walsh, *Fruit of the Vine*, 100–101). Walsh argues that Biblical Hebrew includes two main roots for planting—זרע, "to sow (seeds)," and נטע, "to plant (shoots or twigs)"—and that Jeremiah's use of נטע in this verse indicates his knowledge of proper viticultural practice. She therefore concludes that זרע refers to the vine stock, rather than to literal seeds (103). While Walsh reaches a reasonable conclusion about the meaning of זרע in Jer 2:21, her claim about the uses of זרע and נטע goes too far. E.g., Isa 17:10 describes sowing (זרע) a woody-plant cutting (זמורה) in a line that serves as a semantic parallel to planting (נטע) a plant (נטע). Better support for the conclusion that זרע refers to the vine stock comes from the idiomatic use of זרע to refer to a bloodline or to identify the true members of a particular group, which is well-attested in the biblical corpus (e.g., Gen 3:15; Lev 21:21; 1 Kgs 11:14; Isa 41:8; Jer 7:15; Ps 105:6; Ezra 9:2; Neh 9:2). It may be that the author intentionally employed this bloodline idiom to create a closer connection between the metaphorical image of the vine and its target, the Judahites and their ancestors.

Judah from all other peoples. The concept of a national body also appears in this verse through the planting of the vine.

The second half of 2:21 presents a greater interpretive challenge, as the text appears to have become corrupted during transmission. The phrase סוּרֵי הַגֶּפֶן נָכְרִיָּה is grammatically incoherent. By itself, the construct phrase in the first two words could be translated as "those who turn from the vine," but נכריה disagrees in number with סורי, and in definiteness with הגפן, and therefore cannot modify the phrase as either a predicative or an attributive adjective. The disagreements in number and definiteness also weigh against viewing נכריה as standing in apposition to סורי הגפן. Most scholars now accept the emendation of these lines offered by Bernhard Duhm and Wilhelm Rudolph: וְאֵיךְ נֶהְפַּכְתְּ לְסוּרִיָּה גֶּפֶן נָכְרִיָּה.[27] The new text is achieved primarily through changes in the word division and vocalization. The resulting expression divides cleanly into two phrases: (1) ואיך נהפכת לסוריה, "so how have you been changed into a סוריה"; and, in apposition to סוריה, (2) גפן נכריה, "an alien [i.e., foreign] vine?"

The proposed emendation creates a new problem, however, of how to understand the *hapax legomenon* form סוריה. Two possibilities present themselves as the root for סוריה: סור and סרי. The root סור, "to turn aside," is often used theologically in the sense of turning away from YHWH.[28] Thus, the use of סור would be consistent with Jeremiah's concern with apostasy in the surrounding material (2:20, 23–25). The author may have created a new word to suit his purposes, converting the passive participle of סור into a relational adjective, used as a noun, to express the idea of a turned-aside people: סוּרִיָּה. Granted, the author in this case could simply have used the passive participle of סור, because it conveys a meaning similar to that of the relational adjective, but converting the form creates a closer parallel, in both sound and meaning, with נכריה and more clearly expresses the idea that the term describes a people.[29] An advantage of this solution to

---

27. Holladay, *Jeremiah 1*, 53; Lundbom, *Jeremiah 1–20*, 277–78; and McKane, *Jeremiah*, 42.

28. See, e.g., Exod 32:8; Deut 11:16; 1 Sam 12:20; Jer 5:23; 17:5; 32:40; and Hos 7:14.

29. Jeremiah contains numerous examples of the use of repetition of words and sounds for rhetorical effect (Lundbom, *Jeremiah 1–20*, 122–26). See also the examples of rhyme based on repetition of pronominal suffixes in Jer 9:16–20 and 12:7 in Luis Alonso Schökel, *A Manual of Hebrew Poetics*, SubBi 11 (Rome: Pontifical Biblical Institute, 2000), 24. Watson also comments briefly on the "use of rare or invented words" to create rhyme in poetic lines, citing examples from Isa 22:5 and 30:1. See Wilfred G. E. Watson, *Classical Hebrew Poetry: A Guide to Its Techniques*, 2nd ed.,

the problem of Jer 2:21b is that it acknowledges that the MT has been corrupted, but it credits the tradition with accurately preserving, despite that corruption, both the sense and sound of סור.

The other possible root, סרי, is not attested in the biblical corpus, but it may have existed as a by-form of סור. By-forms of meaning similar to סור exist in Hebrew and Aramaic in the roots סטי/סוט/שטי/שוט, "to deviate; to turn to or away." If the word derives from סרי as a by-form of סור, then the feminine singular active participle would take the form סוֹרִיָּה. The problem with this theory is that סרי is only found in Aramaic with the meaning "to decay, be spoiled."[30] Thus, neither Hebrew nor Aramaic attests to a root סרי that means "to turn aside." In fact, the targum to Jer 2:21 renders סוריה using the root סטי. The evidence from the targum thus suggests that its author interpreted סוריה in Jer 2:21 as having סור's sense of "to turn aside," but that he could not use the same root to translate the passage.

Given that סרי is nowhere attested with the sense of "to turn aside," the more likely solution to the problem of סוריה is that it represents a creative form of the passive participle of סור. Internal to the metaphor, סוריה may draw on plant behavior—that they can turn themselves toward or away from sunlight—as a way of describing Judah's worship of other gods.

JSOTSup 26 (Sheffield: JSOT Press, 1986), 233. On the passive participle for hollow verbs like סור, see Joüon, §80d, 197. Relational adjectives, including gentilic and patronymic adjectives, are formed by adding a sufformative ־ִי to another word. See Joshua Blau, *Phonology and Morphology of Biblical Hebrew: An Introduction*, LSAWS 2 (Winona Lake, IN: Eisenbrauns, 2010), §4.4.6.8, 276. (Such forms are also known by the Arabic name *nisba* or *nisbe*.) For further discussion of the adjectival sufformative ־ִי form, see Joüon, 88Mg, 242.

30. In accepting the Aramaic root, סרי, Holladay (*Jeremiah 1*, 53) notes specifically that it appeals to him as "a synonym for Isaiah's word בְּאֻשִׁים." He cites, without clear explanation, the LXX translation πῶς ἐστράφης εἰς πικρίαν "how did you turn to bitterness" (NETS) as evidence for this interpretation of סוריה, and he further supports this theory by noting that the Syriac and targumim elsewhere use סרי to translate Hebrew באש (53). Two points weigh against this proposed solution. First, the Greek πικρία does not appear to serve as a translation value for Hebrew באש in the LXX. It most often represents Hebrew words from the root מרר, "to be bitter," but it also appears as a translation value for זעם, "cursed" (Jer 15:17), and apparently also for שאון, "noise, roar" (Isa 37:29). In other words, nothing in the LXX connects the senses of πικρία to the senses of Aramaic סרי. Second, while the targumim may use סרי to translate Hebrew באש in some passages, the targum to Jer 2:21 renders the translation using an Aramaic root with a meaning similar to that of Hebrew סור, not באש: סטי, "to deviate, turn to or from" (Jastrow, s.v. "סטי").

That the national vine of Judah did not turn toward YHWH, but away from him, is its flaw. A similar conception of direction of growth indicating loyalty also appears in the vine metaphor of Ezek 17:5–10, which maps Judah's king to a vine that was planted by Babylonia, but that grows toward Egypt.

The brevity of the metaphor in this passage has led some interpreters to supplement its message with details from Isa 5:1–7.[31] This approach is methodologically unsound, in that it may attribute messages to the passage that the author probably did not intend. For example, unlike Isa 5:1–7, Jer 2:21 makes no reference to fruit or produce, so this is not a case of spoiled grapes.[32] Nor is it a case of vines producing low-quality fruit.[33] Rather, the vine itself seems to have developed in a way that is contrary to YHWH's plans.[34] To Jeremiah, the corruption resides in the vine itself, in the very family line of Judah. The national vine grew up wrong. Their

---

31. In some cases, the supplementation may simply reflect the exegete's attempt at elevated prose, employing the language of viticulture to cleverly summarize a conclusion made about the passage. As such, the exegete may not realize that adopting the prophetic author's imagery has had the counterproductive effect of obscuring, or even altering, the prophetic author's message. The analysis and explication of a metaphor may therefore be better served if the exegete avoids employing in the analysis the same source frames that govern the image, thereby allowing the image to remain the exclusive property of the metaphor's creator.

32. Contra Holladay (*Jeremiah 1*, 98–99), who argues that Jer 2:21 summarizes Isa 5:1–7, and as such, סוריה must refer to grapes and must carry a sense similar to באשים. If the author's intent was to summarize Isa 5:1–7, however, why not simply use באש? Jindo (*Biblical Metaphor Reconsidered*, 185) instead claims that Jer 2:21–22 reverses the blessing to Judah in Gen 49:11, but he still supplements the message of Jer 2:21 with that of Isa 5:1–7: "This ironic twist expresses the divine frustration at the 'choicest grape,' expected to be the ultimate symbol of blessing, turning into the utterly corrupt grape. All the efforts and toil of YHWH for the plantation project appear to have been in vain. The annihilation of his 'vineyard' is thus unavoidable." Nowhere in Jer 2:21 does the author mention either a vineyard or its fate. Rather, the metaphor focuses entirely on the vine image as representative of the nation's history up to the (then) present time.

33. McKane (*Jeremiah*, 42) erroneously suggests that the nation "has yielded the bitter and inedible fruit of an uncultivated vine."

34. Wallace ("Harvesting the Vineyard," 117–18) correctly observes that "it is the growth of the vine that is the focus in Jer 2:21." Lundbom (*Jeremiah 1–20*, 277–78) similarly argues that "Israel was once a fine vine but has now changed into something putrid." He also suggests, however, that Isa 5:1–7 provides background to the metaphor in Jer 2:21 (277).

śoreq-stock was carefully selected and planted by YHWH, but the vine that grew from that stock grew facing away from YHWH. The image in Jer 2:21 thus emphasizes Judah's noble origins in the distant past, its prior status as YHWH's chosen nation, and its planting in its homeland. At the same time, the author constructs a subsequent history of ignoble behavior in turning to worship other gods. The metaphor lacks the identity element of a common fate, but it conveys the elements of national origins, national character, common culture, and national body through its depiction of the nation's history. The author thereby transforms the positive image of a national vine, chosen and planted by YHWH, into a negative image of national apostasy.

The third national identity vine metaphor, in Ezek 15, provides some of the best evidence in the biblical corpus that the conception of Israel or Judah as a vine or vineyard became relatively well-known, and that the metaphor, in popular use, carried positive connotations. Rather than addressing the growth or fruitfulness of vines, the passage attacks the nature of vine wood in comparison to other woody plants. The author seeks both to deconstruct the people's positive associations with the image of Jerusalem as a vine and, using the conventional metaphor CONQUEST IS BURNING, to decree destruction for that vine:

ויהי דבר־יהוה אלי לאמר: בן־אדם מה־יהיה עץ־הגפן מכל־עץ הזמורה
אשר היה בעצי היער: היקח ממנו עץ לעשות למלאכה אם־יקחו ממנו יתד
לתלות עליו כל־כלי: הנה לאש נתן לאכלה את שני קצותיו אכלה האש
ותוכו נחר היצלח למלאכה: הנה בהיותו תמים לא יעשה למלאכה אף
כי־אש אכלתהו ויחר ונעשה עוד למלאכה: לכן כה אמר אדני יהוה כאשר
עץ־הגפן בעץ היער אשר־נתתיו לאש לאכלה כן נתתי את־ישבי ירושלם:
ונתתי את־פני בהם מהאש יצאו והאש תאכלם וידעתם כי־אני יהוה בשומי
את־פני בהם: ונתתי את־הארץ שממה יען מעלו מעל נאם אדני יהוה:

[1] The word of YHWH came to me, saying: [2] "O mortal, what becomes of the wood of the vine[35] compared to any of the wood of the cut branch[36] that is from the trees of the forest?[37] [3] Can wood

---

35. The translation offered here interprets מה + היה as an idiom expressing not a comparison, but a question of what will happen (following Greenberg and Block). See Moshe Greenberg, *Ezekiel 1–20: A New Translation with Introduction and Commentary*, AB 22 (Garden City, NY: Doubleday, 1983), 264; and Block, *Ezekiel 1–24*, 453.

36. Walther Zimmerli omits הזמורה from his translation, apparently taking it as a later gloss. In the context of a passage about woodworking, however, the comparison

be taken from it to make into something useful? Could they take from it a peg, to hang upon it any implement? [4] See now, to fire it has been given to consume. Its two ends, the fire has consumed, and its middle has been burned. Will it be useful for woodwork? [5] See, when it was intact, it could not be made into something useful, so how much less when fire has consumed it, and it has been burned. Can it still be made into something useful?" [6] Therefore, thus says my Lord, YHWH, "Just as the wood of the vine among the trees of the forest, which I have given it to the fire to consume, so I have given the residents of Jerusalem. [7] I have set my face against them. From the fire they had come out, but the fire will consume them, and you will know that I am YHWH when I set my face against them. [8] I will make the land a desolation, because they have acted sinfully," says my Lord, YHWH.[38]

Since the author focuses on branches of vine wood compared to those of woody plants that grow in the forest, either a vine or a vineyard could provide the background to the metaphor. In the foreground, however, is the mapping of the city to the VINE frame: הגפן (15:2). The comparison of the vine wood to wood from forest-growing trees might suggest that the vine in the image is a wild grapevine, though the author nowhere describes the vine so. This interpretation would make little sense in the

---

of wood from a vine to a branch from a tree makes sense, and Zimmerli's proposal seems unwarranted. See Walther Zimmerli, *Ezekiel 1: A Commentary on the Book of the Prophet Ezekiel, Chapters 1–24*, trans. Ronald E. Clements, Hermeneia (Philadelphia: Fortress, 1979), 317.

37. The noun עץ, rather than the feminine הזמורה, serves as subject to the 3ms verb היה. The translation of בעצי היער, "from the trees of the forest," reflects the locative sense of the preposition. It describes where the branch was before it was taken from the tree (cf. Amos 6:6: השתים במזרקי יין, "those who drink from the bowl of wine").

38. Some scholars see 15:7b–8 as a later addition, because it repeats the line about YHWH setting his face against Jerusalem using two different verbs (נתן versus שום) and because 15:8 adds an accusation of sinfulness that suggests a different complaint about Jerusalem than that suggested by the image of the uselessness of the vine wood in the rest of the passage (see Zimmerli, *Ezekiel 1*, 318–20; and Block, *Ezekiel 1–24*, 454, who argues that 15:7b is original, but 15:8 is a later addition). The problem for such claims is that the uselessness of vine wood in 15:2–5 does not provide sufficient information by which to evaluate the cause of Jerusalem's punishment. Thus, without 15:8, it is not clear why the people are destined for the fire.

context of the passage, though.[39] Wild vines produce grapes that are inferior to those of domesticated vines. If the author is seeking to denigrate a positive image of Judah as a vine, presenting the vine as wild would undercut that message. The reference to the forest in 15:2 is therefore better understood as defining the types of wood that the author wishes to compare to the vine wood.

The first part of the metaphor strikes directly at a self-conception of Jerusalem as a vine by declaring that vine wood is useless. Such a declaration would make no sense in the absence of a preexisting notion of the city as a vine. The author takes that conceptualization of the city as a given and then sets out to disparage the image.[40] To that end, the author hides the vine's positive attributes of producing grapes and focuses instead on the inherent weaknesses of vine wood for building or woodworking (15:3–5). Employing the CONQUEST IS FIRE conceptual metaphor allows the author to remain within the VINE frame throughout the delivery of this evaluation (15:4–7). The author expresses his perspective on Jerusalem by arguing that vine wood, by its very nature, is useless; it is useless when freshly cut and useless after it has been burned in a fire (15:5). By means of this metaphor, Ezek 15 declares that not only was the nation worthless in the past, before the conquest by the Babylonians, but what remains of it, that which survived the conquest, is also worthless.

Ezekiel 15 thus implicitly rejects conceptualizations of the vine like that of Jer 2:21, which attributes to the vine a noble heritage. The author also rejects metaphors that compare the nation with metal that can be refined (e.g., Isa 1:25; Zech 13:8–9). Unlike metal, whose impurities can be burned off, burning a vine does not improve its quality.[41] Ironically,

---

39. So also Greenberg, *Ezekiel 1–20*, 265.

40. Many scholars see in this passage a reaction against the Jerusalemites' pride or their confidence in their self-conception as a national vine. See, e.g., Block, *Ezekiel 1–24*, 459; Walther Eichrodt, *Ezekiel: A Commentary*, trans. Cosslett Quin, OTL (Philadelphia: Westminster, 1970), 193; and Zimmerli, *Ezekiel 1*, 319.

41. Block (*Ezekiel 1–24*, 457) mentions the difference between how wood and metal respond to fire, but he does not connect that observation to the metallurgical metaphors in the prophetic corpus, including the one in Ezek 22:17–22. Ezekiel's version of the metallurgy metaphor also suggests a rejection of the possibility that the metal may be purified. The author focuses on the image of punishment by fire, of melting the impure metals of Judah (22:20–22), but unlike the passages in, e.g., Isa 1:25 and Zech 13:8–9, he never describes the outcome of the melting process. The metaphor hides the "refining" element of the METALLURGY frame, thereby also hiding

this passage actually offers evidence that branches pruned from the grapevines probably were useful—as firewood.[42] By describing the vine wood as
useless for woodworking, however, and therefore destined for the fire, the
author transforms a positive feature into a negative, implying that "good
for firewood" is not good enough.[43] The second part of the passage then
decrees doom for those who still reside in the city. They may have survived
the first burning, but since, like the vine wood, they remain useless after
their ordeal, YHWH intends to burn them again.[44]

Arguments that the passage focuses exclusively on the vine's fate, rather
than on how the vine compares to other woody plants, overstate the case.[45]
The nature and fate of the vine stands in the forefront of the metaphor, but
implicit in the demonstrations of the vine's uselessness is the reality that
other types of wood do make useful things. Indeed, by mentioning כל־עץ
הזמורה אשר היה בעצי היער, "any of the wood of the cut branch that is from
the trees of the forest," at the beginning of the prophecy (15:2), the author
invokes the forest trees' frames and primes the audience to consider the
critiques of the vine wood in comparison to other types of wood.

At the same time, the comparison exists less to identify other national
woody plants as superior to Jerusalem's vine than to highlight the con-

---

the possibility that a purer nation will result from the current punishment. Jeremiah
6:27–30 goes even further than Ezekiel in this respect, as the author openly declares
that attempts to refine metal-Judah have failed (6:29–30).

42. Borowski, *Agriculture*; and Matthews, "Treading the Winepress," 26.

43. Contra Eichrodt (*Ezekiel*, 93), who observes that the author has focused on an
aspect of the vine that has nothing to do with its value.

44. While Greenberg (*Ezekiel 1–20*, 268) is probably correct to reject interpretations that attempt to map the details of the burning stick—its two ends and its middle—
to specific historical events (see, e.g., Eichrodt, *Ezekiel*, 194), he does agree with other
scholars that, in general terms, the first burning of the stick probably maps to the Babylonian defeat of Judah in 597 BCE. Notice that the author describes Jerusalem in the
third person but addresses the audience in the second. These elements suggest that
Ezekiel is addressing those in exile with him in Babylonia (Zimmerli, *Ezekiel 1*, 319).

45. Greenberg (*Ezekiel 1–20*, 265) argues that a translation of 15:1 that compares
vine wood to other trees will "import into the opening of the prophecy a polemic
against the pride of the Judahites (supposedly expressed by the figure of Israel as a
vine) that is not found anywhere else in it." Block (*Ezekiel 1–24*, 456) offers a similar critique: "Contrary to virtually all translations, the issue here is not a comparison
between not [*sic*] the quality of a vine and other trees, but a comparison of their desti-
nies.… Here the question is how the fate of the vine branch will be distinguished from
the rest of the trees."

trast between what the national grapevine is and what it could have been had its wood been of higher quality.[46] In making this case, the author has constructed a national character via the description of the Jerusalemites as vine wood. He also constructs a national history and common culture by depicting the people as uniformly producing nothing good, both in the past and in the present.[47] Finally, the burning metaphor contributes to the identity a common fate. The metaphor lacks the element of a national body, perhaps because that element was not necessary to the message that the author wanted to convey in this passage. Ultimately, Ezek 15 takes the people's positive self-conception of the nation and subverts it by showing its inherent weakness: the image they treasure is worthless to YHWH.

5.2. Case Study: Ezekiel 19:10–14a

The final national identity vine metaphor appears in Ezek 19. The chapter consists of two sections of metaphorical material, each of which deals with the royal family of Judah in some way. Ezekiel 19:1 opens with a call to the audience to שא קינה אל־נשיאי ישראל, "raise a funeral lament to the leaders of Israel." Ezekiel 19:2–9 likens Judah's rulers to a pride of lions, while 19:10–14a compares Judah to a vine. Each image begins with a comparison focused on the addressee's mother. Ezekiel 19:2 asks: מה אמך לביא, "How was your mother a lioness?" And 19:10 declares: אמך כגפן, "Your mother was like the vine." The change in imagery from lions to a vine between 19:9 and 19:10, and the references to the mother figure in 19:2 and 19:10, create a clear break between the two sections of the chapter. Ezekiel 19:14b closes the unit by describing the preceding text as a lament. Ezekiel 19:1 and 14b thus form a simple *inclusio* that brackets the chapter. Following 19:14, Ezek 20:1 opens with a date formula, indicating the beginning of a new textual unit.

---

46. Despite his protest that the passage lacks comparative language, Greenberg (*Ezekiel 1–20*, 268–69) notes the implications of the useless vine wood image as a description of "Israel's 'congenital' baseness" and as "an analogy to Israel's moral inferiority to the nations," arguing that both attacks are consistent with themes present in the book as a whole.

47. In a way, the complaint of Ezek 15 that Jerusalem produces nothing good inverts the accusation of Isa 5:1–7 that the people produce only bad things (see ch. 4).

Though the literary frame presents Ezek 19 as a unified text, the two metaphorical passages were more likely composed independently and combined later.[48] Studies of the chapter routinely highlight the noticeable differences in content and literary structure (including syntax and meter) between its two sections.[49] The passages also differ in their metaphorical structure. In 19:2–9, the author clearly introduces each "lion," describes the beast's misbehavior, and explains its ultimate fate. Ezekiel 19:10–14a, on the other hand, has spawned an endless debate over how many branches the vine has and what their misdeeds and fates are. The vine metaphor in Ezek 17 demonstrates how easily these details could be incorporated as mappings in a metaphor about an individual, so their absence from Ezek 19:10–14a suggests that the passage focuses elsewhere than on individual kings.

Several scholars have argued that the two images parallel the leonine and viticultural imagery associated with Judah in Gen 49:8–12, and they conclude on that basis that the two sections of Ezek 19 were composed together as a single unit.[50] The comparison to Gen 49:8–12 appears misguided, however. While both the lions and vine branches in Ezek 19 represent the ruling family, in Gen 49, only the lion represents Judah. The vine, on the other hand, represents Judah's prosperity and is based on the metonymic relationship between viticulture and prosperity. The parallel to Gen 49:8–12 may have provided some inspiration for the later combination of the two poems in Ezek 19, but the similarities between the two

---

48. So also Eichrodt, *Ezekiel*, 256. Cooke and Zimmerli, on the other hand, view the vine simile in 19:10–14 as secondary to and dependent on 19:1–9. See G. A. Cooke, *The Book of Ezekiel*, 2 vols., ICC (Edinburgh: T&T Clark, 1937), 1:209; Zimmerli, *Ezekiel 1*, 393. This solution is possible, but the significant differences between the two halves of the chapter seem to better support a theory of independent composition.

49. Block (*Ezekiel 1–24*, 594) notes that while the 3:2 meter generally holds for 19:2–9, "the pattern may be maintained in vv. 10–14 only by resorting to drastic emendations." In addition, 19:10–14 make less use of chiasm and no use of word pairs, both of which help to structure 19:2–9. See Corrine Carvalho, "Putting the Mother Back in the Center: Metaphor and Multivalence in Ezekiel 19," in *Thus Says the Lord: Essays on the Former and Latter Prophets in Honor of Robert R. Wilson*, ed. John J. Ahn and Stephen L. Cook, LHBOTS 502 (New York: T&T Clark, 2009), 211. Further, they lack the clear historical details present in 19:2–9 (Block, *Ezekiel 1–24*, 608).

50. Block, *Ezekiel 1–24*, 591; Christopher Begg, "The Identity of the Princes in Ezechiel 19: Some Reflections," *ETL* 65 (1989): 368; and Carvalho, "Putting the Mother," 213.

texts are too superficial to offer compelling evidence for the compositional unity of Ezek 19. Given the weight of the evidence that argues for independent composition of the two passages, the case study that follows focuses only on the vine metaphor in 19:10–14a, which constitutes the most complete and detailed national identity vine metaphor in the prophetic corpus:

אמך כגפן בדמך	[10] Your mother was like the vine of your vineyard,
על־מים שתולה	Planted by water.
פריה וענפה היתה	Fruitful and thick with branches she was,
ממים רבים:	From abundant water.
ויהיו־לה מטות עז	[11] And she had strong staves,[51]
אל־שבטי משלים	[Akin] to scepters of rulers.
ותגבה קומתו	The height of one grew tall,[52]
על־בין עבתים	up between the branches.[53]
וירא בגבהו	He was noticed for his height,
ברב דליתיו:	[And] for the multitude of his shoots.
ותתש בחמה	[12] She was uprooted in anger.
לארץ השלכה	To the ground she was cast,
ורוח הקדים	And the wind of the east
הוביש פריה	withered her fruit.
התפרקו ויבשו	They were torn away and dried up.
מטה עזה	Her mighty staff,

---

51. The translation of מטה/מטות as "staff/staves" in 19:11, 12, and 14 retains the author's decision to use a term from the RULER frame, rather than from the VINE frame, to describe the "mighty branches" of the vine. Both מטה and שבט serve to indicate the authority of a leader or ruler in the biblical corpus (Block, *Ezekiel 1–24*, 609).

52. Lit. "and his height became tall"; 19:11 abruptly shifts from plural to singular between lines 1–2 about the מטות, "staves," and lines 3–6 about one particular staff. The translation offered here suggests that קומתו in line 3 indicates that change of subject.

53. Some translate עבתים as "clouds," based on Driver's theory that the word ultimately derives from עב, "cloud," with both the feminine and masculine plural endings appended to the form. See Walther Zimmerli, *Ezekiel 2: A Commentary on the Book of the Prophet Ezekiel, Chapters 25–48*, trans. James D. Martin, Hermeneia (Philadelphia: Fortress, 1983), 140 n. 3c. The argument is bolstered by the presence of νεφελῶν, "clouds," at this point in the LXX. In the Hebrew Bible, however, עבות otherwise always appears in contexts related to trees, branches, or leaves, suggesting that whatever its relationship to עב (if any), the form עבות carried a sense, perhaps idiomatic, related to trees.

אש אכלתהו: fire consumed him.

ועתה שתולה במדבר ¹³ Now she is transplanted in the wilderness,

בארץ ציה וצמא: In a land dry and thirsty.

ותצא אש ממטה בדיה ¹⁴ Fire issued from her shoot-laden staff.

פריה אכלה Her fruit it consumed.

ולא־היה בה מטה־עז And there is not on her a mighty staff,

שבט למשול A scepter for ruling.

The text of these verses is difficult. It contains several unclear words and phrases, and the metaphorical mappings defy simple explanations. Beyond these issues, the phrase most significant to the history of interpretation of Ezek 19:10–14a is the description of Ezek 19 as a קינה, "lament for the dead" (19:1 and 14b). If this description originally applied to the poem about the vine, the audience might expect to find features typical of a lament, such as: (1) an opening exclamation of grief; (2) a direct address to the deceased; (3) a "'once-now' scheme, by which the glories of the past are contrasted with the pain and loss of the present";[54] and (4) line pairs in which a longer first line is completed by a shorter second line.[55] The content of 19:10–14a does address the "deceased" staves and fruit and does contain a "once-now" message. At the same time, while the author presents the nation's recent history and current state in harsh terms, the passage lacks any explicit exclamation of grief.

In addition, though the poem begins and ends with *qinah*-type parallel lines (19:10–11aα and 14a), the roughly equivalent length of the parallel lines in the middle verses do not follow that pattern. These deviations in the meter have provided the basis for numerous proposed emendations to 19:10–14a. Daniel Block, however, points out that *qinot* often depart from the typical pattern, and other types of songs may use the *qinah* pattern. He therefore cautions against emendations based on solely issues of meter.[56] Moreover, if Ezek 19 is not a compositional unity, and if the content of 19:10–14a do not fit the *qinah* form, there is little reason believe that the *qinah* description in 19:1 and 14b originally belonged to the vine poem.

---

54. Block, *Ezekiel 1–24*, 592–94, esp. 593. For a more extensive discussion of structural aspects of the קינה form, see W. Randall Garr, "The Qinah: A Study of Poetic Meter, Syntax and Style," *ZAW* 95 (1983): 54–75. The classic study of the קינה meter is that of C. Budde, "Das hebräische Klagelied," *ZAW* 2 (1882): 1–52.

55. Carvalho, "Putting the Mother," 208.

56. Block, *Ezekiel 1–24*, 592.

There is also little justification for emending the text to achieve *qinah*-type parallel lines.

Indeed, the only emendation called for in the poem arises from the apparent textual corruption in the first line of 19:10, which reads אִמְּךָ כַגֶּפֶן בְּדָמְךָ, "your mother was like the vine in your blood." The phrase "like the vine in your blood" makes no sense on its face, and no similar idioms are present in the biblical corpus.[57] The translation offered here—"your mother was like the vine of your vineyard"—reflects an emendation of the MT to אִמְּךָ כְּגֶפֶן כַּרְמְךָ, based primarily on graphic exchanges of ב for כ and of ד for ר that would transform the posited original כרמך into the MT's בדמך.[58] After this emendation, the first image created in the poem depicts the Judahites as a vine planted in a vineyard.

Scholars examining Ezek 19:10–14 have debated whether the mother vine simile refers only to the royal family, or whether it refers to Judah as a whole.[59] The solution to the question of the target(s) in 19:10–14 lies in the patterns in the author's use of conventional plant mappings. The passage represents the fusion of two variants of a single conceptual metaphor: A GROUP OF PEOPLE IS A GRAPEVINE. One variant primarily structures the lines related to the "mighty staff" and its "shoots." The other structures the expressions related to the fruit. The lines about the vine bind the two variants together. The gender and number of the verbs, nouns, and pronouns make it possible to trace the mappings for each metaphor. The vine is always female and always of the nation. The mighty staff is always masculine,[60] and it refers to the royal line of Josiah. Finally, the grapes

---

57. The phrase בדמך, "in your blood" appears in Ezekiel in the context of an individual being a newborn child covered in blood (16:6, 22) and in reference to someone shedding blood in violence (22:4). Psalm 30:10 also uses the term to refer to bloodshed. Neither of these contexts fits Ezek 19:10, however, and none of these passages mentions a vine.

58. For an explanation of this emendation, see the excursus at the end of this chapter.

59. Most commentators conclude that the vine represents the nation, and that the branch or branches represent one or more of the recent kings of Judah (Begg, "Identity of the Princes," 368; Block, *Ezekiel 1–24*, 609–10; Cooke, *Ezekiel*, 209–10; Eichrodt, *Ezekiel*, 256–57). Another approach interprets the vine as representing not the nation, but only the "Davidic royal house." See Zimmerli, *Ezekiel 1*, 397–98; G. T. M. Prinsloo, "Lions and Vines: The Imagery of Ezekiel 19 in the Light of Ancient Near-Eastern Descriptions and Depictions," *OTE* 12 (1999): 354–55.

60. Greenberg (*Ezekiel 1–20*, 353) similarly explains the shift from feminine to masculine as an indication that the subject has shifted to one of the staves.

always map to the people, and while פרי, "fruit," itself is a singular noun, the author treats it as a collective singular and pairs it with plural verbs.[61]

From the perspective of viticultural practice, the description of Judah as a well-watered and flourishing "mother" vine—פריה ועָנפה היתה, "fruitful and thick with branches she was" (19:10)—presents another problem. The image is accurate in one sense, because overwatering a vine will result in lush foliage. The excess shoots and leaves, however, may shade the fruit to such a degree that the lack of sunlight will negatively affect its quality.[62] Presumably, the energy the vine devotes to growing the excess foliage would also reduce the energy it has available to produce fruit. Thus, while the vine in 19:10 may be lush from the availability of water, it would be less likely to also be fruitful.

The inclusion of the water mapping may reflect the author's ignorance about this aspect of viticulture. Since the southern Levant has dry summers, and the Israelites and Judahites typically planted their vines on hills, rather than next to water sources, the effect of excess water on vine growth may not have been widely known. On the other hand, the author may have had an opportunity to observe or learn of the effect of excess water on vines in exile in Babylonia. Both the flood-based irrigation and the higher salinity of the soil made southern Mesopotamian a less hospitable environment for practicing viticulture. To compensate for these issues, the grapevines that they did cultivate may have been planted in relatively elevated locations, perhaps even on the slopes of the irrigation canals.[63] Such a location would seem to create the potential for overwatering. In any case, the metaphor maps the presence of water

---

61. Contra Cooke (*Ezekiel*, 210), who argues that the plural verbs in 19:12 conflict with the singular noun, פרי. Cooke also suggests that a reference to "fruit" does not make sense in the context of the passage. Accordingly, he concludes that the line about the fruit actually refers to the vine's branches. Eichrodt (*Ezekiel*, 205) takes a similar approach, emending the singular "fruit" to the plural "branches" Other scholars follow the approach employed here, based in part on the lack of an attested plural form for פרי in the biblical corpus, and treat the word as a collective singular that serves as the subject of the plural verbs (Block, *Ezekiel 1–24*, 607; Greenberg, *Ezekiel 1–20*, 349; Zimmerli, *Ezekiel 1*, 391).

62. Creasy and Creasy, *Grapes*, 71. As a result of this dynamic, modern vintners carefully control their vines' water supply to avoid excessive foliage production. Failing that effort, they must aggressively prune the vine during the growing season to prevent overshading of the grapes (71).

63. Powell, "Wine and the Vine in Ancient Mesopotamia," 104–5.

to prosperity and divine providence, even though this mapping makes little sense in the context of viticultural practice, where prosperity is determined by the amount of fruit produced rather than by extensive growth of vine shoots. The simplest explanation for this imagery is that the author has drawn on conventional mappings used with other types of woody-plant metaphors, for which water would more logically map to prosperity or divine providence.[64]

Finally, as with the description of the well-watered vine, the attribution of great height to the staff in 19:11 makes little sense in the context of ancient Israelite viticulture. Scholars occasionally cite this passage as evidence that the Israelites trellised their vines or trained them to climb trees. Since a domesticated grapevine, on its own, grows low to the ground, only a trellised or climbing vine would grow to a great height. Such interpretations overlook the fact that the practices of trellis- or tree-training domesticated vines probably developed in response to the challenges of grape-growing in more humid or rainy climates. Too much moisture on developing grapes promotes the growth of mold and mildew. Thus, in climates where it rains during the summer, vintners learned to elevate the vines so that more air could circulate around the fruit and carry excess moisture away.[65]

In Israel, however, where the summers are very dry, the vintner's challenge is to retain as much moisture in the earth as possible to nourish the vines and to help promote fruit growth. As Carey Ellen Walsh argues:

---

64. See the discussion of conventional mappings in woody-plant metaphors in ch. 8.

65. Evidence exists for such practices in Rome, Mesopotamia, and Egypt. Vines could be trained to grow on trellises, to grow up other trees (in intercultivated orchards called *arbusta*), or to grow up stakes in the ground (Walsh, *Fruit of the Vine*, 113–14). Evidence for the use of these methods in ancient Israel is mixed. The metaphorical expressions that associate sitting under a vine and under a fig tree with prosperity might suggest knowledge of the method of training vines to grow up fig trees (1 Kgs 5:5; Mic 4:4; Zech 3:10). The extent to which the phrase reflects an actual practice is unknown, however. The metaphor may simply draw on the height and shadiness of fig trees and figuratively apply those same qualities to the vine. (See also the discussion of this metaphor in ch. 7.) Evidence against the practice of elevating vines in Israel and Judah appears in the relief at Nineveh that commemorates Sennacherib's campaign against Lachish in 701 BCE. The image includes low-profile, free-standing vines in the background (Walsh, *Fruit of the Vine*, 114). The agricultural writings of the Roman scholar Varro (first century CE) also describe vines in Palestine growing on the ground (115). Finally, none of the prophetic vine or vineyard metaphors ever mention trellising or training vines on stakes or trees (114).

> The benefit to growing vines on the ground for ancient Israel would have been twofold. First, the foliage would shade the soil from the sun, thereby lessening the evaporation of its moisture.... Second, freestanding vines dispense with the additional labor and timber needs necessary for *arbusta* or staking each vine.[66]

Thus, the height of the staff in 19:11 should not be taken as evidence that the Israelites elevated their grapevines. Rather, the author of this passage has probably again drawn on conventional mappings used with woody-plant metaphors. The staff grows tall not because Judahites trained their vines so, but because in woody-plant metaphors, power, prestige, and pride all map to height. At the same time, it also seems likely that the biblical author's conceptualization of a vine branch growing taller than the surrounding trees could have been inspired or validated by observations of wild vines, which can train themselves to climb the trees (and anything else) in their immediate vicinity.[67]

The author of the poem uses the image in 19:10 of the well-watered mother vine, planted securely in a vineyard, to provide the nation with an idyllic past. The verse also constructs a national character for the people of Judah by attributing to them a common ancestry from a single vine. Finally, 19:10 sets up the two paths of the staff and fruit metaphors as representing Judah's leaders and Judah's people, respectively, by stating that both the fruit and the branches of the vine prospered because of the water. Ezekiel 19:11 continues the historical account by praising unnamed kings of Judah's past via its depiction of the vine's many strong staves. The rise to prominence of one of these rulers appears in the description of the single staff's height in the second half of 19:11, which overtops the rest of the vine in its growth. In turn, the staff's many shoots at the end of the verse represent the royal family, making use of yet another common mapping in woody-plant metaphors: presenting children or heirs as branches.[68]

---

66. Walsh, *Fruit of the Vine*, 115. On *arbusta*, see the previous note.

67. The tendrils of a vine will "latch onto" nearby objects, providing support for the vine as its canes continue to grow in length (Creasy and Creasy, *Grapes*, 35).

68. Greenberg (*Ezekiel 1–20*, 354) posits that the staves represent an "allusion to the many royal scions of Josiah." According to the genealogy in 1 Chr 3:15–16, King Josiah had four sons, and at least two grandsons. Three of Josiah's sons (Jehoahaz, Jehoiakim, and Zedekiah) and one grandson (Jehoiachin) ruled Judah after him (2 Kgs 23–25; 2 Chr 36). For more on branch imagery in woody-plant metaphors, see ch. 8.

The claim in the final two lines of 19:11 that the staff was "noticed" because of its height and shoots constitutes the central accusation against the vine in this metaphor. The criticism is vague. In contrast to the descriptions of the lions in Ezek 19:2–9, 19:10–14 provides scant historical details suggestive of a particular king. The reference to height probably invokes negative associations between pride or prominence and height.[69] That the author describes the staff as becoming visible might allude to various attempts by the Judahite kings to break free from either Egyptian or Babylonian control. In the final decades of Judah's existence as a kingdom, King Josiah (640–609 BCE) was apparently killed by Egyptian Pharaoh Neco II, presumably because Josiah had displeased Neco in some way (2 Kgs 23:29). In addition, two of Josiah's sons, Jehoiakim (608–598 BCE) and Zedekiah (597–586 BCE), rebelled against Babylonian control, resulting in the conquest of Jerusalem in 597 BCE and its destruction in 586 BCE (2 Kgs 24–25). The accusation of "visibility" in Ezek 19:11 may carry the implication that had these kings remained loyal, they would not have attracted the notice (and ire) of their overlords, and the conquest and exile of Judah would not have occurred.

The rest of the poem focuses on the consequences of these actions, as the author first describes Judah's recent history and then sets out a bleak future for the nation. Judah's defeat by the Babylonians appears in the uprooting and casting to the ground of the vine (19:12). The author further elaborates on the fate of the people by noting that when the vine was uprooted, its fruit was torn away and dried up by the eastern wind, a metaphor for Babylonia (19:12). This imagery represents, in general terms, the idea that many people were either killed or forced to flee from the Babylonian invaders. In the same verse, the phrase "her mighty staff, fire consumed him" uses the conventional metaphors CONQUEST IS BURNING and BURNING IS EATING to express the defeat of the royal family in terms of the burning of the mighty cane.

Finally, the story ends in 19:13–14 with a description of the current state of the vine, its mighty staff, and its fruit. Ezekiel 19:13 represents the exile in terms of the transplanting of the vine to the desert. The imagery of the dry land serves less to describe Babylonia in literal terms than to contrast

---

69. Greenberg (*Ezekiel 1–20*, 358–59) also argues that the height of the cane probably represents an accusation of excessive pride. Cooke (*Ezekiel*, 209) comments on the similarity of the description of the tall cane in this verse to the tree metaphor in Ezek 31. See ch. 8 for a discussion of Ezek 31.

the vine's current dry state with its prior well-watered state in 19:10. When a vine is starved of water, either by drought or from excessively hot, windy conditions, the plant will react by closing off the stomata in its leaves that allow it to take in carbon dioxide and to release the oxygen that is produced during photosynthesis. The action preserves the vine's remaining stores of water by not allowing moisture in the cells of the leaves to evaporate and exit through the stomata, but it also effectively shuts down photosynthesis, and therefore ends the vine's ability to produce new growth and fruit.[70] Thus, the new desert location for Ezekiel's metaphorical vine supports the author's claim that the vine will be unable to produce new branches or fruit.[71]

At first glance, 19:14 seems to present a second episode or an alternate view of the people's fate, this time applying to the people two metaphors that were previously used only of the royal family—CONQUEST IS BURNING and BURNING IS EATING:

ותצא אש ממטה בדיה

פריה אכלה

ולא־היה בה מטה־עז

שבט למשול

[14] Fire issued from her shoot-laden staff.[72]
Her fruit it consumed.

---

70. Creasy and Creasy, *Grapes*, 22.

71. Walsh (*Fruit of the Vine*, 29) highlights a study of average rainfall in Israel between 1846 and 1953 CE that suggests that the region may have experienced drought-like conditions frequently: "Roughly 30 percent of a decade will be well below the average rainfall." Thus, the prophetic author of this passage may have had an opportunity to observe first-hand what drought does to a vine.

72. Treatments of this verse often struggle with the phrase ממטה בדיה, lit. "from the staff of her shoots." They respond to this seemingly awkward phrase by either emending it (e.g., Eichrodt, *Ezekiel*, 250–51; Zimmerli, *Ezekiel 1*, 391; Cooke, *Ezekiel*, 210) or by retaining the MT as is and offering an equally awkward translation, such as "from the bough of her shoots" (Block, *Ezekiel 1–24*, 608; Greenberg, *Ezekiel 1–20*, 349). The evidence from the LXX suggests that its *Vorlage* agreed with the MT on the syntax of the first line, placing מטה in construct with בדיה: αἱ ἐξῆλθεν πῦρ ἐκ ῥάβδου ἐκλεκτῶν αὐτῆς, "and fire went out from a rod of its choice parts" (NETS). The translation offered here, "from her shoot-laden staff," treats the phrase as another example in which Weingreen's approach to rendering certain construct chains into English provides a satisfying translation and makes emendation unnecessary (Weingreen, "Construct-Genitive Relation," 50). See also the discussion of this type of construct chain in ch. 4 n. 28.

And there is not on her a mighty staff,
A scepter for ruling.

Indeed, the argument that the verse represents a later addition to the passage has been proposed.[73] The consistency in mappings and message between 19:10–12 and 19:14, however, does not support such claims. Instead, 19:14 explains the implications of the tale just told about the staves and the fruit.[74] The phrase מטה בדיה, "her shoot-laden staff," parallels the description in 19:11 of the mighty staff as having many shoots. That the fire issued from the shoot-filled staff indicates that the actions of the staff *and* its many shoots led to the death and exile of the people, who map to the consumed fruit. At the same time, the destruction of the mighty staff by fire (19:12), and the vine's current desert location (19:13), leave the vine without a current mighty staff and unable to produce a new one in the future. Through this final image, the author suggests that the Judahite kings have been defeated and will never again hold the throne of Judah.[75]

The content of Ezek 19:10–14 fits with the period after the rule of Judah had passed away from the line of Davidic kings. In particular, the reference in 19:14 to the vine lacking a ruling cane seems to reflect the conditions in Judah after the destruction of Jerusalem in 586 BCE, when a Davidic king no longer held the throne of Judah.[76] Moreover, the passage as a whole has a more distant, retrospective tone, looking back on the events of 610–586 BCE and holding the last kings of Judah collectively responsible for the downfall of the nation. Though the prophetic authors could, and did, sometimes forecast the destruction of a nation as a *fait*

---

73. See, e.g., Zimmerli, *Ezekiel 1*, 397–98.

74. Contra Block (*Ezekiel 1–24*, 609), who interprets 19:14 as a new scene about Zedekiah, in which the cane in 19:14 serves as a "replacement branch" for the one destroyed in 19:12. Cooke (*Ezekiel*, 210) similarly argues that the flaming cane in this verse represents Zedekiah's rebellion against Babylonia.

75. Prinsloo ("Lions and Vines," 353–54) notes that the reversal of the staves' fortunes in 19:11 and 14 "strongly underlines the contrast between the prosperous beginning and the disastrous end of the vine."

76. After deposing Zedekiah, the Babylonians appointed Gedaliah, who was not a member of the royal family, to lead Judah. Whether he served as governor or king is not clear from the biblical text. Second Kings 25:22 and Jer 40:7 give him no title, but Jer 41:1 and 41:10 mention the "king" and could refer to either Zedekiah or Gedaliah (Miller and Hayes, *History of Ancient Israel and Judah*, 482–87).

accompli, in this case, the song was most likely composed in the aftermath of the destruction of Jerusalem.[77]

The author has constructed a slightly more sympathetic national identity in this text than the one present in Ezek 15. He begins with an idyllic image of the nation's past, in which both kings and people prospered when they were planted in their homeland. He then uses the vine metaphor to map the disparate reasons for the common fate experienced by the people of Judah. He places the blame for Judah's fate on the sins of its final four or five kings and so depicts the people as victims of these kings' actions. While the whole vine shares in the pain and displacement of exile, its component parts do not share equally in the responsibility for their fate. By the end of the poem, the author has almost totally transformed the identity that he presents in 19:10. The national body, which was a well-watered land, is gone, and the nation is now planted in a land not their own. The head of the vine and its fruit have both been destroyed, and while the vine itself still survives, it no longer has the ability to grow strong staves. In addition, since vines need at least some irrigation in order to produce fruit, the vine's new location bodes ill for the people's future. The song does not construct an image of the end of the nation in the sense of total death and destruction; instead, it presents the nation's future as kingless, impoverished, and fading into obscurity.[78]

Notice, however, that the author leaves the vine's reputation somewhat intact. He has not deconstructed the positive image of the vine as a whole. Rather, he has rehabilitated it, destroying the problematic shoot-filled staff but allowing the vine to survive. As such, the passage serves more to create or activate in the exiled survivors of Judah their sense of having a national identity. Nothing in the content of the poem suggests that the author looks forward to an eventual restoration of Judah, however. Rather, he may have

---

77. On the *fait accompli*, or "prophetic past," see the brief discussion in Greenberg, *Ezekiel 1–20*, 359. The classic example is the city of Tyre, whose destruction by the Babylonians is presented as an historical fact in Ezek 28:12–19, even though the events described never actually occurred.

78. Philippus Jacobus Botha highlights how the chapter as a whole, including the vine episode, "seems to emphasise the contrast between aspirations and outcome, between the honour sought after and the reality of shame experienced" by the nation. Philippus Jacobus Botha, "The Socio-cultural Background of Ezekiel 19," *OTE* 2 (1999): 249–65.

had the more modest goal in mind of fostering a sense of community among those who were living in exile.

5.3. Conclusions: Deconstructing a Positive National Image

As with the vineyard metaphors discussed in the previous chapter, the national vine metaphors appear to be reacting to a preexisting positive conception of the nation. Three of the four passages construct an identity that includes either a noble origin or a prosperous past for the vine (Hos 10:1–2; Jer 2:21; Ezek 19:10–14), and the fourth reacts against a positive notion of the nation as a vine by rejecting the very idea that the vine could have ever had a noble past (Ezek 15). In each case, the author deconstructs or transforms that positive identity. Hosea 10:1–2, Jer 2:21, and Ezek 19:10–14 all reframe the nation's history by locating the source of the vine's present or future troubles in its past behavior. Ezekiel 15, on the other hand, changes the focus of the frame to highlight the vine's inborn and ever-present weaknesses and to hide its strengths.

Among the four passages, only Ezek 19:10–14 avoids ascribing a collective responsibility for the nation's fate. Instead, it places the blame for Judah's downfall on the nation's kings. Judah the vine is not at fault, but its wayward royal shoot-filled staff, with its conspicuous ways, is (19:11). By contrast, Hos 10:1–2, Jer 2:21, and Ezek 15 do not differentiate between leaders and people in their assignment of blame. Like Ezek 19:10–14, Hos 10:1–2 addresses the actions of the vine while it prospered, but Hosea holds the vine and its grapes together accountable for those actions and for the punishment earned as a result. Likewise, the description in Jer 2:21 of the nation as a single deviant, alien vine and the emphasis in Ezek 15 on the worthlessness of all vine wood also suggest that the behavior of the whole nation, as a unified entity or homogeneous group, is the problem.

Excursus: The MT and LXX Versions of Ezekiel 19:10a

The Masoretic Text for the first phrase in Ezek 19:10a reads אִמְּךָ כַגֶּפֶן בְּדָמְךָ, "your mother was like the vine in your blood." Assuming that the phrase does not represent an obscure idiom, the line is incoherent, leading scholars to propose various emendations to the text to resolve the difficult form. The most common approach emends the consonantal text from בדמך to בכרם, thus yielding "your mother was like a vine in a vineyard," but this change is offered without an explanation of how the text evolved from one form to the other.[79] A second proposal, originally offered by Julius Bewer, relies on a combination of defective spelling and a proposed change in the word division of בדמך to בדם כ. The resulting translation of these two versets is "thy mother was like a vine full of shoots, because planted by water."[80] Mitchell Dahood emends the text in the same way as Bewer but translates כ as a relative pronoun: "your mother was like a vine full of shoots, which is planted by water."[81] Neither בדים nor relative כי are attested in the biblical text with defective spelling, however, which weakens the case for these solutions.[82] Walther Zimmerli, following Rashi and Radak, argues that the form derives from דמה, "to resemble." He suggests that the original text may have employed a *niphal* participle or perfect form and offers the translation "your mother was equal to a vine."[83]

While the above proposals would explain the MT, they leave the mystery of the LXX translation unresolved.[84] In the LXX, Ezek 19:10a reads:

ἡ μήτηρ σου ὡς ἄμπελος, ὡς ἄνθος ἐν ῥόᾳ
Your mother was like a vine, like a flower in a pomegranate.
(NETS)

Retroverted into a hypothetical Hebrew *Vorlage*, the consonantal text of this passage would read something like: אמך כגפן כפרח ברמן. Dominique Barthélemy posits that the Hebrew *Vorlage* contained the form כרמן, instead of ברמן, but that solution does not work.[85] Since Hebrew uses the same word for pomegranate and pomegranate tree, if the Hebrew text had read כרמן, the translator could have just rendered the passage as "your mother was like a vine, like a pomegranate tree." In the context of a vine

---

79. See, e.g., Eichrodt, *Ezekiel*, 250. Cooke (*Ezekiel*, 209), on the other hand, says that this solution "looks attractive, but it does not inspire confidence," and he therefore chooses to omit the offending word, rather than offer a solution to it.

80. Bewer, "Textual and Exegetical Notes on the Book of Ezekiel," *JBL* 72 (1953): 158–68.

81. Dahood, "Ezekiel 19,10 and Relative *kî*," *Bib* 56 (1975): 96–99.

82. At least, these forms are not attested unless one accepts additional proposed emendations by Dahood ("Ezekiel 19,10," 97, 99) for Ps 68:24 and Isa 45:9.

83. Zimmerli, *Ezekiel 1*, 390.

84. Greenberg (*Ezekiel 1–20*, 353) mentions these proposed solutions, but retains the MT, commenting that "the word [בדמך] remains a crux."

85. John W. Olley, *Ezekiel: A Commentary Based on Iezekiēl in Codex Vaticanus*, Septuagint Commentary Series (Leiden: Brill, 2009), 358.

planted by water, another woody plant would provide a better parallel than the present LXX translation of "like a flower in a pomegranate." The LXX translation only makes sense if its *Vorlage* included the form ברמן, "in a pomegranate (tree)," with a corresponding term for ὡς ἄνθος, "like a flower," either in the *Vorlage* or added to the LXX by the translator to complete the phrase.

Though BHS notes that two medieval Hebrew manuscripts contain the form כרמך in place of בדמך, scholars have generally either not addressed this evidence or they have rejected the possibility that the form represents the original Hebrew text.[86] Given the distance in time between the creation of these later manuscripts (ca. twelfth century CE and later) and the original composition of the poem, probably in the sixth century BCE, it seems unlikely that the medieval versions *preserve* the original text.[87] However, they may have *arrived* at that original text nonetheless, in that an original syllabic text with the form כרמך offers a path to explaining both the MT and LXX evidence.

The solution rests on graphic similarity between three pairs of letters in the Assyrian script, which was in use by the second century BCE but may date as early as the fourth century BCE.[88] Thus, the script was in use during the period when the MT and LXX traditions would have diverged from each other. It may be that both traditions derive from a common original scroll that contained an unclear word after אמך כגפן, "your mother was like a/the vine…," in 19:10a. The explanation offered here addresses how the scribes who copied the text may have handled that corruption and how their differing solutions were preserved in the MT and LXX. The diagram below shows the development of textual corruption in the MT and LXX of Ezek 19:10a.

MT   כגפן בַּרְמך ← כגפן בַּדְמך ⇒ כגפן בדמך אמך כגפן בדמך

LXX   כגפן בַּרְמך ← כגפן בַּרמן ⇒ ἡ μήτηρ σου ὡς ἄμπελος, ὡς ἄνθος ἐν ῥόᾳ

---

86. Block (*Ezekiel 1–24*, 607) calls the form כרמך "reasonable" on the basis of graphic similarity between ב and כ and between ד and ר, but he still prefers the solution offered by Bewer.

87. On the dating of the Hebrew manuscripts, see the discussion in Emanuel Tov, *Textual Criticism of the Hebrew Bible*, 2nd ed. (Minneapolis: Fortress, 2001), 36–37.

88. Tov, *Textual Criticism*, 137, 219.

As shown in the top row of the diagram, in the MT, exchanges of ב for כ and of ד for ר would transform כרמך into בדמך. Interchanges between both pairs of letters are well-attested in the available Hebrew texts and versions.[89] In the LXX, shown in the bottom row, the error would have originated in the Hebrew *Vorlage* via exchanges of ב for the first כ and of נ for the second כ, thus transforming כרמך into ברמן, "in a pomegranate (tree)." An exchange of כ and נ is not a common orthographic error in the Assyrian script. The forms of the two letters, however, as attested in texts from the second century BCE, when the LXX translation of Ezekiel was most likely created, were similar enough that a copyist struggling with an unclear form might take one letter for the other.[90]

That the two passages share the exchange of ב for כ may indicate that an original copying error or other textual corruption resulted in the form ברמך, which would represent the combination of the preposition ב, plus the infinitive construct of רום, "to be high, exalted," plus a second-person masculine singular pronominal suffix. The resulting phrase could be translated as something like "when you were exalted" or "when you became great." A similar defective spelling of the infinitive construct of רום also appears in Ps 12:9: כְּרֵם. Though BHS proposes emending the form, the LXX translation of the same verse suggests that its *Vorlage* contained the form כרמך, and that the translator understood that form as representing the infinitive construct of רום (Ps 11:9 LXX). The evidence thus indicates the plausibility of the proposed first transmission error in Ezek 19:10a of כרמך to ברמך, in that a similar defectively spelled infinitive phrase was transmitted in the text of Ps 12:9 (11:9 LXX). In other words, the form ברמך would not have been so incomprehensible to the ancient scribes and copyists that it would constitute an impossible error.

The MT and LXX traditions then diverged in their development (or perhaps better, corruption) of the phrase. The MT eventually read ברמך as בדמך, "in your blood," possibly under the influence of a similar expression in Ezek 16, where it refers to Israel's condition as a newborn (16:6, 22). The LXX tradition, on the other hand, read ברמך as ברמן, "in a pomegranate (tree)." The resulting phrase, כגפן ברמן, "like a vine in a pomegranate

89. Tov, *Textual Criticism*, 244–48.

90. See Ada Yardeni, *The Book of Hebrew Script: History, Paleography, Script Styles, Calligraphy and Design*, 3rd ed. (Jerusalem: Carta, 2010), 2; and Tov, *Textual Criticism*, pl. 29, 409.

(tree)," would have been confusing in the context of the vine metaphor in the rest of the passage. Therefore, either the LXX translator or an earlier gloss in its Hebrew *Vorlage* added "like a flower" before "in a pomegranate (tree)" to resolve the difficult phrase.

6

Wine and Intoxication Metaphors

Not all wine metaphors include intoxication in their mappings, nor do all intoxication metaphors explicitly mention wine. It makes sense to study the two together, however, because for the prophetic authors, wine and intoxication appear to have been closely linked. While passages involving drunkenness often fail to specify the intoxicant, when the drink is included, it is almost always יין, "wine." Outside the prophetic corpus, of fifteen references to being drunk—using nominal or verbal forms of שכר, "to be drunk," or סבא, "to drink heavily"—ten lack a specific intoxicant. Of the five that do identify the intoxicant, four (80 percent) use יין.[1] Within the prophetic corpus, of the twenty-four passages employing nominal or verbal forms of שכר or סבא to express drunkenness, twelve do not specify the intoxicant. Among the remaining twelve passages, ten (83 percent) either identify wine or explicitly reject wine as the intoxicant.[2] This pattern suggests that wine served as the default intoxicant for the Israelites, meaning that wine would have likely come naturally to their minds when they heard references to or metaphors of drunkenness.

At the same time, not all metaphors about wine and other alcoholic beverages map intoxication into the image. Table 6.1 summarizes the prophetic metaphors that map people to an element of the WINE, LIQUOR, or INTOXICATION frames.[3] Among the twenty-two such passages, three draw

---

1. One of the four passages mentioning wine pairs it with שכר, "liquor." The fifth passage mentions סבא, another term for liquor.

2. Seven passages employ יין; two use עסיס; and the pairing of יין and שכר appears in one passage. (The term עסיס refers to "new wine" or "just-pressed wine" [Walsh, *Fruit of the Vine*, 197–99].) In addition, two passages in Isaiah describe people as drunk, but not with יין (Isa 29:9; 51:21). The two passages that do not employ a term for wine instead use סבא as the intoxicant (Hos 4:18; Nah 1:10).

3. Passages shown in bold text are discussed in greater detail in this chapter.

on other features of wine and liquor: on the properties of stored wine in Jer 48:11–12 and Zeph 1:12, and on the flavor and strength of liquor in Isa 1:22. The remaining nineteen metaphors all map intoxication into their structure, but otherwise display significant variety in their mappings. Eight of these metaphors specifically describe the intoxicant as wine or like wine, and two explicitly declare that their target is drunk, but not on wine. Thus, over half—ten of nineteen—of the intoxication metaphors about people in the prophetic corpus reference WINE as an element of the source frame.

Table 6.1. Wine, liquor, and intoxication
metaphors in the prophetic corpus

Basic Image	Relevant Biblical Passages
People as alcoholic beverage	Wine: **Jer 48:11–12; Zeph 1:12** Other strong drink: Isa 1:22
Intoxication Metaphors	
People as vessel	Wine vessel to be filled: Jer 13:12–14; Zech 9:15 Wine cup forced on others: **Jer 51:7–9** "Bowl of reeling" forced on others: Zech 12:2
People as intoxicant	Strong drink in cup: **Obad 16**
Intoxicated by drinking from YHWH's cup	Wine: Jer 25:15–29 Unnamed drink: Ezek 23:31–34; Hab 2:16 "Not wine": Isa 51:17–23
Intoxicated by other means	Like wine: Isa 49:26; Jer 23:9 "Not wine": Isa 29:9 Other strong drink: Nah 1:10 From named nondrink source: Isa 19:14; 63:6 From unspecified source: Jer 48:26; 51:39; 51:57; Nah 3:11

The popularity of wine, liquor, and intoxication metaphors in Jeremiah somewhat skews the data regarding their prevalence in the prophetic corpus. Eight of the twenty-two relevant passages appear in Jeremiah, and Jeremiah contributes five of the ten metaphors that explicitly map wine in their structure. The other five passages appear in First Isaiah (one), Second Isaiah (two), Zephaniah (one), and Zechariah (one). Overall, the fourteen wine, liquor, and intoxication metaphors that appear outside of Jeremiah are distributed across nine prophetic sources. Thus, while Jeremiah makes the most frequent explicit use of such metaphors, as it does of viticulture metaphors in general, many prophets drew on WINE, LIQUOR, and INTOXI-CATION as source frames for their metaphors.[4]

6.1. Wine and Other Intoxicants in Ancient Israel and Judah

We do not have much detailed information about names and classifications of intoxicating drinks, other than wine, that were consumed by the ancient Israelites.[5] A number of Hebrew terms for fermented beverages appear in the biblical corpus, but they are generally not accompanied by descriptive words that clarify their full meaning. The term שכר, for example, is paired with יין in several passages (e.g., Lev 10:9; Deut 14:26; Judg 13:4; Isa 5:11; Prov 20:1), but none of them offer details that speak of how שכר is produced. Some scholars associate שכר with beer, based in part on the Akkadian cognate *šikaru*.[6] As Jack Sasson notes, however, "Akkadian terminology for beverages is not always etymologically reminiscent

---

4. The distribution of wine and intoxication metaphors in the prophetic corpus is as follows: three in First Isaiah; two in Second Isaiah; one in Third Isaiah; eight in Jeremiah; one in Ezekiel; one in Obadiah; two in Nahum; one in Habakkuk; one in Zephaniah; and two in Zechariah. Like Jeremiah, Ezekiel also uses a relatively large number of viticulture metaphors. The pattern in Ezekiel is less obvious, though, because the book as a whole contains a smaller number of long metaphorical passages rather than a large number of short metaphorical expressions like those in Jeremiah. It may be, therefore, that viticulture metaphors were generally popular during the periods when many of the prophecies in Jeremiah and Ezekiel were composed (i.e., the late seventh and early sixth century BCE).

5. For an overview of the subject of wine and other intoxicants in the Bible and its ancient Near Eastern context, see Sasson, "Blood of Grapes," 399–419.

6. Michael M. Homan has argued that שכר consistently refers to beer made from barley, but his argument is not convincing. See Homan, "Beer, Barley, and שֵׁכָר in the Hebrew Bible," in *Le-David Maskil: A Birthday Tribute for David Noel Freedman*, ed. Richard Elliott Friedman and William H. C. Propp, BJSUCSD 9 (Winona Lake, IN: Eisenbrauns, 2004), 25–38.

of its West Semitic equivalent."[7] More significantly, while יין is explicitly connected to grapes in the Bible, שכר does not have a similar association with grain, the key ingredient for producing beer.[8] Moreover, *šikaru* in Akkadian may not always refer to beer. Several passages appear to describe wine as "mountain beer (*šikaru*)," suggesting that *šikaru* could refer to fermented drinks other than beer.[9] The meaning of סבא remains similarly unclear. Walsh notes that the root סבא "seems to refer to the *use* of alcohol … rather than the liquid itself," and therefore nominal סבא probably refers to any drink containing alcohol that a person uses to become drunk.[10] Lacking better information, most scholars simply translate terms like שכר and סבא as "strong drink" or something similar.

Though we cannot put a name to most of the fermented drinks consumed in ancient Israel, texts and archaeological findings from neighboring cultures do suggest something about the content of such drinks. Evidence from Egypt and Mesopotamia indicates that they made wine from figs, pomegranates, and dates, and the Israelites may have done likewise.[11] Indeed, all fruit juice needs to begin fermenting is a warm day and a little yeast. Given the hot summers of the southern Levant and the fact that many of the fruits grown in Israel and Judah had yeast on their own skins, it is likely that most fruit juice produced would have begun to ferment fairly quickly after it was pressed from the fruit. That was certainly true of grape juice, which probably began to ferment while the grapes were still being pressed.[12] Converting the fruit to juice and then allowing it to ferment would have been one way to preserve it for later use. Of course, since figs, pomegranates, and dates contain relatively less juice than grapes, it would have taken more fruit to produce wine from them than from grapes. As a result, commoners engaged in subsistence production probably would not have used a significant share of their fruit (other than grapes) to produce juice; the fruit would have been more valuable as food, either fresh or dried, than as drink. Elites,

---

7. Sasson, "Blood of Grapes," 400.

8. Sasson, "Blood of Grapes," 400.

9. Powell, "Wine and the Vine in Ancient Mesopotamia," 101–2.

10. Walsh, *Fruit of the Vine*, 203–5 (emphasis original).

11. Joan Goodnick Westenholz, ed., *Sacred Bounty Sacred Land: The Seven Species of the Land of Israel* (Jerusalem: Bible Lands Museum, 1998), 31, 33, 36; and Walsh, *Fruit of the Vine*, 200–202.

12. Walsh, *Fruit of the Vine*, 189.

however, may have had sufficient surplus to produce luxury goods such as fruit wines.

Finally, the Israelites may have also made beer, which requires only barley or wheat, yeast, and water to produce. The grain would first be used to bake bread, and then the bread would be broken up and placed in the water to ferment, with yeast from the air settling in the container to start the fermentation process. A few days later, after fermentation, the beer could be flavored if desired.[13] Such flavorings represent a different alcohol-related use for juices from fruits like figs, pomegranates, and dates, one that was probably employed by both elites and commoners: as a sweetener. A reduction of a relatively small amount of fruit can produce a syrup that could be used to flavor a variety of foods. Indeed, evidence indicates that such syrups were used to flavor beer as well as wine.[14]

The Israelites and Judahites probably consumed beer and wine quite regularly. For one thing, as Jennie R. Ebeling notes, the "alcoholic content would have made beer safer to drink than water."[15] In addition, water stored in jars or skins would quickly take on an unpleasant taste from the container, making wine or beer a more palatable option.[16] The higher sugar content in grapes, compared to malted grain, means that wine would have had a higher alcohol content than beer.[17] That said, the alcohol content in both the wine and the beer that the Israelites and Judahites regularly consumed was probably lower than that of the wine and beer produced today, in part because processes for distilling fermented drinks to raise their alcohol content were not invented until the Hellenistic period.[18] Given the lower potency of ancient spirits, the frequent denunciations of drunkenness leveled by the prophets, often against the rulers of Israel, suggests that those accused were consuming relatively large quantities of the intoxicating drinks (e.g., Isa 5:12–13; 28:1–4; Hos 4:11; Amos 4:1; Mic 2:11). If so, then the accusations of drunkenness may be as much (or more) about

---

13. Jennie R. Ebeling, "The Contribution of Archaeology to the Study of Women in Biblical Times: Two Case Studies," *RevEx* 106 (2009): 383–98.

14. Sasson, "Blood of Grapes," 400; Powell, "Wine and the Vine in Ancient Mesopotamia," 113.

15. Ebeling, "Contribution of Archaeology," 390.

16. Sasson, "Blood of Grapes," 402.

17. Vernon Singleton, "An Enologist's Commentary on Ancient Wine," in McGovern, Fleming, and Katz, *Origins and Ancient History of Wine*, 72.

18. Sasson, "Blood of Grapes," 400.

the conspicuous consumption of a valuable commodity as they are about objections to the behavior of the intoxicated.

Economically, it would have made little sense for the kings of Israel and Judah to trade large quantities of wine or beer. Beer can be cheaply and easily made, so there would not have been a demand for it from other kingdoms. Wine, on the other hand, can be profitable, but only if it is transported by water.[19] Landlocked Israel and Judah therefore probably produced wine and other intoxicants primarily for their own consumption, though their kings likely exported some quantity of such products via the Philistine trading ports.[20] In Judah, the growth in settlement activity beginning in the mid-eighth century was probably also accompanied by an increase in the number of vineyards cultivated. If much of that wine was held for domestic consumption, the kingdom may well have seemed awash with wine. This development may provide part of the explanation for the growing popularity of intoxication metaphors during this period, as the discussion below demonstrates.

None of the prophetic authors ever uses wine or intoxication metaphors to construct a national identity for Israel or Judah, so unlike chapters 4, 5, and 7, this chapter will not include a case study. Nevertheless, a study of the metaphorical use of wine and intoxication in the prophetic corpus does suggest that the concept grew in popularity over time, perhaps driven by the dual influence of the conventionalization of plant-based viticulture metaphors and the increasing abundance of vineyards and wine in the region.

6.2. Wine Metaphors

Just as vine and vineyard metaphors map the plants to the ATTACKED role in the COMBAT frame, so wine metaphors may also map the drink to the ATTACKED role. Indeed, such expressions constitute a natural extension of the plant-based viticulture metaphors that map people to grapes, in that wine is a product of grapes. The prophetic corpus contains several expressions of this type. For example, Jer 48:11–12 describes Moab as aged wine that is about to be spilled:

---

19. Powell, "Wine and the Vine in Ancient Mesopotamia," 108–12.
20. Faust and Weiss, "Judah, Philistia, and the Mediterranean World," 71–92.

שאנן מואב מנעוריו ושקט הוא אל־שמריו ולא־הורק מכלי אל־כלי ובגולה
לא הלך על־כן עמד טעמו בו וריחו לא נמר: לכן הנה־ימים באים נאם־יהוה
ושלחתי־לו צעים וצעהו וכליו יריקו ונבליהם ינפצו:

[11] Moab has been undisturbed since his youth; he rests on his lees. He has not been poured from vessel to vessel; into exile he has not walked. As a result, his taste stands in him and his smell has not changed. [12] Therefore, see [that] the days are coming, says YHWH, when I will send to him wine-pourers, and they will pour him out. His vessels they will empty, and their jars they will smash.

The author constructs several elements of a national identity for Moab based on its reputation as a wine producer, presenting the nation's peaceful history and future exile in terms of a wine metaphor that draws on aspects of wine-making and wine storage.

The process of wine-making in the ancient world involved several stages. After harvesting the grapes, they would be placed in a wine press. As the grapes were crushed, the juice would run off the pressing floor and into a tank, vat, or other storage container.[21] Fermentation would begin there. Within days, the fermenting wine would be moved to large jars, which would then be placed in a cellar for storage. Wine needs to be sealed away from the open air to prevent it from turning to vinegar. Therefore, the jars would be sealed with a clay stopper. Since fermentation releases carbon dioxide, however, the stoppers would initially have had a hole in them to allow that gas to escape. After fermentation, the hole could be plugged to keep the wine from further contact with the air. The wine would remain in the large storage jars until it was needed, at which point it would be transferred to smaller jars or skins for serving or transport.[22] While in storage, שמרים, "wine lees"—referring to particles, mainly from yeast, that were present in the wine—would form a sediment at the bottom of a wine jar. Shaking or moving the jar would disturb that sediment, causing it to mix in with the wine. Wine resting on its lees thus refers to wine in jars that have not been moved for a long time.

---

21. See the descriptions of the various types of wine press installations in Rafael Frankel, *Wine and Oil Production in Antiquity in Israel and Other Mediterranean Countries* (Sheffield: Sheffield Academic, 1999). See also the discussion of several relevant archaeological sites in Israel in Feig, "Excavations at Beit Ṣafafa," 191–238.

22. Borowski, *Agriculture*, 187–92.

Once decanted from the large jars, contact with the air would begin to affect the wine, eventually turning it to vinegar. The stored wine also degraded over time. Since the large jars and their seals were not air-tight, the wine stored in them would eventually either evaporate or turn to vinegar.[23] These effects suggest that the Israelites would not have aged their wine for any significant amount of time, because time did not improve their wines. The longer the wine aged, the more likely it was to either evaporate to syrup or turn to vinegar. Consequently, the Israelites probably would have needed to consume it within a year or two of its pressing.

In the metaphor in Jer 48:11–12, the scene opens at the point when the wine in the large jars has rested long enough for the lees to settle to the bottom of the jar, but not long enough for the wine to spoil. The author compresses his version of the history of Moab into the span of time between the grape-pressing and the metaphor's opening scene. The unspoken contrast in the image is between Moab as settled, full-flavored, aromatic wine and other wine that has been poured into smaller jars, and that therefore has lost some flavor or turned to vinegar due to its exposure to air. Highlighting the pleasing taste and smell of well-preserved wine suggests that Moab is a desirable target for conquest (48:11b). As a result, YHWH will send invaders to conquer Moab (48:12).[24]

In the context of the metaphor, "resting on one's lees," represents complacency, a sense that just as Moab has always rested peacefully in its land, so the Moabites expect it will ever be. Idiomatically, the phrase may even carry a connotation of inappropriate complacency in the face of a threat. Zephaniah 1:12 contains a similar, though less palatable, image predicting the punishment of certain Jerusalemites הקפאים על־שמריהם, "who are congealing on their lees," perhaps referring to wine that has been stored too long, such that it has partially evaporated and the remaining wine

---

23. Singleton, "Enologist's Commentary," 70–72.

24. William L. Holladay argues that the comment about Moab's flavor and smell must represent a critique, but he glosses over how the statement of praise could be interpreted in this way. See William L. Holladay, *Jeremiah 2: A Commentary on the Book of the Prophet Jeremiah, Chapters 26–52*, Hermeneia (Philadelphia: Fortress, 1989), 358. Jack R. Lundbom captures the stability aspect of the mapping between the wine's taste and smell and Moab's past of having never been exiled, but he does not consider whether the statement of praise may serve less to criticize Moab than to heighten the threat in the author's message by presenting Moab as good wine. See Jack R. Lundbom, *Jeremiah 37–52: A New Translation with Introduction and Commentary*, AB 21C (New York: Doubleday, 2004), 266–67.

has thickened.[25] In this case, the author provides no explanation of the phrase, which suggests that the metaphor of complacent people as "resting on their lees" was conventional enough that an audience would recognize the underlying PEOPLE ARE WINE metaphor. Zephaniah 1:12 indicates that the erring Jerusalemites have declared that YHWH will not intervene in human events to punish (or reward) them for their actions. Thus, the lees metaphors in both Jeremiah and Zephaniah present images of complacency that ignores the reality of an imminent threat.

The metaphor in Jeremiah concludes in 48:12 with a construction of the Moabites' national body and common fate. It maps the cities of Moab to the large storage jars and Moab's deported people to wine that will be poured out. By explicitly associating exile with the pouring of wine from one vessel to another (48:11), the author implies that the wine in 48:12 will not be poured out onto the ground. Rather, it will be poured into some type of container and carried away. The sequence in the phrasing reinforces this message, as the jars will only be smashed after the wine has been poured out. The metaphor thus also appears to reflect the reality of how wine was transported in the ancient Near East, which may have involved shifting the wine to new jars at each major stage of the trip.[26] Conceptually, the metaphor maps each city in Moab to a single large storage jar, and then compresses the forces attacking each city into the image of a single person pouring out the wine and smashing the original jar.[27] The imagery shares little in common with a combat scene; indeed, it may be more

---

25. The concept of age-thickened wine is reflected in ancient writings that confirm that old wines would occasionally evaporate "to the point of being syrupy" (Singleton, "Enologist's Commentary," 72). Lundbom (*Jeremiah 37–52*, 266) suggests that because lees are strained from wine at the end of fermentation, the description of "congealing" in Zeph 1:12 may indicate a wine that has been left to ferment too long. This explanation assumes that the ancient Israelites distinguished between the sediment that was strained from the wine after its initial fermentation and a smaller amount of sediment that would have survived the straining and would have settled in the jars, but it is not clear that they made such distinctions.

26. Powell ("Wine and the Vine in Ancient Mesopotamia," 111) cites evidence that "the transfer of wine from container to container in the course of conveying it to the consumer must have been rather common practice." Texts from Carchemish describe buying and filling empty jars as part of the process of purchasing wine.

27. Holladay (*Jeremiah 2*, 358) notes that as a consequence of smashing the jars and taking the wine, "all the former serenity, all the former identity of Moab will be gone."

reminiscent of a raid, a brief attack whose primary purpose is usually the theft of property. As such, the metaphor lacks the types of mappings for individual combat seen in other plant metaphors, but instead incorporates the damage to and loss of property that would occur during a raid.[28]

6.3. Intoxication Metaphors

The vine and vineyard metaphors studied in chapters 3–5 all share a basic structure in which the plant or its produce occupies the ATTACKED role, and humans or animals, or occasionally YHWH, fill the ATTACKER role. The example of Jer 48:11–12 shows that wine metaphors could employ the same structure. All of these metaphors create an image of the vines and their produce as victims of a more powerful attacker. At the same time, these images of weakness constitute a deliberate manipulation of an original positive conception of Israel and Judah as a vine or vineyard. Thus, it is worth considering whether the positive viticulture metaphors may have been extended in ways that would reinforce their role as a symbol of pride for the two kingdoms. During a time of conflict, having as a national symbol a plant—an entity that cannot be depicted as an attacker—would have created a rhetorical challenge. The tendency toward realism in prophetic plant metaphors makes the plant image especially problematic, as it is not likely that the prophetic authors would have presented the vines or their fruit as aggressors. Intoxication metaphors may have helped meet that challenge by turning wine and other intoxicants into a weapon. When wielded or directed by YHWH, the image allows Israel or Judah, as YHWH's people, to identify with the position of the attacker, rather than the attacked.

Passages in which the drink maps to the ATTACKER express the conceptual metaphor CONQUEST IS CAUSING INTOXICATION. They represent a conceptual contrast to the CONQUEST IS EATING metaphor, in that instead of being consumed, the entity filling the ATTACKED role is forced to con-

---

28. Jeremiah 13:12–14 presents an alternate use of the image of smashed wine jars to convey divine punishment, in the form of internal unrest among the people. There, the people of Judah map to the jars, whom YHWH will fill with drunkenness and then shatter by striking them against each other. The drunkenness maps to emotions associated with conflict, such as anger, and the shattering jars map to the conflict itself that destroys the people. The metaphor PEOPLE ARE POTTERY also appears several times in the book(s) of Isaiah outside of the viticulture context (Isa 29:16; 30:14; 45:9; 64:7).

sume an intoxicant. CONQUEST IS CAUSING INTOXICATION derives much of its coherence in two ways. First, it shares the same structure as other biblical metaphors that map eating or drinking something unpleasant to the idea of distress or punishment: CONQUEST IS FEEDING SOMEONE SOMETHING BITTER and CONQUEST IS POISONING SOMEONE.[29] The terms לענה, "wormwood [a bitter tasting plant]," and ראש, "poison; a poisonous plant; venom," appear in several expressions of these metaphors (e.g., Amos 6:12; Jer 9:14).

Second, CONQUEST IS CAUSING INTOXICATION incorporates the conventional metaphor WARFARE IS INDIVIDUAL COMBAT into its structure via the elements that the INTOXICATION frame shares with the INDIVIDUAL COMBAT frame. In particular, the EFFECTS OF INTOXICATION mimic the EFFECTS OF EXPERIENCING COMBAT. The fillers for these elements may reflect emotional responses of the combatants, such as anger and aggression, or they may represent physical responses to being struck, such as staggering, loss of consciousness, and potentially death. Even vomiting fits within this conceptual relationship, since nausea and vomiting can occur in response to pain and shock from the physical or psychological trauma associated with combat. Prophetic intoxication metaphors frequently make use of one or more of these physical effects (e.g., Isa 19:14; Jer 25:16, 27; Hab 2:16; Zech 9:15).

Jeremiah 51:7–9 offers an example of the weaponized representation of wine. The metaphor in 51:7 maps intoxication to the Neo-Babylonian Empire's conquest, at the end of the seventh century BCE, of the Assyrian Empire and Syria-Palestine:

כוס־זהב בבל ביד־יהוה משכרת כל־הארץ מיינה שתו גוים על־כן
יתהללו גוים:

A cup of gold was Babylon, in the hand of YHWH.[30] She made all the earth drunk. From her wine [the] peoples drank. Therefore, [the] peoples went mad.

---

29. While CONQUEST IS FEEDING SOMEONE SOMETHING BITTER OR POISONOUS summarizes the metaphor from the perspective of the ATTACKER role, in the biblical corpus, expressions of the underlying source-target conceptual relationship may also approach the issue from the perspective of the ATTACKED: BEING CONQUERED IS EATING/DRINKING SOMETHING BITTER OR POISONOUS (e.g., Lam 3:19; Prov 5:4).

30. It may be that the original verse lacked the phrase ביד־יהוה "in the hand of YHWH" (Holladay, *Jeremiah 2*, 396). If so, then image of a weaponized wine would

The verse attributes Babylonia's success not to its own deities but to YHWH, who uses the empire as his instrument.[31] This conceptualization of history allows the author to maintain YHWH's supremacy at a time when he seemingly had failed to protect his own people from conquest. By means of this argument, the conquest of Judah becomes as much a testament to YHWH's power as Judah's survival would have been. Framed in this way, YHWH cannot lose.[32] In subsequent speeches in Jer 51, YHWH declares that he will also intoxicate Babylonia and its leaders in their turn, as retribution for their actions against Judah (51:39, 57).

The passage does not construct a complete national identity for Babylonia, but it does contain several identity elements. Like the Moab metaphor discussed above, the central image maps people to wine in a vessel. However, the mapping in this case probably refers to the armies of Babylonia, rather than to the population of the kingdom as a whole. In Jer 48:11–12, the jars map to the cities of Moab. That may be the case also in Jer 51:7, but the author more likely had in mind a more general conception of the kingdom as the golden cup, its armies spilling over the rim and flooding the world to the point of drunkenness.[33] Since the author's primary interest lies in conveying to the Judahites that the punishment of their conqueror is at hand, the metaphor lacks the element of a national origin narrative for Babylonia, and its history is limited to a span of decades at most. The passage instead focuses on constructing a character for the kingdom by differentiating the conquering wine from the conquered drinkers.

---

still have been part of the original passage, but the idea that the weapon was controlled by the Judahite national deity would be a later development. Lundbom (*Jeremiah 37–52*, 437) notes, however, that the only purpose of deleting the phrase is to "correct" the meter or message of the verse, and "there is no textual basis" for such an emendation.

31. Using a metaphor of a שבט, "rod," First Isaiah also claims that Assyria served as YHWH's instrument (Isa 10:5; Lundbom, *Jeremiah 37–52*, 440).

32. A weaker variation of this concept of YHWH controlling world history appears in Hab 2:15–16, in which Babylonia, who made other peoples drunk, will be made to drink by YHWH. Habakkuk 2:15 describes Babylonia as the driving force behind the intoxication of other peoples. Habakkuk 2:16, however, states that the cup in YHWH's hand will turn around on Babylonia. The effect of the two verses implies that YHWH played a role in Babylonia's victories over other kingdoms, but it does not attribute those acts to YHWH as directly or clearly as Jer 51:7.

33. A similar image of an invading army as a flood of water also appears in the prophets (e.g., Isa 8:7; Jer 46:7).

The salient aspects of Babylonian culture for this author appear to be its wealth (expressed in terms of the golden cup) and its destructiveness (conveyed by the widespread drunkenness and madness that the Babylonian wine caused), both described in 51:7.[34] The image of the empire's current state as fallen and shattered in 51:8 presumably continues the cup metaphor.[35] The goal and effect of the metaphor is to diminish the powerful image of Babylonia and restore the confidence of the exilic audience that YHWH still controls their destiny. The passage accomplishes these ends by placing the cup in YHWH's hand, thereby asserting that everything the Babylonians have accomplished has proceeded according to YHWH's plan. By implication, then, the author conveys that what YHWH has done to prosper Babylonia and make it mighty among the nations, he can also do for his own people.

Finally, Obad 16 represents a clever blending of the conceptualizations of conquest as eating and as causing intoxication. In the context of verses 15 and 17, the passage creates an image of Jerusalem as both the consumed liquid victim of Edom and the intoxicating drink that will attack all other kingdoms:

כי־קרוב יום־יהוה על־כל־הגוים כאשר עשית יעשה לך גמלך ישוב בראשך:
כי כאשר שתיתם על־הר קדשי ישתו כל־הגוים תמיד ושתו ולעו והיו כלוא
היו: ובהר ציון תהיה פליטה והיה קדש וירשו בית יעקב את מורשיהם:

[15] The day of YHWH is near, against all of the nations. Just as you did, so shall it be done to you; your deed shall turn against you. [16] For just as you drank on my holy mountain, all the peoples shall drink continuously. They shall drink and gulp and become as though they had never been. [17] But on Mount Zion there will be a remnant, and it will be holy. The House of Jacob will dispossess those who dispossessed them.

---

34. For the golden cup, see Lundbom, *Jeremiah 37–52*, 439–40.

35. Lundbom (*Jeremiah 37–52*, 441) points out that a cup of pure gold would not shatter from a fall, but he suggests the alternate possibility that the image refers to a cup "overlaid with gold." The language of healing, or lack of healing, in the following verses belongs to an ILLNESS or INJURY frame (Lundbom, *Jeremiah 37–52*, 441), rather than a POTTERY frame. Since the wine metaphor maps the cup to the nation (as a group of people), however, the common element of the HUMAN BODY helps the blend of source frames remain coherent.

Because the author switches from second-person singular address in verse 15 to second-person plural in verse 16, some scholars argue that YHWH here no longer speaks to Edom, but instead has turned to Jerusalem, declaring that just as the city's inhabitants were metaphorically intoxicated when Edom attacked them, so will all peoples become intoxicated when YHWH makes them drink, too. This interpretation is influenced by the intoxication metaphor in Jer 25:15–29, in which YHWH commands Jeremiah to take a cup and force a series of kingdoms, beginning with Judah, to drink.[36]

The idea of passing the cup from one nation or kingdom to another is a fairly common image in the prophetic texts. In Jer 25:15–29, YHWH justifies that action by arguing that if he has forced his own people to drink, then all other kingdoms should also expect to drink in their turn. Similarly, Ezek 23:31–34 declares that YHWH will make Jerusalem drink from Samaria's cup until Jerusalem is drunk, and in Isa 51:17–23, YHWH takes the cup from Jerusalem and gives it to her enemies. Viewed in this way, the metaphor of Obad 16 would approach its subject from the perspective of Jerusalem, whose days of being the victim are about to end.

In Obadiah, however, the context of verses 15 and 17 suggests that the perspective of verse 16 is less about comforting the victim than it is about threatening the attackers. In that sense, its message is similar to that of Jer 51, discussed above, which focuses on Babylonia's actions and fate, rather than on relief for Babylonia's victims. Obadiah 15b addresses Edom in the second-person singular, saying that what they have done will be done to them. But Obad 15a has a broader focus, declaring judgment over all other kingdoms. Obadiah 17a narrowly focuses on the claim that a remnant of Jerusalem will survive, but it follows that statement in 17b with a declaration that Israel will dispossess those (plural) who dispossessed Israel. Since Obad 15 and 17 contain threats of retribution, it seems reasonable to conclude that the metaphor in verse 16 conveys a similar message. The passage switches from the second-person singular address in verse 15b to

---

36. Julius A. Bewer, *A Critical and Exegetical Commentary on Obadiah and Joel*, ICC (Edinburgh: T&T Clark, 1911), 28–29. On the metaphor of the cup of wrath, see the excursus in Paul R. Raabe, *Obadiah: A New Translation with Introduction and Commentary*, AB 24D (New York: Doubleday, 1996), 206–42. See also William McKane, "Trial by Ordeal and the Cup of Wrath," *VT* 30 (1980): 474–92; and Klaus-Dietrich Schunck, "Der Becher Jahwes: Weinbecher—Taumelbecher—Zornesbecher," in *Verbindungslinien: Festschrift für Werner H. Schmidt zum 65. Geburtstag*, ed. Axel Graupner et al. (Neukirchen-Vluyn: Neukirchener Verlag, 2000), 323–30.

the second-person plural in verse 16 because its addressee has shifted from Edom alone to all of the kingdoms that attacked Jerusalem.

The author alludes to the intoxicating effect of drinking alcohol from two perspectives. The first phrase in verse 16—"For just as you drank on my holy mountain"—describes the kingdoms' attack on Jerusalem using a variation on the CONQUEST IS EATING metaphor: CONQUEST IS DRINKING. The reference to drinking not only conveys the sense of conquest, but it also highlights the concept of drinking in celebration over a defeated opponent. Given that Judah was an exporter of wine, the author may have had in mind a double meaning of the kingdoms both literally and figuratively drinking Judahite wine as part of the attack imagery. The remainder of the verse then uses hyperbole to turn the image of drinking in celebration into one of drinking to excess, drinking to death, in this case. The extreme intoxication that the kingdoms will experience maps to their punishment for what was once done to Jerusalem. In this and other intoxication metaphors, the juxtaposition of these aspects of wine consumption—turning the pleasurable effects of intoxication into an image of violence or death—creates a powerful message of divine vengeance for the audience.

6.4. Conclusions: Turning Wine into a Weapon

As the discussion here has shown, the metaphor PEOPLE ARE WINE could be deployed to depict either a victim or an aggressor, and in both cases, the author could use the image to construct elements of a national identity for the target that would map to the WINE element. In most cases, however, both wine and intoxication metaphors primarily address either the current state or the common fate of the target. Only a few of these images develop these and other national identity elements in any significant way. In addition, while these metaphors can map the INTOXICANT to kingdoms or armies (either directly or by implication) for the MEANS OF ATTACK element in the CONQUEST frame, in some passages that element maps to an unspecified filler: the victim will be made drunk, but how that will be accomplished is only vaguely indicated, if at all (e.g., Isa 29:9; Jer 13:12–14; Ezek 23:31–34).

More broadly, when expressions of CONQUEST IS CAUSING INTOXICATION appear in the prophetic corpus, they arise in a variety of contexts and carry a range of messages. At the same time, some mappings appear to have achieved a degree of conventionalization over time. In particular, the association of conquest with the image of intoxication by drinking from a cup or other vessel appears in six passages in five books (Isa 51:17–23; Jer 25:15–29; 51:7–9; Ezek 23:31–34; Hab 2:15–16; Zech 12:2). Also noteworthy are the two passages that use, in very different contexts, the image of someone "settled on their lees" to express the idea of inappropriate complacency. The difference in contexts between the version about Moab in Jer 48:11–12 and the one about certain Jerusalemites in Zeph 1:12 mitigates against literary dependence between the two passages, as does the use of different verbs for the action of the wine in each passage. Rather, both authors appear to have independently drawn on the same conventional lees metaphor.

We cannot determine when and where the CONQUEST IS CAUSING INTOXICATION metaphor first developed from the biblical evidence. The evidence, however, does indicate a pattern in the deployment of this metaphor by the prophetic authors. Relevant to the analysis is the near absence of wine metaphors from those prophets that scholars traditionally date to the eighth century BCE: Amos, Hosea, First Isaiah, and Micah.[37] Several eighth-century passages map grapes to people, but mappings of wine to people appear almost exclusively in later texts. A similar pattern exists with intoxication metaphors. Amos, Hosea, and Micah do not use INTOXICATION as a metaphorical source frame, and First Isaiah uses it only twice, in metaphors that reject wine as the intoxicant (Isa 19:14; Isa 29:9). This pattern suggests that the wine and intoxication metaphors may have

---

37. Translations of Isa 1:22b often render the phrase as something like "your wine is cut with water," which may represent a metaphor for the corruption of Jerusalem's leaders (e.g., JPS, KJV, RSV). The Hebrew term used in the passage, however, is not ייִן, the more common word for wine. Rather, the author uses סבא: כספך היה לסיגים סבאך מהול במים, "your silver has become dross; your liquor is diluted with water." As such, the passage may not be a wine metaphor. Moreover, the context of the passage suggests that a nonmetaphorical interpretation of the passage is as plausible as a metaphorical one. On the one hand, 1:23 speaks of the misdeeds of Jerusalem's leaders, and 1:25 appears to metaphorically describe removing bad leaders as separating dross from silver. Thus, 1:22 could be understood metaphorically as a reference to Jerusalem's leaders. On the other hand, the complaint about the leaders in 1:23 describes them as friends of thieves, suggesting that 1:22 could contain a literal complaint about the leaders engaging in, or at least allowing, unethical trade practices (i.e., using impure silver as pure silver for trade and selling diluted liquor as pure liquor). Indeed, the LXX seems to interpret it just so: τὸ ἀργύριον ὑμῶν ἀδόκιμον· οἱ κάπηλοί σου μίσγουσι τὸν οἶνον ὕδατι, "Your silver has no value; your taverners mix the wine with water" (NETS).

grown in popularity during the seventh century BCE, perhaps under the influence of the conceptualization of Judah as a vine or vineyard.

One explanation for how the use of the wine and intoxication metaphors could have developed as a consequence of the conventionalization of plant-based viticulture metaphors may lie in the very structure of the plant-based metaphors. By convention, plant metaphors are passive. In the prophetic condemnations, the plant always fills the role of the ATTACKED, never the ATTACKER. Wine and intoxication metaphors may have provided a way for the prophetic authors to take their metaphorical vines on the offensive by turning wine into a weapon in YHWH's hands. In this way, a conceptually passive national vine or vineyard image could be transformed into an expression of YHWH's power.

7

Fig and Fig Tree Metaphors

In 1953, the Rev. C. H. Bird argued: "The fig tree in the Old Testament often represents Judaism or the people of Israel.... Very often Israel is compared ... to a fig tree."[1] His suggestion was firmly rejected by J. W. Wenham in a short note published in 1954. Narrowly confining his data set to only those passages that specifically associate the fig tree with a kingdom, and finding that only Hos 9:10, about Israel, and Nah 3:12, about Nineveh, met his criteria, Wenham concluded: "As far as the Old Testament is concerned, is there much better ground for saying that Israel is very often compared to a fig tree, than there is for saying the same of the fortresses of Nineveh?"[2] Wenham had a point; little evidence exists within the biblical corpus for the *fig tree* as a symbol of Israel or Israelite religion. Had he considered *fig fruit* in addition to fig trees, however, he might have reached a different conclusion. As this chapter will demonstrate, both figs alone and figs paired with grapes held symbolic significance for the ancient Israelites, though in very different ways. The combination of figs with grapes, or fig trees with grapevines, symbolizes the concepts of prosperity and of the lands of Israel and Judah. Images of figs alone, however, consistently represent national defeat.

7.1. Figs and Fig Trees in Ancient Israel and Judah

Fig variants range in form from weedy bushes to tall trees, but in the Mediterranean region, the typical common fig tree, *Ficus carica L.*, grows to three to five meters tall and has spreading branches and large leaves with

---

1. J. W. Wenham, "The Fig Tree in the Old Testament," *JTS* 5.2 (1954): 206–7.
2. Wenham, "Fig Tree," 207.

multiple lobes.[3] The wood of a fig tree is brittle, and the tree produces a natural latex that irritates human skin. These properties made fig wood and leaves unsuitable for most purposes in the ancient world.[4] As a result, the fig tree's primary value derived from its fruit.[5] Figs made a nutrient rich and calorie dense contribution to the human diet.[6] They could be eaten fresh in the summer or dried for off-season eating or to carry as travel rations.[7] In the Bible, metaphors in Isa 28:4 and Nah 3:12 describe eating a fig freshly picked from the tree, while 1 Sam 25:18 and 1 Chr 12:41 mention dried figs among gifts of food and provisions brought by Abigail for David and his army. The caloric density and preservability of figs would have made them valuable during times of warfare or siege as well, when food might be scarce.[8] Figs could also be processed for use in other ways. The Egyptians baked fig paste into bread, added figs to grape wine, perhaps as a sweetener, and made fig wine and liqueur.[9] In addition,

---

3. Ed Stover et al., "The Fig: Overview of an Ancient Fruit," *HortScience* 42 (2007): 1083–87. Zohary, *Plants of the Bible*, 58. On figs and fig trees, see also Asaph Goor, "The History of the Fig in the Holy Land from Ancient Times to the Present Day," *Economic Botany* 19 (1965): 124–35; Zohary and Hopf, *Domestication of Plants*, 159–64; and Lytton John Musselman, *A Dictionary of Bible Plants* (Cambridge: Cambridge University Press, 2012), 55–57.

4. Stover et al., "Fig," 1083; and Musselman, *Dictionary of Bible Plants*, 55–56.

5. The nature of figs hampers our ability to examine the extent of fig production and consumption in the ancient Near East. Fig seeds are so small that they may be overlooked at archaeological sites. See Margareta Tengberg, "Fruit-Growing," in *A Companion to the Archaeology of the Ancient Near East*, ed. Daniel T. Potts, 2 vols. (Chichester: Wiley-Blackwell, 2012), 192. Seedless fruit, like the carbonized figs found in a Neolithic village in Gilgal, in the Jordan Valley, would leave even less evidence for archaeologists to find. See Mordechai E. Kislev, Anat Hartmann, and Ofer Bar-Yosef, "Early Domesticated Fig in the Jordan Valley," *Science* 312.5778 (2006): 1372–74.

6. K. K. Sinha, "Figs," in *Encyclopedia of Food Sciences and Nutrition*, ed. Benjamin Caballero, 2nd ed., 10 vols. (Amsterdam: Academic Press: 2003), 2398.

7. Whole figs could be sun-dried individually by laying them out on a flat surface or by hanging them up on strings (Goor, "History of the Fig," 131). The practice of drying figs on strings is also attested in Philistia and Mesopotamia (Westenholz, *Sacred Bounty*, 32, 122).

8. Wright, "Warfare," 423–58.

9. For fig paste, see L. Saffirio, "Food and Dietary Habits in Ancient Egypt," *Journal of Human Evolution* 1 (1972): 303. For adding figs to wine, see Patrick E. McGovern, *Ancient Wine: The Search for the Origins of Viniculture* (Princeton: Princeton University Press, 2003), 94, 101. The figs may also have been added to aid in the wine's fermentation via yeast on the figs' skin. McGovern notes that both features of the pottery and analysis

both biblical and extrabiblical texts attest to medicinal uses for figs and fig leaves.[10] Finally, evidence shows that dried figs were exported to other countries, which suggests that the fruit was a trade item and a potential source of income.[11]

Newly planted fig trees require three to four years to mature before producing their first crop of fruit.[12] Thereafter, most domesticated trees will produce one or two edible crops per year, depending on the fig variety. Figs do not all ripen at once during the growing season. Rather, the individual fruits achieve ripeness over the course of several weeks, with those closest to the tree's trunk maturing first.[13] In common fig trees that produce two annual crops, the figs from the first, smaller crop are known as breba figs.[14] Breba figs begin to ripen in June, while figs from the second, main crop start to ripen in August. Figs from trees that produce only one crop per year will begin to ripen in August.[15]

A typical ripe fig is one to four inches in diameter and may be egg-, cone-, or pear-shaped.[16] Once picked, the entire fig is edible, including the

---

of the wine and grape remains in the wine jars suggest that the wine was imported from the southern Levant. For fig wine and liqueur, see Westenholz, *Sacred Bounty*, 31.

10. A poultice made from dried figs cures King Hezekiah's שְׁחִין "skin inflammation or boil" (2 Kgs 20:7; Isa 38:21; *DCH* 8:322, s.v. "שְׁחִין"). A text from Ugarit that prescribes various treatments for diseases in horses also includes *dblt*, "dried figs," among the ingredients for one of its recipes (RS 17.120:31). For a discussion of this text and of *dblt* in general, see Chaim Cohen and Daniel Sivan, *The Ugaritic Hippiatric Texts: A Critical Edition*, American Oriental Series Essays 9 (New Haven: American Oriental Society, 1983), 9–10, 40–41. See also *DULAT*, s.v. "dblt." In addition, several Mesopotamian ritual texts, including potion recipes and directions for making a bandage, list fig leaves and fig pollen among their ingredients. See Benjamin R. Foster, *Before the Muses: An Anthology of Akkadian Literature*, 3rd ed. (Bethesda, MD: CDL, 2005), 968; and *CAD* 18:435, s.v. "tittu," 1c2′.

11. Westenholz, *Sacred Bounty*, 122.

12. Zohary and Hopf, *Domestication of Plants*, 159; and Ehud Weiss, "'Beginnings of Fruit Growing in the Old World': Two Generations Later," *Israel Journal of Plant Sciences* 62 (2015): 80.

13. Stover et al., "Fig," 1084. As a result of this gradual ripening pattern, the day-to-day volume of available ripe fruit will vary over the course of the harvesting period. Initially, only a few figs will ripen each day, but the daily volume of available ripe fruit will grow as the season approaches its peak.

14. From the Spanish word for early figs, *breva*.

15. Stover et al., "Fig," 1084.

16. Julia F. Morton, "Fig: *Ficus carica*," in *Fruits of Warm Climates* (Miami: Echo Point, 2013), 47–50.

skin and seeds. The fruit will not ripen further after it has been picked, so figs must be tree ripened to achieve their full flavor. As a fig ripens, its neck softens and droops, making it easy to separate the fruit from the tree either by twisting or cutting the neck at the stem.[17] This softness also means that figs are quite delicate. Indeed, if not picked in a timely manner, the fig will fall from the tree. Figs can be harvested that way, either collecting the fruit from the ground or placing a sheet or other receptacle under the tree to collect the ripe fruit as it drops. A large quantity of figs can be collected in a single harvest using this method, particularly if the tree is shaken to encourage the fruit to drop. Allowing them to fall to the ground, however, risks damaging the fruit, thus rendering it less palatable and more likely to spoil quickly. Figs harvested from the ground are therefore best suited for drying.[18] Ripe figs also deteriorate quickly after picking; they must be either eaten or preserved within days to prevent losses from spoilage.[19]

The biblical evidence attests to one general term for the fig tree and its fruit, תאנה, and four additional terms that refer only to the fruit:[20]

- קיץ, "summer," "summer fruits," and possibly "summer harvest";[21] in the context of fruit, קיץ probably usually refers to figs from the main, August crop or to the harvest of those figs;
- פג, "unripe fig";[22]
- דבלה, "dried fig";[23] and

---

17. Sinha, "Figs," 2397; see also A. Aytekin Polat and Muhammad Siddiq, "Figs," in *Tropical and Subtropical Fruits: Postharvest Physiology, Processing and Packaging*, ed. Muhammad Siddiq (Ames, IA: Wiley-Blackwell, 2012), 460.

18. Stover et al., "Fig," 1084.

19. Polat and Siddiq, "Figs," 461.

20. While exceptions occur, customary Hebrew usage appears to have differentiated the singular and plural forms of fruit tree names as an aid to audience comprehension. In most cases, the singular form refers to the tree, either as a single tree (Judg 9:10–11) or as a collective singular. The plural form typically refers to the fruit. That the singular form תאנה parallels גפן, "vine," in several texts (Num 20:5; Hos 2:12; Jer 5:17), but never parallels ענב, "grape," further supports this claim. On the other hand, תאנים as a reference to fig fruit does appear with ענבים, "grapes" (Num 13:23; Jer 8:13). The broad usage of תאנה and תאנים makes it likely that תאנים is a general term for all types of figs, contra *HALOT* (s.v. "בִּכּוּרָה"), which suggests that תאנים refers only to August figs and excludes June figs.

21. *DCH* 7:250, s.v. "קַיִץ."

22. *DCH* 6:648, s.v. "פַּג."

23. Scholars disagree on the exact nature of דבלה, since the biblical corpus

◆ בכורה, "early fig," probably referring to a breba fig.

Borowski argues that קיץ refers to August figs, which were dried for pres-ervation.[24] The association of קיץ with both summer and figs provides some support Borowski's claim. In addition, since fresh figs deteriorate rapidly once they have been picked, it makes sense that most of a large August crop would be preserved for later use. In the context of any given biblical passage, however, קיץ may appear in either fresh (Amos 8:1–2) or dried form (2 Sam 16:1–2).

Neither פג, "unripe fig," nor דבלה, "dried fig," appear in the prophetic condemnations discussed in this chapter, so a detailed examination of these terms is unnecessary. The term בכורה, on the other hand, does require further study, as it appears exclusively in prophetic national meta-phors (Isa 28:4; Jer 24:2; Hos 9:10; and Mic 7:1). The standard lexica agree that בכורה refers to an early fig, but the exact type of early fig—whether a breba fig or the first ripe fruits of the August fig crop—is a complex issue, one not clearly addressed in the scholarly literature.[25] In his 1965 article on figs in Israel, Asaph Goor indicates of breba figs that "only a few local varieties bear the early crop (Bakurot)."[26] If breba figs were rare in Israel fifty years ago, we must consider whether they were similarly rare in ancient Israel, or even whether the fig varieties that produce breba figs were introduced into the southern Levant after the biblical era. In the

---

contains no clear description of the item. *DCH* (2:385, s.v. "דְּבֵלָה") describes it as a "fig-cake" or "lump of figs." Westenholz (*Sacred Bounty*, 122) associates the term with a string of dried figs. Study of the root דבל in Hebrew and cognate languages yields little helpful insight, but evidence from extrabiblical sources seems to support Westenholz's view. In Mesopotamia, figs (GIŠ.PEŠ or *tittu*) were routinely dried and transported on strings (*šerku*). Similarly, a thirteenth-century BCE pottery jar found at Ekron contains spirals of fossilized figs, each pierced through the middle, suggest-ing that the figs were once strung together through those holes. A jar fragment from the eighth–seventh century BCE bearing the letters דבל was also found at Ekron. Westenholz suggests that the jar held strings of figs that were being exported (*Sacred Bounty*, 32, 122).

24. Borowski, *Agriculture*, 115.
25. See, e.g., *DCH* 2:172, s.v. "בְּכּוּרָה"; *HALOT*, s.v. "בְּכּוּרָה"; BDB, s.v. "בְּכּוּרָה."
26. Goor, "History of the Fig," 127. A scarcity of breba figs in modern Israel may explain why scholars writing about figs in Israel omit discussion of them. See, e.g., Zohary, *Plants of the Bible*, 59; Zohary and Hopf, *Domestication of Plants*, 160; and Musselman, *Dictionary of Bible Plants*, 56.

latter case, בכורה would most likely refer to the first figs to ripen from an August crop.[27]

The evidence weighs in favor of בכורה referring to a breba fig, however. First, the phrase כבכורה בטרם קיץ, "like a *bikkurah*-fig before the summertime," in Isa 28:4 is inconsistent with the idea that בכורה refers to the first ripe fruits from the August crop. Trees that produce only one crop of figs per year need time to grow new branches on which to develop fruit.[28] As a result, even the earliest fruit would probably not ripen before the summer. Breba figs, on the other hand, develop on the previous year's branches, and therefore can ripen much earlier.[29] An alternative approach that interprets בטרם קיץ as referring to the August fig crop ("before the summer figs"), rather than to the season ("before the summertime"), would also suggest that the בכורה crop is not part of the August crop, because the בכורה figs ripen before the August קיץ.

7.2. Figs and Fig Trees in the Biblical Corpus

A total of fifty-eight verses in thirty-eight passages in the biblical corpus employ one or more of the Hebrew terms for figs, fig trees, or the fig harvest. References to figs or figs trees occur in multiple genres, including narrative, historiography, prophecy, wisdom, and psalms. Curiously, however, while the legal collections contain regulations regarding leaving unharvested a portion of the grape and olive harvests for the poor to glean, none of them mention figs (e.g., Exod 23:11; Lev 19:10; Deut 24:20). It may be that grapes and olives were grown in greater quantities than the other fruits—grown with the intention of producing a surplus for use in trade or to pay taxes—and it was therefore considered reasonable to ask farmers to leave gleanings from these fruit trees for the poor. The realities of harvesting figs may also have mitigated against their inclusion in the harvesting regulations. Properly tended, grapes will ripen together and must be picked quickly to avoid spoilage. Olives can be picked and consumed or

---

27. The third alternative, that בכורה refers to an early-ripening fig tree variety, seems unlikely, since the use of בכורה in Hos 9:10 suggests that it represents a rare fruit find, an image not consistent with the notion of a tree variety that produces a large crop of early figs each year. See further the discussion of this passage in the case study, below.

28. Stover et al., "Fig," 1084.

29. Stover et al., "Fig," 1084.

processed for oil even when not fully ripe. These features mean that both grapes and olives could be harvested en masse, with some of the fruit left behind for the gleaners. By contrast, figs do not all ripen simultaneously, and they are only edible when ripe. Therefore, a growing season may have more than one harvest period. Differences in weather patterns from year to year would also have affected the pace of ripening. Under such conditions, it would have been difficult to establish a fixed point in time each year when the remaining fruit should be considered gleanings.[30]

Most biblical references to fig trees lack detail.[31] A few passages allude to the height of the tree or to aspects of its leaves, but the majority express a binary choice: the land either does or does not have fig trees.[32] The treatment of fig fruit is somewhat more extensive, but focuses more on the properties of the fruit than on its uses. Even in these cases, though, the biblical authors generally allude to features of the fruit by mentioning human or divine interaction with the fig or fig tree rather than describing those features directly. For example, Isa 28:4b depicts a person eating figs right off the tree.

---

30. Like figs, pomegranate and date palm trees are omitted from the gleaning regulations. Pomegranates face the same constraints as figs, because they behave in similar ways—they must be tree-ripened, and a single growing season typically has more than one harvest period. A different problem occurs with dates, which can ripen off the tree, and which therefore may be gathered in a single harvesting cycle. The date palm, however, grows to ten to twenty meters in height, with the fruit developing in large clusters that hang just underneath the canopy of leaves at the top of the tree (Zohary, *Plants of the Bible*, 60–61). The tree's height meant that significant effort was required to harvest its fruit. Having expended the effort to climb the tree, the harvester may have been reluctant to leave good fruit behind as gleanings. In addition, the height of the tree meant that it could not be gleaned easily, compared to grapevines, which grow low to the ground, and olive trees, which can be beaten to encourage the fruit to drop.

31. This lack of detail in the mappings may explain why few scholars have studied fig imagery in the biblical corpus.

32. Two passages mention fig leaves. The first occurs in Gen 3:7, when Adam and Eve sew fig leaves together to cover themselves after becoming aware, for the first time, of their own nakedness. The second appears in Isa 34:4, which evokes the autumnal image of trees shedding their leaves as a metaphor for defeated enemies. Passages that describe sitting under a fig tree only allude to the tree's height, which would have to be sufficient for such activities, and its numerous large leaves, which provide significant shade (e.g., 2 Kgs 18:31). Even Judg 9:8–15, a parable in which a fig tree serves as a main character, pays little attention to the tree itself, focusing instead on its sweet fruit.

כבכורה בטרם קיץ אשר יראה הראה אותה בעודה בכפו יבלענה:

[They are] like the breba fig before the summer, which he who sees it, when it is still in his hand, swallows it.

In addition, Hos 9:10a describes YHWH spotting a breba on a fig tree, Nah 3:12 describes shaking a fig tree to make the ripe fruit fall, and Amos 8:1 depicts already picked figs sitting in a basket.

כענבים במדבר מצאתי ישראל כבכורה בתאנה בראשיתה ראיתי אבותיכם

Like grapes in the wilderness, I found Israel. Like a breba fig on a fig tree in its first season, I spotted your fathers. (Hos 9:10a)

כל־מבצריך תאנים עם־בכורים אם־ינועו ונפלו על־פי אוכל:

All your fortresses are fig trees with firstfruits. If they are shaken, they fall into the mouth of the eater. (Nah 3:12)

כה הראני אדני יהוה והנה כלוב קיץ:

Thus, my Lord YHWH showed me: There was a basket of figs. (Amos 8:1)

The frame elements mapped in passages like these may include: the fruit's TASTE; the QUALITY or SCARCITY OF BREBA FIGS; the way the RIPE FRUIT SOFTENS AND FALLS FROM THE TREE; the fact that the fruit CAN BE EATEN RIGHT OFF THE TREE; and the fruit's PERISHABILITY. Of the fruit's features, only its sweetness is directly described:

ותאמר להם התאנה החדלתי את־מתקי ואת־תנובתי הטובה והלכתי לנוע על־העצים:

The fig tree said to them: "Have I stopped producing my sweetness and my good yield that I should go to sway over the trees?" (Judg 9:11)

From an interpretive standpoint, the most significant aspect of figs and fig trees in the biblical corpus is that they almost never stand alone. Thirty-two of thirty-eight passages that mention figs also mention one or more other plants, crops, or food items.[33] Fig trees appear alongside other

---

33. This analysis excludes the instance of קיץ in the prophecy against Moab in Isa

crop-producing trees and plants in seven passages, and fig fruit appears with other crops or food items in an additional seven passages.[34] Passages that mention the fig tree or fruit along with multiple other plants often do so in the context of describing the state of the land: Various and flourishing crops and fruit trees indicate a prospering or prosperous land. The other significant context for these combinations is references to food in historiographical narratives. There, also, the list of foods conveys a sense that the individuals in the story have been well provisioned or well-fed.

The most common single partner for figs and fig trees in the biblical corpus is grapes or grapevines. This specific pairing appears independently of other trees, crops, or foods as often as it appears with those items. Eleven passages mention only the pairing of fig trees and vines, while five mention only figs and grapes.[35] The applications of this pairing are not limited to references to crops or food. Song of Songs 2:13 metonymically evokes the frame of springtime through its images of the fig tree putting forth its fruit and of the vines blossoming: התאנה חנטה פגיה והגפנים סמדר נתנו ריח קומי לכי [לך] רעיתי יפתי ולכי־לך: "The fig tree produces its green figs, and

---

16:9 but includes the use of קיץ in the similar prophecy in Jer 48:32. Jeremiah 48:32 pairs קיץ with בציר, which refers to the grape harvest. Both terms refer to summer harvests, so it is likely that the use of קיץ refers to the fig harvest. Evidence in favor of this interpretation lies in Mic 7:1, which explicitly pairs קיץ with בציר in reference to fig and grape harvests. The author of Jer 48:32 deploys the fig and grape pairing to express Moab's loss of prosperity. Jeremiah 48:36 confirms the prosperity connection: על־כן יתרת עשה אבדו, "therefore the abundance it [Moab] has made will be destroyed." Isaiah 16:9, on the other hand, places קיץ alongside קציר, a term that refers to the grain harvest, a winter crop. In this context, rather than describing the harvest of figs and grains, the two words are better understood as a merism referencing "summer and winter harvests." The use of קיץ with קציר to describe summer and winter harvests also occurs in Jer 8:20; Prov 6:8; 10:5; and 26:1.

34. Fig trees: Num 20:5; Deut 8:8; Judg 9:8–15; Jer 5:17; Joel 1:12; Hab 3:17; Hag 2:19. Fig fruit: Num 13:23; 1 Sam 25:18; 30:11–12; 2 Sam 16:1–2; Jer 40:10; Neh 13:15; 1 Chr 12:41. Grape references in these passages often take the form of צמוקים, "raisins," or יין, "wine," while figs may appear as דבלה, "dried figs." See also Amos 4:9, in which the pairing of vineyards and gardens is placed in parallel with that of figs and olives.

35. Fig trees and vines: 1 Kgs 5:5; 2 Kgs 18:31; Isa 34:4; 36:16; Hos 2:14; Joel 1:7; 2:22; Mic 4:4; Zech 3:10; Ps 105:33; and Song 2:13. Figs and grapes: Jer 8:13; 40:12; 48:32; Hos 9:10; and Mic 7:1. (Jeremiah 48:32 pairs the fig and grape harvests.) In addition, figs and drunkenness (which could be interpreted as a condition resulting from drinking wine) appear in close proximity to each other in another two passages (Isa 28:1–4; Nah 3:11–12).

the vines, in blossom, give off scent. Arise, my beloved! My beautiful one, come!" Conversely, Isa 34:4 employs autumnal imagery, when both the fig tree and the vine shed their greenery, to describe YHWH's future defeat of "the hosts of the heavens": וכל־צבאם יבול כנבל עלה מגפן וכנבלת מתאנה, "And all their host shall wither away, like the withering of a leaf from a vine and like it withers from a fig tree."

The order in which the pairing of figs and vines appears suggests a degree of conventionality in their conceptualization.[36] In passages in which the two woody plants appear with other trees, crops, or foods, the order of the two items shows no clear pattern, but in passages that reference only vines and fig trees or only grapes and figs, the fig trees or figs appear second in all but three cases.[37] A possible explanation of the order of גפן and תאנה would be "the law of increasing members," a phenomenon found in several languages, in which language users tend to express a series of consecutive words in order from shortest to longest.[38] The ordering of grapes/vines before figs/fig trees also occurs across multiple terms for each fruit/plant, however, including in cases where the term for grapes is longer than the term for figs, for example, צמקים and קיץ in 2 Sam 16:1. The evidence thus suggests that even if the order in which גפן and תאנה appear originated as a result of the law of increasing members, that order may have become somewhat conventional at a conceptual level as well. The conventionalization of the sequence may also have been influenced by the relative significance of

---

36. C. H. Middleburgh ("The Mention of 'Vine' and 'Fig-Tree' in Ps. CV 33," *VT* 28 [1978]: 481) argues that in some passages, the two trees appear as "conventional representatives of all trees." However, he does not address why these two fruit trees would have been frequently chosen to represent all other trees.

37. Joel 2:22 describes the restoration of the land after the destruction in ch. 1. Joel 1 mentions the loss of vines before fig trees (1:7), so it is reasonable to consider that fig trees appear first in ch. 2 because the author wanted to present the restoration as a reversal of events in ch. 1. Song of Songs 2:13 does not offer an explanation for the appearance of fig trees before grapevines. It may simply be that the development of the imagery in the passage works better in that order, with the passage first mentioning the appearance of the green figs and then turning to both the sight and scent of the blossoming grapevines. The mention of the fig harvest before the grape harvest in Jer 48:32 may also be for poetic reasons, as the following verse primarily expands on the destruction of the grape harvest through wine-making imagery.

38. Shamma Friedman, "The 'Law of Increasing Members' in Mishnaic Hebrew" [Hebrew], *Lěšonénu* 35 (1971): 117–29.

the two crops in Israel and Judah, where viticulture appears to have played a larger role in the culture and economy than fig-growing.

Further evidence for conventionalization of the pairing of figs and vines exists in ancient Egyptian texts showing a similar pattern, but with figs consistently placed in the first position.[39] In an autobiographical memorial stela from the mid-second millennium BCE, a man named Weni describes how he led a military expedition against the "sand-dwellers," who were rebelling against the Egyptian king. As part of their defeat of that land, Weni's army "cut down its figs, its vines." The section of the inscription describing the battle is written in parallel poetic lines, and these are the only two agricultural products mentioned in the poem. The destruction of the enemies' strongholds precedes these lines, and the destruction of their homes follows them. This pattern suggests that the choice to include the destruction of figs and vines had symbolic significance for the author of the poem, most likely representing the best of the enemies' food crops.[40] From approximately the same time period, a Pyramid Text from Pepi I speaks of afterlife inhabitants "living on figs, drinking wine." Again, these are the only two food items mentioned in this poetic (ritual) text.[41]

In the Shipwrecked Sailor, for which we have a manuscript from the first half of the second millennium BCE, an attendant to an Egyptian official who is returning home from a failed mission attempts to comfort his master by telling the tale of how he survived being shipwrecked for three days on an island: "I found figs and grapes there, all sorts of fine vegetables, sycamore figs, unnotched and notched, and cucumbers that were as if tended" (*COS* 1.39:83 [Lichtheim]). Finally, also from the early second millennium BCE, in Sinuhe, the protagonist speaks of serving his master in "a good land called Yaa. Figs were in it and grapes. It had more wine than water. Abundant was its honey, plentiful its oil. All kinds of fruit were

---

39. Also worth noting is that in the Ugaritic hippiatric text mentioned earlier, the treatment ingredient that appears directly after *dblt*, "dried figs," is *ṣmqm*, "raisins" (RS 17.120:31; see Cohen and Sivan, *Ugaritic Hippiatric Texts*, 9–10, 40–41).

40. Miriam Lichtheim, "The Autobiography of Weni," *AEL* 1:20. The location of the sand-dwellers' land is disputed. Some suggest that the name refers to Palestine (Goor, "History of the Fig," 124). Lichtheim ("Autobiography of Weni," 22 n. 5) seems to agree with Hans Goedicke in placing the location in the eastern Nile Delta. The region is known to have supported vineyards during the second millennium BCE. See T. G. H. James, "The Earliest History of Wine and Its Importance in Ancient Egypt," in McGovern, Fleming, and Katz, *Origins and Ancient History of Wine*, 197–213.

41. Lichtheim, "Pepi I Pyramid Texts: Utterance 440," *AEL* 1:44–45.

on its trees" (*COS* 1.38:79 [Lichtheim]). In each of these stories, figs and grapes are the first food items mentioned by the author, and in that order, further attesting to the conventionalization and significance of the pairing.

The most common use of vine and fig tree imagery in the biblical corpus relates the pairing to the concept of prosperity. Archaeological evidence from the biblical era, up through the end of the Iron Age, suggests that even under monarchic rule, while some professional specialization occurred in urban areas, rural communities and subsistence production still predominated in Israel and Judah.[42] Prosperity in this context should therefore not be understood as accumulating vast wealth, but rather as having resources sufficient to meet the requirements of daily life. The bulk of the crops produced each season would have been devoted to food and drink, but surplus crops could be used as trade items or to pay taxes or debts. Thus, prosperity may include both food security and financial security.

For example, grapevines and fig trees appear among the seven species of the land listed in Deut 8:8 as examples of the abundance that the Israelites will enjoy when they settle there:

כי יהוה אלהיך מביאך אל־ארץ טובה ארץ נחלי מים עינת ותהמת יצאים
בבקעה ובהר: ארץ חטה ושערה וגפן ותאנה ורמון ארץ־זית שמן ודבש:
ארץ אשר לא במסכנת תאכל־בה לחם לא־תחסר כל בה ארץ אשר אבניה
ברזל ומהרריה תחצב נחשת:

[7] For YHWH, your god, is bringing you to a good land, a land of streams of water, springs and deeps, coming out in the plain and in the hill country, [8] **a land of wheat and barley, and vines and fig trees and pomegranate trees, a land of olive oil and sweet syrup.** [9] A land that you will not eat bread in it in poverty, and that you will not lack anything in it, a land that its stones are iron and from its hills you will hew copper. (Deut 8:7–9)

The presence or absence of figs and grapes, along with other types of produce, in two other passages about the wilderness period also illustrates the richness of Canaan or the deprivations of the Negev (Num 13:23; 20:5). In addition, several prophetic passages include vines and fig trees with

---

42. Avraham Faust, "The Rural Community in Ancient Israel during Iron Age II," *BASOR* 317 (2000): 17–39; Schloen, "Economy and Society," 433–53; and William G. Dever, *Beyond the Texts: An Archaeological Portrait of Ancient Israel and Judah* (Atlanta: SBL Press, 2017), 464.

other trees, plants, or property as examples of the loss or restoration of prosperity (Jer 5:17; Amos 4:9; Joel 1:12; Hab 3:17; Hag 2:19). A similar conceptual relationship with prosperity appears in the Egyptian texts cited above. Weni destroys his enemies' figs and vines, thereby destroying their most valuable crops, particularly in the case of the grapevines, which were relatively scarce in ancient Egypt.[43] In the Pyramid Text, the afterlife inhabitants luxuriate in the eating of figs and grapes. And for the shipwrecked sailor and Sinuhe, figs and grapes head the list of produce that makes a land good. The biblical and extrabiblical evidence thus suggests that not only was the conceptual relationship of figs and grapes with prosperity conventional, it was also ancient.

The conventionality of the conceptual relationship between prosperity and vines and fig trees in ancient Israel becomes most evident in passages in which having vines and fig trees (or grapes and figs) becomes a metonym for prosperity. Recall from chapter 2 that a metonym is a mapping of elements within a single frame, and that referencing any element of a frame will evoke the entire frame. In this case, because the presence of vines and fig trees had become symbolic of prosperity, the pairing of GRAPEVINES AND FIG TREES became an element of the PROSPERITY frame. Therefore, the biblical authors could use the two woody plants to refer to prosperity. The cliché "it's as American as baseball and apple pie" has created a modern example of this type of metonymic relationship. The pairing of baseball and apple pie has become so closely associated with the United States, and especially with the nebulous concept of "American values," that the combination BASEBALL AND APPLE PIE is now an element of the UNITED STATES frame. Thus, most people in the United States would have no trouble understanding the expression "on this issue, baseball and apple pie lost" as another way of saying that the outcome in some way represents a defeat for the United States or for American values.

Psalm 105:26–36 provides an example of the metonymic use of vines and fig trees. The passage contains a version of the plagues narrative that includes a description of the loss of all food crops in Egypt, expressed primarily in terms of the destruction of the two woody plants (vv. 32–35):

נתן גשמיהם ברד אש להבות בארצם׃
ויך גפנם ותאנתם וישבר עץ גבולם׃

---

43. Zohary and Hopf, *Domestication of Plants*, 158, 164–65.

אמר ויבא ארבה וילק ואין מספר:
ויאכל כל־עשב בארצם ויאכל פרי אדמתם:

[32] He gave their rain hail, a flaming fire in their land.

[33] He struck their vines and their fig trees, and he broke up the trees of their region [lit. border].

[34] He spoke, and a locust swarm came, a grasshopper swarm, and it was without number.

[35] It consumed every plant in their land, and it consumed the fruit of their farmland.

The reference to vines and fig trees in this psalm likely says more about their importance to Israelites than to Egyptians.[44] While the literary evidence shows that both cultures valued these two fruits, the archaeological evidence suggests that they were more readily available to the Israelites. Figs, especially sycamore figs, were grown in Egypt, but inhospitable soil and climate conditions made grapevines much more rare, largely limited to the Nile Delta and grown as a "luxury crop."[45] As a result, wine consumption in Egypt would primarily have occurred among the elites of society and those who had access to wine through their employment by the elites.[46] Grains were the main crop produced in Egypt, and beer the drink of the common people, yet grains are not explicitly named in Ps 105.[47] The closest the text comes to mentioning them is its reference to locusts and grasshoppers consuming all of the plants in the land (105:35). The structure of the passage keeps the Israelite audience's attention on the loss that would strike them hardest—the loss of vines and fig trees—by naming it explicitly and first in 105:33, and then by reminding them again with the reference to fruit in 105:35. The destruction of all other greenery in Egypt in general terms, without naming any other crop or plant, reinforces the message of deprivation, of the loss of food and financial security.

---

44. Middleburgh ("Mention of 'Vine,'" 481) offers a similar argument as a potential explanation for the presence of vines and figs in the psalm but prefers instead to see their inclusion as evidence of the psalmist's dependence on Num 20:5 for information about produce in Egypt. He does not explain why the psalmist would include these two fruit trees specifically, while excluding the other food items in Num 20:5.

45. Zohary and Hopf, *Domestication of Plants*, 158, 164–65.

46. Walsh, *Fruit of the Vine*, 25; and Leonard Lesko, "Egyptian Wine Production during the New Kingdom," in McGovern, Fleming, and Katz, *Origins and Ancient History of Wine*, 215–30.

47. Walsh, *Fruit of the Vine*, 21–27.

Jeremiah 40:9–12 constitutes another such prosperity reference. Following the destruction of Jerusalem in 586 BCE, the people heed the instructions of Gedaliah, whom the Babylonians had appointed to lead Judah, and they return to farming the land. At harvesttime, ויאספו יין וקיץ הרבה מאד, "they gathered wine and figs in great abundance [lit. very much]" (40:12). The passage does not simply neutrally describe the food gathered and produced by the remnant who remained in Judah after the destruction of Jerusalem; rather, the accumulation of these items in large quantities indicates that the people of Judah prospered under the leadership of Gedaliah and the hegemony of Babylonia.[48]

The conceptual relationship between prosperity and vines and fig trees also appears in metaphorical form: PROSPERITY IS BEING UNDER YOUR VINE AND FIG TREE. Consider the following four expressions of this metaphor, which show some evidence of developing a relatively fixed form:

Table 7.1. Comparison of four similar prosperity metaphors

1 Kgs 5:5	
וישב ...	[Judah and Israel] sat/dwelled …
איש תחת גפנו ותחת תאנתו	Each under his vine and under his fig tree.
Mic 4:4	
וישבו ...	They will sit …
איש תחת גפנו ותחת תאנתו	Each under his vine and under his fig tree.
2 Kgs 18:31 = Isa 36:16[49]	
ואכלו ...	You may eat …
איש־גפנו ואיש תאנתו	Each [from] his vine and each [from] his fig tree.
Zech 3:10	
תקראו ...	You will invite …
איש לרעהו אל־תחת גפן ואל־תחת תאנה	Each his fellow under vine and under fig tree.

---

48. The narrative may also contain an implicit critique of the people who remained in the land. It describes Gedaliah telling them to serve the Chaldeans (40:9) and to live in the cities that they have "seized" (תפש; 40:10), thereby perhaps implying that they are prospering on ill-gotten gains and without regard for those whom the Babylonians have deported.

49. Second Kings 18:31 and Isa 36:16 both narrate the same episode, so they are treated here as a single instance of the metaphor.

The verbs in these passages vary, as do other small details, but all four share a common syntactic structure and all distribute the experience to איש, "each [one]." Three of the four employ the preposition תחת, "under," to position the people under their fruit trees, and three of the four employ possessive pronouns—גפנו, "his vine," and תאנתו, "his fig tree"—to express ownership.

In each case, the metaphor evokes a lush image from the VINE AND FIG TREE frame in order to express the concept of prosperity (again in the form of food and financial security). Locating the subject under the woody plants draws on a conventional association between shade and protection, emphasizing the message of safety from food insecurity.[50] Giving the subject ownership of the two woody plants, via the possessive pronouns, highlights the subject's financial security, since ownership of vines and fig trees would imply ownership of land. The three different verb choices—ישב, אכל, and קרא—each refer to a different experience-based element of the VINE AND FIG TREE frame. For example, evidence for a custom of sitting under fig trees and/or eating from them appears in rabbinic sources, which include narratives that depict such scenes.[51] In addition, in the New Testament, Jesus describes having seen Nathanael under a fig tree (John 1:48, 50).

If these narratives from the early first millennium CE reflect a cultural norm, it was probably also operative during the Iron Age. As a result, the VINE AND FIG TREE frame would have included experiential elements such as SITTING UNDER, EATING FROM, and INVITING UNDER A FIG TREE, which could then be expressed in different versions of the metaphorical expression. Zechariah 3:10 constitutes a hyperbolic extension of the version in 1 Kgs 5 and Mic 4, claiming that each man will have enough not only to meet his own needs but also the needs of his neighbor. Second Kings 18:31 and Isa 36:16, on the other hand, pull back from the promises of the other versions of the metaphor, offering only short-term food security in the image of the subject eating from his vine and fig tree.

Contrary to claims that the pairing of figs and grapevines symbolizes both prosperity and peace, the biblical passages in which the pair appears

---

50. The conceptual connection between shade and protection is not limited to plant metaphors. It also appears, e.g., in expressions that depict YHWH as a bird placing protective wings over a person (e.g., Ps 17:8, בצל כנפיך תסתירני, "hide me in the shadow of your wings"; see also Pss 36:8; 57:2; 63:8). See further the discussion of shade in woody-plant metaphors in ch. 8.

51. See, e.g., b. Taʿan. 24a; Tanḥuma Teṣaveh 13:4.

generally include explicit mappings only to a PROSPERITY frame, and not to a PEACE frame.[52] The situation may be akin to the status of the date palm in ancient Mesopotamia; because of its value both as a food item and for building material in a wood-poor region, the date palm was also known as ʿiṣ mašrê, "the tree of wealth."[53] The wood of vines and fig trees is not suitable for building materials, but ownership of these woody plants would have meant consistent access to calorie- and nutrient-rich food and drink.

The misconception about biblical vines and fig trees representing peace may have arisen in part from commentaries on the passages in which "each [from] his vine and each [from] his fig tree" appear. Only in the version in Zech 3:10 can we credibly argue that peace is incorporated into the metaphor. The image does not address external threats, but inviting your fellow under vine and fig tree does convey a sense of community harmony.[54] In the other passages of this type, the mappings to the PEACE frame occur in the text surrounding the metaphor, not in the metaphor itself. A commentary on these other passages could therefore reasonably argue that, as a whole, they offer a message of peace and prosperity.

The evidence from the metaphors themselves helps correct the misperception that vines and fig trees are associated with peace. Second Kings 18:31 (= Isa 36:16) represents prosperity, in the form of food security, without true peace, as the Assyrian envoy, the Rabshakeh, tells the Judahites that they can eat from their vines and fig trees only temporarily. He urges them to surrender and return to their homes עד־באי ולקחתי אתכם אל־ארץ כארצכם ארץ דגן ותירוש ארץ לחם וכרמים ארץ זית יצהר ודבש וחיו ולא תמתו, "until I come and take you to a land like your land, a land of grain and new wine, a land of bread and vineyards, a land of olive oil and sweet syrup, so that you may live and not die" (18:32a).[55]

---

52. Among those who suggest that they represent prosperity and peace, see, e.g., Borowski, *Agriculture*, 114–115; Westenholz, *Sacred Bounty*, 30; and Macintosh, *Hosea*, 64. Here I define peace in the sense of "absence of war or conflict." The peace *of mind* that one might reasonably associate with food and financial security would be an element of the PROSPERITY frame, and not itself an independent frame.

53. Cole, "Destruction of Orchards," 30.

54. Carol L. Meyers and Eric M. Meyers, *Haggai, Zechariah 1–8: A New Translation with Introduction and Commentary*, AB 25B (Garden City, NY: Doubleday, 2004), 212–13.

55. The parallel verse in Isa 36:17 omits the references to oil and sweet syrup and the promise of living and not dying.

Second Kings 18:31 does evoke the PEACE frame, but outside the metaphor, when the Rabshakeh offers the people the chance to make peace so that the siege of Jerusalem will end and prosperity will return:

אל־תשמעו אל־חזקיהו כי כה אמר מלך אשור עשו־אתי ברכה וצאו אלי
ואכלו איש־גפנו ואיש תאנתו ושתו איש מי־בורו:

"Do not listen to Hezekiah, for thus said the king of Assyria, 'Make a treaty with me, and come out to me, and eat, each from his vine and each from his fig tree, and drink, each the water of his cistern.'" (2 Kgs 18:31)

Moreover, before he makes this offer of peace, the Rabshakeh suggests that if the siege continues, a lack of food and water in the city will eventually require the people לאכל את חריהם ולשתות את־שיניהם, "to eat their dung[56] and drink their urine" (18:27). Thus, the vine and fig tree metaphor that follows in 18:31 primarily provides a contrast to the people's current experience of deprivation as the siege makes food scarce. In addition, in 18:32a, the Rabshakeh describes the land to which the Judahites will be deported as having vines and grain, but he omits figs from his description.[57] With this wording, the author highlights the association of vines and fig trees with prosperity and provides a subtle suggestion to the audience that the Judahites would not prosper in Babylonia as they have done in Israel.[58]

In two other instances of this metaphor, the biblical authors add the sense of peace to that of prosperity by including declarations of peace

---

56. For the qere-ketiv, חריהם, the qere is צואתם "filth" (DCH 3:305, s.v. "חֶרֶא").

57. Grain was abundant in Mesopotamia, and figs were also grown there. Wine was rarer, in part because the climate and soil conditions, especially in southern Mesopotamia, are not ideal for growing grapevines, and therefore successfully cultivating a vineyard would have been difficult and expensive. Textual evidence indicates that the grapes grown in Babylonia were generally either used to produce grape syrup, as a sweetener, or preserved as raisins. Viticulture and the production of wine are well-attested in the mountains and foothills along the northern borders of Assyria in the first millennium BCE, however, making the Rabshakeh's promise to deport the people to a land of "grain and new wine" plausible. See Powell, "Wine and the Vine in Ancient Mesopotamia," 97–122.

58. Given the associations of vines and fig trees with the lands of Israel and Judah (see discussion below), the author may also be indicating that the land to which the people will go will not be like their homeland of Judah.

alongside the metaphor. First Kings 5:5 states that וישב יהודה וישראל
לבטח איש תחת גפנו ותחת תאנתו, "Judah and Israel lived **in security**, each
man under his vine and under his fig tree," while Mic 4:4 says that וישבו
איש תחת גפנו ותחת תאנתו ואין מחריד, "they will live, each man under his
vine and under his fig tree, **and no one will make [them] afraid**."[59] Thus,
these passages as a whole represent a blend of the PEACE and PROSPERITY
frames, but it appears that the vine and fig tree metaphor contributes only
prosperity to that blend.

Collectively, the passages discussed in this section demonstrate two
conceptual metonymic relationships relevant to understanding the use of
vine and fig tree imagery in prophetic national condemnations. The first is
the relationship of vines and fig trees with prosperity, discussed at length
above. The variety of passages participating in this theme, both within the
prophetic corpus and outside of it, suggests that this conceptual relationship was broadly understood within Israelite culture. Many of the same
passages explored thus far also point to a second conceptual relationship:
the association of vines and fig trees with the lands of Israel and Judah. For
the biblical authors, the experience of feast and famine, of war and peace,
of settling down and traveling the land, of springtime and harvest—all are
frequently told in part through images of their grapevines and fig trees
and what happens to them.[60] This pattern suggests that vines and fig trees
were viewed as representative of the lands of Israel and Judah, much like
the example discussed above of baseball and apple pie as representative of
the United States.

This development in the conceptualization of vines and fig trees
makes sense. The Israelite association of prosperity with vines and figs
trees derives from their lived experience in the agrarian societies of Israel
and Judah. Having vines and fig trees (and land on which to grow them)
was part of prospering in the land. As such, vines and fig trees developed
associations both with *living* in the lands of Israel and Judah and with *prospering* there. As these associations became conventionalized, the pairing

---

59. The final phrase in this verse, ואין מחריד, also appears in Lev 26:6; Deut 28:26;
Isa 17:2; Jer 7:33; 30:10; 46:27; Ezek 34:28; 39:26; and Zeph 3:13, usually at the end of
the verse.

60. To be clear, when vine and fig imagery appears in accounts of war and peace,
its contribution to the narrative lies in its ability to evoke the experience not of peace,
but of either deprivation or sufficiency arising as a result of war or peace, respectively.

of GRAPEVINES AND FIG TREES became an element in the frames of ISRAEL and JUDAH, just as it became an element of the PROSPERITY frame.

The prophetic authors exploited these shared conceptual relationships in their condemnations of Israel and Judah. In expressions of collective punishment, several broad descriptions of destruction within the land include the loss of vines and fig trees.[61] Joel 1:7 and 12 describe a plague of locusts that destroys vines and fig trees, among other crops: שם גפני לשמה ותאנתי לקצפה, "they have made my vines a wasteland, and my fig trees stumps" (Joel 1:7a).[62] Amos 4:9 treats past losses of vineyards and figs to blight, mildew, and locusts as attempts by YHWH to punish Israel and correct the nation's behavior:

הכיתי אתכם בשדפון ובירקון הרבות גנותיכם וכרמיכם ותאניכם וזיתיכם
יאכל הגזם ולא־שבתם עדי נאם־יהוה:
"I struck you with blight and with mildew, many of your gardens and your vineyards and your fig trees and your olive trees the locust consumed, but you did not return to me," says YHWH.

The author here conceptualizes the crop diseases in terms of the metaphor DIVINE-HUMAN CONFLICT IS A PHYSICAL BLOW.

The vehicle of destruction in the examples above is a natural or supernatural disaster, but such losses could also be attributed to enemy action, as in Jer 5:17, which describes a loss of prosperity via an invader who will metaphorically consume all that the Judahites have, including their vines and fig trees:

ואכל קצירך ולחמך יאכלו בניך ובנותיך יאכל צאנך ובקרך יאכל גפנך
ותאנתך ירשש ערי מבצריך אשר אתה בוטח בהנה בחרב:
He will consume your grain harvest and your bread. They will consume your sons and your daughters. They will consume your flocks and your herds. He will consume your vines and your fig trees. He will smash your fortified cities, in which you trust, with the sword.

---

61. Habakkuk 3:17 and Hag 2:19 depict an alternate scenario, in which the vines and fig trees have not produced fruit, and the prophets await their renewal by YHWH.

62. *DCH* 7:284, s.v. "קְצָפָה." Restoration occurs in Joel 2:12–22 when the people return to proper worship of YHWH.

This extended example of the conventional metaphor CONQUEST IS EATING (which ends with an expression of CONQUEST IS INDIVIDUAL COMBAT) conveys the sense of a total military defeat, with the enemy taking control over, and profiting from, Judah and everything in it.[63]

Finally, Hos 2:14 creatively expresses the relationship of vines and fig trees to prosperity by blending the vine and fig tree metonym with the metaphor APOSTASY IS PROSTITUTION.

והשמתי גפנה ותאנתה אשר אמרה אתנה המה לי אשר נתנו־לי מאהבי
ושמתים ליער ואכלתם חית השדה:

I will make desolate her vines and her fig trees, [of] which she says, "They are my fee, which my lovers gave to me." I will make them a thicket, and the beasts of the field will consume them.

Through this blend, the author declares that, since the kingdom of Israel has attributed the prosperity that they have enjoyed to their worship of other deities, YHWH therefore intends to end their period of prosperity, represented metonymically by the image of the desolation and destruction of the vines and fig trees that (they believe) the other deities have given them.[64] The author's use of שמם to describe YHWH's action, which carries the sense of desertion in addition to destruction, suggests an underlying conception of a depopulated land.[65] The abandoned vineyards and orchards will then grow wild, and wild animals will feed on them.

7.3. National Condemnation Vine and Fig Tree Metaphors

As with biblical fig imagery in general, the six metaphorical national condemnations based on fig trees or vines paired with fig trees tend to focus on the fruit more than the plant. Excluded from this count is the metaphor

---

63. Not all commentators address this verse in detail, but those that do often incorrectly attempt to interpret each line independently, rather than viewing the whole through the CONQUEST IS EATING metaphor that structures the first half of the verse (see, e.g., Lundbom, *Jeremiah 1–20*, 396–97; and McKane, *Jeremiah*, 125).

64. Contra Andersen and Freedman (*Hosea*, 251–56), who argue that the fees from prostitution in this verse refer to the children of the woman in the passage, not to the vines and fig trees.

65. *DCH* 8:443–46, s.v. "שמם."

of the two baskets of figs in Jer 24:1–9, which primarily represents a restoration metaphor. As table 7.2 below shows, most of the condemnation metaphors draw on the HARVESTING frame to depict the outcome for the nation, with the fruit mapping to the people.

Table 7.2. Vine and fig tree metaphors in
prophetic national condemnations

Harvest Outcome	Vines and Fig Trees	Figs Alone
Gathered from Plant	Jer 8:13–17; Mic 7:1–7	
Eaten from Tree		Isa 28:1–4; Nah 3:12
Placed in Basket		Amos 8:1–2
Other Plant Outcome	Hos 9:10–17	

In passages that include the vines and fig trees, the plants represent the connection of the national character or culture with the national body, represented by the land. The imagery derives from the conception of the nation as planted in the land. Hints of this idea appear in the passages discussed above, which view attacks against the nation through the lens of what happens to the land and its agriculture. The discussion that follows begins with an analysis of the three grape (vine) and fig (tree) metaphors— Jer 8:13–17; Mic 7:1–7; and Hos 9:10–17—all of which construct a national identity. In contrast to the viticulture metaphors, there does not appear to be a pattern of chronological development in the expressions that include figs. Therefore, the analysis will address the metaphors in order of increasing complexity, culminating with an in-depth case study of Hos 9:10–17. Following the case study, the chapter will address the three condemnation metaphors that depict figs without grapes.

In Jer 8:13–17, YHWH declares his intention to destroy Judah, whose people the author metaphorically describes as grapes and figs that have been gathered:

אסף אסיפם נאם־יהוה אין ענבים בגפן ואין תאנים בתאנה והעלה נבל ואתן
להם יעברום:

"Gathered, I will end them," says YHWH. "There are no grapes on the vine, and there are no figs on the fig tree, and the leaf withers. [What] I have given them will pass away from them." (Jer 8:13)

The vines and fig trees in this metaphor, picked clean by the hand of YHWH, represent both the families of Judah and their connection to the land (body) of Judah. The grapes and figs map to the people. The withering of the vine and fig leaves is not a harvest phenomenon; rather it occurs postharvest, as winter approaches. The picture thus painted by the verse describes the vines and fig trees in decline, with everything of value being stripped away from them. The passage presents an image of total conquest, the people killed or exiled, and their land desolated. Some scholars argue that the last line about YHWH's gifts represents a later addition to the passage, because it is absent from the LXX.[66] Nothing in the content of the line necessitates that it be viewed as secondary, however. Rather, it serves well as a summary of the metaphorical message. The prophetic author suggests that all that the people have—children, property, land—are gifts from YHWH, which he is now taking away from them.

As a construction of national identity, this passage conveys the message that in the past, YHWH ensured the prosperity of the nation of Judah, but they now face a common present of conquest and a future of death or exile. The author does little with the issue of a national culture in the metaphor, but he expresses the national character in terms of the imagery of vines and fig trees as the families of Judah. That both have been harvested creates the impression that the vines and fig trees are planted in a single orchard, which maps to the land of Judah. At the same time, by removing the fruit from the trees, the author preemptively deconstructs the national identity that the rest of the passage constructs. A scattered and dying people have no nation. As is typical of deconstructing national identity strategies, the author offers nothing to replace the identity he has demolished. The verses that follow the metaphor present a dialogue among the prophet's audience regarding their coming doom (8:14–15) and a depiction of the approaching conquerors (8:16–17). The latter appropriately includes an expression of CONQUEST IS EATING: ויבואו ויאכלו ארץ ומלואה עיר וישבי בה, "they come and they consume a land and what fills it, a city and those who dwell in it"

---

66. The two most common interpretations of this verse are: (1) that it describes the literal destruction of Judah's vines and fig trees; or (2) that it refers metaphorically to the destruction of Judah. Scholars who interpret the passage literally tend to treat the last line, whether original or secondary, as confirming or emphasizing the loss of vines and fig trees. Those who interpret the verse metaphorically suggest that the final line is a later addition from an editor who interpreted the verse literally (Lundbom, *Jeremiah 1–20*, 523–24).

(8:16b). The imagery in 8:14–17 lends new meaning to the first line of 8:13: YHWH has gathered all of his people-fruit into Jerusalem, and now they await their own destruction-consumption.

Micah 7:1–7 also employs an image of picked fruit and fruit trees, constructing a national identity within a lament spoken by the city of Jerusalem.[67] The city describes its state as like that of an orchard after the harvest, with the fig trees and vines nearly empty of fruit:

אללי לי כי הייתי כספי־קיץ כעללת בציר אין־אשכול לאכול בכורה אותה
נפשי:

Alas for me! For I have become like a summer harvest, like gleanings of a vintage. There is not a cluster to eat, [nor] a breba fig that my soul desires. (Mic 7:1)

The orchard metaphorically represents the national body, the land, in which the national family of trees is planted. The lack of either an אשכול, "cluster of grapes," or a בכורה, "breba fig," in the second half of the verse indicates that the harvest of the good fruit, referring to the death of the good people of a prior generation, has occurred. The rest of the passage clarifies and extends the meaning of the initial harvest metaphor. Micah 7:2–3 and 5–6 describe the situation in literal terms: the good people are gone, leaving behind only scoundrels.[68] In 7:4, the author extends the original harvest metaphor, describing the people who remain as thorny plants that have grown up in the now deserted orchard, ironically refer-

---

67. Also identifying the speaker as the city of Jerusalem are Daniel L. Smith-Christopher, *Micah: A Commentary*, OTL (Louisville: Westminster John Knox, 2015), 140; and James Luther Mays, *Micah: A Commentary*, OTL (Philadelphia: Westminster, 1976), 150. Francis I. Andersen and David Noel Freedman reject the idea that the speaker is the barren land, and instead argue that he represents a "disappointed farmer" whose vines and fig trees have yielded no fruit. See Andersen and Freedman, *Micah: A New Translation with Introduction and Commentary*, AB 24B (New York: Doubleday, 2000), 566–68.

68. The passage presents an image similar to that in Jer 5:1–5, in which the prophet seeks in vain to find one good person in the land. See Delbert R. Hillers, *Micah: A Commentary on the Book of the Prophet Micah*, Hermeneia (Philadelphia: Fortress, 1984), 84–85. Another metaphor of good people as good fruit appears in the restoration metaphor of the two baskets of figs in Jer 24:1–9. The Babylonians have deported the good people, represented by good figs, while the bad people, represented by bad figs, remain in the land. See the additional discussion of Jer 24:1–9 in n. 103 below.

ring to the best of them as כחדק ישר ממסוכה, "briars more upright than a thorn hedge."[69]

In this constructed national identity, the national body is again the land, represented by the orchard in which the family-trees are planted. The fruit still represents people, but only those of the past. The mention of the prior generation provides the nation with a narrative of its past righteousness, while its present seems frozen in the image of the postharvest orchard. The national character and culture develop over the course of the metaphor: What once was righteous now has become lawless, what once was an orchard teeming with good fruit has now been picked over and has been left to sprout thornbushes. Moreover, the implication of the multiple plants incorporated into the image is that those who remain in the land are of a different kind than those who have passed on. The nation is bound together by the shared history of being planted in the land, but they do not derive from a shared genetic stock. Collectively the author has constructed a thoroughly disreputable national identity for Judah. His focus remains on the present, so he offers little sense of the nation's future. The passage closes in 7:7 with the author stepping out of the orchard image and declaring his intent to trust in YHWH despite the present circumstances in the nation. Thus, the purpose of the passage seems to be mainly to convey to the audience the author's perspective on the nation and to bemoan its fallen state.

7.4. Case Study: Hosea 9:10–17

Among the prophetic condemnations, the most complete construction of national identity involving grapes and figs occurs in Hos 9:10–17.[70] The passage opens with an idyllic scene of Israel's founding before launching into a review of Israel's apostasy, past and present, and an announcement

---

69. See the discussion of the image of briars and thorns as a way of depicting troublesome people in ch. 8.

70. Scholars generally agree that Hos 9:10 marks the beginning of a set of prophecies that interpret the present through the lens of the past, so identifying 9:10 as the start of this textual unit is uncontroversial. Following 9:17, Hos 10:1 backtracks in time to reflect, metaphorically, on a time when the vine of Israel was fruitful. The new metaphor is thematically related to 9:10–17, but temporally inconsistent, which suggests that 10:1 begins a new unit. See Eidevall, *Grapes in the Desert*, 147; and Mays, *Hosea*, 132.

that YHWH's abandonment of the nation is at hand. The eight verses divide naturally into two sections, each opening with an historical reference (9:10 and 15) and each addressing themes of apostasy, divine abandonment, and divine punishment in the form of infertility and childlessness. Hosea 9:15–17 in the second section adds to these themes an additional punishment: the loss of the Israelite homeland. The narrative arc between 9:10 and 9:17 connects the two sections; the passage opens in the distant past, with the Israelites dwelling outside of Israel in the time before YHWH became their god. It ends with YHWH rejecting the Israelites and expelling them from the land of Israel, thereby symbolically returning them to their original state.[71] Rhetorically, the author incorporates into his message both imagery that is symbolic of the land of Israel and significant aspects of Israelite culture. He then reframes these inputs to serve his purposes: (1) to delegitimize the Israelites' current cultic practices by presenting them as a betrayal of an original, idealized, Yahwistic identity, whose roots extend back to a period before the Israelites began to worship other deities; and (2) to convince his audience that their cultic practices represent an existential threat to Israel.

As with the two vine and fig tree national identity metaphors discussed above, Hos 9:10–17 combines figurative and nonfigurative material to construct the identity elements.[72] In this case, the text pairs nonmetaphorical accusations of wrongdoing by the Israelites with an opening grapes and figs simile (9:10), which the author later extends to an image of an unspecified fruit-bearing woody plant that could represent either a grapevine or a fig tree (9:16).

כענבים במדבר [10] Like grapes in the wilderness,
מצאתי ישראל I found Israel.

---

71. Deborah Davies Krause ("Seeing the Fig Tree Anew: The Exegesis of Hosea 9:10–17 in Mark 11:12–25" [PhD diss., Emory University, 1996], 166–75) notes the reversals in this passage, with Israel presented in 9:10 as fruitful and then being cursed with fruitlessness (9:16), and with Israel's history starting in the wilderness and the nation then being returned to the wilderness (9:17).

72. Exactly why the grape and fig national identity metaphors all include a mix of literal and figurative elements is unclear. Perhaps the strong conceptual connections between the land, prosperity, and the fruit in some way inhibited the prophetic authors' ability to creatively exploit the metaphor, making it harder for them to conceptualize aspects of Israelite or Judahite national identity in terms of the two woody plants and their fruit.

כבכורה בתאנה בראשיתה	Like a breba fig on a fig tree in its first season,
ראיתי אבותיכם	I spotted your fathers.
המה באו בעל־פעור	They went to Baal-Peor,
וינזרו לבשת	And they consecrated themselves to Shame,
ויהיו שקוצים כאהבם:	And they became abhorrent like what they loved.
אפרים כעוף	[11] O Ephraim,[73] like a bird
יתעופף כבודם	Shall their glory fly away—
מלדה ומבטן ומהריון:	From giving birth, and from pregnancy, and from conception.
כי אם־יגדלו את־בניהם	[12] Even those who are raising their children,
ושכלתים מאדם	I will make them childless among humanity.
כי־גם־אוי להם	Indeed woe to them
בשורי מהם:	When I depart from them!
אפרים כאשר־ראיתי	[13] O Ephraim, just as I saw
לצור שתולה בנוה	Tyre planted in a field,[74]
ואפרים להוציא	So Ephraim will lead forth
אל־הרג בניו:	To a killer his sons.
תן־להם יהוה	[14] Give to them, O YHWH—
מה־תתן	What will you give?
תן־להם רחם משכיל	Give to them a miscarrying womb
ושדים צמקים:	And two dry breasts.

---

73. The book of Hosea employs two different names for the kingdom of Israel: Israel and Ephraim, the latter term taken from one of the major tribes in Israel. For a discussion of the potential political circumstances behind the two names, see H. J. Cook, "Pekah," *VT* 14 (1964): 121–35.

74. The translation offered here reflects the MT, as well as the Peshitta, Vulgate, and Targum. Other scholars prefer to follow the LXX variant to verse 13a, which reads: Εφραιμ, ὃν τρόπον εἶδον, εἰς θήραν παρέστησαν τὰ τέκνα αὐτῶν, "Ephraim, as I saw, presented their children for prey" (NETS; e.g., Harper, *Amos and Hosea*, 338; and Mays, *Hosea*, 134). Anthony Gelston offers more than one potential explanation for the difference between the MT and the LXX, the most plausible of which is that the LXX *Vorlage* read לצוד שתו לה בנוה as compared to the MT's לצור שתולה בנוה. This solution reflects a one-letter difference (underlined above) between the two *Vorlagen* and a different word division. Gelston's explanation would also require the LXX translator to have misread לצוד as לציד ["prey"], based on the graphic similarity of *waw* and *yod*. See Gelston, *The Twelve Minor Prophets*, BHQ 13 (Stuttgart: Deutsche Bibelgesellschaft, 2010), 65*. A few commentators understand צור as related to Arabic *ṣawrun*, "(small) palm trees" (e.g., Macintosh, *Hosea*, 371), but the arguments in favor of that interpretation are not compelling.

כל־רעתם בגלגל   ¹⁵ All of their evil at Gilgal—

כי־שם שנאתים   For [what happens] there, I hate them.

על רע מעלליהם   For the wickedness of their deeds

מביתי אגרשם   From my house I will drive them.

לא אוסף אהבתם   No longer will I love them;

כל־שריהם סררים: All of their princes are rebels.

הכה אפרים   ¹⁶ Stricken is Ephraim,

שרשם יבש   Their root is dried up,

פרי בלי־יעשון   Fruit they cannot produce.

גם כי ילדון   Even if they beget,

והמתי מחמדי בטנם: I will cause the death of the precious things of their wombs.

ימאסם אלהי   ¹⁷ My God will reject them,

כי לא שמעו לו   Because they have not heeded him;

ויהיו נדדים בגוים: And they will be fugitives among the peoples.

Hosea 9:10 offers an origin myth for Israel, as YHWH nostalgically compares Israel's forefathers to grapes found in the wilderness and to early ripe figs. In both cases, the image connotes a rare, unexpected, and delightful find. The climate and soil in Israel provide growing conditions sufficient to support viticulture. As such, wild grapevines could have grown anywhere with sufficient irrigation, such as a ravine, but finding them in any particular location would have been a matter of happenstance. By specifying that the grapes are like those found in the desert, the author describes the forefathers, and by extension their Israelite descendants, as rare, special, and found by YHWH.[75]

A potential problem with the image of wild grapes is that their quality varies widely; in most cases, wild grapes would be inferior to domesticated grapes—smaller, less sweet, and more acidic and astringent.[76] As a result, a simile that simply compares Israel to wild grapes could be interpreted as

---

75. Eidevall (*Grapes in the Desert*, 150) correctly notes that while most commentators focus on YHWH's "attitude" toward the fruit, the metaphor itself focuses on the "qualities" of the fruit. He errs, however, in stressing the sweetness of the fruit as the main element mapped by the author to indicate the quality of Israel's ancestors. The sweetness of grapes and figs would certainly be part of the frames evoked by the two fruits, but the wording of the verse emphasizes the rarity of the find, not the features of the fruit.

76. Olmo, "Origin and Domestication," 33.

a critique of the nation, a message of its inferior quality.[77] Evidence from the biblical corpus, however, suggests that even if ענב could refer to any type of grape, it generally connoted good, edible grapes. For example, Isa 5:1–7 contrasts the rotten grapes, which it calls באשים, with ענבים, the good grapes (5:2, 4).[78] The author of Deut 32:32 does use ענבים to refer to bad grapes, but he explicitly primes the interpretation of the ענבים from the vine of Sodom and Gomorrah by indicating that they are inedible: ענבמו ענבי־רוש אשכלת מררת למו, "its grapes are grapes of poison, it has clusters of bitter things." In all other cases in the biblical corpus, ענבים refers to edible grapes, to be either consumed fresh (e.g., Num 6:3; Deut 23:25) or made into wine (e.g., Gen 40:11; Hos 3:1). Therefore, the use of the word ענבים in Hos 9:10 at least implies to the audience that the grapes found are edible.

The inclusion of a בכורה, "breba fig," further primes the audience to understand both fruit similes as representing praise of Israel. In fact, the entire phrase, כבכורה בתאנה בראשיתה, "like a breba fig on a fig tree in its first season," emphasizes the rarity and delightfulness of the find in several ways. As discussed earlier, trees that produce breba figs may have been rare in ancient Israel.[79] In addition, the breba crop tends to be smaller than the August crop, and the breba crop of a tree producing fruit for the first time smaller still.[80] Moreover, since fig trees need several years to develop before producing fruit, that first year of fruit would represent the culmination of years of waiting.[81] Finally, breba figs would constitute the first fresh

---

77. Indeed, on the grounds of the inferiority of wild grapes, Andersen and Freedman (*Hosea*, 539) reject the notion that the passage compares Israel to wild grapes. In order to sustain their argument, however, they also have to reject the fairly obvious parallelism present in these lines (see n. 81). In addition, they do not consider the practical reality that for subsistence farmers, any food source would be welcome. Such a traveler in the wilderness would respond positively to finding an edible source of energy and hydration in an unexpected location.

78. On באשים, "stinking grapes," see the case study of Isa 5:1–7 in ch. 4.

79. Goor, "History of the Fig," 127.

80. Cristina Pereira et al., "Agronomic Behaviour and Quality of Six Fig Cultivars for Fresh Consumption," *Scientia Horticulturae* 185 (2015): 121–28.

81. Andersen and Freedman (*Hosea*, 540) note that "ראשית can mean the first productive season of a tree." Most commentators argue that בראשיתה disrupts the poetic structure of the first four lines of 9:10 and therefore should be considered a gloss, most likely added to explain the rare term בכורה (see, e.g., Harper, *Amos and Hosea*, 336; Macintosh, *Hosea*, 360; Mays, *Hosea*, 133; and Wolff, *Hosea*, 160). The

fruit of the new season, and as such, would be a source of both anticipation and delight.[82]

The choice of grapes and figs in the simile would also evoke their conventional metonymic mappings: to the ISRAEL frame on the one hand, and to the PROSPERITY frame on the other. Since vines and fig trees were emblematic of Israel, representing the Israelites' ancestors as grapes and figs indicates their belonging to and in the land. At the same time, it also suggests that just as vines and fig trees represent the best of the land of Israel, so the ancestors represent the best of the people of Israel. The conception of vines and fig trees as conferring prosperity on their owners similarly conveys that these ancestral fathers, and by implication their relationship with YHWH, are the source of the Israelites' prosperity in the land.

The description in 9:10 of Israel as כענבים במדבר, "like grapes in the wilderness," also raises the question of whether the passage refers to traditions, like those preserved in the Pentateuch, of the wilderness period. According to these traditions, after leaving Egypt, the Israelites spent forty years living as nomads in the Negev region before they entered Canaan.[83] The sense that the prophetic author has drawn on wilderness traditions is heightened by the mention of Baal-Peor in the second half of the verse.

---

word may indeed be a gloss, since the other words in these four lines each have a semantic *and* syntactic parallel (כענבים במדבר || כבכורה בתאנה; ראיתי || מצאתי ישראל אבותיכם). Another possibility, however, is that the original author wanted to heighten the sense that the figs were a rare find.

82. The description of the find may also highlight another aspect of Israel's identity: the kingdom's small size relative to that of some of its neighbors. Regarding modern grapes and figs in Israel, Macintosh (*Hosea*, 362) observes: "Grapes grown in the desert areas at the present time are described as small and exceptionally sweet. Where the second simile is concerned, reference is to the small figs which can appear as early as May–June and … are regarded as a great delicacy." If the grape and fig varieties grown in ancient Israel have any relation to those grown today, then the choice of two small fruits would suggest an additional mapping from the VINE AND FIG TREE frame to the small size of Israel relative to her imperial neighbors.

83. Placing Israel's national origins in the Negev would be slightly inconsistent with other passages in Hosea that set the beginning of Israel's relationship with YHWH in Egypt (see, e.g., Hos 2:15; 11:1; 12:9, 13; 13:4). Mays (*Hosea*, 133) notes Hosea's references to Egypt as the site of Israel's origin, but argues that the mention of the wilderness in this verse does not represent a separate origins tradition. Andersen and Freedman (*Hosea*, 540) make a similar argument, and they suggest that the author places events in the wilderness period because of its proximity in time to the Baal-Peor incident.

References to Baal-Peor elsewhere in the Bible associate the name with a tradition about Israel worshiping the god Baal in the Transjordan region toward the end of the wilderness period (Num 25:1–5; 31:16; Deut 4:3; Josh 22:17; Ps 106:28–31). These traditions show variations in their details, the most significant of which is that some accounts describe YHWH ordering the execution of the idolaters (Num 25:4–5; and possibly Deut 4:3) while others say YHWH sent a plague to punish Israel (Num 31:16; Josh 22:17; Ps 106:29). Hosea 9:10 makes no mention of punishment, so we cannot be certain whether it draws on one of the biblical traditions or an alternate account about Baal-Peor, perhaps even one not associated with the wilderness period, that has not been preserved in the biblical corpus.

If 9:10 does not draw on wilderness traditions, then the reference to the wilderness in this passage may constitute an exercise in poetic license on the part of the author, with "wilderness" loosely referring to wherever the people lived before YHWH planted them in the land of Israel. In any case, the simile in this passage depicts a once idyllic relationship that began when YHWH discovered the people of Israel. Because national identities are constructed, the specific tradition, or whether it referred to a historical reality, matters little for the interpretation of this passage. The significant factor is the author's claim that YHWH initiated the relationship when he found Israel.

Though the portrait of Israel's origins in 9:10a praises the ancestors as a rare find by YHWH, the author does not allow his audience long to revel in that proud image. Instead, he immediately reframes Israel's past as a long history of illegitimate cultic practices. In effect, 9:10b acknowledges that the Israelites have always worshiped other deities, but it presents that reality as a perversion of YHWH's intent. In these lines, Baal-Peor most likely refers to a manifestation of the god Baal.[84] The phrase באו בעל־פעור should therefore be understood in the sense of "visiting Baal of Peor" at a cult site devoted to the god.

After stating that the Israelites went to Baal of Peor, the author indicates in the next line that they consecrated themselves (נזר) to shame (בשת).[85] The use of the verb נזר in this line to describe how Israel related to Baal sug-

---

84. Mays, *Hosea*, 133.

85. Several commentators credit Hosea with coining the epithet בשת for Baal, which was then taken up by later biblical authors (e.g., Macintosh, *Hosea*, 360–61; Mays, *Hosea*, 133; and Wolff, *Hosea*, 165).

gests a level of devotion that involves deference and self-sacrifice.[86] At best it implies that the Israelites split their loyalties between YHWH and Baal; more likely is that they abandoned YHWH in favor of Baal. By placing Baal-Peor in parallel with בשת, the author argues that in worshiping Baal, the Israelite ancestors devoted themselves to something shameful. The passage reinforces that message in the last line of 9:10, when the author declares that those who worship Baal are as despicable as the deity whom they serve. The verb אהב, "to love," in the last line, carries a specific sense of exclusive loyalty.[87] Like נזר in this passage, אהב emphasizes the level of devotion shown to Baal by the Israelites, implying that their devotion to Baal necessarily excludes the possibility of their continuing to serve YHWH.[88]

The prophet's second accusation against the Israelites appears in 9:15, this time referencing an unspecified evil originating at Gilgal. The verse has invited several different interpretations. The biblical text preserves two traditions about events at Gilgal. First, the Israelites camped there after they entered the land of Canaan (Josh 4:19). Second, Saul's inauguration as king of Israel occurred at Gilgal (1 Sam 11:14–15). Nothing in the content of Hos 9:15 seems to refer to the encampment at Gilgal tradition. Some scholars do suggest, because of Hosea's complaints elsewhere about the monarchy (Hos 7:3–7; 8:4; 10:3, 7, 15), that 9:15 refers to the traditions about Saul's kingship.[89] Most of Hosea's complaints refer to recent kings of Israel, however, who reign in Samaria, so it is not clear why Hosea would focus on Gilgal for a complaint about the monarchy.

The passage thus probably refers to a tradition not otherwise preserved in the biblical corpus. Both Hosea and Amos speak negatively

---

86. *HALOT*, s.v. "נזר."

87. In the context of ancient Near Eastern treaties, אהב, "to love," refers to the exclusive loyalty due between king and vassal. That same conception of love as exclusive loyalty also appears in the biblical corpus, particularly in Deuteronomy and Deuteronomic texts, in reference to the ideal relationship between YHWH and his people (e.g., Deut 7:9–11; 10:12–13; 30:15–20; Josh 22:5; 1 Kgs 11:1–3). See William L. Moran, "The Ancient Near Eastern Background of the Love of God in Deuteronomy," *CBQ* 25 (1963): 77–87; and Moshe Weinfeld, *Deuteronomy and the Deuteronomic School* (Oxford: Clarendon, 1972), 81–91.

88. Macintosh (*Hosea*, 360) notes that the act of dedicating oneself to something also means separating oneself from something else (see also Wolff, *Hosea*, 165). Mays (*Hosea*, 133) describes this change of status with respect to YHWH as a change in Israel's identity.

89. Mays, *Hosea*, 136.

about Gilgal as a cult site, so the mention of Gilgal may relate to cultic practices that were current there during Hosea's day (Hos 12:12; Amos 4:4; 5:5).[90] The cult site at Gilgal is associated with Yahwism, leading James Mays to argue that Hosea's objection relates to the form of the Yahwistic cult at Gilgal.[91] His claims appear to be based solely on biblical depictions of the site, though, and thus do not consider that those depictions of Isra-elite cultic practices may not accord with the historical reality of those practices. More helpful, perhaps, is to consider whether the cult at Gilgal included other deities in addition to YHWH. For the prophetic author, Gilgal may have represented the cultic practices that the texts of Hosea so vehemently denounce (e.g., Hos 2:15, 19; 10:1–2).

Whatever the sin committed at Gilgal, the author again uses the lan-guage of politics, as he does in 9:10, to express the final break between Israel and YHWH. Whereas in 9:10, YHWH accuses the Israelites of loving (אהב) Baal, in 9:15 YHWH declares his hatred (שנא) of Israel, and his intent to love (אהב) them no longer. Hatred in this political context refers to disloyalty to or rejection of an alliance.[92] YHWH here indicates that after a long period of maintaining his loyalty to Israel, even as Israel worshiped other deities and showed no loyalty to him, YHWH has finally decided to end his commitment to Israel.

The remaining verses in Hos 9:10–17—verses 11–14 and 16–17—focus on the punishment that YHWH intends to inflict upon his people. The author contends that on account of Israel's apostasy, which began with Baal-Peor, but which continues to the present at Gilgal, YHWH has at last decided to abandon his people. The passage describes the conse-quences of apostasy literally, through descriptions of death, childlessness, and infertility, on the one hand (9:11–14, 16), and exile and wandering on the other (9:15, 17).[93] In 9:16, it also returns to the horticultural meta-phor introduced in 9:10. It makes no further specific reference to grapes or

---

90. Contrast these verses with Hos 4:15, which appears to view Gilgal as a proper Yahwistic site.

91. Mays, *Hosea*, 136.

92. See the discussion in n. 87, above.

93. Most scholars agree on this basic outline for the passage, though they may differ on the details of how the author crafts this message. Macintosh (*Hosea*, 361–62), e.g., emphasizes a theme of love and betrayal running through the passage. Eidevall (*Grapes in the Desert*, 148–55) highlights the family themes that extend throughout, in both the metaphorical and historical material. Harper (*Hosea*, 339) views the passage as criticiz-ing not only Israel's apostasy, but also its pride in its wealth and population growth.

figs, but it employs a general image of fruit and of the Israelites as a fruit-bearing plant. The passage employs the conventional metaphor (DIVINE) WARFARE IS INDIVIDUAL COMBAT within the horticultural metaphor, as it depicts YHWH's attack in terms of a physical blow. That blow damages the national plant's roots and makes it unable to produce fruit. In other words, there will be no more grapes or figs. The loss of fruitfulness also suggests that Israel's long history of prosperity, provided by YHWH, will come to an end.[94]

The discussion to this point has focused on the national narrative constructed in this passage. Shortly after YHWH found Israel's forefathers, they betrayed him and began to worship other deities. Because their descendants have continued these cultic practices to this day, YHWH has finally had enough. He intends to abandon them, render them childless and infertile, and drive them from the land. The author has thus constructed a collective past, present, and future for the nation. The description of the Israelites as a fruit-bearing woody plant in 9:16 also implies, in the context of 9:10, that the plant that represents the current generation of Israelites has descended from the fruit YHWH found long ago. That 9:10 presents the ancestors as *like* grapes and figs, rather than as *being* grapes and figs, gives the author the freedom to present the nation in 9:16 as an unnamed type of fruit-bearing plant, which may or may not be grapes or figs. In effect, the passage hides the reality that a single plant cannot produce both grapes and figs so that it can construct a unified national character for the Israelites as a people descended from a common stock. The metaphor also provides the nation with a body by planting the Israelites in the land of Israel. Finally, Israel's cultic practices contribute the common culture that completes the national identity presented in this passage. The announced punishments threaten to bring Israel—both kingdom and nation—to an end.

Yet this passage does more than just declare YHWH's intention to wipe Israel off the map; it also thoroughly wipes away the national identity that it has constructed. The author first recasts the current national culture, defined here in terms of the people's cultic practices, as an existential threat to the nation. In both metaphorical fruitfulness terms and literal

---

Finally, Andersen and Freedman (*Hosea*, 536–38) suggest that objections to the practice of child sacrifice underlie the condemnations and the choice of punishment.

94. Harper (*Hosea*, 339) includes Israel's pride in its prosperity, i.e., its wealth and population growth, among the sins condemned in this passage.

terms, YHWH and his prophet declare that because of their polytheistic practices, YHWH will abandon Israel's population to be destroyed by infertility and war and to be expelled from their homeland.[95] The comparison of Tyre's fate with that of Israel in 9:13 drives home the threat by declaring that the calamities that befall other peoples who do not serve YHWH could also occur in Israel.

In describing Israel's neighbors, the prophets occasionally employ metaphors based on features of the kingdom. Thus, the laments over Moab in Isa 16:9 and Jer 48:32 describe the kingdom as the "vine of Sibmah," and both texts continue with descriptions of Moab as a producer of grapes and wine (Isa 16:9–11; Jer 48:32–33). Prophecies against Edom refer to it by its location, on Mount Seir (Ezek 35:2–3) and include images of rocks and cliffs (Jer 49:16; Obad 3–4). Passages about Egypt metaphorically compare it to the waters of the Nile (Jer 2:18; 46:7–8), in addition to referencing scenes associated with rivers and living near a river (Isa 19:5–8; Ezek 29:3–4). References to Assyria also include river images, in this case relating to the Euphrates (Isa 8:7; 11:15; Jer 2:18).

Hosea's declaration about Tyre takes a similar approach. Biblical passages about Tyre focus on its position on the coast of the Mediterranean and its role in international trade. Isaiah 23 speaks of its ships and wealthy traders. Within the set of prophecies against Tyre in Ezek 26–28, 26:3 draws on Tyre's coastal location, with YHWH raising armies against Tyre כהעלות הים לגליו, "like the sea sends up its waves," and 27:3–11 metaphorically depicts Tyre as a trading ship. In Hos 9:13, the image of planting or transplanting Tyre into a field conveys the idea that Tyre has been metaphorically removed from its home, the sea.[96] Evidence suggests that during Tiglath-pileser III's campaign of 734–732 BCE, Tyre submitted to Assyrian authority rather than risk total defeat.[97] That action would have symbolically transferred Tyre's power to Assyria: the lord of the seas thus became

---

95. YHWH's intent to abandon Ephraim (9:15, 17) constitutes a threat, because in the ancient Near East, the loss of divine presence meant the loss of divine providence. See the discussion of divine abandonment in Block, "Divine Abandonment," 73–99.

96. If this interpretation of the line about Tyre is accurate, then the imagery also belongs to a theme in the prophetic texts, especially Jeremiah, that associates the military defeat of a kingdom with the uprooting of a plant (Jer 12:14–15; Ezek 19:12; Amos 9:15).

97. Peter Dubovský, "Tiglath-pileser III's Campaigns in 734–732 B.C.: Historical Background of Isa 7; 2 Kgs 15–16 and 2 Chr 27–28," Bib 87 (2006): 153–70.

landlocked. An alternate explanation may lie in a more literal landlocking of Tyre by Shalmaneser V (727–722 BCE), if Josephus's account of the Assyrian king's five-year siege of Tyre has a historical basis.[98] Regardless of whether one of these events, or some other unrecorded defeat of Tyre, provides a true historical background for the passage, the description of Tyre in 9:13 creates not a semantic parallel, but a semantic progression. Just as YHWH has ensured the conquest of Tyre, so will he see Ephraim, which has not served him properly, lead its sons to defeat in war. In both cases, the metaphor conveys the message of defeat at the hands of an enemy.[99]

In addition to delegitimizing the current national culture, the author also deconstructs the rest of Israel's identity. In 9:10, presenting Israel's ancestors as grapes and figs, two fruits closely associated with the region of Israel, makes a literary connection suggestive of the Israelite homeland. In 9:16, Israel is a fruit-bearing plant that is planted in the land, but with damaged roots. In other words, the Israelites are no longer firmly rooted in the land. By driving the people out of their land (9:15), the author eliminates the link between the people and the land and thus destroys the national body. Hosea 9:17 again addresses the threat of exile by revisiting the birds simile from 9:11, which declares that Israel's glory (כבוד), its future generations, will fly away like a bird. Now 9:17, continuing the bird imagery, states that the current generation of Israelites will also flee (נדד) from the land.[100] In effect, the author scatters the people so that they no longer represent a community with a common national history and character, and he sterilizes them to cut off the nation's collective future.

Hosea 9:10–17 paints a picture of a nation in danger of permanently losing the identity that its national deity intended for it. On the one hand, the author disparages worship of other deities and presents that as a

---

98. Jeffrey K. Kuan, "Hosea 9.13 and Josephus, Antiquities IX, 277–287," PEQ 123 (1991): 103–8. This siege is known to us only from Josephus's Antiquities; we cannot corroborate it with any of the Assyrian records found to date, because nothing legible has been recovered relating to the reign of Shalmaneser V (Kuan, "Hosea 9.13 and Josephus," 107 n. 6).

99. Kuan ("Hosea 9.13 and Josephus," 107) reaches a similar conclusion about the author's intention to compare Tyre and Samaria in parallel lines. He argues that the passage relates to the need of both kingdoms to send out their armies to defend against the Assyrians, but he does not explain how his translation of the metaphor of "Tyre planted in a pleasant place" presents an image of military defense or of sending an army out to slaughter.

100. Wolff, Hosea, 168.

betrayal of YHWH. On the other hand, the author describes the consequences to Ephraim of having rejected an exclusively Yahwistic identity. He constructs the Yahwistic identity using a grape and fig simile about Israel's ancestors, imagery that brings with it the metonymic associations of vines and fig trees with Israel and with prosperity. That nexus of ancestors, figs and grapes, the land of Israel, and YHWH presents the Yahwistic identity as characteristic of the true Israelite and as the source of the nation's prosperity from the beginning. According to this author, therefore, the blessings that Israel has enjoyed to this day have come from their Yahwistic identity, but the punishment that is about to descend derives from their betrayal of that identity. The blessings have come from what made the Israelites unique, but the punishment comes from them acting like all the peoples around them in not worshiping YHWH. The author thus ultimately conveys not only the sinfulness and consequences of the Israelites current cultic practices, but also the ways that those practices diminish Israel from what it was meant to be.[101]

7.5. Collective Condemnation Fig Metaphors

Having addressed the passages that explicitly pair grape (vines) and fig (trees), I will now turn to a pair of passages that focus solely on figs: Isa 28:4 and Amos 8:1–2.[102] Neither of these passages employs fig imagery to construct a national identity. Nor do they map to the PROSPERITY frame. Instead, they present simple condemnation metaphors that map elements

---

101. The image constructed in Hos 9:10–17 shows conceptual parallels with the metaphor in Hos 2:14. Both passages describe a nation attributing prosperity to other deities when they should have attributed it to YHWH. Hosea 2:14 destroys prosperity, conceptualized as the destruction of vines and fig trees. By contrast, in Hos 9:10–17, the people become the grapes and figs, their children the prosperity that ends with the destruction of the national woody plant.

102. Only two of the eight passages in which the fig appears without grapes or vines are relevant to the study of prophetic national condemnations of Israel and Judah. The remaining six passages include: Gen 3:7, in which Adam and Eve sew fig leaves together to cover their nakedness; Prov 27:18, which compares tending a fig and profiting from its fruit with guarding one's master and being honored for it; 2 Kgs 20:7 and the parallel passage in Isa 38:21, in which the prophet Isaiah indicates that a dried fig poultice will heal King Hezekiah's boil; Nah 3:12, which condemns Babylonia, not Israel or Judah; and Jer 24:1–9, and the reference to it in Jer 29:17, which essentially constitutes a restoration metaphor.

of the FIG frame to the CONFLICT frame. The same pattern holds true for the fig simile in Nah 3:12, which presents Babylonians as figs ripe for picking. The evidence thus suggests that for figs and fig trees, it is the pairing with grapes or grapevines that may evoke the PROSPERITY frame.

When the fig stands alone, the unique properties of the tree and its fruit come to the fore, and the perspective is often negative.[103] The most prominent features of figs—that they are delectable but fragile and that the fruit is easy to pick—represent weaknesses of the fruit in absolute terms. Edibility, in particular, constitutes a weakness to the extent that taste can influence a potential predator. A tree whose raw fruit is inedible has stronger defenses against predation than a tree whose fruit tastes good. Olives, for example, contain a bitter chemical, oleuropein, a natural defense that makes the raw fruit nearly inedible.[104] Those same fig features, however, when viewed from a human point of view, become the main reasons why the fruit appeals to humans: figs are a delicious and easily obtained food.

That combination of weaknesses that benefit humans also makes the fig a useful source for expressions of CONQUEST IS EATING, since the fea-

---

103. The fig metaphor in Jer 24:1–9, which envisions the conquered people of Jerusalem as two baskets of picked figs—one delicious and one inedible—provides one example of a (mostly) positive image of people as figs. The passage constructs a national identity for the Judahites in the context of restoration, rather than condemnation. The author transforms the basket of good figs into the first generation of a new nation to be founded after the exile, when the people return to the land. Central to the metaphor in this passage is its clever reversal of the negative connotations associated with the EASILY PICKED element of the FIG frame. Instead of focusing on the weakness of the fig's neck that allows it to be easily picked, Jer 24 turns its attention to the delectability of ripe figs. Figs become easiest to pick when they are ripe, and therefore when they are at their peak flavor. The exiles were not plucked out of Judah because they were weak; they were chosen because they were Judah's best. On the other hand, those who remained in Judah were not even good enough to eat, and therefore they were left behind—not because they were too strong to be conquered, but rather because those left behind were not worth taking. The author thus employs a familiar blend of fig imagery with the conventional metaphor CONQUEST IS EATING, but he uses it in a counterintuitive way. As discussed above, the vine and fig metaphor in Mic 7:1–7 also draws on the concept of good people as harvested fruit, except its author treats the absence of good people as permanent.

104. Indeed, olive oil was used in antiquity to deter pests on other crops. Asaph Goor, "The Place of the Olive in the Holy Land and Its History through the Ages," *Economic Botany* 20 (1966): 228.

tures map easily to CONQUEST frame elements such as DESIRE TO ATTACK, WEAKNESS VS. STRENGTH, CONQUEROR VS. CONQUERED, and VICTORY. It is easy to see how a kingdom could exploit this metaphor in rhetoric against its enemies, as in Nah 3:12: כל־מבצריך תאנים עם־בכורים אם־ינועו ונפלו על־פי אוכל, "all your fortresses are fig trees with firstfruits;[105] if they are shaken, they fall into the mouth of the eater." From the perspective of the conqueror, viewing the enemy as easy and profitable to defeat would be consistent with the positive image of figs as easy and profitable to pick.

In the hands of the prophetic authors, however, when the viewpoint shifts to the experience of the conquered, rather than the conqueror, the image takes on a different significance. One passage that exploits this conceptual relationship is the fig simile in Isa 28:4b:[106]

כבכורה בטרם קיץ אשר יראה הראה אותה בעודה בכפו יבלענה:
[They are] like the breba fig before the summer, which he who sees it, when it is still in his hand, swallows it.

Elaborating on the conceptual metaphor CONQUEST IS EATING, Isa 28:4 compares Samaria's leaders to a breba fig that is consumed right from the tree. Once again, the simile highlights the weaknesses of the fig fruit, in this case to emphasize both the enemy's desire to attack Samaria's leaders (and by extension, their city) and the weakness of Samaria as an opponent easily conquered. Isaiah 28:4 thereby converts the pleasing image of a ripe fig into a devastating account of the fall of Israel.

The final passage in which fig imagery appears without vine imagery in a prophetic national condemnation is Amos 8:1–2:

כה הראני אדני יהוה והנה כלוב קיץ: ויאמר מה־אתה ראה עמוס ואמר
כלוב קיץ ויאמר יהוה אלי בא הקץ אל־עמי ישראל לא־אוסיף עוד עבור לו:
[1] Thus my lord YHWH showed me: Look, a basket of figs! [2] And he said, "What do you see, Amos?" And I said, "A basket of figs."

---

105. בכורים, "firstfruits," here suggests that the fruit is ripe for picking.

106. In the condemnation of Samaria in 28:1–4, the fig simile in 28:4b follows a much longer and more developed image of wine-induced drunkenness (28:1, 3). Nahum 3:12 similarly contains a drunkenness metaphor immediately followed by a fig simile, which raises the question of whether the pairing of vines and fig trees was so ingrained that the biblical authors and editors used it subconsciously even when they had no rhetorical purpose for doing so.

And YHWH said to me, "The end has come to my people Israel; I will not again pardon them [lit. pass it by]."[107]

The passage employs the image of a basket of figs, but the author does not extend the imagery with specific mappings from the FIG source frame. Commentaries on this passage focus on the play on two words in the second verse that, in the Northern Kingdom, would have been pronounced similarly: Israel as קיץ, "figs"; and הקץ, "the end," as coming to Israel.[108] They note in particular that קיץ, when referring to the summer harvest, may have been thought of as the end of the agricultural year in ancient Israel.[109]

While such interpretations no doubt have uncovered part of the message of the passage, they do not address the image of the basket of figs in the metaphor, which would have evoked the whole FIG frame, giving both the author and the audience access to that frame, especially to elements associated with harvesting figs. Since figs are picked only when fully ripe, the choice of this particular image of figs, as opposed to an image of a fig still on the tree, conveys that just as the time for picking figs has come, so the time for conquering Israel has come. The other biblical metaphors that depict conquest in terms of eating figs suggest an additional nuance to this passage. In 8:2, YHWH declares that he will no longer pardon Israel using a phrase that could also describe passing by the basket. This expression would evoke a frame and a scenario of someone not passing by a basket of ripe figs, which hints that the person may stop to eat the figs.[110]

---

107. *DCH* 6:235, s.v. "עבר."

108. Evidence from the Samaria ostraca suggests that diphthongs were monophthongized in the northern Hebrew dialect. Shalom M. Paul, *Amos: A Commentary on the Book of Amos*, Hermeneia (Minneapolis: Fortress, 1991), 253–54.

109. The term קיץ, in reference to the harvest of summer fruit (especially figs), appears in the last line of the Gezer calendar. In that text, it represents the last harvest of the agricultural year. Göran Eidevall, *Amos: A New Translation and Commentary*, AB (New Haven: Yale University Press, 2017), 214; see also Andersen and Freedman, *Amos*, 796; and Paul, *Amos*, 253–54.

110. Further supporting this interpretation are two other passages in which Amos applies the root עבר to YHWH. In 5:16–17, YHWH declares his intention to attack Israel—אעבר בקרבך, "I will pass through the midst of you" (5:17)—the result of which will be wailing in the towns and vineyards. In 7:6–9, YHWH shows the author a vision of a tin wall and of YHWH with tin in his hand, and YHWH declares: הנני שם אנך בקרב עמי ישראל לא־אוסיף עוד עבור לו, "See, I am putting tin in the midst of my people,

The viewpoint of all of these fig passages focuses on the harvested, not the harvester, suggesting that the primary conceptual mapping should be expressed in terms of the fig fruit. Converted to a submetaphor within the CONQUEST IS EATING structure, we might express this relationship as A WEAK ENEMY IS A RIPE FIG—with EASY TO PICK and DELECTABLE TO THE HARVESTER being the standard elements mapped from the FIG frame.

7.6. Conclusions: The Fig as an Image of Weakness

This review of the fig and fig tree imagery in the biblical corpus has demonstrated that this imagery operated within three fairly narrowly defined lanes. First, instances of the combination of vines and fig trees (and occasionally figs and grapes) demonstrate the association of the pairing with prosperity. This conceptual relationship is often expressed in terms of either the presence or the absence of vines and fig trees, with little or no detail drawn from the source frame of VINE AND FIG TREE. The association also appears in both metonymic and metaphoric expressions that map vines and fig trees to prosperity.

Second, that the biblical authors employed the pairing of vines and fig trees so many times in narratives and poetry about Israel and Judah—in everything from the food that the narrative characters consume, to the scenery against which a story plays out, to depictions of both prosperity and deprivation in the land—suggests that the people viewed the two woody plants, as a pair, as representative of the lands of Israel and of

---

Israel. I will not again pardon them [lit. pass it by]" (7:8). Tin, which is a component of bronze, metonymically refers to the bronze of weapons, so by declaring his intent to put tin among the people, YHWH is describing a military attack. The author then makes that threat explicit in 7:9 when YHWH says: וקמתי על־בית ירבעם בחרב, "I will stand over the house of Jeroboam with a sword." The author thus directly connects the expression לא־אוסיף עוד עבור לו, "I will not again pardon them," to the consequence of the lack of pardon: a military attack. The announcement in 5:16 of YHWH's intent to "pass through the midst" of Israel, coupled with the declarations that he will not "pass by" it in 7:9 and 8:2, strongly suggest that 8:1–2 also intends to present an image of divine attack. On אנך as "tin," in contrast to the usual interpretations of the term as referring to lead or a plumb line, see Cor Notebaart, *Metallurgical Metaphors in the Hebrew Bible*, ACEBTSup 9 (Bergambacht: 2VM, 2010), 91–100. Cf. *DCH* 1:342, s.v. "אֲנָךְ": "*lead* i.e., plumbline." Notebaart comments on the similarity of the three passages, but focuses on the metallurgical metaphor, and therefore does not address the broader implications of how each passage uses עבר to threaten a divine attack.

Judah, and that this conception had become at least somewhat conventional. It is not surprising, then, that the combination of vines and fig trees remains connected to the land of Israel in national identity metaphors. In this respect, returning to Wenham's claim that the fig tree does not represent Israel, we can conclude that this claim is narrowly true, but broadly untrue, as vines and fig trees together represent Israel and Judah, with the people as their fruit. Third, in the few cases in which figs appear alone in figurative passages, they carry their own set of connotations unrelated to the conceptualization of grapes and figs as a pair. Instead, they tend to constitute expressions of the metaphor CONQUEST IS EATING.

The question then becomes, given the significance of vines and fig trees together, and as the previous chapters have demonstrated, of viticulture alone, why do fig trees alone not hold a prominent position in prophetic national identity metaphors? Here two factors seem pertinent. First, the properties of the tree itself may have mitigated against the tree becoming a national symbol. The tree's skin-irritating latex and brittle wood would be generally incompatible with national pride, which may explain why we have no evidence of the Israelites or Judahites conceptualizing their kingdoms as a fig tree. More importantly, it appears that the fig fruit's less appealing aspects—including its weak-neck, its often seedless fruit, and the speed at which figs spoil—lend themselves well to images of weak nations or kingdoms, rather than strong ones. Consequently, figs may have proven better suited to imagining conquered peoples than national pride.

The second, and related, factor is that, as the discussion of vine and vineyard metaphors in the preceding chapters has shown, the prophetic authors tend to construct their national identity metaphors by reframing a preexisting conception of Israel or Judah held by their audience. Biblical vine and fig tree national identity metaphors draw on the close association of the lands of Israel and Judah with grapevines and fig trees. Conversely, since we have no evidence of the Israelites or Judahites conceptualizing either kingdom exclusively as a fig tree, we should not expect to find prophetic national identity metaphors based on the fig tree.

8

Other Plant Metaphors

The preceding chapters have examined prophetic viticulture and fig metaphors in close detail. This chapter will now take a step back to consider the broader context of plant metaphors in the prophetic corpus. The metaphorical sources examined in this chapter are divided into two broad domains: GRASSES (especially grains) and WOODY PLANTS (including trees, bushes, and grapevines). While plants that are neither grasses nor woody occasionally make an appearance in the prophetic condemnations, they generally serve as parallels or complements to either grasses or woody plants.[1] As the discussion below will show, none of the prophetic condemnations construct a national identity based on the metaphor A NATION IS A TYPE OF GRASS.[2] Grasses are employed purely for the expression of collective or national punishment. By contrast, and as the previous chapters have already demonstrated, woody-plant metaphors receive a more varied treatment and include among their number several national identity metaphors.[3]

---

1. See, e.g., Isa 1:8, which compares Jerusalem to סכה בכרם, "a booth in a vineyard," and מלונה במקשה, "a hut in a cucumber field." Each simile maps the city of Jerusalem to a building in a field of vines, but the primary image is the first one, the vineyard; the cucumber field simply serves as a parallel to the more common conception of Judah as a vineyard.

2. The one potential exception lies in Isa 28:23–29, which compares the punishment of Israel and Judah to the harvesting of various grains. While the passage primarily claims that the two nations will not share the same fate, a case could be made that the way the author treats the different grains in this extended metaphor also serves to create a distinction between the national identities of Israel and Judah, though the details of those identities are only vaguely defined.

3. In the prophetic condemnations, five passages refer to kingdoms or nations in general terms as being נטע, "planted," or נתש, "uprooted" (Jer 12:14; 18:7; 45:4; Hos 9:13; and Zeph 2:4). Given that none of the explicit national identity metaphors invoke

8.1. Grass Metaphors

The category of grasses includes field grasses and various edible grains (i.e., cereals). In prophetic condemnations, GRAINS, which constituted the primary field crops in the diet of peoples of the ancient Near East, provide the most popular source frame among the grasses metaphors, representing at least twenty-eight of the thirty-two such passages examined for this chapter. Most of the grain metaphors do not specify the cereal within the metaphor, but since wheat and barley were the two main grains grown in ancient Israel and Judah, the prophetic authors likely had one of these plants in mind when crafting their metaphors.[4] In most cases, metaphors based on the GRAINS frame are conflict metaphors that place either YHWH or a kingdom in the role of the ATTACKER, with the GRAIN mapping to the role of the ATTACKED. Israel or Judah fills the role of the ATTACKED in eleven grain passages, and in the remaining seventeen passages, the ATTACKED is either another kingdom or a group of people who oppose YHWH in some way. Babylonia fills the role of the ATTACKED in four passages (Isa 21:10; Jer 50:26, 51:2, 33), Moab in one (Isa 25:10), and Edom in one (Obad 18). The remaining eleven passages describe the defeat of groups or unnamed enemy kingdoms. Thus, the image of people as grains could be broadly applied to numerous targets; it was not restricted to use with Israel or Judah.

Within these metaphorical expressions, the grain is always a passive participant: It does not act, and it has neither history nor motivations. In addition, while many of the grain metaphors center on harvesting processes that remove the edible grain kernels from the inedible stalks and

---

the GRASSES frame, it seems unlikely that these "planting" and "uprooting" metaphors derive from a conceptualization of kingdoms or nations as types of grass. Rather, the author probably had in mind the planting or uprooting of a tree or vine. In addition, three passages conceptualize Israel or Judah as a field or plot of land but contain no mappings to specific types of plants (Jer 4:17; Mic 3:12; and the quotation of Micah in Jer 26:18).

4. Zohary, *Plants of the Bible*, 41. Of the grasses metaphors that do not rely on cereals, Isa 1:31 refers to sinners as flax fibers (נערת) that will be destroyed by fire, and Isa 37:27 (and its parallel in 2 Kgs 19:26) employs field-grass terms as a metaphor for the people of conquered towns, who are destroyed by wind. In addition, both Isa 36:6 and Ezek 29:6 describe Egypt, in derogatory terms, as משענת הקנה, "a reed staff" that is broken or splintered (רצץ). In both cases, the image expresses the foolishness of Judahite leaders relying on Egyptian support.

ears, the prophetic authors generally avoid explicitly mapping the grain kernels. Instead, they hide the grain kernels by focusing on the processes of harvesting and on what happens during harvesting either to the whole grain plant or to its inedible parts. This pattern highlights a feature of how grain metaphors are deployed; they almost always constitute images of scattering or destruction of a homogeneous opponent, with no mitigating implication that a virtuous remnant will escape punishment.[5]

As shown in table 8.1, most grain metaphors rely on one of four means of destruction.[6]

Table 8.1. PEOPLE ARE TYPES OF GRAIN in the prophetic corpus

Action	Relevant Biblical Passages
Reaping	Isa 17:5; **Jer 9:21**; Hos 6:11; Joel 4:13
Threshing	Isa 21:10; 25:10; 28:23–29; 41:15–16; Jer 50:11; 51:33; **Amos 1:3**; Mic 4:12–13
Winnowing	Isa 17:12–14; 29:5; 40:23–24; 41:2; 41:15–16; Jer 13:24; **15:7**; 51:2; Hos 13:3
Burning	Isa 5:24; 33:11; 47:14; **Obad 18**; Nah 1:10; Zech 12:6; Mal 3:19

The first three actions shown in the table—reaping, threshing, and winnowing—are harvest activities; the fourth, burning, probably derives not from a harvesting context, but rather from the flammability of grasses.

---

5. One exception appears in Isa 17:5, which presents an image of a harvested field in which a small number of grain stalks will be left behind by the harvesters. The metaphor is not overly positive, however, since the next verse describes the survivors as עוללת, "gleanings" (17:6). According to biblical law and narrative, the poor and disadvantaged of society would gather such gleanings after the main harvest was done (Lev 19:9–10; 23:22; Deut 24:19–21; Ruth 2; see also Borowski, *Agriculture*, 61). The image in Isa 17:6 therefore suggests that those who escape the initial harvest must still expect to be picked off by a second wave of gleaners.

6. The analysis here covers twenty-eight passages containing twenty-nine grain metaphors. Isaiah 41:15–16 appears twice in the table, because it combines a threshing metaphor with a winnowing metaphor. The one PEOPLE ARE TYPES OF GRAIN metaphor not included in table 8.1 presents Babylon as a heap of grain in a granary destined for destruction (חרם) by unspecified means (Jer 50:26). Passages shown in bold text indicate examples of the metaphor type that are discussed in this chapter.

8.1.1. Reaping Metaphors

The grain harvest (קציר) begins with reaping (קצר), either pulling the standing stalks (קמה) out of the ground by the root or cutting them with a sickle (חרמש or מגל).[7] Among the grain metaphors, those that focus on reaping best evoke the visual experience of combat, via mappings through the WARFARE IS INDIVIDUAL COMBAT metaphor. The image of cutting grain stalks corresponds to that of striking a human with a weapon, and the falling plant maps to the falling bodies of those killed in combat. The prophetic corpus includes four reaping metaphors, the most elaborate version of which appears in Jer 9:21:

דבר כה נאם־יהוה ונפלה נבלת האדם כדמן על־פני השדה וכעמיר מאחרי
הקצר ואין מאסף:

Say, "Thus is the utterance of YHWH, 'The corpse of the man will fall like dung on the surface of the field, and like a bundle of cut grain after the reaper, and there will be no gatherer.'"

The simile in this verse employs singular forms, but both the content and the surrounding context indicate that many will die. Therefore, the simile expresses a collective punishment. In this passage, which describes the punishment of Judah at the direction of YHWH, the mappings occur not just in concepts but also in images. The cut grain maps to the combat victims, but even more evocative is the mapping of the image of a falling bundle of cut grain, from the GRAIN REAPING frame, to the image of a falling body, from the INDIVIDUAL COMBAT frame.

When harvesting grains, such as wheat or barley, the reaper would grab a bundle of grain stalks (עמיר), cut the stalks below where he was holding them, and then drop the bundle and move on to the next patch of standing grain. Additional harvesters would follow behind, gathering up the bundles of grain and binding them into larger sheaves.[8] In Jer 9:21, the weight of one of these bundles of grain stalks conveys the heaviness of a human body falling in a way that a single falling grain stalk cannot. In saying that "the corpse of the man will fall … like a bundle of cut grain after the reaper," the author maps the actions of grabbing, cutting, and

---

7. Borowski, *Agriculture*, 58–62.
8. Lundbom, *Jeremiah 1–20*, 567.

dropping a bundle of grain from the GRAIN REAPING frame to the INDI-VIDUAL COMBAT frame actions of a soldier seizing, striking, and killing a human, whose body falls to the ground. Within the simile, the ungathered grain bundle further maps to an unburied body.[9]

The incorporation of the metaphor WARFARE IS INDIVIDUAL COMBAT within the passage creates a vivid scene that superimposes the image of a defeated kingdom over the image of a single fallen victim. The metaphor expresses both multiple individual deaths, through the cutting of multiple grain stalks, and the death of the kingdom as a whole, through the map-ping of the grain bundle to that of a single human body. With these few words, the prophetic author constructs an image of total destruction.[10] Notice, however, that the passage focuses entirely on the shared punish-ment of the Judahites; as discussed above, grain metaphors do not address the nation's history, culture, or land, and therefore they contribute little to the construction of a national identity.

8.1.2. Threshing Metaphors

A second set of grasses metaphors centers on the next stage of the harvest-ing process. After the grain is cut and bundled into sheaves, it is brought to an open space or threshing floor (גֹּרֶן) to be threshed (דּוּשׁ).[11] Grain

---

9. The focus in this analysis is the grain mappings in the metaphor, but the com-parison of corpses to "dung on the surface of the field" in the verse adds to the image by conveying the sense of unburied bodies. Jeremiah frequently holds out the threat of not receiving a proper burial, but the theme also appears in numerous other biblical passages (e.g., 2 Kgs 9:37; Isa 34:3; Jer 36:30; Amos 8:3). The imagery often includes the idea of being eaten by birds and wild animals (e.g., Deut 28:26; 1 Sam 17:46; Jer 7:33; 19:7; 34:20; Ps 79:2–3), but the larger consequence of not being properly buried was not having access to funerary offerings or to the normal comforts of the nether-world (e.g., Isa 14:18–20; Jer 16:4). For a brief discussion of other ancient Near East-ern texts that employ this threat, see Lundbom, *Jeremiah 1–20*, 499. See also Frances Dora Mansen, "Desecrated Covenant, Deprived Burial: Threats of Non-Burial in the Hebrew Bible" (PhD diss., Boston University, 2015).

10. Reaping metaphors apparently generated colorful imagery in the minds of non-Israelite scribes as well. E.g., an inscription of the Assyrian king Sennacherib (704–681 BCE) declares: "All of the Arameans, I reaped their skulls like withered grain and piled (them) up like pyramids" (230, ll. 111–112). See A. Kirk Grayson and Jamie Novotny, *The Royal Inscriptions of Sennacherib, King of Assyria (704–681 BC), Part 2*, RINAP 3.2 (Winona Lake, IN: Eisenbrauns, 2014), 335.

11. Borowski, *Agriculture*, 58–61.

grows in ears at the top of long stalks. The ears are structurally tough, such that they do not break apart when the wheat is cut down.[12] Threshing achieves two ends: it separates the grain ears (שבלים) from the stalks; and it separates the inner grain kernels from the outer ear spikelets. Threshing methods include beating the grain stalks with a stick or rod, using cattle to trample the sheaves, and using a threshing sledge (חרוץ or מורג) or wheel-thresher (אופן עגלה) drawn by cattle over the sheaves. A threshing sledge is a flat platform with rows of sharp stones or blades on the bottom side. A wheel-thresher is similar to a sledge, except the blades are attached to rows of wheels rather than to the bottom of a platform. Regardless of the method employed, the remains of threshing the grain ears are the grain (בר), the grain stalks or straw (קש), the crushed ear spikelets and bits of straw (תבן), and the lightweight grain husks (מץ).[13]

In terms of their underlying conceptual structure, threshing methods that involve beating the grain come closest to the imagery of individual combat, as the person threshing maps to a soldier striking, the threshing stick to a weapon, and the grain threshed to the defeated opponent. Those threshing metaphors that employ cattle or a threshing sledge or wheel are more visually abstracted from the image of physical combat. They replace the person threshing with the cattle or tool threshing and therefore may lack any intermediate mapping through the INDIVIDUAL COMBAT frame. In the case of the sledge or wheel, however, its blades may introduce the role of a combat weapon into the metaphorical structure.

Amos 1:3 presents an example of war expressed in terms of threshing grain:[14]

כה אמר יהוה על־שלשה פשעי דמשק ועל־ארבעה לא אשיבנו על־דושם
בחרצות הברזל את־הגלעד:

Thus said YHWH, "For three transgressions of Damascus and for four, I will not reverse it—for their threshing of Gilead with threshing sledges of iron."

---

12. Zohary and Hopf, *Domestication of Plants*, 29, 33, 50–51.

13. Borowski, *Agriculture*, 62–65, 69.

14. Three of the eight passages that employ a threshing metaphor use a stick, threshing sledge, or wheel to accomplish the task (Isa 28:23–29; 41:15–16; Amos 1:3), three employ the method of cattle treading down the grain (Isa 25:10; Jer 50:11; Mic 4:12–13), and two lack any reference to the means of threshing (Isa 21:10; Jer 51:33).

YHWH declares his intention to punish Aram (whose main city was Damascus) for having conquered the Transjordanian region of Gilead. Whether the prophecy refers to a specific historical event is not clear.[15] Both the threshing metaphor and the harsh tone of judgment in the passage do suggest, however, that whatever historical memory might lie behind the prophecy, the author associated it with extreme violence.[16]

Commentators in the past have argued that "threshing" refers to a literal type of torture inflicted upon a defeated enemy, but no direct textual evidence for such a practice has been found.[17] The presence of multiple threshing similes and metaphors in both biblical and extrabiblical texts also argues against this theory. Such passages attest instead to a conceptualization of military conquest in terms of the act threshing. For example, an inscription of the Assyrian king Tiglath-pileser III (744–727 BCE) recounts his conquest of Chaldea:

> Like a threshing sledge (*kīma dayyašti*), I trampled down (*adīš*) the lands Bīt-Silāni (and) Bīt-Saʾalli, (and) captured their [king]s. I destroyed the cities Sarrabā[nu] (and) Dūr-Baliḫāya, their large cities, (making them) like a mound of ruins. I brought [all of th]eir [people] to Assyria. (40, ll. 11b–15a)[18]

---

15. The prophecy continues in 1:4 with expressions of the metaphors CONQUEST IS BURNING and BURNING IS EATING: שלחתי אש בבית חזאל ואכלה ארמנות בן־הדד, "I will send fire into the house of Hazael, and it will consume the fortresses of Ben-Hadad." The Aramean kings Hazael and his son, Ben-Hadad, ruled in the second half of the ninth century BCE. That YHWH threatens "Hazael's house," meaning his royal line, and "Ben-Hadad's fortresses," rather than threatening either king directly, suggests that the prophecy could derive from a conflict between Israel and Aram either during or after the reigns of these two kings (cf. 2 Kgs 10:32–33; 13:1–7).

16. Nili Wazana ("'War Crimes' in Amos's Oracles," 479–501) argues that Amos's complaint refers not to an extremely violent single attack on Gilead, but to a pattern of behavior by the Arameans against Gilead that the prophet viewed as unwarranted.

17. Andersen and Freedman, *Amos*, 237. Even if threshing in this context did refer to a type of torture, it would still be a metaphor, since literal threshing happens to grains, not humans. For additional examples of threshing metaphors in ancient Near Eastern texts, see Paul, *Amos*, 47; and Eidevall, *Amos*, 104.

18. Hayim Tadmor and Shigeo Yamada, *The Royal Inscriptions of Tiglath-pileser III (744–727 BC) and Shalmaneser V (726–722 BC), Kings of Assyria*, RINAP 1 (Winona Lake, IN: Eisenbrauns, 2011), 100.

The description of his actions using the simile "like a threshing sledge," as opposed to "with a threshing sledge," makes clear the figurative nature of the expression.[19]

In Amos 1:3, the act of threshing maps to Gilead's defeat, with the iron blades on the threshing sledge mapping to the weapons of the Arameans.[20] The metaphor in this case makes no claim of wrongdoing by Gilead, so it cannot properly be called a collective condemnation metaphor for Israel. Instead, it represents a collective condemnation of Aram for having attacked Gilead. Metaphors of this type, where Israel or Judah fills the ATTACKED role in the metaphor, but neither of them is the accused nation in the prophetic condemnation, are relatively rare, but not unheard of in the prophetic corpus. A similar dynamic occurs in Jer 50:11, another threshing metaphor, which accuses Babylonia of threshing Jerusalem.

8.1.3. Winnowing Metaphors

A third set of grasses metaphors draws on aspects of the winnowing (זרי) of grain after it has been threshed. Winnowing separates the grain kernels from the rest of the grain plant (the straw, ear spikelets, and chaff). The grain kernel is the heaviest of these items, so when the threshed grain is thrown into the air—first with a winnowing fork (מזרה) and then with a cloth "basket"—the kernels fall to the ground first and the wind helps to carry the rest of the grain plant away from the kernels.[21]

---

19. The verb for threshing, דוש in Hebrew and *dāšu* in Akkadian, carries the basic sense of "to trample," leaving open the possibility that some metaphorical uses of the verb refer to trampling an enemy rather than threshing it. Many such expressions, however, clarify their context by including additional terms from the GRAIN THRESHING frame, such as the references to a threshing sledge in the texts cited here. See the examples of trampling and threshing metaphors in *CAD* 3:121, s.v. "dāšu."

20. Historically, the blades of a threshing sledge were made from flint or basalt, not iron. By the Iron Age, sledges with metal blades were also available, but stone blades also remained in use (Borowski, *Agriculture*, 65). Eidevall (*Amos*, 104) suggests that the reference to the iron blades on the threshing sledge highlights "brutality" in the image.

21. Borowski, *Agriculture*, 65–69. While the wind would have carried off at least some of the straw, ear spikelets, and especially the lightweight chaff during the winnowing, the inedible parts of the grain plants were otherwise often kept for other purposes, including as a component of cattle fodder and as a binding agent in making mud-bricks for construction (69).

Winnowing metaphors seem to operate by a different set of rules than other grain harvesting metaphors, which may indicate that they appeared in more than one context prior to their adoption by the prophetic authors.[22] They often lack mappings to the INDIVIDUAL COMBAT frame, and they occur in a broader range of contexts than reaping or threshing metaphors, which focus on the defeat of a kingdom, nation, or region as a whole. In addition, while most winnowing metaphors map to CONFLICT in some way, in two cases, the blown chaff is a metaphor for death or the notion that life is fleeting or tenuous: of kings in Isa 40:23–24; and of the Ephraimites in Hos 13:3.[23]

Finally, though all of the winnowing expressions related to warfare convey an image of emptying a location or nation, differences exist in how the prophets who use the WINNOWING frame deploy their metaphors. First Isaiah does not apply the image to any kingdom, nation, or city. Instead, its two winnowing metaphors map the blown chaff to the flight of a defeated army (17:12–14; 29:5).[24] Second Isaiah and Jeremiah, on the other hand, do map winnowing to the defeat or destruction of nations (Isa 41:2; 41:15–16; Jer 13:24; 15:7; 51:2). Jeremiah 15:7, for example, describes the punishment of Judah's towns by YHWH:

ואזרם במזרה בשערי הארץ שכלתי אבדתי את־עמי מדרכיהם לוא־שבו:
I will scatter them with a winnowing fork among the gates of the land. I will deprive [them] of children, I will obliterate my people. From their ways they have not turned back.

Here, the gates, meaning city gates, serves as a metonym for towns, while the land refers to the world outside of Judah. The image of winnowing maps to exile. YHWH thus describes the scattering of the people of Judah all over the known world, effectively emptying the land and destroying the nation by separating the people from each other and from their homeland. Moreover, the reference to the winnowing fork brings the INDI-

---

22. The metaphors discussed here are limited to those that specifically employ fillers from the GRAINS frame. They exclude other metaphors in which the wind scatters people (e.g., Jer 18:17; Isa 64:5).

23. So also Andersen and Freedman, *Hosea*, 633. By contrast, Macintosh (*Hosea*, 525) argues that the target in Hos 13:3 is Ephraim's idols.

24. Isaiah 17:13 places tumbleweed in parallel to chaff, with both driven away by wind.

VIDUAL COMBAT frame into the metaphoric structure, mapping the fork to a weapon.

8.1.4. Burning Metaphors

In addition to the grain metaphors that employ methods belonging to the GRAIN HARVESTING frame, burning constitutes a fourth method of destruction among the grasses metaphors. Since besieging armies sometimes torched the fields or grain stores of an opponent as punishment or incentive to surrender, we might expect to find metaphors that draw on such imagery.[25] Only one of the seven burning metaphors actually does so, though: Zech 12:6 maps burning עמיר, "cut grain," to people destroyed. The remaining six passages focus on the flammable nature of grasses, placing קש, "straw," in the role of the element that is burnt and mapping it to destroyed groups. For example, Obad 18 describes a future defeat of Edom by Israel and Judah in which the latter two kingdoms are fire that burns straw-Edom:

והיה בית־יעקב אש ובית יוסף להבה ובית עשו לקש ודלקו בהם ואכלום
ולא־יהיה שריד לבית עשו כי יהוה דבר:

The house of Jacob will be fire, and the house of Joseph flame, and the house of Esau will be straw. They will burn them and consume them, and there will be no survivor for the house of Esau, for YHWH has spoken.[26]

The phrase ודלקו בהם ואכלום, "they will burn them and consume them," represents a combination of the conventional conflict metaphors CON-

---

25. For references to these siege practices in ancient Near Eastern texts, see Trimm, *Fighting for the King and the Gods*, 367–79.

26. The reference to Esau in the verse relates to a patriarchal tradition, a version of which appears in the narratives in Genesis, that Esau, Isaac's son and Jacob's brother, founded the kingdom of Edom (Gen 25:20–34; 27:1–40). The enmity between the two kingdoms probably derives from relations between Israel and Edom in the exilic and postexilic periods, when the Edomites occupied portions of southern Judah and the Negev. Elie Assis, "Why Edom? On the Hostility towards Jacob's Brother in Prophetic Sources," *VT* (2006): 1–20. See also Assis, *Identity in Conflict: The Struggle between Esau and Jacob, Edom and Israel*, Siphrut 19 (Winona Lake, IN: Eisenbrauns, 2016).

FLICT IS BURNING and CONQUEST IS EATING, a combination made coherent by the existence of a third conventional metaphor: BURNING IS EATING.[27]

The reference to the straw alone, and not the whole grain stalk, suggests that the image in the verse represents neither a grain field nor a completed harvest. Indeed, since burning metaphors of this type lack specific references to the GRAIN HARVESTING frame (and three of seven cases pair the straw with a nongrain element), they may not relate to the harvesting process at all. Rather, these metaphors probably reference the burning of straw in nonharvesting contexts.[28] This burning theme may have arisen as an elaboration of the combination of the conventional conceptual metaphors PEOPLE ARE PLANTS and CONFLICT IS BURNING, with straw chosen as the source because of its flammability.

8.1.5. Conclusions: Grasses Metaphors

The preceding analysis of the grain metaphors in the prophetic condemnations shows that they almost always have groups, not individuals, as their targets, which makes sense conceptually, since grains are grown whole fields at a time. All of the reaping and threshing metaphors appear to invoke the WARFARE IS HARVESTING metaphor, and they may incorporate the INDIVIDUAL COMBAT frame within their metaphoric structure. On the other hand, winnowing metaphors may have originated independently of the WARFARE frame. The variety and distribution of winnowing metaphors in the prophetic condemnations suggests that they had two primary uses: to express the idea that something is ephemeral; and to convey the sense of scattering. Since winnowing depends on wind power to facilitate the scattering of the straw and chaff, metaphors based on this frame may not pair well with the INDIVIDUAL COMBAT frame, though the example of the winnowing fork in Jer 15:7 provides one exception to that rule. On the other hand, burning grain metaphors may have developed because the flammable nature of straw and chaff made them a convenient vehicle for connecting the metaphor PEOPLE ARE PLANTS to a different conventional conflict metaphor: CONFLICT IS BURNING.

---

27. On the conventionality of BURNING IS EATING, see ch. 2 n. 52.

28. Borowski (*Agriculture*, 69) claims that the קַשׁ was used for kindling, though the only evidence he cites lies in the biblical burning קַשׁ metaphors. Outside of burning it as kindling, it is unlikely that the Israelites would have simply destroyed the straw at the end of the harvest instead of using it for other purposes (see n. 21).

An additional aspect of these metaphors resides not in what they highlight about harvesting, but what they hide: the grain. Threshing, winnowing, and burning metaphors focus on the inedible (by humans) parts of the grain. They thereby hide the good, edible grain kernels that survive the various stages of the harvesting process. Even reaping metaphors, which include the whole grain stalk, avoid mention of the grain kernels themselves. In addition, the threshing and winnowing metaphors tend to present the straw and chaff as useless by-products of the harvest, best carried off by the wind, thereby hiding the other uses that farmers would have had for these items. Downplaying and hiding these elements of the GRAINS frame serves to heighten the condemnation by emphasizing the worthlessness of what is destroyed and by denying that anyone will survive the coming disaster. Finally, in all cases, the grasses are passive recipients of harm. They have no history, no motivations, and they take no actions prior to or in response to their own destruction or scattering. As such, none of the grasses metaphors examined here constructs a national identity for its target.

8.2. Woody-Plant Metaphors

The second source domain employed in the prophetic texts to characterize individuals, groups, kingdoms, and nations is WOODY PLANTS, a category that includes trees, bushes, and vines. The prophetic authors used frames from the WOODY PLANTS domain to express the notions of individual or collective punishment, but they also employed some of the same frames to construct national identities. Biblical woody-plant metaphors share a common structure and set of elements that can be employed with most types of woody plants. The analysis of viticulture and fig metaphors has already addressed several of these mappings. The conceptualization PEOPLE ARE WOODY PLANTS engenders variations in two directions: (1) A PERSON IS A WOODY PLANT; and (2) A GROUP OF PEOPLE IS A WOODY PLANT. Most national identity metaphors derive from the second variant, with the group of people being the nation. Table 8.2 below summarizes the set of mappings drawn from the WOODY PLANTS domain that both metaphor variants may share:[29]

---

29. These mappings are not restricted to prophetic metaphor; they also appear in metaphors elsewhere in the biblical corpus (e.g., Num 24:5–7; Judg 9:8–15; Pss 1:3; 80:9–17).

Table 8.2. Shared elements in variations on PEOPLE ARE WOODY PLANTS

PLANT Frame Role/Element	Woody-Plant Metaphor Variant	
	A PERSON IS A WOODY PLANT	A GROUP OF PEOPLE IS A WOODY PLANT
ROOTS	connection to the land and to water as source of nourishment	connection to the land and to water as source of nourishment
WATER	divine providence or prosperity	divine providence or prosperity
FRUIT	children	group members
BRANCH	child (esp. an heir)	person (esp. a leader)
HEIGHT	power, prestige, or pride	power, prestige, or pride
SHADE	power, influence, or protection	power, influence, or protection

The mappings above all derive either from features of the woody plant or, in the case of the presence or absence of water, from the resources available to it. While most expressions of woody-plant metaphors employ only one or two of these elements, national identity metaphors tend to map several of them.

The woody plant's ROOTS connect it to the land and allow it to draw water for nourishment. The prophetic corpus contains numerous passages that depict a kingdom or nation as metaphorically planted in its land (e.g., Jer 12:14; 18:7; Amos 9:15; Zeph 2:4). Mappings expressing that link to the land, to a claimed territory, may appear as part of the "national body" element in national identity metaphors. In addition, images of a woody plant nourished by water sources in the land express the conception of the subject's prosperity or enjoyment of divine providence. In prophetic condemnations, destroying the roots, uprooting the woody plant, or transplanting it all express the notion of separating the woody plant from the land, or from its water source, either through death or displacement. Children typically fill the role of FRUIT, but when the tree represents a group, the FRUIT role may also be filled by group members. A BRANCH role similarly takes the fillers of child or group member, but often carries the additional connotation of heirship or leadership.[30]

The basic metaphors POWER IS UP, PRESTIGE IS UP, and PRIDE IS UP provide the foundation for filling the HEIGHT role in woody-plant metaphors.[31] An author can express the power and prestige of the subject by describing the height of the woody plant, especially in comparison to other woody plants in its vicinity. Similarly, a tall plant that overtops the plants around it will naturally cast shade over its neighbors, thereby influencing how much sun those neighboring plants receive. In that sense, the taller plant has the power both to deny its neighbors the benefits of sunlight and to protect its neighbors from the harshness of sunlight.[32] Thus, the role of SHADE maps to notions of power and influence in woody-plant metaphors. The concept of HEIGHT can also be turned to a negative. In such cases, the height of the woody plant, or of its branches, may be used to accuse the subject of inappropriate pride or arrogance.

In addition to the variety of expressions available through the choice of elements to map, the metaphor A PERSON IS A WOODY PLANT also allows elaborations in the form of A GROUP OF PEOPLE IS A GROUP OF WOODY PLANTS. By means of such elaborations, authors can differentiate among the people in a group by presenting them as different types of plants, which map to characteristics such as different social strata or distinctions between "good" people and "bad" people. For example, cedar trees may represent leaders or royalty (e.g., Ezek 17:3–4, 22–23). Likewise, thorns, thornbushes, and thistles appear in several metaphors in reference to troublesome people (e.g., Isa 9:17; 27:4; Ezek 28:24; Mic 7:4). Similar

---

30. The concept of a branch as a leader also helps to explain the metaphor in Isa 7:4, which denigrates Rezin of Aram and Pekah (the son of Remaliah; 2 Kgs 16:5) of Ephraim as the stubby remains of two burning sticks—damaged, diminished, no longer connected to their tree, and no longer able to even sustain a fire. The passage apparently refers to the Syro-Ephraimite crisis, a failed attempt by Aram and Ephraim to seize control of Judah. The branch metaphor and its mappings are flexible, however. E.g., in Amos 4:11 the image of a stick saved from burning represents the kingdom of Israel, rather than a specific individual.

31. These conceptual metaphors appear frequently in the biblical corpus. E.g., statements of praise based on POWER IS UP or PRESTIGE IS UP occur in Isa 52:13; Pss 18:47; 21:14; and Job 36:7. Examples of condemnations based on PRIDE IS UP appear in Deut 8:14; Isa 3:16; Hos 13:6; Prov 18:12; and 2 Chr 26:16.

32. In ancient Near Eastern literature, shade is associated with royal protection (Greenberg, *Ezekiel 21–37*, 639).

metaphors of troublesome or unpleasant people as thorn-bearing plants also appear outside the prophetic corpus (Num 33:55; 2 Kgs 14:9 = 2 Chr 25:18; Song 2:2; and probably Ps 58:10), suggesting that the conceptual relationship had achieved a degree of conventionality.[33]

For purposes of analyzing and explaining the variety of woody-plant metaphors in the prophetic corpus, it is helpful to differentiate between woody plants that do not bear fruit and those that do bear fruit.[34] The distinction highlights similarities and differences in the actions taken against each type of woody plant. In addition, fruit-bearing woody plants are much more productive in prophetic national condemnations that construct national identities than are those that do not bear fruit.

8.2.1. Woody Plants That Do Not Bear Fruit

The category of fruitless woody plants includes named trees and woody plants that do not bear fruit and unnamed trees and woody plants for which the fruit element is not mapped. Of the twenty-one passages of this type examined, only three belong to the variant A GROUP OF PEOPLE IS A WOODY PLANT. Two of the three clearly have a tree as their source frame, while their target frames are ISRAEL (Isa 6:13) and ASSYRIA (Ezek 31).[35] The rest of the fruitless woody-plant metaphors belong to the category of A PERSON IS A WOODY PLANT, and especially its extension, A GROUP OF PEOPLE IS A GROUP OF WOODY PLANTS. Most of the fruitless woody-plant metaphors have as their target a group rather than a kingdom or nation—groups such as leaders, armies, or wrong-doers of various kinds.[36]

---

33. An inscription of the Assyrian king Assurbanipal (668–631 BCE) also uses two types of thorn-bearing plants to describe the bodies of Assyria's defeated Elamite enemies: "I blocked up the Ulāya River with their corpses (and) filled the plain of the city Susa with their bodies like *baltu*-plant(s) and *ašagu*-plant(s)" (3, v 90–92). Translation from Jamie Novotny and Joshua Jeffers, *The Royal Inscriptions of Ashurbanipal (668–631 BC), Aššur-etal-ilāni (630–627 BC), and Sîn-šarra-iškun (626–612 BC), Kings of Assyria, Part 1*, RINAP 5.1 (University Park, PA: Eisenbrauns, 2018), 71.

34. "Fruit" in this context refers to the commonly understood sense of the term as fleshy, edible produce, such as figs, grapes, or olives. It does not refer to the broader botanical sense of fruit as any seed-bearing produce of a flowering plant.

35. The third passage, Isa 64:5, depicts Judahites as withering leaves, which suggests that the community is a type of woody plant that sheds its leaves.

36. This total excludes the two branch metaphors in Isa 7:4 and Amos 4:11. See n. 30 for a brief discussion of these passages.

Table 8.3 lists the passages included in this analysis, organized again according to the method of destruction employed in the prophetic condemnation:[37]

Table 8.3: PEOPLE ARE FRUITLESS WOODY PLANTS in the prophetic corpus

Plant Outcome	Relevant Biblical Passages
Burnt	**Isa 9:17**; 10:17–19; **Jer 5:14**; Ezek 21:1–4; Nah 1:10; Zech 12:6
Burned and cut down	**Isa 6:13**; Jer 22:7; Zech 11:1–2
Cut down	**Isa 10:33–34**; Jer 46:22; **Ezek 31**
Other	Isa 1:30; 2:13; 17:13; 64:5; Jer 17:5–8; Ezek 2:6; 17:3; 28:24; Mic 7:4

In nine of the prophetic condemnations, the means of punishment for the woody plant(s) is burning, including three that are both burnt and fallen or cut down. Among the remaining metaphors, which do not involve fire, three have woody plants that are cut down, in five the plants are damaged by other means, and in four they are not damaged at all.[38] Put another way, more than 50 percent (nine of seventeen) of the metaphors that include damage or destruction of the source plant use fire as a means of attack. This pattern suggests that the use of CONFLICT IS BURNING in fruitless woody-plant metaphors about warfare or divine attacks may have been conventional to some degree.

Isaiah 6:13 is an expression of the metaphor A GROUP OF PEOPLE IS A WOODY PLANT that employs both burning and cutting down as an image of the collective punishment of Israel:

ועוד בה עשריה ושבה והיתה לבער כאלה וכאלון אשר בשלכת מצבת בם
זרע קדש מצבתה:

---

37. Again, the metaphors that receive more extensive treatment in this chapter are shown in bold text.

38. For the passages classified as "other," two present fruitless woody plants that are denied water (Isa 1:30; Jer 17:5–8), two depict damage by wind (Isa 17:13; 64:5), one describes a transplanted plant (Ezek 17:3), and four express no negative outcome for the plants (Isa 2:13; Ezek 2:6; 28:24; Mic 7:4).

Though still a tenth [remain] of her, she will again be burnt,[39] like
the terebinth or the oak tree, which when felled, a stump is [left]
of them. (A holy seed her stump will be.)

This verse has engendered significant debate, in part because variations
exist in the available texts and versions.[40] As these variants do not offer
compelling evidence in favor of emendation, the analysis here follows the
MT and interprets the verse in the context of Isa 6:8–12, which speaks of the
total destruction of Israel.[41] The author here describes Israel as כאלה וכאלון,
"like the terebinth or the oak tree." Expressed in terms of tree-removal, the
passage announces doom for more than 90 percent of the people; even the
tree's stump will be burnt away after the tree itself has been felled. Only the
final phrase offers a message of survival for a remnant of the tree.

The image in Isa 6:13 probably derives from the context of clearing
land. When gathering firewood from a forest or thicket, it is sufficient to
simply cut down a tree and haul the wood away. Clearing land for agriculture or construction, however, would generally require removing the
whole tree. Burning is an effective method for eliminating the stump that
remains after a tree has been cut down. Thus, Isa 6:13 fills the ACTION
role in the PLANT frame with clearing land and fills the OUTCOME role
with complete removal of the tree, which is first felled and then the stump
is burnt. Paired with the conceptual metaphor A GROUP OF PEOPLE IS A
WOODY PLANT, the imagery of the cleared land would be consistent with
the content of the preceding verses in 6:8–12, which speak of houses without residents (6:11) and of banishing the people from the land (6:12).

---

39. The feminine pronouns refer back to the feminine singular הארץ, "the land,"
in 6:12. Whether the passage presents a condemnation metaphor or a restoration
metaphor depends, in part, on the interpretation of ושבה. Some translations render
ושבה as "she [Israel] will repent" (e.g., JPS). The translation here takes ושבה והיתה as
a hendiadys meaning "to do or be again." This use of שוב is well attested (HALOT, s.v.
"שוב").

40. E.g., the LXX reflects a Vorlage without the words מצבת בם זרע קדש, "a stump
is [left] of them. A holy seed," from the second half of the verse. On the other hand,
1QIsaᵃ has משלכת, "causing to fall," instead of בשלכת, "when felled," and במה, "high
place," instead of בם, "of them." On the basis of this variant, some scholars emend אשר,
"which," to אשרה, "cultic pole," and interpret the verse as referring to removing a
sacred pole from a high place. Wildberger (Isaiah 1–12, 251) rightly notes the strange-
ness of such a comparison in the larger context of the verse and passage.

41. So also Childs, Isaiah, 57–58.

The above explanation still leaves out the final phrase in the verse: זרע קדש מצבתה, "a holy seed her stump will be." The notion of a holy seed suggests that the tree will survive even being cut down and having the stump burnt out, a message that stands at odds with the total destruction otherwise described in 6:8–13. For this reason, and because the note about the holy seed is missing from the LXX, many commentators consider the phrase to be a later addition.[42] Conceptually, however, the idea that a shoot could yet sprout from the apparently destroyed tree stump has a basis in reality. As Michael Zohary notes: "The work of clearing forests in this country [Israel] required then, and still does, very hard labor. In the stony and rocky ground, the roots of the trees penetrate deep crevices which enable the tree to sprout and reappear even after being cut or burnt."[43] Zohary's observation does not prove that the final phrase is original to 6:13, but it does indicate that each claim in the verse is grounded in human experience.

A second example of a fruitless woody-plant metaphor appears in Jer 5:14, in which YHWH declares that he will empower the prophet Jeremiah to declare YHWH's words of accusation and judgment against the Judahites:

לכן כה־אמר יהוה אלהי צבאות יען דברכם את־הדבר הזה הנני נתן דברי
בפיך לאש והעם הזה עצים ואכלתם:

Therefore, thus says YHWH, God of Hosts, "Because you have spoken this word, see I am turning my words in your mouth to fire, and this people is wood, and it [the fire] will consume them."

The broad semantic range of עץ, which can refer to both woody plants and to wood in various forms, leaves open the possibility that the phrase והעם הזה עצים could be understood as comparing people either to woody plants or to firewood (from one or more woody plants).[44] The underlying con-

---

42. See the discussion of the authorship, editing, and dating of this verse in Nielsen, *There Is Hope for a Tree*, 145–47.

43. Zohary, *Plants of the Bible*, 103. Zohary does not clarify his reference to burning trees, so he may not have the idea of burning out the tree's stump in mind. Nevertheless, his comment on both the difficulty of clearing land in Israel and the hardiness of the trees there is consistent with the interpretation of Isa 6:13 offered here.

44. Most translations render עצים in this passage as "wood" or "kindling" (Lundbom, *Jeremiah 1–20*, 392). Lundbom notes that the image is conceptually consistent

ceptual relationship in this verse could thus be either A GROUP OF PEOPLE IS A WOODY PLANT or A GROUP OF PEOPLE IS A GROUP OF WOODY PLANTS, depending on how the author envisioned the עצים. The basic sense of the metaphor remains the same in either case, however. As in the burning straw expression in Obad 18, the metaphor BURNING IS EATING makes coherent the combination of the conflict metaphors CONFLICT IS BURNING and CONQUEST IS EATING in this verse. The nature of the conflict in this verse is that of divine punishment, which Jeremiah invokes by speaking the messages of YHWH to Judah.

As discussed above, the extension of A PERSON IS A WOODY PLANT to A GROUP OF PEOPLE IS GROUP OF WOODY PLANTS makes possible elaborations that rely on groups of different types of woody plants to describe different types of people. For example, Isa 9:17 presents the people of Israel as a wilderness comprising thornbushes, thistles, and other plants and trees that grow in a thicket:

כי־בערה כאש רשעה שמיר ושית תאכל ותצת בסבכי היער ויתאבכו גאות
עשן:

For wickedness burns like fire. Thornbush and thistle it consumes. It has kindled in the thickets of the forest, and they have billowed up in a plume of smoke.

The passage combines the conventional metaphors PEOPLE ARE PLANTS and CONFLICT IS BURNING to depict internal strife in the kingdom as a wildfire spreading in a forest, with each plant burning any others that come into contact with it. Drawing on the association between troublesome people and thorny plants, the author describes the fire of wickedness starting among the troublesome people, the שמיר ושית, "thornbushes and thistles," and then spreading to other groups of people who belong to סבכי היער, "the thickets of the forest." As such, the passage contains a rare example in which plants fill the roles of both the attacked and the attacker.

Another example of A GROUP OF PEOPLE IS GROUP OF WOODY PLANTS appears in Isa 10:33–34, which describes the defeat of either Assyria or Judah by YHWH in terms of razing a forest:[45]

---

with Jer 1:9, which describes YHWH putting his words into Jeremiah's mouth, and with Jer 23:29, which refers to YHWH's word as fire (395).

45. The passage currently sits between an anti-Assyrian prophecy and a restoration prophecy for Judah. The identity of the target of the forest metaphor—either

הנה האדון יהוה צבאות מסעף פארה במערצה ורמי הקומה גדועים
והגבהים ישפלו: ונקף סבכי היער בברזל והלבנון באדיר יפול:

[33] See, the Lord, YHWH of Hosts, is lopping off a bough with ter-rifying power.[46] The lofty of height will be cut off, and those who are high will become low. [34] The thickets of the forest will be cut down with iron, and Lebanon, in [its] might, will fall.

The conceptual structure of this metaphor allows rulers and leaders to retain their status as trees or tree branches via descriptions of the lofty being brought low and of branches being cut off. At the same time, the image also incorporates their social inferiors as additional members of the FOREST frame: סבכי היער, "the thickets of the forest." In contrast to the previous passage, the destruction of the forest here occurs entirely in the context of felling trees and other woody plants. The passage contains no mention of fire. Similar to the reaping metaphors discussed in the grasses section above, the metaphor incorporates battle imagery via the INDI-VIDUAL COMBAT frame, with woodsmen felling trees with iron mapped to soldiers killing opponents with weapons.

8.2.2. National Identity Construction in Fruitless Woody-Plant Metaphors

Among the metaphors of woody plants that do not bear fruit, only Ezek 31 constructs a national identity, though the absence of any conception of the people as an empowered community in the passage suggests that we should instead view the metaphor as constructing a kingdom identity. While the author frames the chapter as a whole as a prophecy against the Egyptian pharaoh (31:1–2, 18), its core in 31:3–17 contains an extended metaphor of the Assyrian kingdom as an ארז בלבנון, "a cedar tree in Leba-non" (31:3).[47] The passage begins with a long description of past Assyrian

---

Assyria or Judah—depends on whether 10:33–34 concludes the prophecy in Isa 10 or begins the prophecy in Isa 11. See Nielsen, *There Is Hope for a Tree*, 123–44.

46. Many translators assume that the passage contains an error in במערצה, but Nielsen (*There Is Hope for a Tree*, 129) argues that מערצה, "terrifying power," consti-tutes a deliberate wordplay on מעצדה, "axe," intended to lead the audience "to think of both the implement itself and the terror the use of it provokes."

47. Greenberg (*Ezekiel 21–37*, 637), noting that where the MT has "Assyria" (in 31:3) the Syriac and the Vulgate have "the Assyrian," considers Assyria here to be a metonymic reference to the king, with the king then metonymically representing the kingdom. He does not address the circular logic of this claim, nor does he dis-

prosperity and might, with the kingdom depicted metaphorically as a well-watered and flourishing cedar tree (31:1–3). The tree achieved a stature greater than all the trees around it, casting its shadow over all other peoples, and it provided shelter for the birds and beasts and peoples of the earth (31:5–6). YHWH then takes credit for Assyria's prosperity, claiming that by his actions, Assyria became larger and more beautiful than all other trees בגן־אלהים, "in God's garden" (31:7–9).

The passage shifts from poetic lines to prose beginning in 31:10, where the author indicates that Assyria's success made it arrogant, expressed, as in other woody-plant metaphors, in terms of the tree's height (31:10):

יען אשר גבהת בקומה ויתן צמרתו אל־בין עבותים ורם לבבו בגבהו:

Because you were tall in height[48]—he put out his crown up between the branches and his heart was uplifted because of his height.

The middle clause ויתן צמרתו אל־בין עבותים, "he put out his crown up between the branches," conveys the image of a tree's crown growing up through the branches of the surrounding trees, eventually to overtop them.[49] In the final clause, a comparable modern idiom to the Hebrew רם לבבו, "his heart was uplifted," would be "he puffed up his chest," an embodied depiction of a person's excessive pride over his own accomplishments. That 31:9 credits YHWH for the tree's height, which maps to its power

---

cuss whether the Syriac and Vulgate may represent a harmonization to create a more direct comparison in the passage between pharaoh and the Assyrian king. Neither emendation nor metonymic reference is needed for conceptual coherence, however. Figurative language can accommodate such discrepancies as long as the metaphoric structure—the relationships between the elements of the metaphor—holds. Thus, a comparison between a group (Assyria) and an individual (pharaoh) as a metonymic reference to a group (Egypt), would not disrupt the logic of the metaphor. That said, if the prophecy's address, אל־פרעה מלך־מצרים ואל־המונו, "to pharaoh, the king of Egypt, and to his multitude" (31:2), is taken at face value, then the comparison offered in the passage is between two groups, not between an individual and a group.

48. Hebrew גבהת, a 2ms perfect verb, is the only second-person verb in this section. Otherwise, the passage describes Assyria in the third person. The Syriac and Vulgate reflect a 3ms verbal form, but the difference may be the result of a later harmonization rather than deriving from an original Hebrew text. See Daniel I. Block, *The Book of Ezekiel: Chapters 25–48*, NICOT (Grand Rapids: Eerdmans, 1998), 189 n. 57.

49. See the discussion of עבותים in the case study of Ezek 19:10–14 in ch. 5.

and prestige, suggests that the complaint in 31:10 attributes to Assyria an unseemly arrogance.

As punishment, YHWH claims that he allowed an even greater kingdom to conquer Assyria (31:11).[50] Continuing the tree metaphor, the destruction of Assyria takes the form of the felling of the tree, with the kingdoms that sheltered under it abandoning it, and with its branches scattered across the earth (31:12).[51] Consistent with other biblical woody-plant metaphors, the branches here probably map to people. The images in 31:12–13 map to the WARFARE frame via roles in the INDIVIDUAL COMBAT frame: the ACTION roles that are filled by cutting down the tree, having it hit the ground, and then having birds and animals nest on its remains map to the MEANS OF ATTACK roles filled by a soldier striking an opponent, the opponent falling dead, and the body remaining unburied, respectively. The rest of the passage shifts the setting to the netherworld and focuses on the fallen tree as an object lesson to all of the other trees (i.e., kingdoms) of the world (31:14–18).

The author of Ezek 31 has constructed an identity for Assyria that incorporates the kingdom's origins, history, and fate and that includes elements suggestive of the Assyrian homeland and culture.[52] Since Assyria was the dominant power in Mesopotamia and the Levant for much of the seventh century BCE, the prophetic author's opinion of Assyria would derive from his Judahite perspective on that period. The choice of the

---

50. Ezekiel 31:1 dates the prophecy to the eleventh year after the beginning of Jehoiachin's exile in Babylonia, which corresponds to 586 BCE, during the Babylonian siege of Jerusalem. Thus, while the author does not name the greater kingdom, the context indicates that the metaphor reflects backward on the Babylonian defeat of Assyria in the seventh century BCE (Block, *Ezekiel 1–24*, 29).

51. The metaphorical mappings of the animals in this chapter are somewhat muddled. Where the birds and animals sheltering under the tree serve as an image of peace and prosperity in 31:6, in 31:13 similar imagery of birds and animals sheltering among the branches expresses a sense of the tree's abandonment by humans.

52. Changes in content and form(s) across the text of Ezek 31, differences among the versions, and linguistic inconsistencies in a few words suggest that the text is composite and not entirely attributable to a single exilic author. The verses most frequently excised on the basis of such arguments are 31:5 and 31:9 (Block, *Ezekiel 25–48*, 178 n. 1). Removing these verses would not significantly alter the analysis offered here, except to slightly weaken the kingdom's origin myth, as 31:9 directly attributes Assyria's rise to power to YHWH. The passage would still retain its attribution of Assyria's downfall to YHWH, however (31:10–11).

cedar tree probably relies in part on the use of cedar in the construction of palaces and temples, leading the cedar tree to be generally associated with royalty and the divine.[53] The choice of a tall tree may also draw on the conventional connection between height and power or prestige.[54] Indeed, several prophetic metaphors employ cedar imagery. In some passages, the cedar appears to be a metaphor for the leader (Isa 2:12–13; Ezek 17:3–4), while in others it may be a metonymic or metaphoric reference to the royal palace or to other important buildings (Jer 22:6–7; Zech 11:1–2).[55]

Imagining Assyria as a cedar tree not only serves to identify the kingdom with prestige and wealth, but it also makes those associations part of Assyria's destiny in history; the kingdom is a cedar tree, and it therefore was destined to rule from its beginning. At the same time, the author carefully attributes Assyria's past dominance to YHWH both by outright declaration (31:9) and by comparing it to the trees בגן־אלהים, "in the garden of God" (31:8–9), as though the Assyrian cedar was also part of that garden. This combination of narrative elements creates an origin myth for Assyria as a kingdom nurtured to full power by YHWH.

The author then moves on to other aspects of Assyria's identity. He describes its history prior to the Babylonian conquest as one of dominance over other kingdoms, who depended on Assyria for protection. The author expresses these aspects through the cedar tree's height exceeding that of other trees and through the sheltering of people and animals under the cedar tree or in its shade (31:3–6).[56] The Assyrian homeland, between the Tigris and Euphrates Rivers, appears in the lengthy descriptions of the cedar tree's abundant water sources (31:4–5, 7), thus supplying a body element for the constructed identity. Its culture, from the perspective of the biblical author, lies in the descriptions of the kingdom's arrogance (31:10–11), with the implication that Assyria did not acknowledge YHWH's role in its success (31:9). Finally, the destruction and abandonment of the tree express a common fate, not just for Assyria but for all the other king-

---

53. Block, *Ezekiel 25–48*, 185; and Greenberg, *Ezekiel 21–37*, 645.

54. Zohary (*Plants of the Bible*, 105) notes that a cedar tree can grow to thirty meters in height.

55. For a discussion of imagery referencing (the cedars of) Lebanon, see Jack R. Lundbom, *Jeremiah 21–36: A New Translation with Introduction and Commentary*, AB 21B (New York: Doubleday, 2004), 124.

56. The imagery may draw on the association of shade with royal protection in ancient Near Eastern literature (Greenberg, *Ezekiel 21–37*, 639).

doms that depended upon Assyria or that benefited from Assyria's might (31:12–18).[57]

An underappreciated aspect of this passage is the blending of the image of Assyria with a schematic image of Egypt. Interpretations that focus on this text as a depiction of Egypt may overlook the significance and rhetorical effect of constructing an Assyrian identity, with Egypt appearing only in comparison to Assyria.[58] The metaphor creates a kingdom identity for Assyria in order to deconstruct Egypt's kingdom identity. By equating the two kingdoms, the author turns Egypt from a powerful kingdom in its own right into just another arrogant, river-irrigated empire that has not shown proper deference to YHWH. Just as Egypt has enjoyed Assyrian-like levels of prosperity and power, so Egypt will experience an Assyrian-like downfall. The author thereby doubly insults Egypt. Not only is Egypt destined to destruction; it is also denied the prestige, the token of respect, of being credited with a unique identity based on its own characteristics. In the world according to Ezek 31, Egypt is not special; it is merely one of many trees in the forest, rising or falling according to YHWH's design.

Of course, the Egyptians likely were not the target audience for this prophecy. Rather, this prophecy probably aimed to influence the people

57. Block (*Ezekiel 25–48*, 186) argues that the kingdoms conquered by the Assyrians would probably not have described Assyria as their protector. The picture is not so simple, however. Both biblical and extrabiblical texts attest to Assyrian vassals seeking Assyrian aid when they were threatened by internal or external pressures. See Amélie Kuhrt, *The Ancient Near East c. 3000–330 BC*, 2 vols., Routledge History of the Ancient World (London: Routledge, 1997), 2:460–62, citing the Kilamuwa (= Kulamuwa) and Panammu (= Panamuwa) inscriptions. For translations of the texts, see "The Kulamuwa Inscription," trans. K. Lawson Younger Jr., *COS* 2.30:147–48; and "The Panamuwa Inscription," trans. Younger, *COS* 2.37:158–60. In the Bible, see 2 Kgs 15:19–20; 16:7–9; and 2 Chr 18:16. Moreover, viewed from the perspective of the Judahite author, any kingdoms who benefited from Assyrian power, especially at Judah's expense, could easily be portrayed as sheltering under Assyria's tree. Philistia, e.g., acquired portions of western Judah from Assyria after the invasion of 701 BCE (Faust and Weiss, "Judah, Philistia, and the Mediterranean World," 71–92).

58. See, e.g., Zimmerli (*Ezekiel 2*, 149, 153), who notes that the poem's content does not fit the characteristics of Egypt, but who nevertheless emends אשור, "Assyria," in 31:3 to an "original" תאשור, "cypress," and then treats the poem as referring entirely to pharaoh. Block (*Ezekiel 25–48*, 187–88) recognizes Assyria as the subject of 31:3–16, but when he analyzes the content of the verses, he at times fails to maintain a distinction between Assyria and Egypt, instead framing his analysis as applying to "Assyria (Egypt)."

of Judah who advocated accepting Egyptian assistance against Babylonia.[59] After the conquest of Jerusalem in 597 BCE, the Babylonians installed their own choice of king over Judah, Zedekiah, and they left the kingdom as a vassal state.[60] Both Jeremiah and Ezekiel indicate the existence of a pro-Egypt faction in Judah at this time, and both texts firmly reject the idea of relying on Egypt in a fight against Babylonia (Jer 2:12–19, 36–37; Ezek 17:11–20).[61]

In that context, Ezek 31 contains two messages for the Judahites. On the one hand, it denigrates Egypt as an ally, both by declaring that YHWH is against Egypt and by replacing whatever identity Egypt held in the minds of its adherents with an identity that reduces Egypt's stature to that of Assyria, a kingdom that has already been conquered. On the other hand, the passage attributes to YHWH the fall of Assyria, Judah's one-time overlord, thereby implying that YHWH can also end the Babylonian hegemony over Judah, Babylonia being yet another arrogant, river-irrigated empire. Ezekiel 31:16–17 may indirectly refer to Babylonia, as it depicts all the trees that drink water (31:16) and all that lived under the tree of Assyria (31:17) as sharing Assyria's fate. The description fits Babylonia's proximity to the Tigris and Euphrates Rivers and Assyria's rule over Babylonia prior to Assyria's demise. This may be the cleverest aspect of the passage. The author would probably have found it difficult to incorporate a message about Babylonia within a metaphor focused on Egypt, but by making Assyria his focus, the author can indirectly condemn both Egypt and Babylonia to a similar fate.

8.2.3. Fruit-Bearing Woody Plants

The category of fruit-bearing woody plants includes generic fruit trees as well as named trees and plants, such as the olive tree, the fig tree, and the grapevine. The discussion that follows focuses on plant metaphors of this type that have not been covered in previous chapters. Metaphors based on these plants constitute a separate class from both grass and fruitless woody-plant metaphors, both in terms of the methods of destruction

---

59. See Block, *Ezekiel 25–48*, 196; and Greenberg, *Ezekiel 21–37*, 647.

60. Miller and Hayes, *History of Ancient Israel and Judah*, 468–69.

61. Miller and Hayes, *History of Ancient Israel and Judah*, 469, 475–75; and Greenberg, *Ezekiel 21–37*, 647.

mapped in the metaphors and with respect to their employment in the construction of national identities.

Amos 2:9 provides an example of an unspecified fruit-bearing woody-plant metaphor based on the metaphor A GROUP OF PEOPLE IS A WOODY PLANT. In this passage, YHWH claims to have aided Israel when they conquered the land of Canaan:

ואנכי השמדתי את־האמרי מפניהם אשר כגבה ארזים גבהו וחסן הוא
כאלונים ואשמיד פריו ממעל ושרשיו מתחת:

I destroyed the Amorite from before them, whose height was like the height of cedar trees, and who was strong like the oak trees. I destroyed his fruit above and his roots below.

Here the author describes the Amorites collectively in terms of a single fruit tree. The Amorites' former power and prestige appear in the description of the tree as being as tall as a cedar tree and as strong as an oak tree. Even though these trees do not bear fruit, at least not in the common sense of the term, no conceptual contradiction occurs in the subsequent description of the Amorite tree as having fruit, because the comparisons occur in simile form and are limited to specific aspects of the cedar and oak that could also apply to a fruit tree. The metaphor maps destructive OUTCOMES to both the FRUIT and ROOTS elements of the WOODY PLANT frame, suggesting that the people were killed (FRUIT) and the nation dispossessed of its land (ROOTS).[62] At the same time, the MEANS OF ATTACK

---

62. H. L. Ginsberg has argued that פרי in Amos 2:9 and elsewhere refers to branches, not fruit. See "'Roots Below and Fruit Above' and Related Matters," in *Hebrew and Semitic Studies: Presented to Godfrey Rolles Driver in Celebration of His Seventieth Birthday, 20 August 1962*, ed. D. Winton Thomas and W. D. McHardy (Oxford: Clarendon, 1963), 72–76. Three problems weaken his argument. First, he (74) notes that פרי and שרש form a word pair that constitutes a merism referring to a whole tree (cf. 2 Kgs 19:30 [= Isa 37:31], Ezek 17:19, and Hos 9:16). In the merism, however, while the word pair represents the whole tree, the two terms retain their literal senses as referring to the upper and lower extremes of that tree. In other words, פרי does not mean *branches* simply because the merism of פרי and שרש includes the tree's branches. Second, the biblical authors also paired שרש with terms that mean *branch*, including קציר (Job 14:8–9; 18:16; and 29:19), פארה (Isa 10:33–11:1), ענף (Mal 3:19), and דלית (Ezek 17:6 and 31:7). Rather than taking these root-branch forms of the merism as further evidence that פרי also refers to branches when paired with שרש (Paul, *Amos*, 89), it seems more likely that they represent alternate formulations of

role remains essentially unfilled; the tree is destroyed in some way, but the metaphor does not specify the method of destruction.

The destruction of the tree in Amos 2:9 is consistent with some biblical rhetoric about the fate of the Amorites when the Israelites took control of Canaan, but the imagery is also somewhat unusual.[63] The preceding chapters have already demonstrated that in prophetic metaphors, fruit-bearing woody plants are seldom destroyed. In fact, they are never cut down and only rarely burnt. Rather, the majority of such metaphors go no farther than harvesting the woody plant's fruit or damaging its boughs. As discussed in chapter 3, the relative lack of fruit tree destruction in these metaphors may reflect a combination of an aversion to destroying a food source and a tendency toward realism in metaphorical imagery.

While fruitless woody plants contribute only one identity metaphor to the prophetic condemnations (and grasses none), fruit-bearing woody plants appear in at least nine national identity metaphors. The distribution of the source domains/frames for these metaphors is shown in table 8.4.

Table 8.4. National identity in fruit-bearing
woody-plant metaphors in the prophetic corpus

Source Domain/Frame	Relevant Biblical Passages
VITICULTURE	VINEYARD: Isa 5:1–7; GRAPEVINE: Jer 2:21; Hos 10:1–2; Ezek 15; 19:10–14
GRAPEVINE AND FIG TREE	Jer 8:13–17; Hos 9:10–17; Mic 7:1–7
OLIVE TREE	Jer 11:16–17

---

the merism: "roots and branches" for woody plants in general; and "roots and fruit" for fruit-bearing woody plants. Third, all of the passages that employ a version of the merism are metaphorical, making it likely that the terms were chosen more for creative reasons than for technical precision in referring to the parts of a woody plant. As such, we have no reason to assume that פרי carried a sense other than *fruit* in Amos 2:9 and similar passages. (See also the discussion of whether פרי refers to fruit or branches in the case study of Ezek 19:10–14 in ch. 5.)

63. For an overview of the varied and sometimes inconsistent traditions about the Amorites in the biblical corpus, see Andersen and Freedman, *Amos*, 329.

All nine of these national identity metaphors have either ISRAEL or JUDAH as their target. (The depiction of Moab as aged wine in Jer 48:11–12 is also an identity metaphor and a viticulture metaphor, but since it focuses on wine rather than grapes or vines, it is not technically a woody-plant metaphor.)[64] Chapters 3–7 examined in detail the condemnation metaphors based on the source domain of VITICULTURE and the source frame of FIG TREE. The following discussion will therefore focus on how the other major fruit-bearing woody plants of the Levant are, or are not, represented in prophetic condemnations.

8.2.4. Fruit-Bearing Woody Plants Chosen as Symbols of Israel and Judah

The most frequently mentioned fruit-bearing woody plants in the prophetic corpus are: grapevines (גפן); fig trees (תאנה); olive trees (זית); pomegranate trees (רמון), and date palms (תמר).[65] Any of these products could have provided a source frame through which to view a nation, but for the prophetic authors, it appears that not all crops were created equal. Pomegranates and dates are not well represented in the prophetic corpus. Jeremiah 52:22–23 mentions images of pomegranates decorating the bronze pillars in the temple that were taken by the Babylonians when they conquered Jerusalem, while date palms figure extensively in the decorations on the doors and walls in Ezekiel's vision of the rebuilt temple in chapters 40–41 (40:16, 22, 26, 31, 34, 37; 41:18–20, 25–26). Beyond these cultic references, pomegranates appear with vines, fig trees, and olive trees in Hag 2:19 in reference to trees that YHWH will begin to bless as soon as the temple is rebuilt, and Joel 1:12 includes both pomegranate trees and date palms among the trees stricken by a plague of locusts. The pomegranate and the date palm, however, are never employed in a PEOPLE ARE PLANTS metaphor in the prophetic corpus.[66]

---

64. Chapter 6 includes a discussion of this passage.

65. While גפן may refer to any vine or climbing plant, most biblical instances of this noun are references to grapevines. These five fruits also appear in the list of שבעת המינים "the seven species"—wheat, barley, grapes, figs, pomegranates, olives, and dates—traditionally seen as the most important agricultural products of the land of greater Israel (Westenholz, *Sacred Bounty*, 13–14). Rabbinic tradition views these seven products as the only acceptable first-fruits offerings in the Jerusalem temple (14).

66. The date palm did achieve status as symbolic of Judea centuries later, when Roman coins from Judea were stamped with the image of a date palm on their face (Zohary, *Plants of the Bible*, 53). In addition, the idiomatic phrase ראש וזנב כפה ואגמון,

The use of dates and pomegranates in cultic decorations may explain the prophetic authors' decision not to employ such imagery in their condemnations of Israel and Judah. Beyond the prophetic passages already mentioned, 1 Kgs 6–7 speaks of King Solomon decorating the walls and doors of the temple in Jerusalem with images of palm trees (6:29, 32, 35; 7:36) and the pillars in the temple entryway with pomegranates (7:18, 20, 42).[67] Second Kings 25, which contains a shorter version than Jer 52 of the temple looting by the Babylonians, also mentions the pomegranates decorating the pillars (25:17). Finally, Exod 28:33–34 and 39:24–26 speak of adorning priestly robes with pomegranates. The prophets may not have wanted to employ imagery closely associated with YHWH and the temple in any derogatory conceptualizations of Israel and Judah.

In the case of the date palm, another factor may have made the tree less appealing as a metaphor for Israel or Judah. As noted in chapter 2, emphasizing dissimilarity with other nations is one of the core strategies used in constructing national identities. Date palms grew prolifically in both Egypt and southern Mesopotamia. In Mesopotamia in particular, dates and date palms held great economic and symbolic significance. For example, in the poem Erra and Ishum, the Babylonian god Marduk speaks a lament over the city of Babylon, which he describes as a date palm:

Ah, Babylon, whose crown I made as splendid as a palm tree, but the wind has dried it up/carried it away!
Ah, Babylon, that I filled with seed like a (date)-cone, but I could not have enough of its delights![68]

Another text, a hymn, compares the city to a date.[69] The significance of the date palm, especially to Mesopotamia, thus means that the tree would not have provided the prophetic authors with imagery that was distinctive of Israel.

"head or tail, (palm) branch or reed" (Isa 9:13; 19:15), might constitute a metaphorical use of the date palm, but the image is not entirely clear, since כפה may not always mean "palm branch" (see *DCH* 4:453, s.v. "כִּפָּה"). The metaphor refers to leaders for the first term in each word pair (ראש // כפה) and prophets or sages for the second term (זנב // אגמון).

67. See also the version of this account in 2 Chr 3–4.
68. Wisnom, *Weapons of Words*, 233, citing Erra and Ishum 4.40–41.
69. Wisnom, *Weapons of Words*, 233.

The relative absence of personified olives or olive trees in the prophetic condemnations is more puzzling, given the prominence of the trees and their fruit in the biblical corpus, both in literal and symbolic contexts. Several passages associate ownership of olive trees with prosperity (Deut 6:11, Josh 24:13; Neh 5:11) and treat the loss of olive trees as evidence of deprivation (1 Sam 8:14; Amos 4:9; Hab 3:17). The biblical authors also considered olives to be important enough to include in laws governing the harvest (Exod 23:11; Deut 24:20), and the olive leaf had symbolic significance in the flood story in Gen 6–9 as the item that the dove brought back to Noah after the flood as evidence that the waters were receding from the earth (8:11).

In addition, several passages personify olives in a positive sense. The olive tree takes pride of place in Jotham's fable in Judg 9:8–15. In the story, the trees of the land seek one of their members to anoint as king over themselves. The first tree that they approach is the olive tree, who declines, preferring to maintain the productive role of making oil that honors both gods and humans rather than "swaying over the trees" (9:8–9).[70] In Ps 52:10, the speaker, for trusting in YHWH, describes himself as זית רענן בבית אלהים, "a lush olive tree in the house of God." Psalm 128:3 blesses the man who obeys YHWH, saying: בניך כשתלי זיתים סביב לשלחנך, "your sons will be like olive shoots around your table." Within the prophetic corpus, Zech 4 includes a vision in which YHWH's attendants appear as שני הזיתים, "the two olives/olive trees" (4:11), or שתי שבלי הזיתים, "the two olive clusters" (4:12). Finally, Hos 14:7 declares that if Israel returns to YHWH, ויהי כזית הודו, "its [the nation's] beauty will be like the olive tree."

Yet within the prophetic condemnations, olive trees appear only three times. Two passages describe the survivors of YHWH's punishment as כנקף זית, "like the beating of an olive tree," referring to the remnants left on the tree after an olive harvest (Isa 17:6; 24:13). Isaiah 17:6 goes on to explain the image in greater detail:

ונשאר־בו עוללת כנקף זית שנים שלשה גרגרים בראש אמיר ארבעה חמשה בסעפיה פריה נאם־יהוה אלהי ישראל:

Only gleanings shall be left on it, like the beating of an olive tree—two, three berries on the top branch, four, five on its fruitful boughs—declares YHWH, the god of Israel.

_____

70. Here again, HEIGHT maps to concepts of pride or arrogance in the PEOPLE ARE PLANTS metaphor that structures the fable.

The image of beating the tree derives from the typical process for harvesting olives, but in these passages, it represents a near total devastation of the target of the metaphor. The preceding verse employs an individual combat metaphor within a grain-reaping expression (17:5), which primes the audience to interpret the beating of the olive tree as also mapping to INDIVIDUAL COMBAT.

The third and final olive tree metaphor in the prophetic corpus begins with an image of collective punishment. Jeremiah 11:16 declares:

זית רענן יפה פרי־תאר קרא יהוה שמך לקול המולה גדלה הצית אש עליה
ורעו דליותיו:

"A lush olive tree, beautiful of form,"[71] YHWH called you. With a sound of a great crowd, he set fire to her, and his branches were ruined.[72]

The textual unit in which this metaphor resides, Jer 11:14–17, may contain one or more corruptions that create challenges for interpreting the passage. In 11:14, YHWH commands Jeremiah not to intercede with him on Judah's behalf. Jeremiah 11:15 accuses Judah of some form of cultic transgression, though the verse does not provide details about the nature

---

71. The noun תאר means "appearance" or "form" (*DCH* 8:584–85, s.v. "תֹּאַר"). Elsewhere in the biblical text, the term appears in adjectival constructs similar in form to the phrase found in this verse: פרי־תאר (cf. יפת־תאר "beautiful of form" meaning "beautiful" [Gen 29:17], טוב־תאר "pleasing of form" meaning "handsome" [1 Kgs 1:6]). The comparable passages suggest that the term preceding תאר in Jer 11:16 should be an adjective, rather than a noun. The absence of a reference to fruit in the LXX translation of this verse raises questions about whether a textual corruption has occurred at this point. *DCH* (4:250, s.v. "יפה"; citing יפיפית in Ps 45:3) notes the existence of a *pealal* stem attested for the verb יפה "to be beautiful." Multiple Hebrew manuscripts also attest to a related adjectival form, יפיה, rather than the MT's יפה־פיה, in Jer 46:20, in a metaphor about Egypt as a beautiful heifer. The translation here thus adopts *HALOT*'s conjectural emendation in Jer 11:16 from יפה פרי to the construct form יפיפה (*HALOT*, s.v. "יְפֵיפִיָּה").

72. While the referent of the pronoun on עליה must be the tree, it is not clear why the pronoun is feminine, when the other pronouns used of the tree are all masculine. One potential solution is to emend the final verb, ורעו, to align with the Vulgate, which describes the branches as burnt. This change is questionable, however, because the LXX appears to agree with the MT on ורעו, though the two texts differ at other points in the verse. Ultimately, whether or not the text is emended, the phrase's intended message—that the branches are destroyed—is fairly clear.

of the offense. In this context, 11:16 constitutes a metaphorical expression of the punishment awaiting the nation for these misdeeds. It provides little detailed information about the present state of its target, though the image of a beautiful, full tree suggests prosperity.

Jeremiah 11:16 includes a rare instance of a condemnation metaphor about a fruit-bearing woody plant that employs CONFLICT IS BURNING in its metaphorical structure. The reference to the destroyed branches may map to the deaths either of people in general or of the kingdoms' leaders. The verse provides no information to clarify its intended mapping on this point. That the branches are ruined suggests that the tree survives. As in the burning of the vine in Ezek 19:10–14, the destruction of the olive tree may be limited. By itself, Jer 11:16 represents a simple condemnation metaphor. In the larger context of 11:14–17, however, 11:16 contributes the element of a common fate to a national identity metaphor. Since Jer 11:14–17 contains a set of originally independent verses that have been subsequently combined, the passage thus demonstrates how a national identity can be constructed progressively through the stages of editing a text.

While the passage now exists as a textual unit, it probably does not represent a compositional unity.[73] The speakers and addressees in 11:14–17 change in ways that seem more random than planned, and the verses' content contains little to interconnect them. It seems likely that a later editor joined 11:15–16 and then framed them with 11:14 and 11:17 to create the textual unit. The inclusion of 11:17 at the end of the unit is critical to the construction of a national identity within this condemnation metaphor:

ויהוה צבאות הנוטע אותך דבר עליך רעה בגלל רעת בית־ישראל ובית
יהודה אשר עשו להם להכעסני לקטר לבעל:

YHWH of Hosts, who planted you, has decreed disaster for you, "because of the wickedness of the house of Israel and the house of

---

73. Lundbom (*Jeremiah 1–20*, 627) defines the unit as 11:14–17 on the basis of its similarities to the prophecy in Jer 7:16–20, in which an admonition against Jeremiah praying for the nation introduces the textual unit about apostasy. Jeremiah 7:16–20, however, contains a speech by YHWH that is directed at Jeremiah, while Jer 11:14–17 contains more diverse material, which suggests that 11:14–17 may be the product of editorial activity designed to create a textual unit similar in form and message to 7:16–20.

Judah, what they have done for themselves, angering me by burning offerings to Baal."

The planting metaphor in 11:17 has no direct ties to the olive tree metaphor in 11:16. Rather, the image in 11:17 derives from the generic
metaphoric theme of uprooting and planting that appears repeatedly in
Jeremiah and elsewhere in the biblical corpus.[74] By placing that common
metaphor immediately after 11:16, the editor completes the national identity construction begun with the collective punishment metaphor in 11:16.
Jeremiah 11:17 contributes the national origins (planted by YHWH), culture (apostate), and claimed territory (planted in the land) to the identity.

Jeremiah 11:16–17 also establishes that Israel or Judah *could* be both
identified with an olive tree and condemned as such, which raises the
question of why they were not more often depicted so. On this point,
the historical reality of olive cultivation in ancient Israel may offer some
insight. Olive trees grow well even where the soil is poorly nourished or
rocky, and in ancient Israel, they flourished both in the mountains and on
the coastal plain. The trees are slow to produce fruit, needing five to six
years of growth before yielding their first crop, but thereafter a well-tended
tree can continue producing fruit for hundreds of years.[75] While the fruit
and its oil were used for food, the oil was also used in lamps and for ritual,
medicinal, and personal grooming purposes.[76]

The hardiness of olive trees and the uses of their fruit argue in its
favor as a national symbol, but the trees' weaknesses create a counter-
point to their image of longevity and beauty. The olive tree trunk hollows
out with age, making the wood unsuitable for building purposes, though
it was useful for crafting smaller household items.[77] In addition, the
tree's yield is inconsistent from year to year, providing abundant fruit
only every other year, while the yields in the alternate years are poor.[78]
Finally, even when fully ripe, olives are bitter; they technically can be

---

74. See n. 3, above.

75. Zohary and Hopf, *Domestication of Plants*, 145.

76. Zohary, *Plants of the Bible*, 56.

77. On the hollowing out with age, see C. L. van W. Scheepers, "An Archaeological Investigation into the Production of Olive Oil in Israel/Palestine during Iron Age
I and II," *JSem* 15 (2006): 566. For its usefulness, see Zohary, *Plants of the Bible*, 56.

78. Scheepers, "Archaeological Investigation," 566.

eaten fresh, but their palatability improves significantly with processing to reduce the bitterness.[79]

While the features and uses of the olive tree suggest that it may have seemed a less-than-ideal choice to represent the nations of Israel or Judah, economic and political factors may have played a greater role in influencing the extent to which the biblical authors' and their audiences associated the olive tree with Israel and Judah. The kingdom of Israel had a flourishing olive oil industry in the ninth–eighth centuries BCE, but the Assyrian conquest at the end of the eighth century largely wiped out these sites, and they were apparently not rebuilt during the period of Assyrian control of Samaria.[80] The evidence suggests that Judahite production of olive oil in the Shephelah expanded toward the end of the eighth century, but these installations, too, were destroyed by the Assyrians, during their campaign against Judah in 701 BCE. In the seventh century, it was primarily Philistia, not Judah, that expanded its olive oil production, especially at Ekron, thus filling the gap in supply left by the destruction of the Israelite and Judahite olive oil installations.[81] Zephaniah's prophecy against Philistia may contain a late-seventh-century polemical pun against Ekron's olive oil industry in its claim that ועקרון תעקר, "Ekron will be uprooted" (2:4).[82] The passage suggests the

---

79. Westenholz, *Sacred Bounty*, 39, 43. Also creating potential difficulties for the use of the olive tree as a national symbol in prophetic condemnations is the role of olive oil and olive wood within the cultus. As discussed above, the oil was used for anointing and as fuel for lamps in the temple. In addition, 1 Kgs 6:31–33 describes temple doors made from olive wood. Similar to the case of the pomegranate and date palm, it may be that the connection of olive trees to the cultus contributed to the biblical authors' avoidance of using the image in a negative way.

80. Avraham Faust, "The Interests of the Assyrian Empire in the West: Olive Oil Production as a Test-Case," *JESHO* 54 (2011): 62–86. Pollen analysis of sediment cores taken from the Sea of Galilee and the western shore of the Dead Sea (in the Ze'elim Ravine) support the theory that olive cultivation in Israel sharply declined at the end of the eighth century BCE, likely as a result of the abandonment of olive groves in the aftermath of the Assyrian campaigns in the region (Finkelstein and Langgut, "Climate, Settlement History, and Olive Cultivation," 153–69).

81. Faust, "Interests of the Assyrian Empire," 69, 77–78. Olive oil produced in Judah during the seventh century would probably have been mostly for domestic consumption rather than foreign trade (Faust and Weiss, "Judah, Philistia, and the Mediterranean World," 82).

82. Eric Lee Welch, "The Roots of Anger: An Economic Perspective on Zephaniah's Oracle against the Philistines," *VT* 63 (2013): 471–85.

existence of some negative feelings associated with Philistine olive production. With Judah ceding much of its olive oil industry, and profits, to
Philistia, it is unlikely that the Judahites would have chosen the olive tree
as a symbol of national pride.

From the perspective of the prophets seeking to craft condemnations
of Israel or Judah, a weakened olive oil industry might have made the olive
tree seem ideal as a symbol of the nations' punishment. Indeed, the only
positive representation of Israel as an olive tree in the prophetic corpus is
in Hos 14:7, a text that may predate the Assyrian campaign against Judah
in 701 BCE and the subsequent rise of the Philistine oil industry. As the
preceding chapters have demonstrated, however, the prophetic authors
tended to select plant imagery that was positively associated with Israel
and Judah for their metaphors about the kingdoms. If the olive tree did not
have the requisite status as a national symbol, then it probably would not
have served the prophets' rhetorical needs.

8.2.5. Conclusions: Fruit-Bearing Woody Plants

The examination of woody-plant metaphors in the prophetic condemnations has demonstrated that both fruit-bearing and fruitless woody
plants could be used for the construction of national identity, but that the
prophetic authors displayed a decided preference for fruit-bearing woody-
plant metaphors for that purpose. In addition, while fruitless woody-plant
metaphors frequently employ the destruction methods of cutting down
or burning, fruit-bearing woody-plant metaphors generally avoid destruction of the plant and instead focus on harvesting or destroying the fruit.
Even in the national identity metaphors, where burning of the woody
plant occurs in a few cases, the plant typically survives. Finally, despite
the differences in the implementation of metaphors based on fruit-bearing
versus fruitless woody-plant frames, most woody-plant metaphors appear
to draw from a common set of roles and relations at the domain level.

8.3. Conclusions: Framing National Plant Metaphors

The analysis in this chapter provides both methodological lessons for
metaphor analysis and insights into the use of PLANT-BASED frames in
prophetic national condemnations. On the one hand, studying the grain
metaphors at the frame level, expressed in terms of frames related to the
method of destruction, demonstrates the limits of relying on broad source

domains, such as GRASSES, for categorizing metaphors. When examined below the domain level, images that employ the same source domain may have independent origins and they may find expression through different source frames. On the other hand, whereas the importance of frame-level analysis becomes apparent in the study of grain metaphors, the importance of domain-level analysis shows itself in the study of woody-plant metaphors. Metaphors that differ at the source frame level—expressed either in terms of the plant type or method of destruction—may share mappings when compared at the domain level, as woody-plant metaphors share a common set of roles no matter what the specific source frame. In other words, the search for patterns in metaphorical expressions requires study of metaphors at both the domain level and the frame level.

The pattern of source frames and mappings discussed in this chapter also offers some potential explanations for the prophetic authors' choices of plant source frames in their identity metaphors about Israel and Judah. The common association between height and prestige may have mitigated against using low-profile plants, like grasses, for national identity. On the other hand, grapevines also grew low to the ground, so height was not the only relevant factor. The fact that grain metaphors were already conventionalized to describe defeated enemies probably provides a better explanation for the lack of grain-based national identity metaphors. The absence of national identity metaphors from the various fruitless woody-plant frames is harder to explain. While the cedar tree was not native to Israel or Judah, and therefore not a likely choice as a national symbol, both kingdoms abounded in trees. The most impressive in height and strength were the oak tree (אלון) and the terebinth (אלה).[83] Perhaps the fact that these trees were most valuable when cut down (and exported) mitigated against their use as a symbol of national pride. The prevalence of trees and groves in cultic imagery (and practice) may also have prevented the development of a general association of these trees with the concept of a nation.[84] As discussed above, a similar issue of cultic significance may have inhibited the use of some fruit trees as national symbols.

The evidence also suggests that while economic importance to the kingdom may have factored into the choice of images, it was not determinative. Israel and Judah exported both lumber and olive oil to other

83. Zohary, *Plants of the Bible*, 28–33, 103–111.
84. Zohary, *Plants of the Bible*, 28–33, 45, 103–111.

countries, yet neither their lumber trees nor the olive tree became significant sources of national imagery. On the other hand, the two kingdoms also exported figs and wine, and they do constitute the most commonly used woody-plant frames for constructing national identity. Perhaps a better measure of the economic importance of these crops would be to consider their value to the common people of Israel and Judah, where ownership of fruit-bearing woody plants would have represented greater food and financial security to those engaged in subsistence production.

9
Conclusions

This project originated as an attempt to determine whether patterns exist in the metaphors about Israel and Judah in the prophetic corpus. The exploration of this question has uncovered a wealth of conceptual connections linking different types of plant metaphors to each other and to the lands of Israel and Judah. Fundamentally, the metaphorical condemnations of kingdoms or nations (i.e., metaphors about groups of people) examined in the preceding chapters all rely on the conventional metaphor PEOPLE ARE PLANTS. Within the prophetic corpus, the number of PEOPLE ARE PLANTS metaphors and their creative application in a range of contexts and with numerous target frames creates challenges for identifying patterns in the ways the authors have deployed these images. The analysis of over one hundred condemnation passages that personify plants, however, has yielded several insights.

First, while the prophetic authors occasionally engage in hyperbolic imagery, their metaphors generally remain grounded in reality; there are no sword-swinging trees or fire-wielding farm implements in these texts. Rather, the authors employ scenes of common agricultural or forestry practices. This realism extends even to the level of only employing CON-QUEST IS EATING with plant elements that may be eaten right off the plant: grapes and figs. Realism also appears in the choices that the prophetic authors made about how to depict other kingdoms using fruit-bearing woody plant imagery. While they associated vines and fig trees with their own homelands, the authors felt free to employ similar imagery with two other kingdoms of the southern Levant that also cultivated grapevines or other fruit trees: Moab and Edom.[1] Wine and intoxication metaphors

---

1. For reasons that I cannot ascertain, the prophets did not apply this imagery to Philistia, with the possible exception of the "uprooting" pun about Ekron in Zeph

receive an even broader geographic application, perhaps because wine is transportable in a way that vines and fig trees are not. Thus, the wine image works well for presenting any kingdom as a victim of YHWH's wrath, or for depicting conquerors as instruments of YHWH's will.[2]

Second, national vine metaphors share many features with other woody-plant metaphors. They may map many of the same elements, such as WATER, BRANCHES, FRUIT, and HEIGHT. They may also adapt woody-plant mappings to the unique features of grapevines, as in the cases of converting the element of HEIGHT to the LENGTH or DIRECTION OF GROWTH of a vine's running canes. The national vine metaphors may even employ imagery from the WOODY PLANT frame that makes little sense in the context of viticulture as it was likely practiced in ancient Israel, including the concepts of a well-watered vine and a vine that grows taller than the surrounding trees. The pattern suggests that the national vine conception may represent a variant of a more general national woody-plant metaphor, a variant that was adopted because of the prevalence of viticulture in Israel and Judah (and their neighbors).

At the same time, the depictions of conquest in vine metaphors differ from fruitless-woody-plant metaphors. Whereas the typical conquest mappings in fruitless-woody-plant metaphors describe burning or cutting them down, vine metaphors employ images of pruning or harvesting. Fundamentally, this pattern further demonstrates the prophetic authors' tendency toward realism in their metaphors. Fruitless woody plants are routinely cut down for lumber or burnt, either in forest fires or as fuel. Grapevines, on the other hand, are typically neither cut down nor burnt. Rather, they are pruned to maximize fruit production, and then the grapes are harvested. Granted, the yield from a typical grapevine will diminish

---

2:4 (see the discussion of olive tree imagery in ch. 8). Yet during the seventh century, Ekron was a significant producer of olive oil and Ashdod a significant producer of wine (Faust and Weiss, "Judah, Philistia, and the Mediterranean World," 71–92). Similarly, only one of the viticulture or vine and fig tree passages uses that imagery with Egypt (Isa 18:5), and none use it of Mesopotamia, even though both regions did produce figs and grapes.

2. In addition, both Mesopotamia and Egypt did import wine, so employing wine metaphors with either region is not outlandish. Given the challenges and risks of transporting wine over land, wines imported to Mesopotamia came primarily down river from Aram and Anatolia (Powell, "Wine and the Vine in Ancient Mesopotamia," 97–122). Exports to Egypt, on the other hand, could be shipped by sea (Faust and Weiss, "Judah, Philistia, and the Mediterranean World," 85–86).

after approximately twenty years, so it is possible that in reality they would have been cut down at that point. None of the prophetic authors exploit this stage in a vine's life cycle, however. The notable exceptions to this overall pattern in the use of vine metaphors both appear in Ezekiel. Ezekiel 15 exploits the one area in which vine wood probably was burnt—to make use of pruned branches. Ezekiel 19:10–14, on the other hand, presents the closest example we have of an unrealistic situation, with a branch of the vine catching fire and burning the rest of the plant.

Third, most of the plant metaphors in prophetic condemnations express the method of punishing or destroying the people in terms of an action related to tending, harvesting, or burning plants. Since the action is directed against them, the plants in these metaphors always represent the attacked party. The only metaphors in which plants fill the role of the attacker are those that present plant-on-plant aggression, such that plants are both the attacker and the attacked. Examples of this latter situation include the forest fire metaphor in Isa 9:17–19, in which fire spreads by contact between plants, and Ezek 31, in which one tree towers over the others. Fourth, many of these metaphors draw on conventional metaphors for conflict to depict military conquest or a divine attack in terms of a plant-based source frame. Fifth, the prophetic authors employed grapevines and fig trees, and in one case, an olive tree, to construct national identities, but most other plant-based source frames appear only in simple metaphors that express a collective condemnation—that is, an accusation of wrongdoing, a pronouncement of doom, or a combination of the two.

Sixth and finally, the evidence from both the vineyard metaphors in First Isaiah (Isa 5:1–7; 3:13–15) and the vine-wood metaphor in Ezek 15, texts that reside at nearly opposite ends of the time frame spanned by this study, suggests that the prophetic authors were responding to preexisting conceptions held by their audiences. Indeed, the basic viticulture metaphors examined here—ISRAEL or JUDAH IS AN ORCHARD (OF VINES AND FIG TREES); ISRAEL or JUDAH IS A VINE; and JUDAH IS A VINEYARD—probably reflect not just realistic, but also common ways of speaking about the two kingdoms. In the case of the eighth-century passages, even if the metaphors were not yet conventionalized, the conception of a kingdom as a vine was intelligible as an extension of PEOPLE ARE PLANTS, and the image of the land of Judah as a vineyard was at least well-known enough in Jerusalem that Isa 3:13–15 and 5:1–7 could employ the image without defining the vineyard mapping for the audience. By the late seventh century, on the other hand, viticulture imagery as representative of kingdoms had become conventional enough that the prophetic authors did not always identify whether the underlying image was that of a vine or vineyard.

9.1. Patterns in the National Identity Metaphors

The investigation thus far has included discussion of how the prophetic authors employed each of the fruit-bearing woody-plant source frames, but a broader comparison of the evidence yields additional insights about the origins and development of these conceptualizations. Table 9.1 summarizes the identity elements present in the national identity metaphors examined in chapters 4, 5, 7, and 8, organized by source frame and arranged chronologically by prophetic book.

Among the metaphors about kingdoms, the vineyard image applies only to Judah (or, in the case of Isa 5:1–7, to a Judah-centered conception of a greater Israel). In addition, as discussed in chapter 4, three of the four vineyard passages about Judah appear in the eighth-century texts of First Isaiah. By comparison, the six national identity passages that use the image of a single woody plant (i.e., the four vine metaphors, the olive tree metaphor, and Hos 9:10–17) reside in Hosea and the prophets of the seventh and sixth centuries and apply to either Israel or Judah.[3] Finally, the two orchard scenes, one from the eighth century and one from the seventh to sixth century, apply only to cities in Judah: Jerusalem (Mic 7:1–7) and the walled towns of Judah (Jer 8:13–17).

An explanation of this pattern may lie in the reach of the kingdoms at the times that these prophecies were created. For much of the late eighth through early sixth centuries BCE, both Israel and Judah were rump city-states. In Israel during the period covered by Hosea, internal conflict and external forces had reduced the territory controlled by the king of Israel to Samaria and its immediate environs. Judah's reach was similarly limited in the seventh century, as much of its western territory had been under Philistine control since Sennacherib's invasion of 701 BCE. The conceptualization of a nation or kingdom as a woody plant thus seems to rest on the nature of a city-based state—one plant mapping to one city. The conceptualization of Jerusalem and Judah's walled towns as orchards, on the other hand, probably derives from the practice of enclosing a vineyard, and perhaps also an orchard, in which

---

3. Hosea 9:10–17, which begins with a potential orchard scene in the mention of both grapes and figs, ultimately presents the nation as a single fruit-bearing woody plant.

Table 9.1. Constructed national identities in prophetic plant metaphors

Passage	National Past	National Character	National Culture	National Body	Common Present and Fate
		Grape and Fig			
Hos 9:10–17	Found, planted by YHWH	From common fruit-bearing woody plant	Apostasy	Planted in land	w/o YHWH, barren, exiled; CONQUEST IS UPROOTING
Mic 7:1–7	Righteous past; DYING IS BEING HARVESTED	From common orchard (and the weeds in it)	All are criminals and liars	Planted in land	Lawlessness and strife
Jer 8:13–17	Prospered by YHWH	From common orchard	n/a	Planted in land	CONQUEST IS HARVESTING, EATING
		Vineyard			
Isa 5:1–7	Chosen, planted by YHWH	From elite common vine stock	Injustice, unrighteous-ness	Vineyard walls, planted in land	w/o YHWH; overrun by cattle, weeds, drought-stricken
		Vine			
Hos 10:1–2	Prolific vine	From common vine	Apostasy	Planted in land	Loss of prosperity
Jer 2:21	Chosen, planted	From elite common vine stock	Apostasy	Planted in land	n/a
Ezek 15	Always use-less vine wood	From common vine	Producing nothing good	Jerusalem	CONQUEST IS BURNING
Ezek 19:10–14a	Prospered when planted by water	From common vine	n/a	Planted in land	CONQUEST IS UPROOTING, CONFLICT IS BURNING
		Olive Tree			
Jer 11:14–17	Planted by YHWH	From common tree	Apostasy	Planted in land	CONQUEST IS BURNING

vines may have been intercultivated with other fruit trees, within a protective wall or hedge. That walls are common to the source and target frames in these metaphors facilitates the other mappings between orchard and city or town.

Conversely, most of the vineyard metaphors appear in texts from a brief period of expanded territorial control in Judah, under Hezekiah, after the fall of Samaria. Some may argue that the vineyard expressions are structured like orchard metaphors, with a walled vineyard mapping to the city of Jerusalem. In at least two eighth-century cases, however, the vineyard image explicitly extends beyond the walls of Jerusalem: in Isa 1:4–9, Jerusalem sits in the midst of the vineyard: ונותרה בת־ציון כסכה בכרם, "and Daughter Zion is left like a booth in a vineyard" (1:8), and in Isa 5:1–7, the vineyard maps to all of Israel and Judah. Isaiah 3:13–15 also hints at a broader conceptualization of the vineyard, since presumably the exploitation of the poor by Jerusalem's elites is not restricted to the poor living in Jerusalem. The cumulative weight of the evidence thus further supports the claim introduced in chapter 4 that the image of a nation as a vineyard arose specifically in reference to a conceptualization of the land of Judah as a vineyard. This difference in the origins of the two metaphors probably also explains the differences in their mappings. Vine metaphors represent an extension of the conventional PEOPLE ARE WOODY PLANTS metaphor, and therefore they draw liberally on the typical mappings of woody-plant metaphors. Vineyard metaphors, on the other hand, began with a conceptualization of the land. As a result, while they could draw additional woody-plant mappings into their structure (e.g., Isa 3:13–15), they could also omit such mappings altogether (e.g., Isa 1:4–9).

The arrangement of the metaphors in table 9.1 also highlights an additional pattern in the data. All of the plant-based national identity metaphors derive from authors who probably lived, at some point in their lives, in preexilic Israel or Judah. Moreover, the earliest of the prophetic texts, Amos, does not appear on the list, and the latest passage on the list dates to the exilic period. Aligned with what we know of historical events in Israel and Judah in the eighth–sixth centuries BCE, this distribution suggests that the period in which viticulture and fig tree imagery operated as ideal vehicles for depicting Israel or Judah is limited to times in both kingdoms when they faced an existential threat or experienced a devastating military defeat.[4] Perhaps the threats to the homeland made the features

---

4. To fully prove this claim would require a detailed analysis of all prophetic plant metaphors about Israel and Judah, rather than just the condemnations included within the scope of this study. My initial assessment of the evidence, however, suggests

and images that the people positively associated with that homeland particularly salient to the prophetic authors.

The discussion of the biblical material has, to this point, largely avoided the issue of whether the prophetic authors responded to each other's work in favor of developing a clear understanding of what the individual authors intended to convey and how they constructed their messages. An analysis of patterns of metaphor, however, requires consideration of interactions among the texts. Our ability to address this issue is hampered, however, in two respects. First, with one or two questionable exceptions, we have little evidence of direct literary dependence among any of the metaphors examined in detail.[5] Second, if national viticulture metaphors were known and became conventional, the mere fact that two prophets employ the same image provides insufficient evidence to support a claim that one text is responding to another. The lack of evidence of literary dependence among the texts means that great uncertainty attaches to any conclusions we may draw about how the texts relate to each other. Even if we believe that a later text knew an earlier one, in the context of conventional metaphors, it may be difficult to determine that the later author is responding to the earlier text rather than to the conventional metaphor behind that text. In addition, a later metaphor can respond to any part of an earlier text; it is not limited to responding to a similar metaphor. For example, Jeremiah or Ezekiel could use a viticulture metaphor to respond to the ideology of Hosea or Isaiah without specifically responding to the viticulture metaphors in those earlier texts.

With all of these caveats in mind, the discussion here will focus simply on a few ideological similarities and differences between the prophets that

---

that while the imagery of vines and fig trees as representative of the lands of Israel and Judah existed before Hosea's time and remained salient into the Persian and Hellenistic eras, within the biblical corpus, the metaphorization of that imagery to represent Israel or Judah as nations is largely limited to the period between Hosea and Ezekiel. Isaiah 27:2–6, which scholars generally date to the Persian (or Hellenistic) period represents one exception, but that passage appears to have been composed specifically as a response to Isa 5:1–7 (Sweeney, "New Gleanings," 51–66; and Willis, "Yahweh Regenerates His Vineyard," 201–7). Therefore, it may not indicate a broader pattern in later prophetic conceptualizations of Israel and Judah.

5. Holladay (*Jeremiah 1*, 98–99) has argued that Jer 2:21 summarizes Isa 5:1–7, and Marvin Sweeney (*Tanak: A Theological and Critical Introduction to the Jewish Bible* [Minneapolis: Fortress, 2012], 304) claims that Jer 12:7–13 refers to Isa 5:1–7. The connections in both cases are weak. See the discussions in chs. 4 and 5.

find expression in their metaphors. In each of the nine complex metaphors listed in table 9.1, the prophetic authors use preexisting positive associations between grapevines and fig trees (and their fruit) and the lands of Israel and Judah to condemn the kingdoms for a failure to properly serve their deity, YHWH. Each author constructs a national identity for the people that incorporates their view of their current culture into a broader national narrative that, in most cases, begins in the past and extends to the future. Almost all of the constructed national identities draw on elements of the VINE frame to present the people as descended from a common stock and as planted in the land, but otherwise the narratives vary on the details of the nations' past and future fate. In addition, the authors all found different ways to express their personal perspective on the degenerate state of the kingdoms' current culture.

As I have already noted in the analysis of Ezek 15 in chapter 5, Ezek 15 seems to invert the claims of Isa 5:1–7 that the people, descended from good stock, are producing bad fruit by claiming instead that they are, and have always been, incapable of producing anything good. More broadly, Ezek 15's claim that the people have been worthless from the very beginning constitutes a break from earlier prophetic conceptualizations in which Israel and Judah had an idyllic past, with their descendants representing a perversion of what the nations were at the beginning (Hos 9:10–17; Isa 5: 1–7; Mic 7:1–7; Jer 2:21; 11:14–17).

At the same time, Ezek 15 also breaks with the claim in Ezek 19:10–14 that the kings of Judah are to blame for the exile, not the people. Two possibilities suggest themselves for this internal disagreement in Ezekiel's metaphors. First, the two passages may present a difference of opinion about the culpability of the Judahites for their present circumstances, indicating either two authors or a single author who changed his view of the nation over time. A second, more likely, possibility is that the passages reflect different attitudes about those deported in 597 BCE and those who remained in the Judah. The messages in this case would be consistent with the view expressed in Ezekiel that those who remained are more degenerate than the exiles (Ezek 14:12–23).[6] By this reckoning, Ezek 19:10–14 would represent a perspective on the deportees of 597, while Ezek 15 condemns those remaining in Jerusalem, who are even more useless than those already in exile.

---

6. Dalit Rom-Shiloni, "Ezekiel and Jeremiah: What Might Stand behind the Silence?," *HBAI* 1 (2012): 203–30.

The various identity metaphors also present different perspectives on the future of the nations. Hosea 10:1–2 and Ezek 19:10–14 seem to offer a degree of hope, Hosea by suggesting a potential alternate future if the people change their apostate ways, and Ezekiel at least leaving the people alive in exile, rather than destroying them utterly. Other passages use the imagery not to reform the nation, but to destroy it. Hosea 9:10–17 utterly dismantles Israel and disperses the people. Isaiah 5:1–7 sees YHWH abandoning the nation and allowing it to be overrun by all enemies, foreign and domestic, and Jer 8:13–17 presents a similar image of a nation overrun. Finally, fire consumes the olive tree in Jer 11:14–17.

The authors of these passages did not assume that the nation had a right to continue to exist, and their constructions of national identity did not serve a goal of presenting a better future for the nation. In this way, they contrast with modern nationalist movements, which usually exploit positive national symbols to unify the nation in service of goals that they believe will benefit their conception of the nation. In fact, the wine and intoxication metaphors, while not actually constructing a national identity, better represent the tactics of modern nationalist movements, as they engage the association of Israel and Judah with viticulture to assert the power of their national deity over all other deities and kingdoms. Ultimately, the examination of national identity construction in the prophetic plant metaphors has shown that even drawing on conventional imagery, the prophetic authors all found ways to shape the metaphors to suit their own messages and goals.

9.2. Directions for Future Research

The analysis offered in this study represents only a first step in systematically mapping the use of metaphor in the construction of national identity in the prophetic corpus. Yet to be analyzed is the set of national condemnation prophecies that draw on the image of a woman. Whereas the prophetic plant metaphors appear to constitute creative elaborations on, and extensions of, existing conventional metaphors already known and used by the Israelites and Judaeans, the evidence from the woman metaphors suggests that the promiscuity mappings were innovative and driven by the prophetic authors. Beginning with the expressions of Israel as YHWH's unfaithful wife in Hosea, we can trace the development and increasing conventionalization of the metaphorical use of זנה, "to be a prostitute, fornicate," to refer to apostasy. Thus, where the agriculture metaphors aided our understanding of how the prophetic authors engaged the perspectives of their audiences, promiscuity metaphors provide an opportunity to trace the spread of a new idea, captured first in the prophetic texts and then later in other biblical genres.

A second area for additional research lies in the restoration prophecies, which appear to draw on a different set of images than the condemnations. For example, they make less frequent use of viticulture metaphors and more frequent use of pastoral imagery. At an instinctive level, it makes sense that the image of regathering a scattered flock would find a prominent place in the restoration prophecies. A few prophetic passages also take up again the metaphor of the nation as a woman, this time focusing on images such as a widow or grieving mother, and therefore often avoiding the need to rehabilitate the promiscuous past that characterizes many of the earlier woman metaphors. Perhaps further analysis of the later prophetic texts will yield additional insights into the relative absence in these texts of the viticulture metaphors that were so central to the construction of national identity for the preexilic prophets and Ezekiel.

9.3. On Methodology

As noted above, the genesis of this project was a desire to systematically study patterns in prophetic metaphors about Israel and Judah. Its methodological approach, however, developed in response to a pattern I found in the existing scholarship on viticulture metaphors. As I began my research, I found that many studies of this material fail to draw a clear distinction between vine and vineyard metaphors. I wanted to solve that problem, and I hoped that frame semantics would provide the answer. It did do so, but in an unexpected way. The structure provided by the concepts of frame roles and relations highlights how many such roles and relations go undefined in prophetic metaphor, including what appear to be fundamental questions of whether or not the underlying image in a metaphor is that of a vine or a vineyard. The fault for not clearly distinguishing between these two images, therefore, lies not with the interpreter, but rather with the nature of the metaphorical expressions, many of which are more interested in depicting what happens to the metaphor's target than in describing that target.

Also illuminating in the analysis is blending theory's concept of a generic space, which facilitates consideration of the shared features of the source and target frames at a schematic level. The mapping of PLANTS to

WARFARE is made possible through the schematic elements that the two frames share. Both involve processes of destruction, such as chopping, killing, and burning. From an experiential perspective, the inspiration for some plant metaphors may have been the actual damage that an invading army does to the invaded landscape. In addition, and specific to the situation in ancient Israel and Judah, farming lends itself particularly to warfare situations in which a significant imbalance of power exists between the two combatants, because plants are relatively defenseless against any action taken by a human to clear them from the land. I say relatively defenseless, because anyone who has tried to clear a particular plant or weed from their land knows how stubbornly persistent plants can be in refusing to die and in regenerating from a bare minimum of remaining root or seed. As such, the PLANTS frame also lends itself well to hope for restoration.

Having identified the shared generic material between the PLANTS domain and the WARFARE frame, I then turned to consider how that material shapes each of them separately. The result was the discovery of the conventional conflict metaphors: WARFARE IS INDIVIDUAL COMBAT, CONFLICT IS BURNING, and CONQUEST IS EATING. In a general way, some figurative uses of burning, and, to a lesser extent, eating and striking a physical blow have long been recognized, as evidenced by the discussions of this imagery in the relevant entries in the Hebrew lexica and in works such as the *Theological Dictionary of the Old Testament* and the *Dictionary of Biblical Imagery*.[7] Specifically analyzing how such imagery provides structure within the prophetic metaphors, however, highlights aspects of the plant metaphors that might otherwise go overlooked. For example, pruning metaphors, from the VITICULTURE domain, have less in common with grape-harvesting metaphors from the same domain than they do with reaping metaphors from the GRAINS frame. Both pruning and reaping metaphors incorporate similar violent imagery of a knife-wielding attacker from WARFARE IS INDIVIDUAL COMBAT into their structure, while grape-harvesting metaphors offer a milder image of carefully gathered grapes. A similar relationship holds between wine-making metaphors,

---

7. *Theological Dictionary of the Old Testament*, ed. G. Johannes Botterweck, Helmer Ringgren, and Heinz-Josef Fabry, trans. John T. Willis et al., 17 vols. (Grand Rapids: Eerdmans, 1974–2021); and *Dictionary of Biblical Imagery*, ed. Leland Ryken, James C. Wilhoit, and Tremper Longman III (Downers Grove, IL: InterVarsity Press, 1998).

which involve crushing grapes, and those threshing metaphors that depict crushing the grain under foot or threshing sledge.

Given these patterns and relationships among the metaphors, an understanding of how the ancient Israelites and Judahites conceptualized warfare via plant-based frames should take into consideration not just which plants they drew into their metaphors, but which actions as well. Counting and analyzing metaphors based on underlying imagery of combat, burning, or eating may yield meaningful results that could be overlooked in analyses that only focus on how many times a particular plant appears in metaphor. For example, the twenty-seven grains metaphors slightly outnumber the twenty-six plant-based viticulture metaphors in the prophetic corpus, and the eight threshing metaphors outnumber the three grape-treading metaphors in the prophetic corpus. Yet, as this study has shown, viticulture metaphors in general hold a much more prominent place in the prophetic conceptions of Israel and Judah.[8] At the same time, focusing on the more significant viticulture metaphors could lead to missing the greater degree of conventionality in the grains metaphors as images of warfare. Moreover, setting the two sources against each other—grains versus viticulture—might result in missing the conceptual similarities, discussed above, between expressions derived from the two sources.

Finally, the detailed frame analysis has also brought into relief a small subset of viticulture metaphors that are not like the others. As discussed earlier, most plant metaphors are logically consistent with literal interactions with plant life—the condemnations simply draw on those aspects that may be exploited to express conflict. That tendency toward logical consistency explains why the prophetic metaphors often liken the destroyed opponent to those elements of the PLANT domain most susceptible to collection, damage, or disposal. Crops are harvested, woody plants pruned, cut down, or burnt, and both may be trampled or eaten by cattle. In several national identity metaphors, however, the plant metaphors represent a sort of anti-farming, in which the farmer acts against his crops or farmland in ways that would be counterproductive in a literal farming context. The actions taken still reside within the range of normal, in the

---

8. The discrepancy is probably best explained as resulting from threshing metaphors being more conventional, and thus a more common, natural way of speaking about warfare, as evidenced by their relatively frequent appearance in extrabiblical texts from the ancient Levant and Mesopotamia (see the discussion of Amos 1:3 in ch. 8).

sense that a literal human could take such actions. A wise human would not do so, though. The most prominent example of this theme occurs in Isa 5:1–7. YHWH spends years cultivating a vineyard and then, after one bad harvest, he destroys its defenses and allows nature to ravage it. In a similar vein, in Hos 9:10–17 YHWH uproots his fruit-bearing woody plant, and in Jer 11:16, he sets fire to his own olive tree. A literal human would probably be regarded as insane for taking such actions, but for YHWH and his prophets, such is the prerogative of divinity.

Bibliography

Aharoni, Yohanan. "Beth-haccherem." Pages 171–84 in *Archaeology and Old Testament Study: Jubilee Volume of the Society for Old Testament Study, 1917–1967*. Edited by D. Winton Thomas. Oxford: Clarendon, 1967.

Albertz, Rainer, Beth Alpert Nakhai, Saul M. Olyan, and Rüdiger Schmitt, eds. *Family and Household Religion: Toward a Synthesis of Old Testament Studies, Archaeology, Epigraphy, and Cultural Studies*. Winona Lake, IN: Eisenbrauns, 2014.

Albertz, Rainer, and Rüdiger Schmitt. *Family and Household Religion in Ancient Israel and the Levant*. Winona Lake, IN: Eisenbrauns, 2012.

Allen, Leslie C. *Jeremiah: A Commentary*. OTL. Louisville: Westminster John Knox, 2008.

Alt, Albrecht. "Judas Gaue unter Josia." *PJ* 21 (1925): 100–117.

Andersen, Francis I., and David Noel Freedman. *Amos: A New Translation with Introduction and Commentary*. AB 24A. New York: Doubleday, 1989.

———. *Hosea: A New Translation with Introduction and Commentary*. AB 24. New York: Doubleday, 1980.

———. *Micah: A New Translation with Introduction and Commentary*. AB 24E. New York: Doubleday, 2000.

Anderson, Benedict. *Imagined Communities: Reflections on the Origin and Spread of Nationalism*. Rev. ed. London: Verso, 2006.

Ashmore, Richard D., Kay Deaux, and Tracy McLaughlin-Volpe. "An Organizing Framework for Collective Identity: Articulation and Significance of Multidimensionality." *Psychological Bulletin* 130 (2004): 80–114.

Assis, Elie. *Identity in Conflict: The Struggle between Esau and Jacob, Edom and Israel*. Siphrut 19. Winona Lake, IN: Eisenbrauns, 2016.

———. "Why Edom? On the Hostility towards Jacob's Brother in Prophetic Sources." *VT* (2006): 1–20.

Austin, Steven A., Gordon W. Franz, and Eric G. Frost. "Amos's Earthquake: An Extraordinary Middle East Seismic Event of 750 B.C." *International Geology Review* 42 (2000): 657–71.

Avrahami, Yael. "Foul Grapes: Figurative Smells and the Message of the Song of the Vineyard (Isa 5:1–7)." *VT* 67 (2017): 341–56.

Bar-Asher, Moshe. "יְדִידָה—וה' אֲהֵבוֹ: The Morphology and Meaning of the Word יָדִיד." Pages 23–46 in *Studies in Classical Hebrew*. SJ 71. Berlin: de Gruyter, 2014.

Barata, André, Alda Pais, Manuel Malfeito-Ferreira, and Virgílio Loureiro. "Influence of Sour Rotten Grapes on the Chemical Composition and Quality of Grape Must and Wine." *European Food Research and Technology* 233 (2011): 183–94.

Barstad, Hans M. "Hosea and the Assyrians." Pages 91–110 in *"Thus Speaks Ishtar of Arbela": Prophecy in Israel, Assyria, and Egypt in the Neo-Assyrian Period*. Edited by Robert P. Gordon and Hans M. Barstad. Winona Lake, IN: Eisenbrauns, 2013.

Begg, Christopher T. "The Identity of the Princes in Ezechiel 19: Some Reflections." *ETL* 65 (1989): 358–69.

Berges, Ulrich. "Isaiah: Structure, Themes, and Contested Issues." Pages 153–70 in *The Oxford Handbook of the Prophets*. Edited by Carolyn J. Sharp. Oxford Handbooks. New York: Oxford University Press, 2016.

Bewer, Julius A. *A Critical and Exegetical Commentary on Obadiah and Joel*. ICC. Edinburgh: T&T Clark, 1911.

———. "Textual and Exegetical Notes on the Book of Ezekiel." *JBL* 72 (1953): 158–68.

Black, Max. "Metaphor." *Proceedings of the Aristotelian Society* 55 (1955): 273–94.

Blau, Joshua. *Phonology and Morphology of Biblical Hebrew: An Introduction*. LSAWS 2. Winona Lake, IN: Eisenbrauns, 2010.

Blenkinsopp, Joseph. *Isaiah 1–39: A New Translation with Introduction and Commentary*. AB 19. New York: Doubleday, 2000.

———. *Isaiah 56–66: A New Translation with Introduction and Commentary*. AB 19B. New York: Doubleday, 2003.

Block, Daniel I. *The Book of Ezekiel: Chapters 1–24*. NICOT. Grand Rapids: Eerdmans, 1997.

———. *The Book of Ezekiel: Chapters 25–48*. NICOT. Grand Rapids: Eerdmans, 1998.

———. "Divine Abandonment: Ezekiel's Adaptation of an Ancient Near Eastern Motif." Pages 73–99 in *By the River Chebar: Historical, Liter-*

ary, and Theological Studies in the Book of Ezekiel. Cambridge: Clarke, 2014.

Bodel, John, and Saul M. Olyan. *Household and Family Religion in Antiquity.* The Ancient World: Comparative Histories. Malden, MA: Wiley-Blackwell, 2008.

Borowski, Oded. *Agriculture in Iron Age Israel.* Winona Lake, IN: Eisenbrauns, 1987.

Botha, Philippus Jacobus. "The Socio-Cultural Background of Ezekiel 19." *OTE* 2 (1999): 249–65.

Brettler, Marc Zvi. *God Is King: Understanding an Israelite Metaphor.* JSOTSup 76. Sheffield: JSOT Press, 1989.

Bright, John. *Jeremiah: Introduction, Translation, and Notes.* AB 21. Garden City, NY: Doubleday, 1965.

Budde, C. "Das hebräische Klagelied." *ZAW* 2 (1882): 1–52.

Carroll, Robert P. *Jeremiah: A Commentary.* OTL London: SCM, 1986.

Carvalho, Corrine. "Putting the Mother Back in the Center: Metaphor and Multivalence in Ezekiel 19." Pages 208–21 in *Thus Says the Lord: Essays on the Former and Latter Prophets in Honor of Robert R. Wilson.* Edited by John J. Ahn and Stephen L. Cook. LHBOTS 502. New York: T&T Clark, 2009.

Chaney, Marvin L. "Whose Sour Grapes? The Addressees of Isaiah 5:1–7 in Light of Political Economy." *Semeia* 87 (1999): 105–22.

Childs, Brevard S. *Isaiah.* OTL. Louisville: Westminster John Knox, 2001.

Cienki, Alan. "Frames, Idealized Cognitive Models, and Domains." Pages 170–87 in *The Oxford Handbook of Cognitive Linguistics.* Edited by Dirk Geeraerts and Hubert Cuyckens. Oxford: Oxford University Press, 2007.

Cohen, Chaim, and Daniel Sivan. *The Ugaritic Hippiatric Texts: A Critical Edition.* American Oriental Series Essays 9. New Haven: American Oriental Society, 1983.

Cogan, Mordechai. *1 Kings: A New Translation with Introduction and Commentary.* AB 10. New York: Doubleday, 2001.

Cole, Steven W. "The Destruction of Orchards in Assyrian Warfare." Pages 29–40 in *Assyria 1995: Proceedings of the Tenth Anniversary Symposium of the Neo-Assyrian Text Corpus Project, Helsinki, September 7–11, 1995.* Edited by Simo Parpola and Robert M. Whiting. Helsinki: Neo-Assyrian Text Corpus Project, 1997.

Cook, H. J. "Pekah." *VT* 14 (1964): 121–35.

Cooke, G. A. *A Critical and Exegetical Commentary on the Book of Ezekiel.* ICC. Edinburgh: T&T Clark, 1937.

Creasy, G. L., and L. L. Creasy. *Grapes.* Crop Production Science in Horticulture 16. Wallingford: CABI, 2009.

Croft, William, and D. Alan Cruse. *Cognitive Linguistics.* CTL. Cambridge: Cambridge University Press, 2004.

Dahood, Mitchell. "Ezekiel 19,10 and Relative *kî.*" *Bib* 56 (1975): 96–99.

Dancygier, Barbara, and Eve Sweetser. *Figurative Language.* CTL. New York: Cambridge University Press, 2014.

David, Ohad, and Daniel Bar-Tal. "A Sociopsychological Conception of Collective Identity: The Case of National Identity as an Example." *Personality and Social Psychology Review* 13 (2009): 354–79.

Davies Krause, Deborah. "Seeing the Fig Tree Anew: The Exegesis of Hosea 9:10–17 in Mark 11:12–25." PhD diss., Emory University, 1996.

Deignan, Alice. *Metaphor and Corpus Linguistics.* Converging Evidence in Language and Communication Research 6. Amsterdam: Benjamins, 2005.

Dever, William G. *Beyond the Texts: An Archaeological Portrait of Ancient Israel and Judah.* Atlanta: SBL Press, 2017.

Dobbs-Allsopp, F. W. "Isaiah's Love Song: A Reading of Isaiah 5:1–7." Pages 149–66 in *Biblical Poetry and the Art of Close Reading.* Edited by J. Blake Couey and Elaine T. James. Cambridge: Cambridge University Press, 2018.

Dorsey, David A. *The Roads and Highways of Ancient Israel.* Baltimore: Johns Hopkins University Press, 1991.

Dubovský, Peter. "Tiglath-pileser III's Campaigns in 734–732 B.C.: Historical Background of Isa 7; 2 Kgs 15–16 and 2 Chr 27–28." *Bib* 87 (2006): 153–70.

Ebeling, Jennie R. "The Contribution of Archaeology to the Study of Women in Biblical Times: Two Case Studies." *RevExp* 106 (2009): 383–98.

Eichrodt, Walther. *Ezekiel: A Commentary.* Translated by Cosslett Quin. OTL. Philadelphia: Westminster, 1970.

Eidevall, Göran. *Amos: A New Translation and Commentary.* AB. New Haven: Yale University Press, 2017.

———. *Grapes in the Desert: Metaphors, Models, and Themes in Hosea 4–14.* ConBOT 43. Stockholm: Almqvist & Wiksell, 1996.

Eph'al, Israel. *The City Besieged: Siege and Its Manifestations in the Ancient Near East.* CHANE 36. Leiden: Brill, 2009.

———. "On Warfare and Military Control in the Ancient Near Eastern Empires: A Research Outline." Pages 88–106 in *History, Historiography, and Interpretation: Studies in Biblical and Cuneiform Literatures.* Edited by Hayim Tadmor and Moshe Weinfeld. Jerusalem: Magnes, 1983.

Fauconnier, Gilles, and Mark Turner. *The Way We Think: Conceptual Blending and the Mind's Hidden Complexities.* New York: Basic Books, 2002.

Faust, Avraham. "The Interests of the Assyrian Empire in the West: Olive Oil Production as a Test-Case." *JESHO* 54 (2011): 62–86.

———. "The Rural Community in Ancient Israel during Iron Age II." *BASOR* 317 (2000): 17–39.

———. "Settlement, Economy, and Demography under Assyrian Rule in the West: The Territories of the Former Kingdom of Israel as a Test Case." *JAOS* 135 (2015): 765–89.

Faust, Avraham, and Ehud Weiss. "Judah, Philistia, and the Mediterranean World: Reconstructing the Economic System of the Seventh Century B.C.E." *BASOR* 338 (2005): 71–92.

Feig, Nurit. "Excavations at Beit Ṣafafa: Iron Age II and Byzantine Agricultural Installations South of Jerusalem." *Atiqot* 44 (2003): 191–238.

Fillmore, Charles J. "Frame Semantics." Pages 613–20 in *Encyclopedia of Language and Linguistics.* Edited by Keith Brown. 2nd ed. New York: Elsevier, 2006.

Finkelstein, Israel, and Dafna Langgut. "Climate, Settlement History, and Olive Cultivation in the Iron Age Southern Levant." *BASOR* 379 (2018): 153–69.

Forshey, Harold O. "The Construct Chain *naḥalat YHWH/ᵖᵉlōhîm.*" *BASOR* 220 (1975): 51–53.

Foster, Benjamin R. *Before the Muses: An Anthology of Akkadian Literature.* 3rd ed. Bethesda, MD: CDL, 2005.

Frankel, Rafael. *Wine and Oil Production in Antiquity in Israel and Other Mediterranean Countries.* Sheffield: Sheffield Academic, 1999.

Friedman, Shamma. "The 'Law of Increasing Members' in Mishnaic Hebrew" [Hebrew]. *Lĕšonénu* 35 (1971): 117–29.

Frymer-Kensky, Tikva. "The Planting of Man: A Study in Biblical Imagery." Pages 129–36 in *Love and Death in the Ancient Near East: Essays in Honor of Marvin H. Pope.* Edited by John H. Marks and Robert M. Good. Guilford, CT: Four Quarters, 1987.

Garr, W. Randall. "The Qinah: A Study of Poetic Meter, Syntax and Style." *ZAW* 95 (1983): 54–75.

Gelston, Anthony. *The Twelve Minor Prophets*. BHQ 13. Stuttgart: Deutsche Bibelgesellschaft, 2010.

Gibbs, Raymond W., Jr., ed. *The Cambridge Handbook of Metaphor and Thought*. Cambridge: Cambridge University Press, 2008.

———. "Evaluating Conceptual Metaphor Theory." *Discourse Processes* 48 (2011): 529–62.

Ginsberg, H. L. "'Roots Below and Fruit Above' and Related Matters." Pages 72–76 in *Hebrew and Semitic Studies: Presented to Godfrey Rolles Driver in Celebration of His Seventieth Birthday, 20 August 1962*. Edited by D. Winton Thomas and W. D. McHardy. Oxford: Clarendon, 1963.

Goor, Asaph. "The History of the Fig in the Holy Land from Ancient Times to the Present Day." *Economic Botany* 19 (1965): 124–35.

———. "The Place of the Olive in the Holy Land and Its History through the Ages." *Economic Botany* 20 (1966): 223–43.

Grady, Joseph E., Todd Oakley, and Seana Coulson. "Blending and Metaphor." Pages 101–24 in *Metaphor in Cognitive Linguistics: Selected Papers from the Fifth International Cognitive Linguistics Conference, Amsterdam, July 1997*. Edited by Raymond W. Gibbs Jr. and Gerard J. Steen. Amsterdam: Benjamins, 1999.

Gray, George Buchanan. *A Critical and Exegetical Commentary on the Book of Isaiah: I–XXXIX*. ICC. New York: Scribners, 1912.

Grayson, A. Kirk, and Jamie Novotny. *The Royal Inscriptions of Sennacherib, King of Assyria (704–681 BC), Part 2*. RINAP 3.2. Winona Lake, IN: Eisenbrauns, 2014.

Greenberg, Moshe. *Ezekiel 1–20: A New Translation with Introduction and Commentary*. AB 22. Garden City, NY: Doubleday, 1983.

———. *Ezekiel 21–37: A New Translation with Introduction and Commentary*. AB 22A. New York: Doubleday, 1997.

Greenfeld, Liah, and Jonathan Eastwood. "National Identity." Pages 256–73 in *The Oxford Handbook of Comparative Politics*. Edited by Charles Boix and Susan C. Stokes. Oxford: Oxford University Press, 2009.

Guibernau, Montserrat. "Nationalism without States." Pages 592–612 in *The Oxford Handbook of the History of Nationalism*. Edited by John Breuilly. Oxford: Oxford University Press, 2013.

———. *Nations without States: Political Communities in a Global Age*. Cambridge: Polity, 1999.

———. "Nations without States: Political Communities in the Global Age." *Michigan Journal of International Law* 25 (2004): 1251–82.

Hammack, Phillip L., Jr., "Theoretical Foundations of Identity." Pages 11–30 in *The Oxford Handbook of Identity Development*. Edited by Kate C. McLean and Moin Syed. Oxford Library of Psychology. Oxford: Oxford University Press, 2015.

Harper, William Rainey. *A Critical and Exegetical Commentary on Amos and Hosea*. ICC. New York: Scribner, 1905.

Hecke, Pierre J. P. van. "Pastoral Metaphors in the Hebrew Bible and in Its Ancient Near Eastern Context." Pages 200–217 in *The Old Testament in Its World: Papers Read at the Winter Meeting, January 2003, The Society for Old Testament Study and at the Joint Meeting, July 2003, The Society for Old Testament Study and Het Oudtestamentisch Werkgezelschap in Nederland en België*. Edited by Robert P. Gordon and Johannes C. de Moor. OTS 52. Leiden: Brill, 2005.

Hellman, Edward W. "Grapevine Structure and Function." Pages 5–19 in *Oregon Viticulture*. Edited by Edward W. Hellman. Corvallis: Oregon State University Press, 2003.

Hillers, Delbert R. *Micah: A Commentary on the Book of the Prophet Micah*. Hermeneia. Philadelphia: Fortress, 1984.

Holladay, John S., Jr. "Hezekiah's Tribute, Long-Distance Trade, and the Wealth of Nations ca. 1000–600 BC: A New Perspective." Pages 309–32 in *Confronting the Past: Archaeological and Historical Essays on Ancient Israel in Honor of William G. Dever*. Edited by Seymour Gitin, J. Edward Wright, and J. P. Dessel. Winona Lake, IN: Eisenbrauns, 2006.

Holladay, William L. *Jeremiah 1: A Commentary on the Book of the Prophet Jeremiah, Chapters 1–25*. Hermeneia. Philadelphia: Fortress, 1986.

———. *Jeremiah 2: A Commentary on the Book of the Prophet Jeremiah, Chapters 26–52*. Hermeneia. Philadelphia: Fortress, 1989.

Homan, Michael M. "Beer, Barley, and שֵׁכָר in the Hebrew Bible." Pages 25–38 in *Le-David Maskil: A Birthday Tribute for David Noel Freedman*. Edited by Richard Elliot Friedman and William H. C. Propp. BJSUCSD 9. Winona Lake, IN: Eisenbrauns, 2004.

James, T. G. H. "The Earliest History of Wine and Its Importance in Ancient Egypt." Pages 197–213 in *The Origins and Ancient History of Wine*. Edited by Patrick E. McGovern, Stuart J. Fleming, and Solomon H. Katz. Food and Nutrition in History and Anthropology 11. Amsterdam: Gordon & Breach, 1995.

Jindo, Job Y. *Biblical Metaphor Reconsidered: A Cognitive Approach to Poetic Prophecy in Jeremiah 1–24*. HSM 64. Winona Lake, IN: Eisenbrauns, 2010.

Johnson, Benjamin J. M. "'Whoever Gives Me Thorns and Thistles': Rhetorical Ambiguity and the Use of מי יתן in Isaiah 27.2–6." *JSOT* 36 (2011): 105–26.

Joosten, Jan. "A Note on the Text of Deuteronomy xxxii 8." *VT* 57 (2007): 548–55.

Kaiser, Otto. *Isaiah 1–12: A Commentary*. Translated by John Bowden. 2nd ed. OTL. Philadelphia: Westminster, 1983.

———. *Isaiah 13–39: A Commentary*. Translated by R. A. Wilson. OTL. Philadelphia: Westminster, 1974.

Kelm, George L., and Amihai Mazar. "Seventh Century B.C. Oil Presses at Tel Batash, Biblical Timnah." Pages 243–47 in *Olive Oil in Antiquity: Israel and Neighboring Countries from the Neolithic to the Early Arab Period*. Edited by David Eitam and Michael Heltzer. HANE/S 7. Padova: Sargon, 1996.

———. "Three Seasons of Excavations at Tel Batash: Biblical Timnah." *BASOR* 248 (1982): 1–36.

King, Philip J., and Lawrence E. Stager. *Life in Biblical Israel*. LAI. Louisville: Westminster John Knox, 2001.

Kislev, Mordechai E., Anat Hartmann, and Ofer Bar-Yosef. "Early Domesticated Fig in the Jordan Valley." *Science* 312.5778 (2006): 1372–74.

Kletter, Raz. "Chronology and United Monarchy: A Methodological Review." *ZDPV* 120 (2004): 13–34.

Kloppenborg Verbin, John S. "Egyptian Viticultural Practices and the Citation of Isa 5:1–7 in Mark 12:1–9." *NovT* 44 (2002): 134–59.

Knauf, Ernst Axel. "Masrekah." *ABD* 4:600.

———. "Was There a Refugee Crisis in the Eighth/Seventh Centuries BCE?" Pages 159–72 in *Rethinking Israel: Studies in the History and Archaeology of Ancient Israel in Honor of Israel Finkelstein*. Edited by Oded Lipschits, Yuval Gadot, and Matthew J. Adams. Winona Lake, IN: Eisenbrauns, 2017.

Köcher, F. "Ein spätbabylonischer Hymnus auf den Tempel Ezida in Borsippa." *ZA* 53 (1959): 236–40.

Koller, Aaron. *The Semantic Field of Cutting Tools in Biblical Hebrew: The Interface of Philological, Semantic, and Archaeological Evidence*. CBQMS 49. Washington, DC: Catholic Biblical Association of America, 2012.

Kövecses, Zoltán. *Metaphor: A Practical Introduction*. 2nd ed. Oxford: Oxford University Press, 2010.

———. "Recent Developments in Metaphor Theory: Are the New Views Rival Ones?" *Review of Cognitive Linguistics* 9 (2011): 11–25.

Kuhrt, Amélie. *The Ancient Near East c. 3000–330 BC*. 2 vols. Routledge History of the Ancient World. London: Routledge, 1997.

Kuan, Jeffrey K. "Hosea 9.13 and Josephus, Antiquities IX, 277–287." *PEQ* 123 (1991): 103–8.

Lakoff, George. "The Contemporary Theory of Metaphor." Pages 202–51 in *Metaphor and Thought*. Edited by Andrew Ortony. 2nd ed. Cambridge: Cambridge University Press, 1993.

Lakoff, George, and Mark Johnson. *Metaphors We Live By, with a New Afterword*. Chicago: University of Chicago Press, 2003.

Lakoff, George, and Mark Turner. *More Than Cool Reason: A Field Guide to Poetic Metaphor*. Chicago: University of Chicago Press, 1989.

Leeuwen, Cornelis van. "Meaning and Structure of Hosea X 1–8." *VT* 53 (2003): 367–78.

Lesko, Leonard. "Egyptian Wine Production during the New Kingdom." Pages 215–30 in *The Origins and Ancient History of Wine*. Edited by Patrick E. McGovern, Stuart J. Fleming, and Solomon H. Katz. Food and Nutrition in History and Anthropology 11. Amsterdam: Gordon & Breach, 1995.

Lipschits, Oded, Yuval Gadot, Benjamin Arubas, and Manfred Oeming. "Palace and Village, Paradise and Oblivion: Unraveling the Riddles of Ramat Raḥel." *NEA* 74.1 (2011): 1–49.

Lipschits, Oded, and Nadav Na'aman. "From 'Baal-Perazim' to 'Beth-Haccerem': Further Thoughts on the Ancient Name of Ramat Raḥel" [Hebrew]. *Beit Mikra* 51 (2011): 65–86.

Lundbom, Jack R. *Jeremiah 1–20: A New Translation with Introduction and Commentary*. AB 21A. New York: Doubleday, 1999.

———. *Jeremiah 21–36: A New Translation with Introduction and Commentary*. AB 21B. New York: Doubleday, 2004.

———. *Jeremiah 37–52: A New Translation with Introduction and Commentary*. AB 21C. New York: Doubleday, 2004.

Machinist, Peter. "Assyria and Its Image in the First Isaiah." *JAOS* 103 (1983): 719–37.

Macintosh, A. A. *A Critical and Exegetical Commentary on Hosea*. ICC. Edinburgh: T&T Clark, 1997.

Maeir, Aren M., Oren Ackermann, and Hendrik J. Bruins. "The Ecological Consequences of a Siege: A Marginal Note on Deuteronomy 20:19–20." Pages 239–44 in *Confronting the Past: Archaeological and Historical Essays on Ancient Israel in Honor of William G. Dever*. Edited by Seymour Gitin, J. Edward Wright, and J. P. Dessel. Winona Lake, IN: Eisenbrauns, 2006.

Maier, Christl M. *Daughter Zion, Mother Zion: Gender, Space, and the Sacred in Ancient Israel*. Minneapolis: Fortress, 2008.

Mansen, Frances Dora. "Desecrated Covenant, Deprived Burial: Threats of Non-Burial in the Hebrew Bible." PhD diss., Boston University, 2015.

Matthews, Victor H. "Treading the Winepress: Actual and Metaphorical Viticulture in the Ancient Near East." *Semeia* 86 (1999): 19–32.

Maxwell, Alexander. "Primordialism for Scholars Who Ought to Know Better: Anthony D. Smith's Critique of Modernization Theory." *Nationalities Papers* 48 (2020): 826–42.

Mays, James Luther. *Hosea: A Commentary*. OTL. Philadelphia: Westminster, 1969.

———. *Micah: A Commentary*. OTL. Philadelphia: Westminster, 1976.

McCormick, C. Mark. "From Box to Throne: The Development of the Ark in DtrH and P." Pages 175–86 in *Saul in Story and Tradition*. Edited by Carl Ehrlich and Marsha C. White. FAT 47. Tübingen: Mohr Siebeck, 2006.

McGovern, Patrick E. *Ancient Wine: The Search for the Origins of Viniculture*. Princeton: Princeton University Press, 2003.

McKane, William. *Introduction and Commentary on Jeremiah I–XXV*. Vol. 1 of *A Critical and Exegetical Commentary on Jeremiah*. ICC. Edinburgh: T&T Clark, 1986.

———. "Trial by Ordeal and the Cup of Wrath." *VT* 30 (1980): 474–92.

Mendoza Ibáñez, Francisco José Ruiz de, and Lorena Pérez Hernández. "The Contemporary Theory of Metaphor: Myths, Developments and Challenges." *Metaphor and Symbol* 26 (2011): 161–85.

Meyers, Carol L., and Eric M. Meyers. *Haggai, Zechariah 1–8: A New Translation with Introduction and Commentary*. AB 25B. Garden City, NY: Doubleday, 2004.

Middleburgh, C. H. "The Mention of 'Vine' and 'Fig-Tree' in Ps. CV 33." *VT* 28 (1978): 480–81.

Millard, Alan R. "Ezekiel xxvii. 19: The Wine Trade of Damascus." *JSS* 7 (1962): 201–3.

Miller, J. Maxwell, and John H. Hayes. *A History of Ancient Israel and Judah*. 2nd ed. Louisville: Westminster John Knox, 2006.

Moder, Carol Lynn. "*It's Like Making a Soup*: Metaphors and Similes in Spoken News Discourse." Pages 301–20 in *Language in the Context of Use: Discourse and Cognitive Approaches to Language*. Edited by Andrea Tyler, Yiyoung Kim, and Mari Takada. CLR 37. Berlin: Mouton de Gruyter, 2008.

Moore, Anne. *Moving beyond Symbol and Myth: Understanding the Kingship of God of the Hebrew Bible through Metaphor*. StBibLit 99. New York: Lang, 2009.

Moore, Megan Bishop, and Brad E. Kelle. *Biblical History and Israel's Past: The Changing Study of the Bible and History*. Grand Rapids: Eerdmans, 2011.

Moran, William L. "The Ancient Near Eastern Background of the Love of God in Deuteronomy." *CBQ* 25 (1963): 77–87.

Morton, Julia F. "Fig: *Ficus carica*." Pages 47–50 in *Fruits of Warm Climates*. Miami: Echo Point, 2013.

Moughtin-Mumby, Sharon. *Sexual and Marital Metaphors in Hosea, Jeremiah, Isaiah, and Ezekiel*. OTM. Oxford: Oxford University Press, 2008.

Moyal, Yigal, and Avraham Faust. "Jerusalem's Hinterland in the Eighth–Seventh Centuries BCE: Towns, Villages, Farmsteads, and Royal Estates." *PEQ* 147 (2015): 283–98.

Musselman, Lytton John. *A Dictionary of Bible Plants*. Cambridge: Cambridge University Press, 2012.

Nielsen, Kirsten. *There Is Hope for a Tree: The Tree as Metaphor in Isaiah*. JSOTSup 65. Sheffield: JSOT Press, 1989.

Nissinen, Martti. "Prophetic Intermediation in the Ancient Near East." Pages 5–22 in *The Oxford Handbook of the Prophets*. Edited by Carolyn J. Sharp. Oxford Handbooks. New York: Oxford University Press, 2016.

Notebaart, Cornelius Wilhelmus. *Metallurgical Metaphors in the Hebrew Bible*. 2nd ed. ACEBTSup 9. Bergambacht: 2VM, 2010.

Novotny, Jamie, and Joshua Jeffers. *The Royal Inscriptions of Ashurbanipal (668–631 BC), Aššur-etal-ilāni (630–627 BC), and Sîn-šarra-iškun (626–612 BC), Kings of Assyria, Part 1*. RINAP 5.1. University Park, PA: Eisenbrauns, 2018.

Olley, John W. *Ezekiel: A Commentary Based on Iezekiēl in Codex Vaticanus*. Septuagint Commentary Series. Leiden: Brill, 2009.

Olmo, H. P. "The Origin and Domestication of the *Vinifera* Grape." Pages 31–43 in *The Origins and Ancient History of Wine*. Edited by Patrick E. McGovern, Stuart J. Fleming, and Solomon H. Katz. Food and Nutrition in History and Anthropology 11. Amsterdam: Gordon & Breach, 1995.

Ortony, Andrew, ed., *Metaphor and Thought*. Cambridge: Cambridge University Press, 1979. 2nd ed., 1993.

Pallavidini Marta, and Ludovico Portuese, eds. *Researching Metaphor in the Ancient Near East*. Philippika 141. Wiesbaden: Harrassowitz, 2020.

Pantoja, Jennifer Metten. *The Metaphor of the Divine as Planter of the People*. BibInt 155. Leiden: Brill, 2017.

Paul, Shalom M. *Amos: A Commentary on the Book of Amos*. Hermeneia. Minneapolis: Fortress, 1991.

———. "Amos 3:15—Winter and Summer Mansions." *VT* 28 (1978): 358–60.

———. *Isaiah 40–66: Translation and Commentary*. ECC. Grand Rapids: Eerdmans, 2012.

Pereira, Cristina, Manuel Joaquín Serradilla, Alberto Martín, María del Carmen Villalobos, Fernando Pérez-Gragera, and Margarita López-Corrales. "Agronomic Behaviour and Quality of Six Fig Cultivars for Fresh Consumption." *Scientia Horticulturae* 185 (2015): 121–28.

Polat, A. Aytekin, and Muhammad Siddiq. "Figs." Pages 455–77 in *Tropical and Subtropical Fruits: Postharvest Physiology, Processing and Packaging*. Edited by Muhammad Siddiq. Ames, IA: Wiley-Blackwell, 2012.

Pond Hall, Megan Edina. "Sour Rot on Grapes: Understanding the Etiology and Developing Management Strategies." PhD diss., Cornell University, 2018.

Powell, Marvin A. "Wine and the Vine in Ancient Mesopotamia: The Cuneiform Evidence." Pages 97–122 in *The Origins and Ancient History of Wine*. Edited by Patrick E. McGovern, Stuart J. Fleming, and Solomon H. Katz. Food and Nutrition in History and Anthropology 11. Amsterdam: Gordon & Breach, 1995.

Prinsloo, G. T. M. "Lions and Vines: The Imagery of Ezekiel 19 in the Light of Ancient Near-Eastern Descriptions and Depictions." *OTE* 12 (1999): 339–59.

Raabe, Paul R. *Obadiah: A New Translation with Introduction and Commentary*. AB 24D. New York: Doubleday, 1996.

Radner, Karen. "Fressen und gefressen werden: Heuschrecken als Katastrophe und Delikatesse im Alten Vorderen Orient." *WO* 34 (2004): 7–22.

Rahmouni, Aicha. *Divine Epithets in the Ugaritic Alphabetic Texts.* Translated by J. N. Ford. HdO 93. Leiden: Brill, 2007.

Roberts, J. J. M. *First Isaiah: A Commentary.* Hermeneia. Minneapolis: Fortress, 2015.

Rollston, Christopher A., ed. *Enemies and Friends of the State: Ancient Prophecy in Context.* University Park, PA: Eisenbrauns, 2018.

Rom-Shiloni, Dalit. "Ezekiel and Jeremiah: What Might Stand behind the Silence?" *HBAI* 1 (2012): 203–30.

Rose, Martin. "Names of God in the OT." *ABD* 4:1001–11.

Ryken, Leland, James C. Wilhoit, and Tremper Longman III, eds. *Dictionary of Biblical Imagery.* Downers Grove, IL: InterVarsity Press, 1998.

Saffirio L. "Food and Dietary Habits in Ancient Egypt." *Journal of Human Evolution* 1 (1972): 297–305.

Samet, Nili. "On Agricultural Imagery in Biblical Descriptions of Catastrophes." *JAJ* 3 (2012): 2–14.

Sasson, Jack M. "The Blood of Grapes: Viticulture and Intoxication in the Hebrew Bible." Pages 399–419 in *Drinking in Ancient Societies: History and Culture of Drinks in the Ancient Near East.* Edited by Lucio Milano. HANE/S 6. Padua: Sargon, 1994.

Scheepers, C. L. van W. "An Archaeological Investigation into the Production of Olive Oil in Israel/Palestine during Iron Age I and II." *JSem* 15 (2006): 564–89.

Schloen, J. David. "Economy and Society in Iron Age Israel and Judah: An Archaeological Perspective." Pages 433–53 in *The Wiley Blackwell Companion to Ancient Israel.* Edited by Susan Niditch. Wiley-Blackwell Companions to Religion. Chichester: Wiley & Sons, 2016.

Schökel, Luis Alonso. *A Manual of Hebrew Poetics.* Translated by Adrian Graffy. SubBi 11. Rome: Pontifical Biblical Institute, 2000.

Schroeder, Christoph. "'A Love Song': Psalm 45 in the Light of Ancient Near Eastern Marriage Texts." *CBQ* 58 (1996): 417–32.

Schunck, Klaus-Dietrich. "Der Becher Jahwes: Weinbecher–Taumelbecher–Zornesbecher." Pages 323–30 in *Verbindungslinien: Festschrift für Werner H. Schmidt zum 65. Geburtstag.* Edited by Axel Graupner, Holger Delkurt, Alexander B. Ernst, and Lutz Aupperle. Neukirchen-Vluyn: Neukirchener Verlag, 2000.

Schwartz, Joshua. "Treading the Grapes of Wrath: The Wine Press in Ancient Jewish and Christian Tradition." *TZ* 49 (1993): 215–28, 311–24.

Singleton, Vernon. "An Enologist's Commentary on Ancient Wine." Pages 67–76 in *The Origins and Ancient History of Wine*. Edited by Patrick E. McGovern, Stuart J. Fleming, and Solomon H. Katz. Food and Nutrition in History and Anthropology 11. Amsterdam: Gordon & Breach, 1995.

Sinha, K. K. "Figs." Pages 2394–99 in *Encyclopedia of Food Sciences and Nutrition*. Edited by Benjamin Caballero. 2nd ed. 10 vols. Amsterdam: Academic Press: 2003.

Smith, Anthony D. "When Is a Nation?" *Geopolitics* 7.2 (2002): 5–32.

Smith-Christopher, Daniel L. *Micah: A Commentary*. OTL. Louisville: Westminster John Knox, 2015.

Smoak, Jeremy Daniel. "Building Houses and Planting Vineyards: The Inner-Biblical Discourse of an Ancient Israelite Wartime Curse." PhD diss., University of California, Los Angeles, 2007.

Sommer, Benjamin D. "Conflicting Constructions of Divine Presence in the Priestly Tabernacle." *BibInt* 9 (2001): 41–63.

Stover, Ed, Malli Aradhya, Louise Ferguson, and Carlos H. Crisosto. "The Fig: Overview of an Ancient Fruit." *HortScience* 42 (2007): 1083–87.

Sullivan, Karen. *Frames and Constructions in Metaphoric Language*. Constructional Approaches to Language 14. Amsterdam: Benjamins, 2013.

Sweeney, Marvin A. "New Gleanings from an Old Vineyard: Isaiah 27 Reconsidered." Pages 51–66 in *Early Jewish and Christian Exegesis: Studies in Memory of William Hugh Brownlee*. Edited by Craig A. Evans and William F. Stinespring. Atlanta: Scholars Press, 1987.

———. *Tanak: A Theological and Critical Introduction to the Jewish Bible*. Minneapolis: Fortress, 2012.

Tadmor, Hayim, and Shigeo Yamada. *The Royal Inscriptions of Tiglath-pileser III (744–727 BC) and Shalmaneser V (726–722 BC), Kings of Assyria*. RINAP 1. Winona Lake, IN: Eisenbrauns, 2011.

Tengberg, Margareta. "Fruit-Growing." Pages 181–200 in *A Companion to the Archaeology of the Ancient Near East*. Edited by Daniel T. Potts. 2 vols. Chichester: Wiley-Blackwell, 2012.

Tov, Emanuel. *Textual Criticism of the Hebrew Bible*. 2nd ed. Minneapolis: Fortress; Assen: Van Gorcum, 2001.

Trimm, Charlie. *Fighting for the King and the Gods: A Survey of Warfare in the Ancient Near East*. RBS 88. Atlanta: SBL Press, 2017.

Tull, Patricia K. "Persistent Vegetative States: People as Plants and Plants as People in Isaiah." Pages 17–34 in *The Desert Will Bloom: Poetic Visions in Isaiah*. Edited by A. Joseph Everson and Hyun Chul Paul Kim. AIL 4. Atlanta: Society of Biblical Literature, 2009.

Ullendorff, Edward. "Is Biblical Hebrew a Language?" Pages 3–17 in *Is Biblical Hebrew a Language? Studies in Semitic Languages and Civilizations*. Wiesbaden: Harrassowitz, 1977.

Viezel, Eran. "A Note to ויעזקהו (Isaiah 5,2)." *ZAW* 123 (2011): 604–7.

Wallace, Howard N. "Harvesting the Vineyard: The Development of Vineyard Imagery in the Hebrew Bible." Pages 117–29 in *Seeing Signals, Reading Signs: The Art of Exegesis; Studies in Honour of Antony F. Campbell, SJ, for His Seventieth Birthday*. Edited by Mark A. O'Brien and Howard N. Wallace. JSOTSup 415. London: T&T Clark, 2004.

Walsh, Carey Ellen. *The Fruit of the Vine: Viticulture in Ancient Israel*. HSM 60. Winona Lake, IN: Eisenbrauns, 2000.

Watson, Wilfred G. E. *Classical Hebrew Poetry: A Guide to Its Techniques*. 2nd ed. JSOTSup 26. Sheffield: JSOT Press, 1986.

Way, Kenneth C. *Donkeys in the Biblical World: Ceremony and Symbol*. HACL 2. Winona Lake, IN: Eisenbrauns, 2011.

Wazana, Nili. "Are the Trees of the Field Human? A Biblical War Law (Deut 20:19–20) and Neo-Assyrian Propaganda." Pages 274–95 in *Treasures on Camels' Humps: Historical and Literary Studies from the Ancient Near East Presented to Israel Eph'al*. Edited by Mordechai Cogan and Dan'el Kahn. Jerusalem: Magnes, 2008.

———. "'War Crimes' in Amos's Oracles against the Nations (Amos 1:3–2:3)." Pages 479–501 in *Literature as Politics, Politics as Literature: Essays on the Ancient Near East in Honor of Peter Machinist*. Edited by David S. Vanderhooft and Abraham Winitzer. Winona Lake, IN: Eisenbrauns, 2013.

Weinfeld, Moshe. *Deuteronomy and the Deuteronomic School*. Oxford: Clarendon, 1972.

Weingreen, J. A. "The Construct-Genitive Relation in Hebrew Syntax." *VT* 4 (1954): 50–59.

Weiss, Ehud. "'Beginnings of Fruit Growing in the Old World': Two Generations Later." *Israel Journal of Plant Sciences* 62 (2015): 75–85.

Welch, Eric Lee. "The Roots of Anger: An Economic Perspective on Zephaniah's Oracle against the Philistines." *VT* 63 (2013): 471–85.

Wenham, J. W. "The Fig Tree in the Old Testament." *JTS* 5 (1954): 206–7.

Westenholz, Joan Goodnick. "The Good Shepherd." Pages 281–310 in *Schools of Oriental Studies and the Development of Modern Historiography: Proceedings of the Fourth Annual Symposium of the Assyrian and Babylonian Intellectual Heritage Project, Held in Ravenna, Italy, October 13–17, 2001*. Edited by Antonio Panaino. Melammu Symposia 4. Milan: Mimesis, 2004.

———, ed. *Sacred Bounty Sacred Land: The Seven Species of the Land of Israel*. Jerusalem: Bible Lands Museum, 1998.

Westermann, Claus. *Isaiah 40–66: A Commentary*. Translated by David M. G. Stalker. OTL. Philadelphia: Westminster, 1969.

Wildberger, Hans. *Isaiah 1–12: A Commentary*. Translated by Thomas H. Trapp. CC. Minneapolis: Fortress, 1991.

———. *Isaiah 13–27: A Commentary*. Translated by Thomas H. Trapp. CC. Minneapolis: Fortress, 1997.

Willis, John T. "Dialogue between Prophet and Audience as a Rhetorical Device in the Book of Jeremiah." *JSOT* 33 (1985): 63–82.

———. "The Genre of Isaiah 5:1–7." *JBL* 96 (1977): 337–62.

———. "Yahweh Regenerates His Vineyard: Isaiah 27." Pages 201–7 in *Formation and Intertextuality in Isaiah 24–27*. Edited by J. Todd Hibbard and Hyun Chul Paul Kim. AIL 17. Atlanta: Society of Biblical Literature, 2013.

Wisnom, Selena. *Weapons of Words: Intertextual Competition in Babylonian Poetry; A Study of Anzû, Enūma Eliš, and Erra and Išum*. CHANE 106. Leiden: Brill, 2020.

Wodak, Ruth, Rudolf de Cillia, Martin Reisigl, and Karin Liebhart. *The Discursive Construction of National Identity*. Translated by Angelika Hirsch, Richard Mitten, and J. W. Unger. 2nd ed. Edinburgh: Edinburgh University Press, 2009.

Wolff, Hans Walter. *Hosea: A Commentary on the Book of the Prophet Hosea*. Hermeneia. Philadelphia: Fortress, 1974.

Wright, G. Ernest. "The Good Shepherd." *BA* 2.4 (1939): 44–48.

Wright, Jacob L. "Warfare and Wanton Destruction: A Reexamination of Deuteronomy 20:19–20 in Relation to Ancient Siegecraft." *JBL* 127 (2008): 423–58.

Wyatt, Nicolas. "'Jedidiah' and Cognate Forms as a Title of Royal Legitimation." *Bib* 66 (1985): 112–25.

Yang, Kon Hwon. "Theological Significance of the Motif of Vineyard in the Old Testament." PhD diss., Golden Gate Baptist Theological Seminary, 1996.

Yardeni, Ada. *The Book of Hebrew Script: History, Paleography, Script Styles, Calligraphy and Design*. 3rd ed. Jerusalem: Carta, 2010.

Yee, Gale A. "A Form-Critical Study of Isaiah 5:1–7 as a Song and a Juridical Parable." *CBQ* 43 (1981): 30–40.

Zevit, Ziony. *The Religions of Ancient Israel: A Synthesis of Parallactic Approaches*. London: Continuum, 2001.

Zimmerli, Walther. *Ezekiel 1: A Commentary on the Book of the Prophet Ezekiel, Chapters 1–24*. Translated by Ronald E. Clements. Hermeneia. Philadelphia: Fortress, 1979.

———. *Ezekiel 2: A Commentary on the Book of the Prophet Ezekiel, Chapters 25–48*. Translated by James D. Martin. Hermeneia. Philadelphia: Fortress, 1983.

Zohary, Michael. *Plants of the Bible*. Cambridge: Cambridge University Press, 1982.

Zohary, Daniel, and Maria Hopf. *Domestication of Plants in the Old World: The Origin and Spread of Cultivated Plants in West Asia, Europe, and the Nile Valley*. 3rd ed. Oxford: Oxford University Press, 2000.

Zwickel, Wolfgang. "Weinanbaugebiete in alttestamentlicher Zeit." Pages 311–23 in *Ein pralles Leben: Alttestamentliche Studien; Für Jutta Hausmann zum 65. Geburtstag und zur Emeritierung*. Edited by Petra Verebics, Nikolett Móricz, and Miklós Köszeghy. ABIG 56. Leipzig: Evangelische Verlagsanstalt, 2017.

Ancient Sources Index

Modern Authors Index

Printed in the USA
CPSIA information can be obtained
at www.ICGtesting.com
JSHW021047181223
53901JS00002B/103